P9-CTA-798

OCT 3 0 2015

324.27104 Boy

Boyer, J.
The big blue machine.

PRICE: $35.00 (3559/he   )

THE BIG BLUE MACHINE

OTHER BOOKS BY J. PATRICK BOYER

Our Scandalous Senate

Another Country, Another Life : Calumny, Love, and the Secrets of Isaac Jelfs

Raw Life : Cameos of 1890s Justice from a Magistrate's Bench Book

Solitary Courage : Mona Winberg and the Triumph over Disability

Local Library, Global Passport : The Evolution of a Carnegie Library

A Passion for Justice : How 'Vinegar Jim' McRuer Became Canada's Greatest Law Reformer [revised paperback edition]

A Man & His Words

Leading in an Upside-Down World [contributing editor]

"Just Trust Us" : The Erosion of Accountability in Canada

The Leadership Challenge in the 21st Century [contributing editor]

Accountability and Canadian Government

Boyer's Ontario Election Law

A Passion for Justice : The Life and Legacy of J.C. McRuer [hardcover edition]

Direct Democracy in Canada : The History and Future of Referendums

The People's Mandate : Referendums and a More Democratic Canada

Hands-On Democracy : How You Can Take Part in Canada's Renewal

La Democratie pour tous : Le citoyen ... artisan du renouveau Canadien

Local Elections in Canada : The Law Governing Elections of Municipal Councils, School Boards and Other Local Authorities

Election Law in Canada : The Law and Procedure of Federal, Provincial and Territorial Elections. Vol. I

Election Law in Canada : The Law and Procedure of Federal, Provincial and Territorial Elections. Vol. II

Money and Message : The Law Governing Election Financing, Advertising, Broadcasting and Campaigning in Canada

Lawmaking by the People : Referendums and Plebiscites in Canada

The Egalitarian Option : Perspectives on Canadian Education [contributing author]

J. PATRICK BOYER

THE BIG BLUE MACHINE

How Tory Campaign Backrooms
Changed Canadian Politics Forever

DUNDURN
TORONTO

Copyright © J. Patrick Boyer, 2015

All rights reserved. No part of this publication may be reproduced, stored in a retrieval system, or transmitted in any form or by any means, electronic, mechanical, photocopying, recording, or otherwise (except for brief passages for purpose of review) without the prior permission of Dundurn Press. Permission to photocopy should be requested from Access Copyright.

Editor: Dominic Farrell
Design: Courtney Horner
Cover design: Gary Long
Front cover image: 123RF Stock Photos
Back cover image: PC Party/Paul Curley Collection
Back flap image: J.Patrick Boyer photographed by David Leadbitter
Printer: Marquis

Library and Archives Canada Cataloguing in Publication

Boyer, J. Patrick, author
    The big blue machine : how Tory campaign backrooms changed Canadian politics forever / J. Patrick Boyer.

Includes bibliographical references and index.
Issued in print and electronic formats.
ISBN 978-1-4597-2449-5 (bound).--ISBN 978-1-4597-2450-1 (pdf).--ISBN 978-1-4597-2451-8 (epub)

    1. Progressive Conservative Party of Canada. 2. Political campaigns--Canada--History--20th century. 3. Campaign management--Canada--History--20th century. 4. Communication in politics--Canada--History--20th century. 5. Politics, Practical--Canada--History--20th century. 6. Canada--Politics and government--1935-. I. Title.

JL197.P7B69 2015   324.27104   C2015-900569-8
                                             C2015-900570-1

1 2 3 4 5   19 18 17 16 15

  Canada

We acknowledge the support of the **Canada Council for the Arts** and the **Ontario Arts Council** for our publishing program. We also acknowledge the financial support of the **Government of Canada** through the **Canada Book Fund** and **Livres Canada Books**, and the **Government of Ontario** through the **Ontario Book Publishing Tax Credit** and the **Ontario Media Development Corporation**.

Care has been taken to trace the ownership of copyright material used in this book. The author and the publisher welcome any information enabling them to rectify any references or credits in subsequent editions.
                                                        — *J. Kirk Howard, President*

The publisher is not responsible for websites or their content unless they are owned by the publisher.

Printed and bound in Canada.

VISIT US AT
Dundurn.com | @dundurnpress | Facebook.com/dundurnpress | Pinterest.com/dundurnpress

Dundurn
3 Church Street, Suite 500
Toronto, Ontario, Canada
M5E 1M2

Dedicated to the memory of

John A. MacNaughton
(1945–2013)

Douglas M. Fisher
(1919–2009)

Keith D. Davey
(1926–2011)

whose friendship and counsel
guided my own sojourn
through politics

TABLE OF CONTENTS

THE HUMAN FACE OF "MACHINE" POLITICS

The Big Blue Machine is about the struggle for political power in Canada during the second half of the twentieth century by those attached to the Progressive Conservative Party, both at the federal level and in many provinces. But, rather than focusing on the politicians whose names and faces are known to the public, this book presents the perspective of individuals in the campaign backrooms.

Political parties and their election campaigns have changed beyond recognition from what one would have found even a few decades ago. Those responsible for this transformation operated in tandem with the advent of television, the emergence of opinion pollsters, and advertising agencies that could shape and manipulate election outcomes. Paralleling these changes came three others: campaign publicity to "brand" the party and emphasize its leader to the exclusion of others; election finance reforms that broke the corrupt link between money and power and replaced it with an entirely new system for campaign funding; and the centralization of control over political operations that diminished local autonomy and reduced individuality. These new approaches abetted the rise of professional campaign organizers. All the while, new sources for public policy replaced traditional party-developed programs. The pace of electioneering accelerated with computers, fax machines, and mobile phones. This overall transformation set the stage for the second revolution in Canadian campaigns that would arrive with the digital age and politics in cyberspace.

In the decades covered by this book, even ordinary events like a party leader's tour became transformed beyond recognition. John Diefenbaker's stately election travels aboard a special train morphed into media-focused campaign caravans with chartered airplanes, fully equipped buses, the "Dirty Dozen" shock-troop advance men, and the Tories' in-house band, Jalopy. New campaign characteristics appeared: televised leaders' debates; the use of direct mail to solicit campaign funds; and more permissive rules for political commercials that led to "attack ads." Both the nature and context of these changes cumulatively reinvented public affairs as we now experience them, altering people's expectations and changing Canada's political culture.

———

The story begins with one man, Dalton Camp, whose career and motivations became absorbed in the unique role of his disciple, Norman Atkins. Out of that team, a legendary campaign organization was born. Their machine was no campaign organization assembled for just a single election or a one-off leadership race, but, rather, it was a juggernaut, one that came closer to being institutionalized — within the Albany Club and the Camp Agency, through the Spades and Rough-Ins, fused within the Tory party — than any political formation in Canadian history. The course of their lives became inextricably meshed with the roller-coaster fortunes of the Progressive Conservative Party itself, to whose cause they devoted themselves. It consumed their best efforts, produced government advertising contracts to sustain them, and required remarkable personal sacrifice.

"No one person was responsible for all that took place during the period of the big blue machine," emphasized Ross DeGeer, himself a dynamo in the Camp-Atkins campaign organization, "but Norman empowered his team to strive for the best, and our best was punctuated with innovation."

Ontario's premier Bill Davis was explicit about the larger nature of the big blue machine. "You have to make clear that Norman was key," he told me, "but you have to go beyond Norman."

This legendary Tory campaign organization was not just an Ontario-based operation during the Bill Davis era of the 1970s, although that is when and where the Camp-Atkins apparatus most tellingly broke through the walls of the backrooms to become part of the conscious operation of government itself, and when journalist Claire Hoy hung that "big blue machine" name on it, which is why many think of the entity in those narrower terms of time and place.

The Camp-Atkins organization operated across Canada, emerging in stages, learning from its mistakes, each phase building upon the one before. It arose initially out of hardball New Brunswick politics in the late 1940s, and developed in the national electioneering that took place during the booming 1950s and counter-culture '60s, whose new style was reflected in the political campaigns in the provinces also. The blue machine really took off with a surge of technical innovations and political psychology introduced and experimented with in PC campaigns throughout the 1970s.

By the mid-1980s, the organization was at its zenith. Looking back, one of its insiders, Brian Armstrong, said the unprecedented Mulroney sweep in 1984 was "pretty much the big blue machine's last hurrah." Another, John Laschinger, however, argues that the machine is still operating today, his view no doubt influenced by the fact this former blue machinist continues to run campaigns as a business, the way he'd first learned from Norman Atkins.

Still another contends the operation was always a bit of a fiction. "The big blue machine did not exist, except in people's minds," asserted Clare Westcott, who worked at the right hand of Ontario premiers Les Frost and Bill Davis. "It was just a bunch of guys," he said, trying to burst an illusion. "Can you imagine the mystique of having something like that? It's like owning the name Coke or Ford."

Clearly, when something becomes a legend, it exceeds the bounds of reality. Atkins himself knew this. Addressing top organizers assembled in the Albany Club on the eve of the 1984 national election campaign he was chairing for Brian Mulroney, Norman said, "Remember, we have a reputation to live up to."

———

Imprecision about the big blue machine's real nature was also fostered by the fact its activities were secretive, often to the point of being covert.

Its operatives sometimes signed into obscure hotels under assumed names. The cover identities by which some of these campaign organizers identified themselves — the Eglinton Mafia, the Spades, the Dirty Dozen, or attendees at "the Rough-In" — changed over time, reflecting the shifting roles they were playing in various power struggles. Using such terms to cloak, rather than reveal, what they were up to was a precaution against discovery by both journalists and Liberals, to be sure. But such cover also provided a buffer during the Progressive Conservative Party's long-running factional warfare between supporters and opponents of Camp's challenge to John Diefenbaker's leadership.

Their use of code names — calling Camp "Mother" and Bob Stanfield "Father" when communicating over walkie-talkies at a 1967 leadership convention — resembled the practices of a security detail or spy cell. Private lingo became part of big blue machine's modus operandi: vague phrases like "research" and "the agency," the "war room" and "the bunker" meant, to them, quite specific activities and venues.

Adding more fog was the name itself. The term *big blue machine* first had currency in the early 1940s, when Ontario PC leader George Drew and his chief organizer, A.D. Mckenzie, used it to describe the new Progressive Conservative election force they were marshalling across Ontario. A speech Drew made in Windsor in 1943, using this very term, was reported in dozens of newspapers. From the 1970s onward, after the "big blue machine" label was re-popularized by *Toronto Star* reporter Hoy, this political shorthand came into wider use with many politicians and journalists, even though few really knew who was in the organization, what it did, or how it operated. Understandably, Wikipedia's entry for "big blue machine" is a sorry mash-up of confusing disinformation.

———

The nature of any political machine is inevitably enriched by legend, its mystique enlarged by tales of patronage-fed campaign organizations controlling elections and directing government operations.

Jimmy Gardiner's Big Red Machine of the Saskatchewan Liberals had been as effective a political operation as the Prairies ever knew. The Union Nationale political machine of Premier Maurice Duplessis in Quebec was a seamless operation that turned out political results as effectively as Montreal's packing houses made sausages. When Dalton Camp in New Brunswick spoke of "the awesome power of the Liberal machine" of Premier John McNair in the 1940s, he was acknowledging the legend of an invincible Grit organization that had become a Maritime model for predetermined election results.

Even within a single constituency, this potent "machine" imagery could sometimes attach itself to certain candidates' partisan squads. At municipal levels, too, such well-oiled operations became renowned. All replicated as best they could the entrenched power networks that ran government and society in colonial times, such as the Château Clique in Lower Canada, the Family Compact in Upper Canada, the Council of Twelve in Nova Scotia, and the Legislative Council members on Vancouver Island.

In twentieth-century Canadian political life, "machine politics" fascinated those aspiring to be players, drew the resentment of vanquished opponents, inspired exposés by journalists, and prompted study by political scientists.

Use of such a term as "big blue machine" to describe the PC's political operation fostered the impression of a single, powerful, well-defined, entrenched entity, further enhancing its intimidating psychological impact as a campaign juggernaut so good it was virtually unbeatable. This reputation often exceeded reality. A fundraising initiative using Canadian art failed. Party leaders arrived late and without having been briefed for momentous public meetings. Sometimes even its most brilliant campaigns failed, unable to overcome the charisma of an especially attractive opponent, the perverse electoral roulette of Canada's voting system, or public fatigue with a spent government.

———

Dalton Camp started life as a Liberal, which contributed a convert's zealousness in "fighting Grits" for the rest of his days. Many whom he and Norman Atkins drew into the blue machine had also been Liberal-inclined. Roy McMurtry voted for Liberal Mitchell Sharp in Eglinton in 1963 before working for PC candidate Camp against Sharp in 1965. Paul Curley voted for Pierre Trudeau in 1968 before he worked at senior party levels for PC leader Bob Stanfield in the 1972 election against Trudeau. Tom Kierans, a blue machine insider in Ontario who was a close policy adviser to Bill Davis from the 1970s on, attended the PC leadership convention at Maple Leaf Gardens in 1967 as an "observer" rather than a delegate because he was, at the time, organizing a leadership campaign for his Cabinet-minister father, Liberal Eric Kierans, who within months would seek to replace Lester Pearson as party leader and prime minister. Dozens of blue machinists came from families with Liberal lineages. Many others had been apolitical before being recruited.

Quite apart from these personal migrations, which served to confuse the distinctions that existed between the parties, it was hard even at the best of times to differentiate between Conservatives and Liberals. When Camp was president of the Progressive Conservative Association of Canada in the 1960s, a dinner discussion with a number of caucus members about party ideology and doctrine led to a conclusion that the PCs simply had to have a clearer enunciation of the party's fundamental principles. Camp excused himself, saying he had a document they might wish to consider. When he returned and handed out copies, the Tory MPs were unanimous in approving the concise statement of support for the monarchy, the rule of law, the primacy of Parliament, the importance of free enterprise as the engine of Canada's economy, the value of the historic partnership between Canada's two founding peoples, the dignity of the individual, and respect for civil rights including freedom of speech and freedom of religion.

"Great work, Dalton," said one, as others nodded in agreement. "That's exactly nailed it!"

"It's a direct lift from the constitution of the Liberal Party of Canada," he replied evenly, looking around the table at the rarely quiet MPs, suddenly silenced.

Conservatives and Liberals embrace the country's foundational institutions and seek a moderating balance on issues of the day because each wants to maximize electoral support across the country's diverse regions. As a result, trying to tell the story of Canadian public affairs by looking only at "fundamental principles" of these two parties is futile. In one election covered in this book — the PC come-from-behind 1988 win in a campaign battle over "free trade" — Tories and Grits even swapped each other's defining, century-old policies.

Instead of dealing much with party platforms and political ideology, this book, instead, concentrates on the three elements that mostly determine the fate of a Canadian party: the character of its leader, the appeal of its specific platform in a particular election, and the strength of its campaign organization. Each is a phenomenon unto itself, but all three interact to produce a singular combined effect. Weakness in one can sometimes be offset by strength in the others, but seldom are electoral triumphs achieved without leader, platform, and campaign organization operating in harmony.

To such elements are added, of course, prevailing economic and social conditions, and Canada's political culture itself, all blending as specific determinants of a particular election campaign. Sometimes quirks of fate also add unexpected good or bad luck that can propel a dismal effort to unexpected victory, or stall an apparently winning romp somewhere short of the finish line. These surprises of democracy help keep anxious campaign organizers awake nights. Norman Atkins, in particular, was a constant fretter.

As well as side-stepping political philosophy, *The Big Blue Machine* also leaves aside the campaigns of parties competing against the PCs. The inter-acting campaigns of different parties significantly determine the outcome of elections, of course. Keith Davey's *Rainmaker* memoirs make clear how the disastrous 1984 Liberal campaign under Prime Minister John Turner con-tributed to victory for Mulroney-led Progressive Conservatives. But because well-rounded accounts of past elections have already been written by others, the focus in this book is instead on how the blue machinists, working behind the scenes, indelibly changed Canadian politics and public affairs through dozens of federal and provincial elections.

Attention to the backrooms does not mean the public side of political life is ignored. Performances by those in office sometimes created issues campaign organizers had to respond to: the Diefenbaker government's indecision over nuclear weapons; Bob Stanfield's fateful decision to campaign on price-and-wage controls; Bill Davis's dramatic cancellation of Toronto's Spadina express-way "because cities are for people, not cars"; and the Mulroney government's contentious free trade treaty with the United States.

Finally, the impact of Canada's electoral system on politics and political campaigns is assuredly considered here. The difference between "historic land-slide victories" and "humiliating defeats" was sometimes a shift of only eight or ten percentage points in popular support, as translated through the iron determinism of an electoral system lacking proportionality between how cit-izens vote and are represented in legislative assemblies. The electoral system's distorting impact caused backroom strategists to engineer vote-splitting among rivals, and to exploit the vagaries of a two-party electoral system still being used for multi-party elections.

———

Dalton Camp and Norman Atkins were at the forefront of those who devel-oped new techniques to benefit from Canada's imprecise electoral system — in their case for the partisan advantage of the PC Party.

For years, the two men were at the very core of the inner circle of the Progressive Conservative Party, wielding power thanks to all the campaigns they ran, party offices they held, and control at Toronto's Albany Club. But they were equally at home in the universe of commercial advertising, thanks to their Toronto-based agency with its impressive roster of clients. This nexus placed them in crossover positions, pivotal players with a transformative role in Canadian public life.

With a cadre of other backroom players, such as Malcolm Wickson, Ross DeGeer, and John Thompson, they pioneered new methods for campaigning that included techniques lifted from the American political campaigns of Republicans and Democrats. When applied to Canadian elections, their advances set precedents other parties followed, as soon as they could figure out how.

Tories traditionally looked to Britain for "best practices," but both Camp and Atkins were openly sympathetic to, and inspired by, American ways, which they found far more relevant to North American society. The same outlook was shared by those recruited to the blue machine, such as Phil Lind and Allan Gregg, who imported the latest fundraising and opinion polling arts from the United States. Their adoptive adeptness between the 1950s and the 1980s changed campaigns, reconfigured the nature of parties and, by extension, transformed public affairs.

———

Parties are to election campaigns what an ice surface is to hockey; without the two together, there's not much of a game.

Although Dalton Camp first skated with the Liberals, he became a free agent and traded himself to the Conservatives, which is how our country's longest running political formation, dating from the mid-1800s, became intrinsic to this saga. At the time, ironically, the Conservatives' future was so dark many believed the party had run its course. Its dismal plight and the deep pessimism of the Tories were forces Dalton had to contend with, in the era when this story of his unique campaign organization began to take shape.

Over ensuing decades, Camp worked hard to change the party's fortunes. Many others joined him in this quest. Despite many operational and personality changes in the organization, one constant imperative energized the blue machine: *winning*. Camp distinguished three types among the political throng: "gentlemen, players, and politicians." The individuals he and Atkins hand-picked for campaign positions were *players*.

The blue machinists bonded into a cohesive force at the Albany Club of Toronto, in private homes and smoky hotel rooms, at relaxing weekend retreats in the countryside, intense elections at urban campaign headquarters, and Atkins's renowned campaign meetings at the back of a restaurant or in his "war room." He transformed disparate yet talented individuals into an enthusiastic and unified team that came to treasure winning an election as the biggest prize in the most competitive sport of all. They were, as Tom Kierans observed, "a band of happy warriors who loved what they were doing, who were part of an organization with well-defined roles, and who carried out those roles with remarkable success."

As the blue machine's organization kept getting deeper, stronger, and more innovative through the 1960s and 1970s, the enterprise gradually transferred from Camp's hands into those of his understudy brother-in-law. Brian Armstrong, who'd started as a student volunteer and ended up a Tory éminence grise, described Atkins as "the gold standard" for campaign managers.

There is no shortage of testimonials. Another recruit who became a close friend and political partner of Atkins, Paul Curley, concluded, "He was the best organizer up to that time, and probably since."

Ross DeGeer said, "Norman was outstanding at putting a campaign together, and developing personal relationships with people across the country was probably his strongest suit."

Bill Saunderson, who started into politics filling ice buckets in hospitality suites, then helped the blue machine keep track of money, and went on to become an Ontario Cabinet minister, said "Norman and Dalton really democratized Canadian political parties."

Pollster Allan Gregg, after working in over fifty far-flung campaigns, was unequivocal about those run by Norman: they "were the best because there was no one else like him in Canadian politics." Atkins, added Gregg, "was the only person who could get the best of the best — be it a strategist, adman, or policy analyst — into the same room and have all of them accept his leadership without question."

Yet behind Norman's emergence as Canada's most durable campaign organizer was his unbreakable connection to his brother-in-law's tortured evolution. In some respects, Atkins resembled a clone of the older man, who, from first encounter, became his hero. Camp's complex personality — alternating between brilliant, brazen, and baffling — was a central presence throughout Norman's own life.

This rare relationship accounted for how Camp remained a luminous presence, even after he withdrew from direct campaign operations and daily operations of his advertising agency for other pursuits. The continuity and cohesiveness displayed in the multi-purpose advertising and campaigning organization that Dalton had first launched in the 1950s were the direct results of Norman's unshakable embrace of his mentor's values; he remained deferential to him, even in absentia. Many who became part of the big blue machine through the 1970s and 1980s never saw Camp in action and only knew of him by reputation, with Norman the zealous keeper of his flame.

Across the board, blue machinists were driven by a passion for adapting new technology and innovative techniques to achieve more effective political results, believing their actions important for Canadian democratic politics and for the country itself.

If public service fused with politics was their religion, an election campaign was its most hallowed sacrament.

J. Patrick Boyer
July 1, 2015
Bracebridge, Ontario

CHAPTER 1

CAMPAIGN ARTISTRY

Uncertainty hung in the morning autumn air around Parliament Hill. Converging toward the Gothic Revival splendour of the West Block, 210 members of Parliament, most elected for the first time, some forty of them now Cabinet ministers, gathered in the cavernous Room 200.

Seeming confident and unsure in about equal measure, they introduced themselves to each other, all the while glancing around, looking for someone more important. The rising din of nervous chatter added to the morning's heady excitement, reminding some of a first day back at school. When they heard cheers erupting from the long entrance corridor, the MPs began crowding into the rows of green leather chairs, keen as theatre-goers to get the best available seat, straining for a sightline to witness the arrival of the most famous of them all, the 211th member of Canada's Thirty-Third Parliament, the first among equals, the new prime minister.

Exuding smooth confidence, Brian Mulroney made his ceremonial entrance, floating into Parliament Hill's largest meeting room upon a cushion of sustained clapping and cheers. He relished his slow progression up the centre aisle amidst his caucus multitude, shaking this hand, touching that elbow, pointing with acknowledging smile to someone, whether real or virtual, further away. Mulroney rode the unrelenting tide of lusty emotion. Cheers morphed into a mantra-like rhythmic chant: "Bri-an! Bri-an! Bri-an!"

The MPs were replicating what they'd witnessed only weeks before in their far-flung ridings, when thronging supporters had transformed the leader's campaign visit into a ritual of celebrity adulation. Although this morning's jubilation was spontaneous, it was equally a manifestation of an artful campaigner's shrewd calibration. In achieving this feisty spirit, Mulroney was melding even this huge and diverse Tory caucus into single-minded group, and extracting from it a unified emotional response.

Other leaders might have arrived on time, walked to their place, merely smiling, or waving, or nodding a brief acknowledgement before taking their seat to conclude the standing ovation. Not this prime minister. A master at milking maximum effect from an anticipated appearance, Mulroney stood, soaking it all in, before finally taking his place at the front table, flanked by a half-dozen prominent Progressive Conservative personalities who'd been waiting, despite their venerable seniority, like primed altar boys. He continued standing, prolonging the ovation, pointing to individuals, smiling and waving, radiating companionable warmth.

At last, with his signal nod, everyone sat down. A chairman began speaking. Some MPs fumbled to plug in unfamiliar earpieces for simultaneous translation. Most just drank in the raw immediacy of a scene they still could not believe themselves part of. The chamber's high, vaulted ceiling and its walls bearing oversized foggy mirrors only heightened their dreamy sense of occupying a front-row seat for history in the making.

Like at an orchestrated stadium concert, several performers had warm-up roles, to pump the atmosphere before the star himself would rock them all. One of those was Norman Atkins. Heavy-set, like a cop, with brown hair cut trim and brown shoes polished to glistening, he seemed strangely shy. The man's awkwardness appeared to telegraph a thought that, perhaps, he should not even be taking this role in these Parliament Hill proceedings.

As he reached the podium, Atkins pulled nervously at the microphone. It emitted a loud scrunching noise that required no translation. The little smile he managed, while making a hasty glance at the wall-to-wall assembly of MPs and senators, hinted that perhaps feelings of pride were beginning to overpower his nervousness, that he was even enjoying an adrenalin rush from this energy-emitting assembly.

"I'm here to tell you that we are all very lucky people," he began.

For many caucus members who'd never heard or even seen the Progressive Conservative Party's national campaign chairman before, the man's voice seemed strange — thinner and higher than expected, given Atkins's stolid appearance.

After a further look across the now hushed assembly, he elaborated, "We're lucky because we have Canada's most exceptional leader at the head of our party."

Cheering erupted.

As Atkins continued, it became clear the man who'd assiduously built and painstakingly operated a state-of-the-art political "machine" for the 1984 election had a unique role at this first caucus meeting of the largest group of a party's MPs ever elected in Canada.

Norman transformed the vast space of Room 200 into a hybrid venue, somewhere between a religious confessional, where closer truth is revealed, and a military debriefing room, where accounts are rendered after a tumultuous battlefield engagement. With quiet voice and matter-of-fact manner, he shifted the mood from sensational to secretive.

In the palpable silence, the Tory organizer selectively shared what had transpired in the election headquarters' secret inner sanctum, "the war room" as insiders called it. He spoke in the flat tone of a sincere man spilling secrets. To this audience of zealous believers, Atkins imparted no mere report on campaign details but, rather, a revelation of true character.

"You all need to know," he said, "just how strenuous were the demands I, as national campaign chairman, and others on the team placed, day after day, week after week, on this man who's now been overwhelmingly elected prime minister of Canada. I've been in this business a long time, a very long time, and I've never seen *anyone* come close to his level of dedication, energy, and leadership performance."

All eyes turned to drink in a new view of Brian Mulroney, sitting neat and erect. The communion was complete as he humbly soaked up the homage, looking down at his hands.

Atkins had artfully turned the spotlight onto the star himself, and the prime minister innately knew how to bathe in such illumination.

Building from this solemn moment of respect and insight, the campaign chairman described how the leader delivered flawlessly, and without cessation, throughout the unrelenting schedule of an intense campaign — whether addressing pulsating crowds, answering hostile journalists, or making a stream of flawless television commercials in French and in English.

"Did he need a break? No, Brian Mulroney just kept going. He was focused, determined, and inexhaustible."

Winding up his cameo performance, Atkins made the essential connection: the leader had campaigned with such stamina, skill, and polish that the result was the largest landslide victory in Canada, ever.

Cheering and applause enwrapped self-effacing Norman Kempton Atkins, chief engineer of the big blue machine, as he quietly resumed his seat, looking relieved. The astute backroom organizer had directed everyone's attention away from his campaign machinery to the leader.

Others of power and influence came to the microphone for brief performances at this opening caucus concert, which culminated at last in a galvanizing, humorous, and moving performance by the prime minister himself, Brian Mulroney addressing the most receptive audience of his entire life.

———

Everyone in this triumphant Progressive Conservative caucus understood that a new chapter in the country's political history was beginning.

Some recent recruits, especially those from Quebec, last-minute candidates stunned to find themselves in Ottawa as MPs, were wide-eyed learners. Surrounding and amongst them were legendary Canadian political figures, prominent characters from prior chapters of national public affairs. Here was George Hees, there Flora MacDonald and Erik Nielsen, and over there, Marcel Masse, Jacques Flynn, and even Joe Clark.

"Who is George Hees?" one puzzled newcomer asked an MP beside her, after his name had been mentioned. Venerable party personalities were strangers to many of these fresh, young Tory MPs, as, indeed, was the history of the PC Party itself, the brand under which they'd come to public office. If neophytes seemed perplexed, others in Room 200, long-time Tories who knew all too well the personalities and plights of their party's past, felt triumphal vindication. They'd soldiered on for years — for many, most of their lifetimes — through bitter campaigns and dismal defeats to finally reach this pinnacle in triumph.

A quarter-century had passed since the previous record high in Canadian electoral politics, now exceeded, had been set in 1958, when the Progressive Conservatives led by John Diefenbaker claimed the greatest number of seats ever in the Commons. For that campaign, Norman Atkins's brother-in-law, Dalton Camp, had worked harmoniously with Diefenbaker to fashion a stunning campaign that ousted the deeply entrenched Liberals. Both record-setting victories displayed an uncommon degree of campaign innovation, professionalism, and wily determination.

The landmark victories of 1958 and 1984 also shared, thanks to a behind-the-scenes connection linking Dalton Camp and Norman Atkins, if not a common paternity, certainly a lot of the same political DNA.

———

Seven months later, *Saturday Night* magazine sought to make sense of the political tornado that had swept through Canada's landscape and turned Ottawa upside down because, for many Canadians, having Tories in office running the country was an aberration. A front-cover feature by Ron Graham told about the campaign organization that brought these Progressive Conservatives to power, the so-called big blue machine, and profiled its chief engineer, Norman Atkins. When describing this powerhouse campaign organization and its greatest achievement, the long-running Progressive Conservative government in Ontario, by then in power for over four decades, Graham called the whole enterprise "the most successful democratic institution in the Western world."

The claim struck humble Canadians as outlandish. *Surely Graham didn't mean the* whole *Western world, did he?* Prideful Liberals recoiled from the notion anyone but their own beloved "Rainmaker," Senator Keith Davey, could be Canada's master campaign organizer. Brian Mulroney took umbrage over the magazine giving Atkins unfiltered accolades for *his* massive election victory. Readers would get the impression the PM's success was the product of political puppetry, that he was on strings pulled by others. Emphasis on Norman diminished Brian's own prowess as an accomplished campaign organizer — especially in Quebec, which had been key to the big win and where Mulroney himself, certainly not Atkins, made all the difference.

Mulroney had been around political backrooms himself and organized enough campaigns to know credit for victory goes to a team and never the leader alone. But the man's instincts also made him want the *backrooms* of politics to stay that way — in the back and out of sight. Yes, he'd asked Atkins to be national campaign chairman, partly on the urging of Ontario's powerful premier, Bill Davis, on whose support Mulroney depended in the seat-rich province, partly knowing himself the talented team that Norman had helped assemble across Canada when Robert Stanfield led the party and Dalton Camp was national PC president. If public credit was to go to backroom organizers at all, the PM felt it should be shared with the veteran campaigners who'd been with him through two leadership races and the Quebec section of the 1984 election. And beside these stalwart loyalists in his personal political base, Mulroney was also fully aware of his debt to the provincial Liberal organization of his friend Premier Robert Bourassa, which had given such a huge boost and helped him to win a majority of Quebec's seats. Atkins could take no credit for that either. The national PC campaign that Norman organized in 1984 was more decentralized, at least in Quebec, than Ron Graham publicly credited.

These sentiments of modest Canadians, proud Liberals, and a sensitive prime minister were really beside the point, however, as were the unbelievable bungles of the Liberal campaign under John Turner that helped the Tories win. Even the brutal determinism of Canada's outdated voting system, which translated the Progressive Conservative's 50 percent support in popular vote nationwide into 75 percent of the Commons' 282 seats, though significant, was not the main story.

What counted, and what political observer Ron Graham's article, "The Unlikely Godfather," about quiet Norman Atkins and the big blue machine sought to show, was the deeper story about Canadian elections: the importance of backroom strategy in setting the context for the public show, and the increasing primacy of those whose names did not appear on any ballots.

The big blue machine, a constantly evolving campaign juggernaut pioneered by Dalton Camp and continued by Norman Atkins, both of them assisted by many well-chosen allies across Canada for over four decades, had become so interwoven with the Progressive Conservative Party that it was often impossible to tell where one ended and the other began.

CHAPTER 2

REQUIEM FOR TORIES

By the Second World War, the "Liberal-Conservative Party," as Canada's Tories called themselves at that time, was an endangered entity languishing in a political wasteland. Parties had gone extinct before. Revival of the poorly adapting Liberal-Conservatives seemed unlikely.

In all the country's provinces, the party had virtually vanished. In Ottawa, the Tories' dire state paralleled how they'd faded provincially. The party's MPs, few in number, were deeply pessimistic.

Ottawa itself was abuzz with the urgency of war. The quietest place in the whole city was the darkened Parliament Hill office of New Brunswick's R.B. Hanson, latest in a succession of hard-luck Conservative Party leaders. With the war's outcome in doubt, the bleak prospects of Canada's Conservatives were of scant interest even to men like Hanson, who had a duty to feel responsible.

A lawyer who'd been mayor of Fredericton and then a minister in R.B. Bennett's Conservative government before its crushing defeat in the 1935 election, Hanson managed to get re-elected in 1940. Having no ambition for higher office, the Maritimer seemed "safe" to the shell-shocked Tory caucus who solemnly named him interim leader. Somebody had to hold the vacant job. Party leader Bob Manion, deeply disillusioned, had quit within weeks of losing the disastrous wartime general election.

In that March 1940 contest, the Conservatives elected only thirty-nine members to Parliament, the party's 30 percent of the popular vote producing 16 percent of the Commons' seats, making Tory support appear even less than it was. Apart from being woefully outnumbered, the party's MPs felt unable to match the overarching psychological power of the supremely confident — some said "smug" — Grits.

The summer before war started, in July 1938, Conservative delegates had convened to replace R.B. Bennett, whose government, its life drained by the Depression's ravages and its supporters split into competing factions, had been flung from office three years earlier. By the second round of balloting, the convention had chosen Dr. Robert Manion as the new leader and, on the surface, things looked promising.

A reassuring man, Manion appealed to Canada's moderates, including Liberals weary of William Lyon Mackenzie King, an incrementalist whose success came from never doing by halves anything he could do by quarters. Bob Manion had even started out as a Liberal, asked by Sir Wilfrid Laurier himself to run for Parliament. But when war came in 1914, Dr. Manion volunteered with the Canadian Army Medical Corps. As war devoured soldiers and pressure grew to force un-enlisted men to the front, the country divided. Conservatives, and Liberals supporting conscription, rallied behind Prime Minister Borden's "Union Government" for the 1917 election. Manion, advocating forced enlistment, was elected from his hometown, Fort William, as a "Liberal-Unionist" candidate. In subsequent elections, he was re-elected as a Conservative, gaining experience in the Cabinets of Arthur Meighen and Richard Bennett.

Manion's balanced focus on social justice and better measures for unemployed Canadians made him an attractive moderate amidst the political extremists with radical solutions to the Depression. The new Conservative leader had specific appeal in Quebec, where the party had not won a majority of Commons seats since 1892. A Roman Catholic, Manion shared the faith of a majority of voters in the province. His wife was French-Canadian, and their children were fully bilingual.

Since the Tories lacked any party structure in the province, however, Manion's only hope lay in striking a deal with Quebec's new Union Nationale premier. Maurice Duplessis had formed his party by absorbing the remnants of the Conservative Party in the province while retaining its robust antagonism towards all things Liberal. Each of Duplessis's elected members, now constituting a large majority in Quebec's assembly following his party's 1936 electoral victory, would work in close collaboration *only* with the Conservative candidate in their riding whenever the next federal election was called.

The federal Tories believed that they'd been handed the keys to the highly effective electoral machine of their *"bleu"* confreres. The national Conservatives, their excitement incubated by electoral desperation, believed they now miraculously possessed a vehicle of great power, ready and waiting to carry them into office.

But one week after Germany's invasion of Poland on September 1, 1939, triggered another world war, Canada's parliamentarians voted to declare war on Germany. In the sombre light of this changed situation, Prime Minister King announced that no wartime election would take place. If need be, Parliament would extend its five-year life, as a number of parliaments and legislatures had done during the 1914–1918 war. Under King's plan, any Commons seat becoming vacant would be filled by whichever party held the riding when the vacancy occurred simply designating a replacement MP.

The Conservatives accepted at face value King's commitment to hold no election during the war. Manion personally agreed to the partisan cease-fire. Conservative organizers and fundraisers, knowing what dismal shape they were in, heaved a sigh of relief. No Tory Party workers at any level made preparations for a general election. Across the country, none of the constituencies lined up candidates. Bagmen ceased trying to raise campaign funds. There were few events even to keep core loyalists together. Toronto Tories shut down their recently opened party office, and in Ottawa the leadership decided to close down the Conservative's national office, fully dismantling the remaining vestiges of organization.

The party that was only a ghost in the provinces had become a phantom nationally.

———

Then, to the Conservatives' dismay, a wartime election did occur — in Quebec.

The federal Tories watched helplessly as the provincial campaign heated up. They listened to Liberals portray the Conservatives as "the party of conscription" — a claim based on the introduction of mandatory military service in the prior world war by a Union Government of both Conservatives *and* Liberals. To answer the Liberals' fear-mongering among Quebec's voters, Manion emphatically stated there would be "no forced enlistment for military service."

Quebec Liberals gave a shrug, expressed disbelief, and claimed to voters that if elected the Conservatives would certainly bring in conscription even though they said they would not. Provincial Liberal leader Adélard Godbout, for his part, categorically pledged that no Liberal government would ever impose conscription. Then, for extra measure, he added that should even one single French Canadian ever be conscripted under Ottawa's Liberal government, he would quit his party and personally fight against the Liberals.

Stoking conscription fears among French-Canadian voters, the Liberals connected the dots for voters: Union Nationale support for the Conservatives in Quebec would lead to a national Conservative government in Ottawa; the Conservatives would impose conscription; thus, the only way to prevent conscription was to defeat the Union Nationale.

In the previous election, Quebec's voters had given a huge majority to the Union Nationale. This time they rewarded the Godbout-led Liberals with seventy seats, a crushing surplus over the Union Nationale's remnant fifteen. Across Quebec, the Union Nationale was decimated. Bob Manion's election prospects in the province lay in smouldering ruins.

How fortunate for the Conservatives, mused Manion, that he'd agreed with the prime minister there'd be no federal election until the war was over.

———

Having gained an upper hand in Quebec, however, the Liberals in Ottawa smiled, broke their promise, and called a wartime election.

Surprising voters and his political opponents alike by launching a general election, King brazenly made a fresh promise to replace his broken one. He now solemnly committed that there would be no military conscription. This line had worked in Quebec, after all, for Godbout's Liberals.

The snap 1940 election caught the Conservatives unprepared, with no candidates recruited, the campaign organization in complete disarray, and the bank account empty. King had six Liberal premiers backing him, Manion none. There were no Conservative lieutenants of stature in the federal caucus, nor even any politically appealing leaders in the remaining provincial Conservative parties. In Ontario, the largest base of the national party, Conservative leader George Drew refused to help Manion and his Ottawa counterparts, repaying the federal party's establishment for its aggressive efforts to thwart his rise in the provincial party.

In desperation, Manion sought to replicate Borden's successful 1917 strategy of forming a coalition Union Government with the Liberals, by re-naming the Conservatives the "National Government Party." But this was cosmetic. In 1917 Borden had the benefit of a fully revamped Election Act that ran roughshod over the political rights of opponents and gave advantage to anyone supporting the war effort and conscription. Manion, in opposition, lacked Borden's ability to change election laws to predetermine the outcome.

The Conservative Party of Canada no longer existed even in name. There was little support for Manion's National Government gambit. Newspapers remained neutral. Dyed-in-the-wool Tories felt abandoned.

As ballots were tallied, political opportunism was seen to pay off. The King-led Liberals won a large majority, with plenty of seats in Quebec, in French-speaking communities elsewhere across Canada, and in farming ridings on the Prairies and southwestern Ontario where voters had bought the solemn Liberal promise of no conscription.

Shattered Conservatives were desperate. Nobody was willing to contribute money to the party. The Commons, in this era, had no budget for caucus support. The only stopgap was an appeal to the remnant caucus members themselves. Manion asked for at least $50 from each MP and senator to cover immediate needs. This raised $3,350.61, which enabled the party to exist a little longer.

———

Two years later, in April 1942, King instituted a wartime national plebiscite asking Canadian voters to "release the government" from its no-conscription mandate.

The plebiscite carried with a majority "yes" vote in all provinces except Quebec, where the answer from four out of every five voters, feeling deeply betrayed, was an angry *"non."* The Liberals brought in conscription, despite having twice committed to voters they would never do so. Adélard Godbout did not resign as Liberal premier of Quebec over the issue as pledged, nor did he campaign against the Ottawa Grits as promised.

Canadian Conservatives were thoroughly disillusioned by politics and embittered by the Liberals' shining success practising electoral dishonesty. The people of Canada, for their part, no longer looked to the Conservative Party for anything. Its death throes had landed the venerable party at the abyss's edge. Few could see any future at all for Canadian political conservatism.

———

The Conservative's most irrepressible warrior, Grattan O'Leary, who'd run for the party in his Quebec home district of Gaspé in 1925 and since become editor of the *Ottawa Journal*, wrote on December 1, 1942, in *Maclean's Magazine*, what read like the party's obituary.

The Liberal-Conservative Party was "at the lowest ebb in its fortunes since Sir John A. Macdonald created it eighty-nine years ago," he lamented. "Orphaned of leadership, unrecovered from shattering defeat in two successive elections, holding power in no single province, nudged into oblivion by the direction of the war, its decline and fall from its once proud eminence of historic achievement is one of the strange tales of politics." O'Leary pondered the cause for such demise. "Is it that the Conservative Party has become a spent force, its philosophy and policies unsuited to our day?"

This seemed to be the case. If Britain's once-great Liberal Party could be destroyed by historic transformations, so, too, could Canada's grand old Liberal-Conservative Party. In Quebec, its formal remains disappeared in 1936 when the Quebec Conservative Party and Action Libérale Nationale merged to form the new Union Nationale of French-Canadian nationalists. For the 1940 federal election, Conservative leader Manion's manoeuvre to hide his party under the name "National Government Party" seemed a last-ditch effort. The party was so far gone that the Conservatives were doing what, in historian Jack Granatstein's words, amounted to little more than "dynamiting the wreckage."

———

Yet, if a wrecked classic automobile can tempt a young mechanic to dream about making it roadworthy again, the remnants of an abandoned political party may likewise appeal to ambitious individuals who envisage someday riding the restored vehicle back into power. And that was how the idea of rebuilding Canada's Conservative Party *from the ground up* began.

This enterprise engaged a small number of true believers at first; against the backdrop of war, these never-say-die partisans, dreaming to rejuvenate Canadian political conservatism, began to discuss bold new directions for the party. Initial gatherings were spontaneous, the groups small. Soon, their efforts became more organized and better defined.

Taking account of both their party's bleak electoral experience and the radical changes sweeping Canadian society, they knew the party's ideology had to be revamped. If society changed, so must a democratic political party that hoped to serve it. To be relevant to citizens, Conservatives had to embrace Canada's contemporary needs, reflect people's core aspirations, and set a specific course toward the future. The more they talked, the clearer the sequence of these steps became. Only a revivified philosophy of political conservatism could generate relevant policies and programs that, in turn, could reconnect the party to the wider public and, eventually, gain enough electoral support to win power, control government, and implement the program.

They decided to gather in central Canada, convenient to like-minded party modernizers from east and west, and chose Port Hope, a town on Lake Ontario's shore east of Toronto, whose name seemed apt in light of their purpose. Wanting frank discussion and open appraisals, they did not invite incumbent party leaders, who'd be more intent on preserving their positions than making bold changes. On September 7, 1942, these aspiring Conservatives, some 115 in number, began arriving for their Conservative Forum and soon dubbed themselves "the Port Hopefuls."

Assembled in the precincts of the town's classic Trinity College, a mood of tentative optimism began taking hold. These Conservatives heard policies advocated by others whose thinking was similar to their own. They felt a liberating spirit of camaraderie. In coming decades these forward-looking Conservatives would hold some of the highest offices in their provinces and nationally: governor general, minister of finance, attorney general, party leader, campaign organizer, and election fundraiser. Yet in this history-making moment, the focus was not on the personal careers of individuals, but on the future of the Conservative Party itself.

Galvanized by time and place, the Port Hopefuls unanimously agreed on proposals that were, in a word, "progressive." Rather than tinkering with details, their broad-stroke resolutions defined a new stage in the evolution of Canadian political conservatism, with a stronger human focus and confident embrace of affirmative government action.

———

Philosophy and policy were fundamental, but the party's organizational structure was just as important.

The gathering at Port Hope was a forum of like-minded individuals. They'd stepped apart from Tory traditionalists, whom they feared would resist change, to revamp the philosophic framework of Conservative Party programs. To effect change, however, the Port Hopefuls knew they could not remain a satellite to the party, but had to engage the Tory organization itself.

The opportunity came just months later, in December 1942, when Conservative delegates converged on Winnipeg for a national convention to debate policy resolutions and elect a new leader. The Port Hopefuls, knowing their next task was to engage voting delegates and fill party offices, arrived resolved to continue their resuscitation operation. Helping their cause was the fact almost every delegate had read Grattan O'Leary's article on the bleak state of the party. To save it, he'd urged Conservatives to avoid extinction by reinventing the party. O'Leary sensed that the resolutions adopted at Port Hope, and the spirit they invoked, offered the only glimmer for political revival.

As the policy debates took place, the efforts by the Port Hopefuls turned the tide for political conservatism. The progressives prevailed, getting enough delegates to adopt most of their resolutions so the party could strike a new course.

———

Reorienting the party still required one thing more: choosing the right leader.

The last time the party had been led by someone from the Prairies, back in 1930, Calgary's R.B. Bennett won a majority government. Since then, three successive leaders from central and eastern Canada had failed: Ontario's Bob Manion, who'd resigned in May 1940; New Brunswick's Richard Hanson; and succeeding him in November 1941, Ontario's Arthur Meighen. When Meighen failed to even gain a seat in the House, Hanson remained interim leader, giving detail to O'Leary's portrait of a party "at its lowest ebb" since inception. A western Canadian would be refreshing.

There were choices. Saskatchewan MP John Diefenbaker, a lawyer from Prince Albert, finally elected in 1940 after many failed efforts, was already in the national caucus. Also in the Commons was British Columbia MP Howard Green, a Vancouver lawyer. A third westerner, M.A. MacPherson, had been a member of Saskatchewan's legislature and attorney general in the province's Conservative government until 1932. H.H. Stevens, a Vancouver businessman who'd been a minister in Bennett's Cabinet, was back in the Tory fold after an ill-fated bolt to lead the Reconstruction Party of Canada, whose only accomplishment had been to draw away enough Tory votes in 1935 to help the Liberals defeat the Conservatives.

Diefenbaker and Green were shunned by the party's hierarchy. Diefenbaker was too radical, Green too idealistic. MacPherson's qualities had only been tested at Cabinet level in Saskatchewan provincial politics, while Stevens could never be forgiven his costly gambit. Instead of these four, Arthur Meighen and other ranking members of the Tory establishment embraced a strange belief that the best person to lead the national party would be a provincial premier. None had ever done so before. Pondering this prospect at the Albany Club in Toronto, where Conservative insiders frequently plotted, they listed three positives: premiers were already successful in winning high public office; they enjoyed established recognition and credibility; and they came with existing political organizations. For a bankrupt party in the wilderness, such notional attributes were appealing.

Infatuated with the novelty of a provincial politician becoming a national leader, these power brokers did not account for the negatives: the circumstances that brought a premier to office might be entirely unrelated to any ability to win elections; popularity in one province would not likely translate into support elsewhere across a highly regionalized country; and experience in provincial politics did not prepare one to deal with national concerns, since Canada's two levels of government exercise different powers under separate jurisdictions allocated by the Constitution.

With no Conservative premier in office, however, Meighen's unusual quest led him to second best; an incumbent premier who was *not exactly* a Liberal. And that's how Manitoba's John Bracken became the Tory's prospective bride.

Born in Ontario farming country, Bracken had attended Ontario Agricultural College and the University of Illinois. In 1910 he became professor of animal husbandry at University of Saskatchewan, leaving in 1920 to become president of the Manitoba Agricultural College. Although he clearly enjoyed farming classrooms more than fields, Professor Bracken did impart helpful lessons to several generations of agriculturalists. Then a crop John had not planted began to sprout.

In 1919 and the chaotic aftermath of the First World War, when farm movements became political organizations to protect rural interests, the United Farmers of Ontario formed a provincial government. Three years later, the

United Farmers of Manitoba similarly came to power in Winnipeg. In neither case did the Farmers have a leader. The Ontario Farmers chose Ernest Drury, a farm leader and son of the province's first agricultural minister, as premier. Those in Manitoba turned to the head of the province's Agricultural College.

John Bracken was a political outsider, but he gave the United Farmers of Manitoba professional grounding and improved credentials. The United Farmers were an agrarian manifestation of the broader "Progressive" movement that had taken hold across much of Canada and the United States before the war. Once in government, Bracken's followers identified themselves as the "Progressive Party of Manitoba," while maintaining affiliation with the United Farmers.

Because Progressives rejected the partisanship of the two old-line parties, they wanted government policies based on independence from vested interests. In Manitoba, although it applied principles of sound business management and frugality in spending, the party's orientation shifted over the ensuing decades as Premier Bracken engineered a number of shifting alliances with other political parties, including a merger of Manitoba's provincial Liberal Party into the Progressives. By 1942, when Arthur Meighen and other senior federal Conservatives came calling, Bracken had been Manitoba's premier for more than twenty years.

As a condition for leading the Liberal-Conservatives, he insisted the party be renamed *Progressive*-Conservative. Long associated with the Progressive Movement and its comprehensive agenda of radical reform, the term *progressive* had also become an alternative name for Canada's Communists when they were outlawed as a political organization. So, by 1942, "progressive" had become a term heavily freighted with political meaning. Even with their major new embrace of rights for organized labour, nobody would have thought the Tories were becoming communists, or even radical agrarian reformers. Yet, by switching its name to Progressive-Conservative, the party was sending an important if somewhat attenuated signal. Certainly the Port Hopefuls were supportive.

Even after the hyphen was dropped, some years later, leaving "Progressive Conservative" as the party's name, it was still a mouthful, and to some even a contradiction. Journalistic practice and practicalities would soon enough streamline it to "PC" — even as headline writers kept alive "Tory" as a concise all-encompassing generic name for the ever-changing entity.

The 1942 name change not only aligned with Bracken's own flexible political orientation but also invoked a precedent other politically savvy Manitobans had set years before. Errick Willis, a candidate in Souris, had successfully campaigned under the blended name Progressive-Conservative as he straddled the Progressive Party and Conservative Party, amalgamating their values and getting himself elected to Parliament as Canada's first PC MP in 1930.

Bracken became leader on the second ballot. His most significant accomplishment in national politics came, just hours later, when the political formation he now headed was rechristened, by vote of the delegates, "The Progressive-Conservative Party of Canada."

––––––

However it was called, the party, as everyone present at the Winnipeg convention knew, was an integrated operation that had grown and evolved, in organic harmony with the country itself, since the 1850s.

Policy was developed at party conventions where delegates debated and voted on resolutions that, if approved, became planks out of which to construct the electoral platform on which Conservative candidates would stand in a coming election. Campaign organization was handled in each riding by elected officers of the party's constituency association, not by any special team assembled by the candidate or run from above by a central campaign commander. Because the Conservative Party had always been based at the riding level, moreover, the provincial and national parties had never been free-standing entities but, rather, umbrella associations of participating riding associations. This relationship incorporated a Conservative belief that public affairs are best grounded in strong community roots. It also reinforced Conservative preference for local people deciding what is best for themselves and their communities. Inherent in this preference, too, was a dislike for distant strangers telling locals what to do.

All this was embedded in the way Conservatives conducted provincial and national elections. Although called general elections, the reality was such events consisted of a series of quite separate constituency battles. The essential autonomy provided by this arrangement appealed to Conservative preference for local decision-making. The concept of a single, integrated election campaign run from a central "war room" would still have been unimaginable, even in 1942.

Even though revamped in name and policy, the Tories would continue on this existing foundation. It was deeply entrenched. The Conservatives were Canada's oldest political formation. General elections would continue to be locally based campaigns, organized and conducted by local party members under the direction of the riding associations' officers. Long-established practices, such as secrecy for raising campaign funds, would continue as well. Party bagmen wanted anonymity while making their rounds to collect cash from government contractors, distillers and brewers, bankers, lumber barons, mining company head offices, and prospering manufacturers. To protect donor secrecy and avoid giving opponents ammunition for allegations of corruption, this *sub rosa* operation for acquiring money also remained, of necessity, a built-in part of the Conservative organization.

Could a party with progressive policies, ambitious Port Hopeful members, traditional structures, entrenched methods, an altered name, and a new leader who'd long been a provincial premier, arise like a phoenix out of its ashes?

CHAPTER 3

CAULDRON OF WAR

Around the world, all the while, the grim threat that Nazi Germany's propaganda minister Josef Goebbels glorified as "total war" had been searing people for three years.

Yet in rural New Brunswick, six-year-old "Kemp" Atkins, an American kid on summer holidays, faced a more immediate battle, struggling to pull his wagon over rough terrain around the family's cottage at Robertson's Point. The boy brightened with surprise to see reinforcements arrive, in the form of a Canadian soldier on a motorcycle.

The soldier was soon pulling the lad in his wooden Flyer and, when ready for something else, the pair played catch with a baseball.

"I immediately liked Dalton, because he gave me the attention a little boy likes to have," Atkins later said about the bond forged that first summer morning. "He was fun!"

Camp's biographer Geoffrey Stevens would describe that spark as the beginning of "a severe case of hero worship." As the relationship between them strengthened over the years, Camp would help Atkins grow from "a snotty-nosed kid" into a political godfather for the Conservative Party.

"He encouraged me to reach beyond what I could do," was how Atkins put it.

Dianne Axmith, who would come to work closely with both men through hard-fought election campaigns and in their Toronto advertising agency, confirmed the enduring strength of this 1942 summer's link. Atkins, she confided, "had a loyalty to Dalton that almost went beyond the reasonable."

Camp himself would one day quip, "If I'd become a socialist, Norman would have followed me into socialism."

Dalton had not come all the way down to Grand Lake to play with a boy, however. He'd materialized at Robertson's Point because he was yearning for the kid's twenty-two-year-old sister. Camp's campaign was for Linda Atkins, whom he'd fallen in love with at Acadia University before enlisting.

They were similar opposites. Camp was an Americanized Canadian who'd lived his formative years in the United States before returning to New Brunswick. The Atkins were American Canadians. Linda and Norman's parents had been born in the Maritimes. They'd met at Acadia, too, then married. After the First World War, the father relocated with his family to New Jersey, but they retained their Canadian connections, and in 1937 built this Robertson's Point cottage and returned each summer.

———

The experience of living in the United States had profoundly shaped Dalton's views on public affairs, sports, and life.

When he was a young boy, his father, Harold, landed work as projectionist for a theatre in Woodstock, New Brunswick, where the son began watching new release movies with riveted fascination. "The inevitable victory of good over evil," Dalton remembered, "unfailingly stirred the heart and confirmed a world of heroic dimension."

When Harold Camp caught religion, the newly ordained Baptist minister moved his family to the United States. After living awhile in New England, the Camps relocated to California. Mixing into American school life, Dalton was exposed to a far broader education than he'd received in New Brunswick. He began emulating his fellow students, who displayed confidence on the sports fields and charm in the dance halls. Virtues of the American way of life, formerly absorbed in a distant Canadian movie theatre, were now drummed into teenage Dalton at school and soaked up from his friends.

Harold Camp emerged as a powerful, popular, and well-paid preacher at major centres on the lucrative speaker's circuit around the United States.

People flocked to hear the charismatic clergyman's inspiring sermons and his compelling oratory on transcending public issues.

As the elder Camp's status rose, the family's living standards soared. Dalton's well-born mother enjoyed plenty of money and pursued its rewards. Aurilla Camp orchestrated the family's relocations to successively bigger homes, until they finally landed in one of Oakland's most exclusive neighbourhoods. In these formative years, Dalton became charmed by the good life, enjoying smart clothes and the latest phonograph records.

Harold Camp was also enthusiastic about sports, particularly boxing, and next thing Dalton knew, his dad had been appointed by the state Democrats to the California Boxing Commission. The clergyman's interest in boxing went fist in glove with his fascination for another fighting sport, Democratic election campaigns. Harold befriended leading party members, like rising star Earl Warren, later California governor and, later still, U.S. Supreme Court chief justice.

Outspoken on world conditions, Harold went to Nazi Germany to see for himself how bad things were becoming for Jews. After returning stateside, his sense of urgency led him to become active in the World Peace Federation. Top Americans, including President Franklin Roosevelt, now asked Camp's advice.

Like his father, Dalton, too, was sensitive to oppression and social injustice, particularly the raw injustice that he saw existing in America. "Growing up," Dalton would later write, "I developed an instant sympathy for the underdog, for the put-upon, the unemployed, the disadvantaged, and the luckless." He learned what "every white American child inevitably learned, which was to look without seeing, to hear without listening." America was "not one nation, but two," he observed, "one 'indivisible,' the other, invisible." It was accepted as natural "that Negroes were porters or maids (where they were not entertainers), Japanese were gardeners, Chinese were cooks and laundrymen, Filipinos were houseboys, and Mexicans worked the fields."

Dalton's thinking about society based on such observations was given even sharper focus by his intensive, constant reading. Laid up for almost a year because of a foot infection, he initially listened to popular songs on his radio until his father sternly admonished his bed-ridden son to read books by important thinkers instead. His edict led Dalton to Walter Lippmann's *A Preface to Morals*, next a biography of Abraham Lincoln, then more biographies of famous and heroic men, until he was fully launched into a private universe of serious reading — a portable space in which he would remain transported, engaged, and inspired the rest of his days.

These beliefs, values, attitudes, and memories — all contending within young Camp and becoming self-arranged as a distinct world view — would have held no significance for Canadians had Dalton not carried them back to Canada intact and applied them, for decades, at high levels in election campaigns, political party affairs, newspaper columns, broadcasting commentaries, and public policy development.

What triggered Dalton's return, and transformed his life more than anything, was the blow fate delivered one August morning in 1937. His father fell dead in the prime of life at age forty-three. Dalton was devastated, first by the loss of his larger-than-life father, then by the changes that followed in rapid succession.

The steady flow of money underwriting the family's high-rolling life dried up overnight. His mother, a widow with few prospects, decided to retreat "home" by train, with her boys Dalton and Red, to the quiet safety of the Maritimes. Her oldest son, Sandy, resolved to stay behind and make his own way.

A sensitive youth, just shy of seventeen, Dalton was overwhelmed by melancholy. "Everything I loved and held dear had been wrenched away," he wrote. "Not only had I lost my father, friends, school, the family home, my room and the pleasures and comforts which had surrounded me, but, as well, I was leaving America for an unknown country where I would be a stranger."

Camp did retain, and carried north with him, an instinctive passion for social justice, a deep distrust of surface appearances, and his on-going love affair with books about serious subjects. Back in Canada, he soon noticed, and lamented, how "there just weren't any heroes. In America we had one a week, people like Lindberg." Dalton craved someone to believe in.

———

Living in New Brunswick meant adjusting to a society secured by familiar customs and unchallenged traditions. Staid Maritime provincialism presented a big hurdle for Dalton, still intoxicated by the dynamic nature of the United States.

He'd felt in synch with the hard-hitting rhythms of American public affairs. He'd enjoyed the direct, earthy humour of America's people. While repelled by the cruelty and excesses of racism within American society, Dalton remained enthralled by America's demanding arenas of baseball, football, journalism, and politics. At least he was still Canadian enough to be charmed by paradox: Dalton liked how Americans appeared to treat life as just a game, but played for keeps.

Realizing they were back in New Brunswick for good, restless Dalton and his cultured mother suffocated in Woodstock's narrow society. They felt stymied by the limited scope of small-town intellectual curiosity. The place, Dalton observed in dismay, had few Jews but plenty of anti-Semites.

Dalton's mother made the best plans she could for him, arranging enrolment in a private academy in the fall of 1937. It would offer better education than her well-read but rebellious son could get at Woodstock High. And sending him to a private school, just across the border in Maine, could help Aurilla maintain some semblance of a cherished station in society's higher ranks.

Dalton lasted only two days. Then he progressed to another private school, Horton Academy in Wolfville, operated in affiliation with Nova Scotia's Acadia University, a Baptist institution. But wherever he found himself, he did not fit in. An active state of rebellion had become Dalton Camp's personal norm.

Despite his campaign of insurgency against all school rules, he managed to graduate in May 1939, just as world war appeared imminent. Before departing to New Brunswick for another Woodstock summer, he headed over to the registrar's office at adjacent Acadia to sign up. Dalton had decided to return to Wolfville in the fall for university education. Acadia seemed the best option for someone lacking money. No tuition fee was charged to the son of a Baptist minister who declared interest in becoming one himself.

Back in Woodstock, strolling down a street that summer "on a still, airless afternoon," Dalton heard German leader Adolf Hitler's voice over the radio, "coming out from behind a screen door." He paused in his tracks, listening to the announcer explain Hitler's speech "and why people were cheering." In Ottawa that fall, the House of Commons voted to declare war on Germany.

By September Dalton returned to Wolfville, his always awkward relationship with the world now troubled even more by uneasy feelings about the war. As campus life at Acadia picked up, Dalton's moody thoughts were eclipsed by Linda Atkins. The attractive cheerleader, gymnastics star, and high-marks economics student dazzled him. While it was Linda's innate qualities that made Dalton fall in love, her essential nature as an American woman further enhanced his rapture. Still aching for America's pulse, he felt it flow through him every time he held her tight.

———

Barely noticed by Dalton, whose thoughts divided up pretty much between Linda and a world at war, was a provincial election taking place over in New Brunswick.

The two-way battle between Liberals and Conservatives, with voting set for November 20, 1939, grew hotter when a Liberal Cabinet minister's allegations about Conservatives engaging in corrupt fundraising caused a sensation. He'd accused the Tories of promising companies that a new Conservative government, if elected, would fix things for them, ranging from liquor sales to lower taxes. But these allegations about prospective future Tory corruption, launched just a week before voting, grew so intense and personal they began to backfire. Many New Brunswickers shrugged in commonsense disbelief. Where, after all, did Liberals get their campaign funds, if not from the same sources, using similar means?

When votes began to be counted on election night, the Conservatives took heart. As the night progressed, they watched their popular vote rising to 45 percent of all ballots cast. Riding-by-riding results were declared through the evening, with the Tories climbing back to nineteen seats from the mere five held after the 1935 election. Still, the party remained in Opposition in the forty-eight-member legislature, ten seats behind the Liberals.

Dalton, unmoved by parochial provincial politics and generally apolitical in the context of Canadian affairs, had not bothered to travel from Wolfville to Woodstock for an election that in no way interested him. Had he taken time from Acadia to vote, it would have been for the Liberals.

———

What did pull at him, though, was the world darkened by a war whose outcome remained in gravest doubt.

Haunted by moral qualms about sitting safe while his friends offered up their lives as soldiers, he left Acadia in November 1941 and enlisted in the Canadian army. An equally persuasive factor was that Linda was no longer around. After graduating, she'd become a financial worker in the dark canyons of New York's Wall Street, commuting daily from her parents' home in New Jersey. With Linda gone, Dalton had no remaining pull to campus life.

From "Camp Utopia," Dalton exchanged electrifying love letters with Linda. By the summer of 1942, this romantic relationship crackled more than ever. At Robertson's Point, after Linda's kid brother had gone to bed, they swam together and sat by a beach fire. They wanted to be together for life. It took another year, but in August 1943, Dalton snagged a four-day pass from the army and married Linda in Fredericton. They travelled by train to Saint John for a short honeymoon, staying in the city's Admiral Beatty Hotel. Two days later, the groom returned to Camp Utopia, the bride to New Jersey.

Private Dalton Camp visited Robertson's Point in 1942 to court Linda Atkins and, in the bargain, became a hero to her kid brother Norman.

Included in Linda's dowry was the kid brother. Dalton Camp and Kempton Atkins, who'd bonded so well the summer before, were now "brothers," in law. It was clear who would wield the influence in this relationship. Soldier Dalton was twenty-three, admiring schoolboy Kemp, only nine. Yet that very difference in age contributed to the caring interest each had in the other.

They were not rivals but good buddies.

CHAPTER 4

FIRE OF POLITICS

In 1945, the war over and his army discharge papers in hand, Dalton signed up for the program giving veterans the university education most of them, himself included, never finished before enlisting. He and Linda moved to Fredericton, where he enrolled at the University of New Brunswick.

At university, he continued reading the works of great writers, and, in tandem, exercised his talent for written expression. Dalton was an instinctive writer, making intelligent sense of a chaotic world through ideas and imagery. Putting views about public issues into print proved to be the shy and rebellious man's preferred method of outreach. By autumn 1946, as editor of UNB's student newspaper, *The Brunswickan*, Dalton was in full flight. Using this weekly platform, he offered forthright commentaries on subjects of the day, opining on current events with profundity, wit, and clarity. Camp's talent for engaging readers lay far beyond the ken of most student journalists.

One day, a sharp knock on the Camp's apartment door startled him. Dalton was even more surprised, opening it, to find a gentleman introducing himself as Robert Tweedie, private secretary to New Brunswick's premier. Tweedie had come, he explained, to invite the student editor to Ottawa. He was extending the invitation, he added, at the joint request of Premier John B. McNair and New Brunswick MP Frank Bridges, minister of fisheries in Prime Minister King's Liberal Cabinet. Both men were impressed by Camp's editorials.

Up to this point, Dalton's interest in public affairs had not extended to politics' earthy realities. He'd been content to observe from a higher plateau, where he could agonize over the human condition, sense history's sweeping currents, and consider leadership as displayed in the actions of men like his father Harold, Franklin Roosevelt, and Winston Churchill. It was time, the Liberal sages believed, for him to descend onto the plains of truer battle and experience the real work of politics.

As these things go, Dalton's coming-of-age induction into Canadian public life was like a poor country kid getting his first automobile ride through big city streets in the front seat of a new Cadillac. Not only did he experience unaccustomed luxury travelling by train to the nation's capital, but Camp was met at the station by "the first in an endless line of ubiquitous men described as executive assistants to the ministers," shown his room in the Château Laurier with two beds, large overstuffed chairs, gleaming white-tiled bathroom, and a bottle of Scotch on the dresser. "It was clear that I had arrived," he said, "both in Ottawa and somewhere — on some upper rung — of the Liberal ladder."

Touching down at the epicentre of Canada's political universe, the student, already on a veteran's accelerated program of study, was now immersed in an additional crash course of special adult education. Up to now, Camp acknowledged, politics had been "a foreign country" to him, and politicians "distant, alien figures." During his intensive visit with Liberal officialdom, Dalton encountered for the first time the human side of politicians.

From the House of Commons public gallery, looking down "on the gently lit, softly coloured chamber below," Camp studied the orchestrated performances of elected representatives. At "burnished desks sat identical men, in charcoal greys and blacks and navy blues, drumming on their desks in unison, laughter rising in throats like a chorus."

———

Back in Fredericton, the Liberal Party's newest recruit responded by doing what he enjoyed most — writing.

The New Brunswick party published a journal called *Liberal Review*, and in it Dalton K. Camp began a column under the title, "A Young Liberal Looks at Politics." Apart from giving his ego a solid boost, the *Liberal Review* column confirmed for Dalton that the writing he most relished was not reporting news,

but instead reflecting on events and commenting on what they forewarned —
now as the writer of columns, someday as author, he envisaged, of books.

A close observer of detail, Dalton could paint with words the exquisite
poetry of life's touching moments and hard truths, free of cant, true to reality.
Being sensitive and still feeling like an outsider, Camp observed with clarity
and dispassion.

Dalton's articles also expressed his rebellious edge. This gave his columns a
seriousness that might have grated, had it not been for his talent in rendering
criticism more palatable by the touching irony in his humour and the counter-
weight of his abiding humanism. He addressed public affairs with a trademark
disdain for the banal. He taunted readers with portents about what lay ahead,
as a consequence of failing to grapple with some current conundrum.

All the while in Ottawa, Cabinet minister Chubby Power, himself a resident
critic of the Liberal government of which he was part, began reading, clipping,
and underlining many of Camp's *Liberal Review* columns.

———

In August 1947, Prime Minister King appointed Milton Gregg, a highly decorated soldier of the Great War who'd become president of UNB, to his Cabinet
as fisheries minister, to replace Frank Bridges who'd died suddenly in Ottawa
from heart failure. King then called a by-election in York-Sunbury for October
so the political novice, already in Cabinet, could get into the Commons.

At the UNB president's invitation, Dalton and Linda joined Gregg for
tea at his campus residence to discuss his campaign. Linda, impressed by this
emerging dimension in her husband's life, felt proud.

With his interest in politics now "broadened and deepened," as he put it,
Camp was eager to accept, a couple of days later, a Liberal organizer's request to
campaign all around York-Sunbury riding with Gregg before leaving for New
York and journalism studies at Columbia University that fall. What Dalton
was to bring to the old war hero's campaign was the voice of a younger soldier
looking to his future.

There was already deep support for Milton Gregg, out of respect for his
courageous determination. During combat in France in 1917 he earned the
Military Cross. The next year, his further "valiant leadership under fire" added
a bar to the Cross. Then in the final weeks of the war, his conspicuous bravery

in battle at Canal du Nord earned Gregg the highest military honour, the Victoria Cross. His outstanding valour prevented many casualties and enabled the Canadians' war-ending advance to continue. Though Dalton held him in respectful admiration, even as a political novice he could see the distinguished soldier needed tips about campaigning.

In their initial outings, the candidate in no way resembled a powerful minister in the Government of Canada. Camp persuaded Gregg to change from his tramp-like dungarees to a suit, instinctively grasping the importance of image for someone seeking election. Dalton, to his own delight and that of others, displayed real skill in campaigning, too, not at shaking hands but at speaking from a platform. At their meetings, he'd follow Gregg's folksy ramblings by speaking as a young veteran, hitting harder on the issues, scoring partisan points against the Tories.

The campaign had not yet ended, although another Liberal win seemed fairly certain, when Dalton and Linda departed for New York. In Manhattan that October he received a cordial telegram from Gregg, announcing his substantial win at the polls.

————

So far, Camp's introduction to ground-level politics had been on the federal level, though provincial politics held greater appeal because he found it "more interesting and vital."

When completing his year at Columbia, which left him aspiring more than ever to a writer's career, Dalton got an invitation from his Liberal pals to return to New Brunswick for the 1948 provincial election. Writing and politics were not, he reasoned, mutually exclusive. They might even be self-reinforcing.

In the campaign's opening days, Dalton, who had been recruited because of his impressive 1947 performance with Milton Gregg, was asked to tour the province with the premier himself. John McNair was bright, articulate, and solidly entrenched in power. The more the young Liberal campaigner witnessed from this unique vantage point at the premier's side, the more he could see how the Grits' province-wide political operation ran with machine-like precision.

The premier, Dalton observed, had no separate headquarters for the election but conducted the entire campaign from his office at the legislature. Dalton was even more fascinated to discover that McNair had quietly imported two men from Toronto's Walsh Advertising, a Grit agency, to handle all campaign publicity.

Although Camp's early duties entailed touring with McNair as an organizer and helper, once the premier discovered the high calibre of some speech material Dalton drafted for him, the premier envisaged a more crucial role for his aide. He reassigned the talented wordsmith to help the Toronto admen, secreted in a suite at Fredericton's Lord Beaverbrook Hotel, to ensure they got the true "Maritime understanding" of things.

Their Liberal campaign consisted entirely of newspaper advertisements. Camp studied how the Walsh men designed the ads, booked space in the dailies and weeklies, and arranged to get the best visibility for the most economic rates. He followed, for the rest of the campaign, how they wrote and re-wrote copy for the series of VOTE LIBERAL notices. He took a hand in it himself, discovering how to hover in a rarefied creative space until finding the perfect phrase to connect with voters who were aware of political realities yet aspired to something better.

On election night, of the fifty-two seats in New Brunswick's assembly, the Liberals claimed all but five.

———

A couple of months later, Dalton took another step up the Liberal ladder.

As one of New Brunswick's most active and increasingly prominent Young Liberals, he'd become a voting delegate to the Ottawa convention selecting a successor to retiring Prime Minister King. Happily back in the capital again, Dalton and other Maritimers, including the Liberal premiers, were busy drafting policy resolutions when suddenly he was summoned out of the committee room to address the plenary session of delegates.

For the party strategists calling on him, Camp's mission "as a Young Liberal" was to put an end, in public, to rumblings of impatient discontent from some of the party's younger members. Dalton, with two others similarly summoned, heard the chairman saying, "I do not know what they wish to talk about, but when three or four men say they have something important to say to a convention of this kind, we should hear them."

Finding those words "embarrassingly gratuitous, and almost completely false," Dalton felt he was "on the end of a string looped around someone's fingers, helplessly manipulated, obliged to respond without thought or calculation to the urgencies of unknown or unseen forces." He looked over the vast audience, searching in vain for the revolt of the young he was called upon to quell. Yet speak he did, offering the most natural thing on his mind — a tribute to the brand of Liberalism practised in New Brunswick by the recently re-elected premier, John B. McNair.

After he finished, Prime Minister King, sitting on the stage behind him, shook Dalton's hand and congratulated him on his message. The next day, the *Montreal Star*'s report would quote him as saying, "If you will not listen to the younger members of this party, then they will leave and join another party." It was a speech in which Camp, speaking without any specific grievance against the Liberal Party and almost on automatic pilot, had given abstract voice to the natural rebelliousness that dwelt within him: *Listen to me, okay? Take my views into account, or I'll leave for another party.*

The following days would give him more genuine cause for grievance. The Maritime delegations had come prepared to push for a better deal for their region, a part of Canada which routinely gave Liberals majority representation but which just as routinely was ignored by Liberal Ottawa on substantive issues that mattered. Camp had joined other true believers, working hard on resolutions which, if adopted as official Liberal policy, could change that. Delegates from Nova Scotia and PEI agreed with New Brunswick's delegates on the strategy. Premier McNair would nominate Nova Scotia's powerhouse premier, Angus L. Macdonald, as a candidate for the Liberal leadership. Premier McNair had a well-crafted speech ready to deliver, and so did Macdonald, who would make the Maritime case with force and eloquence before withdrawing from the race, his point made to the full convention of Canadian Liberals. That, they'd all reasoned, would prepare the way for approval of the Maritime resolutions.

Faced with opposition to Macdonald's candidacy and pressure behind the scenes against their agenda, however, the Maritime delegation's earlier unity disintegrated. Macdonald was not nominated. The two premiers folded and put away their carefully honed speeches. The resolutions never reached the floor for Liberal delegates to debate and approve.

"The fragile wall of resolve many of us had so laboriously improvised," Dalton saw, "was easily breached by a numberless horde whose interests and ambitions lay with the new order. The deeper realities of politics left us exposed, armed with only good intentions."

The business-like efficiency of the convention was not to be marred. The Liberal Party was now "a corporate dynasty," he realized, "and its board of directors was not lacking in zeal for good corporate relations. No delegate felt himself pushed or driven, but gently directed by some benevolent guidance system, deflected in the mists of his confusion from the possibility of harmful collision with more powerful purpose and authority."

The only challenger not derailed was Cabinet minister Charles G. Power, a leadership candidate wedded more to liberalism than to the party's corporatism. He urged delegates, in a nomination speech Dalton eagerly absorbed, that "almost nothing can be accomplished unless we proceed vigorously along the lines of reforming, first, our electoral system; secondly, our parliamentary system; and thirdly, our administrative ministerial system; to make these more readily responsive to the will of the people." He gave more details, with which Dalton heartily concurred: "There must be a complete and final disappearance from our electoral manners, customs and morals of wasteful, unnecessary, and often scandalously corrupt political expenditure."

Dalton cast his ballot for "Chubby" Power, one of the fifty-six votes the western Canadian received as Louis St. Laurent coasted into the prime minister's office with an 848-vote win in the first round of voting, as planned. Camp was unaware that, the year before, Power had avidly read, marked, and kept his article from the New Brunswick *Liberal Review* that included his own similar critique of the Liberal Party.

As the 1948 convention concluded, Camp marvelled at the efficiency of the Canadian Liberal Party, "its splendid imperturbability, the infallibility of both its fortune and its genius. The convention had been summoned to decide everything — to ratify the decision of the directors as to its management for the next decade — and to decide nothing (or as little as possible) and to demonstrate that there are ways to maintain fealty other than through commitment to a cause. It was a new politics of pragmatism made more compelling for its graceful power."

Camp returned to New Brunswick with a changing view of politics.

"Somehow," he reflected, he'd previously "had the notion that power was compassionate and sympathetic." It had not been until encountering the machinations of power in the "dark, noisy, confused convention hall, and in the corridors and stuffy little rooms where groups of men gathered," that he sensed power as being "a blind and omnipresent force" that was "indiscriminate and amoral." He now understood that "men who wield it are also prisoners of it."

He had yet to discover how his insight applied not only in Ottawa, on the upper rungs of power, but equally at all levels of political operations throughout the country.

————

For the rest of the summer, Dalton floated in loose engagement with a small squad of Young Liberals recruited by the party's provincial organizer.

Lacking instructions, they spent their time playing cards in the Liberal Party's dusty, sloped-floor back office. The interlude, like a soldier's rest time behind the front lines, gave Dalton space and time to wrestle "with a growing uneasiness about politics and with the New Brunswick Liberal organization."

He'd come to know "Smiler" McFadgen, "who did for the political chiefs what they did not want to do themselves — the numberless, small, but cumulatively vital tasks of dispensing what is collected, for appropriate purposes and for maximum effect, among the party's forces and elsewhere." Dalton already had learned that while electoral victories are claimed by those whose names are on the ballots, their votes are accumulated at the polling stations "under the shrewd and watchful management of men like McFadgen, who adopt whatever means seem most likely to achieve the best results."

Dalton accompanied Smiler along Fredericton's main street, learning how he dispensed $2 bills to men "clustered on the corners, in their frayed Mackinaw or denim jackets, wool shirts open at the throat, the bottoms of their trousers tucked loosely into the tops of pink-soled, gum-rubber boots." Smiler had "an honest, direct relationship with them all that was neither cunning nor cynical but, in a Calvinistic way, compassionate. He was the unofficial almsman of the Liberal Party."

Between infrequent forays into the field and intense card games in the backroom, Dalton delved into the yellowing copies of old *Synoptic Reports* he found in the office, reading accounts from earlier sessions of the provincial assembly. He "marvelled at the elaborate, mysterious irrelevance of the New Brunswick legislature, the interminable hours of meaningless debate, and the dramatic, highly stylized interventions of McNair ... his caustic wit and bitter irony, all directed at make-believe adversaries in a world of illusion."

It was clear to Dalton that he was only putting in time, that nothing he did during the languid summer months of 1948 would affect the course of

New Brunswick Liberalism before he took off for England where he'd been admitted to the London School of Economics on a Beaverbrook Overseas Scholarship. But already he'd seen too much of the Liberal machine to depart with quiescent equanimity. He'd concluded after this time in the Grits' back-shop that politics "was not for me."

Politics was, he'd concluded, "much too dark and mysterious a business to fathom." He'd come to think that being even a part of politics "deprived you of your balance ... so that you walked in anxious fear of falling and developed hesitancy in speech, as though frankness would have your tongue." All in all, Camp judged politicians to be "afflicted by some rare, obscure passion which they could neither understand nor consummate, doomed to lonely lives devoted to failing in the effort." *Lonely lives, devoted to failing.*

He went to see John McNair at the legislature and, facing him across his large desk, told the New Brunswick premier that he had come to dislike politics. He was unable to list the reasons, but was bold enough to tell the Liberal leader that he'd even come to dislike his party, because "much of my experience in it had been, to my dismay, distasteful."

After a long silence, the puzzled man told Dalton to enjoy the rest of the summer, profit from his year overseas, and that when he returned to New Brunswick, he might feel differently.

By the time Camp got back to the Liberal Party office to say farewell to his Young Liberal colleagues, he encountered the chief organizer, Don Cochrane, who was also a member of the legislature and vice-chairman of the province's Power Commission, handing out their weekly paycheques. When he got to Dalton, there was none.

"It meant that I had been summarily and retroactively removed from the payroll of the Liberal Party."

Dalton, already disenchanted with the Liberals, had now been humiliated before his pals by the Liberal's chief organizer. He hitchhiked from Fredericton back to the Atkins' family cottage. By the time he reached Robertson's Point, the sun was low, its late August rays slanting across Grand Lake's placid surface. He broke its mirror with a running dive, swam far underwater, and finally surfaced with a joyous splash, his baptism of purification complete.

His career in politics, he believed, was over. He was liberated, a free man.

Dalton Camp had quit the Liberal Party.

CHAPTER 5

NEW-ERA DEMOCRACY

In late 1948, seeking a new path, Dalton, Linda, and their infant daughter, Gail, departed with happy anticipation for England. He would study at the London School of Economics, funded by a Beaverbrook scholarship, which seemed especially fitting because "Lord Beaverbrook" was really New Brunswick's very own Max Aiken, a newspaper magnate who'd played a huge role in politics and soared to the top of Britain's wartime government with Camp's hero, Winston Churchill. Even if the intimidating Max Aiken was not someone Camp wanted to emulate entirely, the man had blazed a worthy trail and his largesse now provided his fellow Maritimer with a welcome chance to gain distance from Canada's Liberals and acquire new perspectives.

———

As Dalton was recalibrating his life, developments across Canada's political landscape were shaping the new era of public affairs he might return to. Methods for sampling public opinion were purporting to show those running governments and planning campaigns how voters would cast their ballots months before actually doing so.

The cautious political era of Mackenzie King, begun with him seeking out clairvoyants to guide him on events yet to happen, now included "scientific" opinion sampling enabling him to know in March how an election in June or October would likely turn out. During the war, when King contemplated a nation-wide plebiscite on conscription, Sol F. Rae was a senior official at the Department of External Affairs with a compelling interest in how Canada was going to raise more troops to defeat Nazi Germany. So, to determine, in advance, whether the PM's prospective exercise in direct democracy would help or hinder this objective, Rae invited George Gallup to Ottawa, whose polling organization had been tapping into American public opinion since the mid-1930s, to discuss conducting one of his "scientific polls" for the Canadian government.

A pioneer of survey sampling techniques, he'd invented a statistical method for measuring public opinion, dubbed "the Gallup poll." In 1935 he'd formed his own polling company, the American Institute of Public Opinion, and, one year later, gained a coveted reputation with a prediction that contradicted other polls but proved right. George Gallup foresaw, from the responses of fifty thousand people, that Democrat Franklin Roosevelt would defeat Republican Alf Landon in the 1936 presidential election, contradicting the prediction by the highly respected *Literary Digest* magazine after it polled more than two million readers through questionnaires and announced, in advance, victory for Landon. Suddenly everyone embraced, like religious converts, the new age of "scientific sampling."

Gallup's approach was to not ask a single direct question but present "a basket of topics," including questions about such things as car ownership, the name of a respondent's electoral riding, his views on foreign policy, phone ownership, intended support in the next election, membership in a political party, union membership, and past voting behaviour.

Gallup made polling into a business by selling his findings to newspapers. The "news" of a fresh poll was front-page material, editors discovered, because its "Gee whiz" revelations fascinated readers. Beyond a poll's entertainment value for members of the public, however, or its service as launching pad for an editorial or classroom lecture, the most serious and avid readers of Gallup's findings were individuals trying to shape public thinking and political behaviour.

A poll could show preferences for certain types of service and kinds of products. That, by extension, could influence professionals, manufacturers, and service companies. A poll could reveal people's political views and voting patterns across the country's many social, religious, geographic, and demographic groups. This, in turn, suggested new possibilities for where to campaign, how to do it, and even what to say when addressing voters. Gallup's business expanded through contracts with political parties, candidates, corporations, and government agencies.

Rae explained to the president of the American Institute of Public Opinion that a ballot question on conscription carried profound implications for the war effort in which both Canada and the United States, since 1941, were now united. He described the acute political sensitivity felt on this issue by the Liberals, who had won recent wartime elections, both in Quebec and nationally, with their solemn pledge to never introduce conscription. Maybe the grim state of the war had softened or even changed earlier opposition to conscripting men to fight overseas? Could George find out?

The two men reached an agreement. The American pollster would survey public opinion Canada-wide and then predict the voters' verdict based on what he discovered about public attitudes toward conscription. The results would be kept top-secret by Gallup and reported only to Rae, the prime minister, and, depending on what he found, a couple of other top players in Ottawa.

Despite the work being done "for the government's eyes only," they knew that, even with tight wartime security and press censorship, secrets could circulate, and it would be bad for the King government to be discovered using an American organization to find out what Canadians thought about the politically contentious war effort. Many in Canada resented how the United States had stayed out of the war while Canada's soldiers, sailors, and airmen died, until the Japanese attack at Pearl Harbor finally prompted the Yanks to fight. Canadians would be scandalized if an American was secretly surveying them to help determine whether the Liberals could go about breaking their solemn election promise to not bring in conscription. If it could be ascertained in advance that the plebiscite would fail, it would not be held.

To remove his American taint, Gallup set up a Canadian subsidiary, the Canadian Institute of Public Opinion, whose services the government retained. Because Gallup would also help with plebiscite voting strategy, this inaugurated for Canada the role of pollsters working to direct campaign tactics, based on their samplings. Having started, there would be no end.

Once "in the field" north of the border, Gallup realized he could develop a full-scale polling business in Canada, too. This led to his 1943 Gallup poll on party standings. These poll results, unlike those on conscription, became public, because George sold his findings to newspapers, opening a wider dimension to Canadian democracy. Public opinion had been surveyed in Canada for a decade by this time, but pollsters had used limited methods and only generated market data for advertising firms and statistical reports for government departments. Until Gallup's arrival in the mid-1940s, sampling techniques in Canada had not touched upon citizens' political preferences.

The change Gallup introduced would cause a major shift in Canadian political culture. The country had switched to secret ballots decades earlier, and had since benefitted from how the electorate's undisclosed preferences kept politicians more accountable and responsive. Polling would remove the mystery from an election's outcome, diminish the politicians' short-leash connection with voters, and gradually convert the electoral ritual of participation into a spectacle for detached observation. Campaign news coverage would shift to resemble a horse race: who's ahead, and by how many lengths?

To those planning election strategies in backrooms, a potent new weapon had just been delivered. Use of opinion polls for ranking party standings in the 1940s began to redirect Canada's democratic politics by altering party behaviour, changing campaign tactics, and influencing policy emphasis. If elections included fictions about announced programs, they would now embrace a sort of science fiction as well — a present view of a world to come.

This time warp feature added another dimension to Canadian public life as politicians and campaign organizers, armed with polling results, began to take steps to avoid, or accelerate, what seemed inevitable.

———

A second development transforming democratic politics was how the voting system remained unchanged, and hence out of date, even as the political party system it translated into seats in a legislature had grown more diverse.

Canada's two-party system began to fragment as early as the late 1800s, and by the 1920s the emergence of smaller parties had created a multi-party political system. Canada's political pluralism was trapped, however, inside a voting system designed to work best for, and indeed to perpetuate, a two-party dispensation. More was at stake than a democratic society's healthy diversity of political values. Vote splitting between the candidates of many parties meant one party could get enough candidates elected to form a government without achieving majority support from the electorate.

In Ontario and Manitoba, vote splitting resulted in Farmer governments after the First World War, and Progressives were on the ascendancy in national politics, too. In 1921, Progressives won fifty-eight seats in the Commons, bunting the Conservatives, with forty-nine seats, into third place, while the Liberals, with 118 seats, formed a majority government. Yet in popular support, the Liberals had 41 percent of the total votes, far less than a majority, the third place Tories had 30 percent, and the second place Progressives only 22 percent.

As the twentieth century advanced, many Canadian elections resulted in parties wielding power without ever winning majority support, a reality contributing to voter disenchantment and declining turnouts on election day. Proposals to make representation in the legislature "proportional" to the votes cast by people were advanced, on the democratic principle that representation of the people should correspond to their level of support rather than some distortion of it. But in the immediacy of daily politics, those holding power, or aspiring to get it, set aside fundamental electoral reform and instead wove alliances and coalitions with other parties wherever possible. Even reform-minded parties who eschewed "traditional politics" fell into the pattern. The United Farmers and Progressives proved as adept at deal making as Grits and Tories. In Ottawa, Liberal prime minister King enticed Progressive MPs to merge with his caucus. In the provinces, more effort went into forming political alliances after an election than to reforming the voting system in advance of it.

And in the political backrooms, campaign strategists settled in to leverage vote splitting as a pathway to victory. How to benefit from the perverse electoral system would, of necessity, become a primary calculus for shrewd party organizers.

―――

Entering upon this playing field of shifting democratic politics, the rejigged Progressive-Conservatives were not making much progress.

John Bracken had stepped down as Manitoba's premier shortly after becoming PC national leader in 1942, but did not bother seeking a parliamentary seat until the general election of 1945, three years later. During this lengthy hiatus, Bracken failed, not surprisingly, to establish personal authority over the party organization and its election preparations.

Although a long-term premier, he'd never been close to campaign organizers. Nor had he needed the human talents required to change the electorate's voting patterns by effective campaigning. Although sought by the party's establishment for the job, Bracken brought nothing vital to the tasks of political leadership because he'd never had much to offer in the first place, his main "assets" status as a premier and caché as a "Progressive." Things continued as before. The next Progressive-Conservative election campaign would, again, be run mostly by committees of politically interested lawyers, supplemented by someone from an advertising agency handling the party's publicity. Even by 1944, rumblings in Tory backrooms suggested Bracken had to be replaced before the election that would follow the war.

———

Canadians who had persevered through the Great Depression and were now weathering the Second World War would not, it appeared, be stymied by the country's antiquated political ways. George Gallup's first published poll in 1943 showed the rising CCF ahead of both the Liberals and Progressive-Conservatives nationally, with potential to win as many as 70 to 100 seats and form a minority government in the 245 seat House of Commons. This prospect generated hope for socialists, fear among capitalists, and fascination with the public.

Before that federal election, however, would come provincial votes in Ontario and Saskatchewan.

CHAPTER 6

TO THE POLLS

When the Second World War began, the Liberals under popular premier Mitch Hepburn seemed poised to become a decades-long governing force in Ontario. Then something snapped in the onion farmer. Hepburn's change of character spread turmoil in Liberal circles and promised opportunity to the Tories.

Hepburn got bored heading his own government and abandoned its running to the province's top civil servant, Chester Walters. The premier and his northern Ontario gold mining cronies partied in the Liberal leader's suite at the King Edward Hotel, with jazz on the radio, women companions laughing, and liquor flowing. Whenever his mind wandered back to his government up at Queen's Park, it was only about how to turn the thing over to somebody else. By the time of the 1943 Ontario general election, Hepburn had twice handed his premiership over to other members of his Cabinet, first Gordon Conant, then Harry Nixon, and even tried to form a wartime coalition government with Conservative leader, Earl Rowe. The Ontario Liberal Party that had been re-elected with a big majority in 1937 found itself torn apart.

Handsome and boldly visionary, George Drew was the opposite of Hepburn. The new leader of Ontario's "Progressive-Conservatives," one of the most impatient men in Canadian politics, was also a counterpoint to slow-moving John Bracken, his national leader. Within Ontario Tory circles, Drew, ambitious to lead the provincial party, had been made all the hungrier for the top position after being rebuffed by the Conservative establishment, not once but twice, before finally winning the provincial leadership in December 1938. Once he became leader, Drew worked hard to gain the Ontario premier's office. For his campaign organization he relied, in the pattern of the time, on the strength of the constituency organizations and provincial officers of the party.

Drew knew he needed fresh policies to counter the rising appeal of the Co-operative Commonwealth Federation, or "CCF." Turning to the Port Hope resolutions, he found what he needed for a *progressive* Progressive Conservative platform and fashioned them into his provincial party's Twenty-Two Point Program. The package of policies was extensive, specific, and touched virtually every sector of Ontario society. Drew announced it on radio.

In the midst of Ontario's general election, with voting slated for August 4, 1943, Drew was bullish about his party's prospects. In Windsor, he addressed an afternoon audience in a local movie theatre on July 14, telling his supporters, "We're going to build a big blue machine that will advance from one side of this province to the other and roll up a big majority at Queen's Park." The *Windsor Star* reporter filed his story of the meeting, which was picked up by the Canadian Press wire service. Daily papers across Ontario to Ottawa and north to Fort William quoted the Progressive Conservative leader's imagery of the Ontario Tories as a "big blue machine."

Drew's "machine" metaphor fitted his wartime context. Canada was a major player in the war effort, thanks to a tightly organized, highly disciplined, and resolutely motivated domestic war machine, producing munitions, foodstuffs, and trained soldiers, sailors, and airmen. By blending pragmatism and idealism, resources and planning, Canada had forged a nation-wide mechanism for victory. In these dramatic circumstances, it was easy for "Colonel" Drew to envisage, and portray to others, how the party he led might, likewise, resemble a machine.

The vote tallies on election night gave Drew and the PCs enough MPPs to form a new government for the province, but the blue machine had not rolled up a big victory. It barely eked out the narrowest of wins. The policy was strong. The leader was outwardly confident. And several valuable campaign innovations, such as the artful packaging of almost two dozen major programs and extensive use of radio, greatly helped the Progressive-Conservative's 1943 Ontario campaign. Falling short of a majority resulted from the party's general *organizational* weakness, and the expected spectacular rise of the CCF.

The discredited Liberals plummeted from majority government to third spot. Representation in the legislature was thirty-eight seats for the PCs, thirty-four for the CCF, and fifteen for the Liberals. The CCF surge had helped the PCs get past the Grits, thanks to vote splitting.

The voting system worked to the disadvantage of the Liberals. All three parties were close, with the Progressive Conservatives claiming 35.7 percent of the popular vote, the CCF 31.7 percent, and the Liberals 31.2 percent. Although the PCs won more ridings than the other two parties, the Tory's vote actually dropped more than 4 percent from the prior election in 1937. The Liberals had fallen 20 percent. All gains were by the CCF. Results riding by riding made clear that, by just a handful of votes in a scattering of constituencies, Ontarians had come razor close to electing the first socialist government in North America. That distinction would, instead, belong to Saskatchewanians a year later.

The interplay of circumstances helped the Progressive Conservatives end up on top, and the slight 4 percent difference between the PCs and CCF meant Drew could take power and establish a Progressive Conservative government. The only one in Canada, it was a bridgehead, Tories elsewhere in the country hoped, for the new *progressive* brand of Canadian political conservatism.

Being able to exercise powers of government gave Drew and his small blue machine the ability, over the ensuing months, to turn promised policies into programs, reap the partisan advantages of making appointments and awarding contracts, and ride the crest of people's renewed optimism as the tide of war, at last, seemed to be turning toward an Allied victory.

––––

The 1945 Canadian general election, with voting slated for June 11, featured a battle of the Prairies, where leaders of the country's four strongest parties were each candidates.

The CCF leader since 1942, Saskatchewan's M.J. Coldwell, had been an educator and union activist before getting elected to Parliament in 1935 from Rosetown-Biggar constituency. In Alberta, where Social Credit had come to power provincially in 1935, Solon Low had been leader of the federal Social Credit Party since 1944. Liberal prime minister King was seeking re-election in Saskatchewan's Prince Albert constituency, a seat of convenience he'd held since 1926 after having been beaten in his Ontario riding. The fourth national leader in this Prairie faceoff was, of course, Manitoba's John Bracken of the Progressive-Conservatives.

Bracken won rural Manitoba's Neewapa riding, one of only two seats the Tories claimed in a province where he'd been premier for two decades. A damning measure of the feeble clout a provincial leader wields in the sterner contest of national politics was provided by the CCF winning three more seats in Manitoba than the PCs, the Liberals seven more.

The tallies across Canada from the June 11 election gave the Liberals 118 seats with less than 40 percent of the popular vote, the Progressive Conservatives sixty-seven with 28 percent, the CCF twenty-eight, a majority of them in Saskatchewan, with 16 percent popular support. Social Credit, with only 4 percent support nationally, won thirteen Alberta seats. That was another thing about Canada's voting system: a party strong in one region or province could achieve disproportionate weight in the lawmaking assembly. Mackenzie King formed a government, based on 40 percent support of voters; 60 percent of Canadians had voted for other parties.

The Progressive-Conservatives had garnered only one or two seats per province, except for the anomaly of Ontario, where the party elected forty-eight MPs. This gave them enough seats overall to rank as Official Opposition in the Commons. Ontario stood out in another way, too. Progressive Conservative premier George Drew had called a provincial election to overlap with the federal one, with voting just a week ahead, on June 4, 1945. When the provincial PCs won a massive victory, the national campaign sought to capitalize on this momentum. Large newspaper advertisements across the country exhorted voters heading to the polls on June 11 to rally behind the PC Party: "Ontario shows! Only Bracken can win!"

PC campaign ads suggested it would be impossible to form a majority government in the country without winning a plurality of seats in Ontario, which, the party contended, only the Tories could do. This unappealing stance was more than offset, however, by the arrogance of Liberal prime minister King who, believing only Liberals could, or should, govern Canada, threatened voters that if *his* party did not receive a majority, he'd simply call another election.

The June 11 contest brought fully three-quarters of Canadian voters to the polls. After they'd rendered a collective verdict, the Liberals had lost fifty-nine seats, the Progressive Conservatives gained twenty-two, but both parties saw their share of the popular vote erode from the prior election. At just under 28 percent, the Tories had in fact hit their lowest popular vote in history. The exhilarating promise that filled the air in Winnipeg in 1942, when the Port Hope resolutions had become party policy and the party's name changed to indicate a more progressive nature, had evaporated.

Except for Ontario, the Progressive Conservatives were still in the wilderness.

CHAPTER 7

DALTON CAMP'S RESURRECTION

Late in 1949, Dalton and Linda, returning after his year at the London School of Economics, arrived in New Jersey to stay with her parents. Several days later Dalton heard a knock at the Atkins' front door. But unlike 1947, the caller was not a Liberal operative. Rather, he was a Western Union messenger, although he, too, brought a political organizer's invitation as Robert Tweedie had done.

In the closed-circuit universe of New Brunswick politics, word that Dalton had decamped from the Liberals circulated among the Tories, who hoped a disgruntled partisan might be turned into a valiant warrior against his former side. Camp studied the cable from Ewart Atkinson, president of the provincial Progressive Conservatives, offering him the position of executive secretary with the New Brunswick PC Party. The prospect struck him as "both alluring and forbidding, like a sudden invitation to climb Mount Everest."

His friends, family, and most especially an alarmed Linda, objected with strenuous sincerity to the preposterous idea. Apart from questions of political ideology, the Conservatives were a lost cause, a rag-tag assembly of losers. Everybody knew that. Dalton himself could easily list dozens of reasons to reject Atkinson's offer.

He managed, in fact, to come up with only three positives: return to Canada, live in New Brunswick, and "teach Tories how to fight Grits." What he could not add to that stub column on the Yes side of his ledger, because it remained inarticulate, was his idealism about politics. If anything, his time at LSE had burnished it brighter.

Camp would convert. He decided to enlist with the New Brunswick Tories.

———

A rebel returned to fight his former allies, he now took fuller measure of the province's realities.

Camp saw how many New Brunswickers came to be, and remained, Liberal, "not because of any private convictions, but because their ordinary lives depended upon it. These were not only the select in the higher organizational echelons, nor merely the contractors and entrepreneurs. They included the numberless people who subscribed to the Liberal Party in recognition of whatever they got from it."

In his view, "charity and compassion" once ennobled Liberalism, but what now corrupted the faith was "its expedience and the haunted insecurity that led it to accompany humanitarianism with the menace of fear." The gist of Liberalism had simply become that "everyone was better off being Liberal, everyone would be worse off being anything else."

He was nuanced in this appraisal, adding that "the philosophy was not so simply pejorative as that." It had been "refined and tailored for countless applications, wherever uncertainty could be seeded, wherever there was fear to be fostered. Liberalism had become not a faith but a command." He even suggested Liberalism probably had to be this way, because "no party on earth could treat so many claimants."

But the end result of this kind of politics was bleak and rekindled his outrage about conditions in his home province, "much of it directed at the Liberal Party."

Dalton walked the streets of Woodstock and Fredericton. He saw men "consumed by idleness, their women worn by harsh routine, bearing the pallor of self-neglect, the children with bad teeth, the early beginning of a life cycle of decay; store windows displaying the hideous litter of cheap merchandise, malevolently designed for lives of quiet despair, for an existence amid an abandoned culture, in a ghetto of memory." This wasteland human condition was the result of partisan political conduct of public affairs in which "charity and compassion, cynicism and greed, lived side by side."

Dalton knew the culprits. In New Brunswick, "the merchant class took few risks but prospered, and among the risks it did not take was an involvement in politics." Instead, community service was safely rendered in the safer havens of church activities, charities, and service clubs. Government and commerce "remained at peace, exchanging tributes with graceful facility and tacit understanding." Each operated so as "to avoid colliding in the other's jurisdiction."

Politics was left to lawyers, business to the merchants. Those who benefitted most in terms of personal enrichment were the facilitators who "glided in between" these two worlds, "advertising a common usefulness." To Camp, this was "a classic kind of Liberalism, satisfying and rewarding to the principals, stultifying to the people, suffocating to the province."

The new Progressive Conservative recruit raised his sights to take in, as well, the province's own larger setting. Canada's constitution had, over time, become unrealistic in its allocation of powers. "There was a growing gap between provincial resources and provincial responsibilities," he realized, which meant that while the New Brunswick's government "held title to sovereign responsibilities under the constitution, providence had not provided for the means to discharge them." Like other Maritime provinces, New Brunswick was "a ward of the federal state." That had prompted Camp and other Liberals at the August 1948 national convention to draft policies for regional fairness, which he'd seen overridden by the party's desire to give Canadians nothing more than a perceptibly smooth transition in prime ministerial leadership.

But now he updated his earlier appraisal, noting how constitutional incapacity was itself married to New Brunswick's bankrupt political system. "If politics and the parliamentary system are meaningless ritual, merely a crude public deception, then argument could be made that the condition of New Brunswick, in 1949, was its natural state."

Camp saw a party system that had collapsed, and citizens who'd become fatalistically passive. The capacity for public protest, the claims of those with true grievances, even vigorous political dissent had "all been abandoned, indeed, had devolved upon less than a half-dozen men, no more, each of whom, for one reason or another, lacked the strength, skill, or competence to discharge so large a responsibility. In New Brunswick, the party system was dead."

The refurbished idealist now looked upon the politics of New Brunswick "as a personal challenge and a private duty."

Dalton found the man who'd hired him, Ewart Atkinson, a bulldog-like lawyer and aggressive optimist for all things Conservative, in a hospital bed late on a Sunday afternoon. Atkinson told his fresh recruit that he'd booked fifteen minutes of radio air time the next night. Camp's job was to show up at the station and fill the quarter-hour with a powerful message. It would be entirely up to Dalton what to say.

Over the next twenty-four hours Camp fashioned his first PC political manifesto. As Monday darkness descended, on December 5, 1949, he walked over to radio station CFNB and into the broadcast studio. The red light came on, the microphone was live:

"The business of politics is looked upon by many of us in this province as a practice somewhat unhealthy and sinister," he opened, connecting himself with his listeners. "That this is so is, in itself, mute indictment of the present party in power," he added, making clear the villain was the Liberal Party of New Brunswick. "It should be of little comfort to us that a national Canadian magazine recently listed elections in New Brunswick as among the most corrupt in Canada," he offered by way of external reinforcement, from *Maclean's* magazine, for his allegation.

Now with his audience readied, he hit full bore: "Let me make it clear that the professional Liberal, in power today, is opposed to the collectivist state. He is also self-dedicated to freedom. But the professional Liberal will sell any principle, as he has done throughout history and looks like doing today — if the selling will yield him increased power. If professional Liberalism means anything today, it means an ability to hold power, by the subtle exploitation of fear and suspicion."

He then expressed hope that no sales tax would be introduced by the Liberals in New Brunswick, because people could not afford it and did not want it, only to add his stinger: "But a sales tax is the logical result of the government's postwar fiscal policy."

He took note of rising unemployment in New Brunswick to further condemn Liberals, calling the attitude of the provincial government towards labour as "totally unreal" and "anti-labour."

As for the lop-sided Liberal representation in New Brunswick's legislature, where the government had forty-six members, Camp said he did not doubt their motives or sincerity. If New Brunswickers set aside the leader of the Liberal Party, however, and looked at the crowded benches behind him, they'd see "a startling array of nonentities collected together for the purpose of governing a modern state."

"Surely we have not endorsed one-man government, nor a one-party state," he said. A "political machine" had been put together in the province, he argued, one "highly skilled in the subtle art of patronage, a wealthy machine, a smooth machine" whose masters did not sit in the legislature. "We do not elect them. They do not seek office, but the spoils of office. The greatest task at hand is to crush this machine."

———

The next day, that smooth machine began spreading oily rumours that a disgruntled Camp had left the Liberal Party because Premier McNair refused to name him director of New Brunswick's travel bureau, a plum appointment. Another version put about explained Camp's dark anger as the result of the Liberal premier not supporting his supposed ambition to become editor of the *Daily Gleaner*. In case those two allegations did not stick, another claim to discredit Dalton was that he'd bolted over not getting appointed secretary to the Cabinet.

The Grits added social ostracism to isolate and diminish Camp. "Erstwhile Liberal friends crossed the street," he observed, "or ducked into the nearest store to avoid meeting me."

It had been suspected, he was able to chuckle, that his departure from New Brunswick for the London School of Economics meant he'd "gone off to Britain and returned a socialist, or worse." As his feisty support for Tories confirmed, "it was worse."

———

The executive secretary of the New Brunswick Progressive Conservative Party barely had time to get his feet under his desk and start work when he had to deal with a quick by-election called for January 9, 1950, in Charlotte, a solid Liberal riding. It was as if McNair wanted to humiliate his former confidant.

As the party's new chief operating officer, Camp accompanied provincial PC leader Hugh Mackay to a meeting with the riding's Tory executive, only to hear him plead that they *not* field a candidate. The impoverished provincial Conservatives sole-sourced their campaign funds from the leader, and Mackay was still in debt from the 1948 election.

Being Conservatives, however, a couple of locals resented being told what to do and, anyway, just wanted to fight Grits. So they nominated a candidate, pooling enough dollars to cover the $100 deposit a candidate had to pay, as earnest money, submitting the funds with his nomination papers. Camp found himself twisting between the do-nothing wishes of his leader, the combative desires of a handful of riding association diehards, and, to his dismay, the great reluctance of many Progressive Conservatives to rise and do battle at all.

The only advertisement that the meagre PC campaign could afford was a newspaper ad Dalton prepared. It challenged the Liberal candidate to declare his position on the expected introduction of a provincial sales tax. He actually responded, saying he knew nothing about it.

Dalton took up an offer of free air time and drove the PC candidate from his home to the radio station. During their hour long trip, while Camp reviewed the hottest New Brunswick topics with the candidate and suggested approaches to dealing with them during his thirty-minute address to voters, the candidate mostly sang country and western songs. When he delivered his talk on air, it was not about unemployment or the likelihood of a Grit sales tax, but the importance of the new United Nations in world affairs.

On election day, through a blizzard and freezing temperatures, the Liberal machine hauled supporters to the polling stations and accumulated, for its effort, some 5,547 votes to 3,156 for the PCs. The candidate did not lose his $100 deposit, though several PCs had bet he would. Taking account of "the sour predictions of some of our Tory friends," that small victory alone pleased campaign organizer Camp.

The Progressive Conservative vote would have been somewhat higher if Liberal-appointed returning officers had not moved two polling stations in strong Tory areas. After the election, Camp demanded "full investigation of the gross abuses and violations of the provincial Elections Act."

Premier McNair "seemed only puzzled by this unexpected sign of defiance." He issued a statement filled with patronizing comments about Dalton Camp and his misunderstanding of New Brunswick electoral laws.

Dalton replied, to keep the issue alive in the newspapers and on radio news, but most every other Tory thought he should drop the subject. After all, the election was over and the PCs had lost. One senior Conservative wearily told him, "I don't think anyone cares about it, really."

But they did not understand Liberals the way Camp did. "I knew he was wrong," Camp said. "The Grits cared; they hated it, despised the publicity, the controversy, and 'that son-of-a-bitch Camp' landing on their doorstep." They became what they did not want to be: "cautious, careful about doing things, so that things should not only be done right, but *appear* to be done right. It was an unaccustomed consideration."

Dalton, because he was a Liberal convert among long-time Tories, seemed almost alone in his understanding. He suspected the Liberal machine could be persuaded of the risks and dangers. "If the machine could intimidate people, we had to intimidate the machine." The PCs must, he concluded, "fight fear with fear."

———

Working for the Conservative Party provided a hard apprenticeship in politics.

Linda had been right. The intelligence and energy Dalton expended tilling New Brunswick's barren ground for the Tories, with nothing to show for it, made him ask whether he needed to refocus. The fact the threadbare provincial PCs were out of money, had closed the party office, and could no longer pay him helped answer his question.

"At a mere twenty-eight years of age," he acknowledged, "you do not like to admit defeat. But Don Quixote had broken his lance on the impenetrable armour of New Brunswick Liberalism. Or was it Toryism?"

When he'd arrived in their midst, Dalton had found the Conservatives "racked by dissension, soured by intrigue, demoralized, spiritless, and fragmented." Their makeover in Winnipeg as *Progressive* Conservatives may have portended a better future but, so far, nothing had moved at ground level in the Maritimes. Something would have to change for Dalton though. A married man with a growing family had to buy groceries, pay rent.

CHAPTER 8

ILL-FATED FLIGHT

Dalton was ready to do just about anything.

The Progressive Conservatives, however, were in such shambles nobody in charge knew what to do with so ardent a volunteer. All across Canada, chill provincial political winds continued to buffet the Tories, as they had for so long. By 1950, the eastern provinces of Newfoundland, Prince Edward Island, Nova Scotia, and New Brunswick were each governed by Liberals. Quebec was being run by the Union Nationale machine, a case unto itself. In the West, British Columbia Liberals and Progressive Conservatives had merged into a centre-right coalition to defeat the CCF in 1945, and been re-elected in 1949, but the new formation did not even carry the Conservative name, doing nothing for the party profile. Alberta had a Social Credit government, Saskatchewan a CCF one, and Manitoba, Liberal. Ontario alone had its Progressive Conservative government, elected in 1943 and re-elected in 1945 and, again, in 1948.

With the 1945 federal election, John Bracken had entered Parliament and become leader of the Official Opposition. He and sixty-six other Progressive Conservative MPs tried to challenge the Liberals in a divided House where the Grits were shy of a majority. With sizeable numbers of Social Credit and CCF MPs, the Progressive Conservatives were as weak in Parliament as they were behind the scenes, where nothing much had been developed for constituency organization or national campaign structure, either. Such matters held no interest for Bracken.

The only show of spunk came when others in the party, spotting a potential PC headquarters, bought for little money a rundown Laurier Avenue house in a sirloin section of Ottawa. In hommage to the leader, they dubbed the creaky two-storey structure "Bracken House."

By 1948 it was time for Bracken to take his failures and depart. But he always seemed to have a condition. The premier who'd refused to accept the leadership unless the party changed its name now insisted he would only yield the leadership if given a farm on which to retire. Senior PC bagmen Ed Bickle and Harry Price raised the money and bought the agronomist a handsome spread outside Ottawa.

This backroom deal to facilitate a leadership change sprang directly from an odd turn of events in Ontario. Mackenzie King had shown a leader could be defeated even as his party won majority re-election, and George Drew had pulled off the same stunt, too. The man who'd made the lone Progressive Conservative breakthrough by forming an Ontario government in 1943 and strengthening it in 1945, had lost his own Toronto High Park seat while leading the provincial PCs to a third election victory in 1948.

Ontario's PCs still had a majority, with fifty-three members in the ninety-seat legislature, but had dropped thirteen ridings, all picked up by the CCF, while the Liberals and Labour Progressives held at fourteen and two seats, as before. Should Drew seek to get back into his premier's chair at Queen's Park through a by-election? Or might he instead press ahead for the national party leadership and become prime minister of Canada?

Tory sages at the Albany Club considered Drew a better bet than Bracken. Few, if any, raised concerns about replacing one provincial premier by another. The sweet irony was that a man the party establishment had earlier thwarted at every turn in his efforts to become the provincial leader now wanted to pull strings and orchestrate his ascent to national leadership.

———

A challenge was that, beyond the Albany Club, there did not seem much national interest in a defeated provincial premier.

MP John Diefenbaker was already in the Commons. Though portrayed as a Prairie loner, he had friends in Toronto and elsewhere, including a circle of supporters with enough money to actively promote him for leader. Diefenbaker was gaining publicity and support and was seen by many Conservatives across Canada as a deserving contender. Drew could not just declare his candidacy without appearing rudely ambitious. The Tory premier and his promoters knew a springboard was needed. He should appear to be responding to a "Draft Drew" movement when entering the race.

Drew's close friend and political confidant A.D. McKenzie, also president of the Ontario PC Party, phoned Elmer Bell, the lawyer in Exeter who was party vice-president and his most reliable fixer. Bell was to start a groundswell of support for Drew.

After making arrangements to patch together a coast-to-coast network of private radio stations to broadcast a special political message, Bell called two nearby Progressive Conservatives, Huron County farmer Gerry Godbout and PC Youth member Clare Westcott in Seaforth, asking them to represent two different Progressive Conservative "grass-roots" voices in delivering a radio message.

Bell picked them up in his car and drove into Stratford, pulling up in front of radio station CJCS. Just before going in, he handed each a speech they'd not seen until that moment, written by someone in Toronto at the ad agency handling the PC account. The nervous duo entered the studio, a small room, where they were instructed to say nothing until a red light came on. With that signal they began reading their speeches, first Godbout, then Westcott. Their call for George Drew "to tender his name to the leadership convention" was heard across the country through the national hookup.

Drew declared his candidacy in a race against Diefenbaker and Toronto Eglinton MP Donald Fleming. The October 1948 convention in Ottawa drew some 1,300 delegates, who also voted on some three dozen policy resolutions, most of them perennial Tory favorites such as tax relief, confronting communists, reducing the cost of government, strengthening defence, and a long-term immigration policy, but a number of them were nationalistic vanguard measures: adopting a distinctive Canadian flag, for instance, and creating a national library. Little remained of the Port Hopefuls spirit or the party's progressive policy resolutions from Winnipeg six years earlier.

Drew emerged a clear frontrunner, abetted by the strong provincial Tory organization in Ontario. His speech earned more applause than Diefenbaker's, especially when he called for stronger relations between Quebec and the rest of Canada, criticized centralized power in Ottawa, and advocated a future centred upon personal initiative, saving, and security. Winning on the first ballot by taking two-thirds of the votes, Drew soon entered the Commons in a by-election for Carleton riding near Ottawa.

For a while things seemed more promising for the PCs nationally, but in 1949 the Liberals, smoothly in control and now led by Louis St. Laurent, defeated the Drew-led Progressive Conservatives, gaining another majority. Overall, Progressive Conservative performance remained the same in the provinces. In Nova Scotia, the Liberals swamped the PCs in a 1949 provincial election, taking twenty-seven seats to eight for the Tories. Liberal hegemony in national politics seemed more stable than ever, thanks to the post-war prosperity which folks in general attributed to the presiding beneficence of "Uncle Louis" St. Laurent's government in Ottawa.

It seemed Ontario's Progressive Conservative government was an aberration.

CHAPTER 9

NEW FOOTINGS

With the PC Party in disarray everywhere except Ontario, Camp was in need of something else to occupy him and to pay the bills.

Dalton was adept at capturing complex social realities in easy to grasp images, which meant he might follow a number of different careers, such as journalism, speech writing, advertising, or authorship.

Because his instinct was to integrate rather than segregate, he saw no reason to exclude any of these possibilities. If he could blend political writing, election campaigning, and commercial advertising into a harmonious whole, say, he might even be able to construct a better version of New Brunswick's smooth Liberal machine, whose effective campaign operation he admired, even as he despised its arrogance and double standards in conducting public business.

Camp's desire to get something going was especially fueled by ambition to someday, somehow, rise in politics himself. He'd already watched politicians enough to know someone not born into power and privilege had to make his own way by establishing "a power base." He needed a position that would give him income, influence, and independence, but rather than follow the traditional pattern of, say, Milton Gregg, who'd been decorated for bravery in war and become a university president before venturing into political life, Camp envisaged a swifter and more contemporary route suited to his own interests and temperament.

He might, for instance, earn enough money in one realm of writing, such as commercial journalism or advertising, to subsidize others that, at least for now, did not pay their way. If he could not get income from another a job with the PCs, he could work in one of the other fields and fight Grits pro bono.

———

Though keen to write, Camp knew he'd not be able to fight Grits the way he really wanted if he was a journalist. Rising as a reporter would be hard anyway because the writing he favoured was "not reportorial but opinion informed by a sense of social justice." That meant working as a columnist, something he was not yet positioned to be.

Sidestepping journalism cleared the way to a kindred trade: advertising.

When working for premier McNair in the 1948 election, Dalton had a rare opportunity to directly witness advertising men in elections. He'd first encountered the Walsh agency operatives in the premier's office. Later in the campaign, spending a lot of time "in their improvised offices" of a hotel suite, he'd been fascinated watching Scott Faggans hover over his artist's drawing board and Larry Jones hammer out copy on his portable typewriter. Dalton was mesmerized by their intriguing telephone conversations with the Toronto office, "conducted in the unintelligible idiom of their trade."

It had been a revelation to discover how these advertising paladins, living a special life on the edge of power and creativity, not only worked a particular influence over voters, but even steered campaign strategy itself.

After those encounters, everything about advertising charmed Dalton. The adman's special lingo, his entrées into diverse fields, exercise of power, the brilliant conversation at martini lunches, and artistic flare: all defined an adventurer's calling that mixed ideas and action. Advertising might be his best path forward of all. He'd find work with a major agency and learn everything he could about the business, no longer by watching over the shoulders of Walsh agency men, but acting directly with responsibilities of his own.

In 1950, Camp landed a beginner's job in Toronto as a junior copywriter at the prestigious J. Walter Thompson agency, one of the big international advertising houses. He and Linda moved into a recently built house, on a newly developed street. Joining their five-year-old daughter in this year of fresh beginnings was a second child, David.

Camp's writing talent was soon being deployed, not to influence voters in elections or change people's minds on public policy, but for the benefit of such JWT clients as Wrigley's chewing gum, Labatt's Breweries, and the Bank of Nova Scotia. It was valuable experience, he thought, learning about the wide-ranging activities of the firm's many clients, discovering the range of advertising practices, and working in an intensely focused milieu where talent could rise.

———

When the Camps relocated to Toronto, Dalton brought his zealous new political faith with him. Like a Baptist seeking a new congregation, Dalton sought out in Toronto a local partisan congregation of worn and weary PCs similar to those he'd known in New Brunswick's Charlotte constituency, and discovered them huddled in Spadina riding.

Camp's research convinced him this core city riding was the last Toronto seat a PC candidate would ever win. Even Hollywood-handsome George Hees, well-educated, a war veteran, and a strong athlete whose three seasons with the Toronto Argonauts included winning a Grey Cup, lost in Spadina and had to enter the Commons from a neighbouring riding. However, Dalton, with the sensibilities of a penitent putting on a prickly hair-shirt and smearing ashes onto his face, felt right in Spadina. To embrace the Tory faith, he'd go all the way.

Although legend portrayed the Conservatives as a party for the powerful and privileged, those were the very people Dalton had deliberately left behind when quitting the Liberals. Along Spadina's hard streets lived cousins of men he'd seen standing in rubber boots huddling on New Brunswick's windy street corners with no money, little employment, and few prospects. They were "disarming in their innocence of power, uncorrupted by arrogance or cynicism, endearing in their stoic perseverance, and uncomplicated in their loyalty to that mysterious meaning of conservatism."

Camp had not left the Liberal Party to abandon his liberalism, but in fact to reclaim it. The PC Party's contradictory name might confuse some, but Dalton discovered that as a *Progressive* Conservative, he could serve the people while remaining true to himself. "In politics," as his new national leader George Drew put it, "nothing is sacred but the integrity of our own minds."

———

Dalton was not content to mingle only with defeat-numbed Conservatives in his local congregation, however, because he knew beating Grits demanded much more, and wanted to make it happen.

That summer he travelled to Ottawa and offered himself in higher service, too.

Exceedingly determined, Camp had requested an appointment with George Drew, disregarding how a leader is weary, and wary, of being importuned by an unceasing stream of supplicants for work. Those who considered Camp pushy did not understand the zealousness of his cause.

"I knew only that I had failed to help rally the party in New Brunswick," said Camp of this initial encounter with Drew, "but the ego remained stubborn enough to persuade me that I could do something for the Tory Party, if only it would give me the opportunity."

CHAPTER 10

DALTON'S REACH

In 1951, Ontario's Progressive Conservatives won a resounding electoral victory, claiming seventy-nine seats in the ninety-seat legislature, taking ridings from the three other parties and leaving the Liberals with eight members, the CCF with two, and Labour-Progressive, one. At a deeper level, it was the same story. Despite their win, the PCs were below 50 percent, the other two, together, above.

Dalton Camp's role in this PC triumph was limited to casting a Tory ballot in his Toronto riding, adding one more vote to the PC's popular support. Although happy with the party's victory, he understood, too, that the system that had generated such a big win was flawed. Regardless of how the electoral system operated, though, Dalton wanted into the game. He was chagrined by the lack of a battlefield on which to wage his personal war against Grits. Ontario Tories clearly did not need him. He'd heard nothing from Drew in Ottawa.

———

With little happening for Camp on the political front, where his role seemed dependant on others, he became more engaged with advertising work and his family, where he had direct say.

In 1952, after two years at J. Walter Thompson, he was offered the position of creative director in the firm's Toronto office. But the offer came when Dalton was already contemplating moving to a rival firm, where he hoped to learn still more about commercial communication, but from a different perspective. The Locke Johnson firm had enticed him with a yearly salary exceeding what U.S.-based JWT allowed anyone in its Canadian office. Besides higher income, which was needed now that Linda was expecting their third child, Dalton's belief that he would be more appreciated and could take a larger role in a smaller firm propelled him across town to enlist with JWT's competitor.

If he could shift between political adversaries in New Brunswick, he could certainly move to a rival advertising agency in Toronto.

———

The summer of 1952 was especially hot in New Brunswick and vacationing Dalton was enjoying easy pleasures at Robertson's Point with Linda, her now eighteen-year-old brother, Kempton, and the rest of their family, when news arrived that Premier McNair had just called a New Brunswick provincial election for Monday, September 22. Camp was electrified.

Could this 1952 campaign in his home province be his awaited main chance?

The Progressive Conservatives had a new leader, chosen the year before: shrewd and calm Hugh John Flemming, himself the son of a premier, James Flemming. Dalton had met "Hugh John," as the new leader was invariably called, when he worked at the Flemming family saw mill years before. He knew Flemming could be evasive, in fact so hard to pin down that some of the lumberman's close associates described him as "strange." Despite his position as leader, it seemed Hugh John was, strange but true, uninterested even in advancing his own political interests.

Camp feared "that politics in New Brunswick would resume its accustomed course," with McNair in the legislative building, and Flemming retreated into the woods at Juniper, "each enjoying the seeming tranquility of the summer, neither able to measure the restless unease beneath the placid surface of everyday life."

Dalton sought to reconnect with Flemming and resume his mission of fighting Grits. He would offer the leader his services, just as he had to Drew. Did the PCs want his help with campaign advertising? Dalton had worked for the party, knew the province, and was now in the ad business. With an election ahead, it seemed obvious that someone volunteering crucial help for the campaign would be welcomed.

Yet Flemming was diffident. He saw no benefit from paid advertising. He and his candidates could speak at meetings around the province, he explained. He could also use some free time offered on radio. That should be enough.

Not really, countered Camp. He stressed that the PCs had to have some professional advertising. He knew the Liberals would have plenty.

All he heard from Flemming, though, were evasive expressions of doubt about the value of election publicity, worry about the cost, and hesitancy even about what should be conveyed by campaign messages. "It's a powerful waste of money," asserted the unmoved leader.

Miffed, Dalton got in his car, returning to Grand Lake to pack for Toronto and his work at Locke Johnson, his allotted vacation time drawing to a close anyway. He'd leave Linda and their kids to finish out summer at Robertson's Point. Swelling with discontent, he mentally conceded the fall election to the Liberals. "With less than eight weeks until polling day, the Tories had yet to begin to create a campaign."

He drove straight through Fredericton and up the highway another sixty miles, winding alongside the St. John River, heading out of New Brunswick for Ontario. But he was passing familiar places that tugged at him. A farm came into view where, as boys, he and Billy Chase, "now dead and buried in France," once stalked groundhogs, drove horses, hauled hay, and slept in the orchard at night beneath the stars. He pulled his car over and stopped. He walked inland along a road, and looked at the weather-beaten barns.

Dalton thought about Hugh John Flemming with his principled concern for people. He thought about the New Brunswick Tories and their political despondency. He thought about his earlier "hundred wasted days" in 1948 working for the PCs "searching for a sign of life."

He realized nobody knew Premier John McNair the way he did. Nor did anyone else know so well the Liberal's vulnerabilities. Billy Chase had sacrificed his very life. Dalton could give two months.

"If you leave New Brunswick now," he told himself, "you have quit, for the last time. And New Brunswick will never be the same to you."

He could not leave without a clear answer.

Returning to Fredericton, he found Flemming surprisingly more receptive, but Camp still could not get his ultimate commitment. He was dispatched, instead, to speak with Hugh Mackay, whom the leader obscurely said "knows about these things."

When they connected two days later, the adman outlined his approach to the campaign, which Mackay listened to with nods of approval. "Now to the big question," he said, clearing his throat, "How much?"

Dalton replied he wanted a budget of $25,000, which astonished Mackay. "My God, you can't do much with that, can you?"

"All that needs to be done."

"Is that all you will want?"

"Yes."

"You have it."

———

In the Lord Beaverbrook Hotel on Fredericton's Queen Street, with his new designation of "provincial campaign coordinator," Camp set up his guerilla war encampment in a cramped third-floor room.

In a full suite of rooms two floors above, Larry Jones from Walsh Advertising had already settled in and was overseeing the smooth, incremental release of pre-approved ads urging re-election of McNair's Liberals. His budget was vastly larger, his attitude that of a detached professional.

The two men sometimes passed each other down in the hotel lobby, or stood waiting together by the elevator, exchanging inconsequential chat about hotel services or a baseball game, like men from rival secret service agencies who each know who the other is and what he's up to yet do not want to let on.

Few made it into Camp's room. "I guarded my room," said Camp, "treasuring privacy as essential to work and contemplation." He kept no liquor on hand, a big help in reducing campaign visitations, but "drank black coffee as thick as pitch-blende all day long" and offered nothing but the same to any who did drop by.

One person readily admitted was "Kemp" Atkins (who, following Dalton's suggestion, began using his name "Norman" to reduce confusion between "Kemp" and "Camp"). He was keen to help his brother-in-law with anything that came up, and Dalton trusted him like no other. This was the first time he witnessed his brother-in-law in the storm centre of a mysterious intrigue, operating many lines of activity and channels of communication, all of them woven together in this strange room by a vow to defeat powerful men in control of government. The youth's fascination knew no bounds. Atkins's induction into the high craft of campaigns had begun, his first "real" summer job.

While awaiting orders, he studied the purposeful chaos of the New Brunswick Progressive Conservative command post. Its anesthetizing smell of stale cigarette smoke was permanently etched into old curtains and a grimy carpet. Work seemed to be organized around Dalton's typewriter, apparently a magnet drawing toward it an ever-growing archive of back copies of the *Daily Gleaner*, the *Telegraph-Journal*, and other papers, the *Synoptic Reports* of legislative proceedings, government reports, ashtrays and coffee cups, departmental estimates, draft speeches, copies of press releases, dirty plates, and phone books. As the days passed and the quarters became more cramped and confining, Camp himself would say "only the ceiling was bare."

Besides his brother-in-law, another person with equal and regular access was Ralph Hay. The son of a Liberal organizer, Ralph had been introduced to politics and Grit ways early, but began to have doubts. When his father died, he felt released from any lingering loyalty. Ralph liked hanging out with Dalton. They reinforced each other's sense of righteousness in rebellion against their former party.

Ralph had developed a strong friendship with the Hay family's physician, Dr. Jack McInerney. The Fredericton doctor, outraged over appalling New Brunswick medical services and lack of concern from the officious Liberal health minister, Dr. F.A. McGrand, had become a PC candidate to fight for justice by ousting the Grits. When Dr. McInerney asked Ralph to help him, nothing could restrain his combative enthusiasm.

———

Although New Brunswick's Liberals were experienced and resourceful campaigners, Camp began to take encouragement from the perfunctory slickness of the extensive, and expensive, advertising campaign designed to support them.

"The Liberals employed an unknown professional commentator who sounded," he thought, "like a door-to-door salesman, oozing homilies on the benefits of Liberal legislation addressed to 'you mothers' and those 'older folks' in the listening audience." Beyond that, "the Liberal airwaves were reserved for candidates who gave faithful utterance to agency scripts, written by someone on the moon with a goose-feather quill."

New Brunswick's newspapers, meanwhile, published the growing number of advertisements Larry Jones was steadily releasing from his Lord Beaverbrook suite two floors up. The unrelenting ads formed a marching parade of mind-numbing statistics. Camp doubted if people measured their lives by numeric tables. "Do they really see themselves parading amidst armies of statistics, marching in column of route across the landscape, joining on the horizon's line to form millions of dollars, tons, or pounds: cyphers aggregating to make symbols of mystical meaning to politicians?" Such advertisements would not foster a sustainable sense of prosperity, if one could trump it by a specific grievance.

Camp's advertising for the PCs was not extensive, but it was sharp, deadly like a sniper's single shot. He looked for the specific grievance. The Liberals began to respond to Dalton's hits, even as their main campaign continued to unfold with mind-numbing boilerplate ads, prepared and signed off on by a full committee well in advance of the election. Camp, acting alone, was able to respond with stunning swiftness, the very next day, to any turn of events that gave the PCs an opening.

He attacked the Liberals with direct and specific revelations of their failings, rather than campaigning the way predictable Tories had before, infected by a "loser syndrome" that soured their message. Camp's instinct for campaigns was to combine surprise attack with unfamiliar methods.

The Conservatives had been dull campaigners, Dalton felt, "spending half their time reacting to Liberal attacks on them, and showing themselves overly sensitive." A Tory voice typically expressed airs of wounded pride, advanced pieties about the horror of debt and the burden of taxes, and was just "no fun at all."

Why not attack, instead? "Was ever a Liberal government or party more vulnerable?"

He planned a three-week campaign, which would consume his limited budget but, if handled right, would be enough. Camp brooded on the fact New Brunswick's newspapers and radio stations were apolitical, offering the public little or no election coverage, until he thought up a way to turn this weakness into an advantage. He'd write his *own* editorial comments on the election, then run them as paid advertisements in the province's six dailies.

Camp's edgy style, focused targets, and ever changing content in a standard format would give the PC campaign continuity. His criticisms of the Liberals provided ammunition to PC candidates in the field, who needed only to check their newspaper for each day's new message. The frequency would give "a nearly immediate opportunity for comment." Dalton's daily columns could even build readership about the upcoming vote, in a province where "there wasn't much else to read."

The Tory slogan was "Let's Clean House!" so Camp, with a twinkle in his eye, signed the editorials "L.C. House" and had his art director, Bill Kettlewell, in Toronto, write the signature in a large, bold hand and send it, together with an attention-getting border of question marks to go around each ad, to every New Brunswick daily.

Camp knew political advertising had to be different from the commercial messages he created to sell cosmetics, cars, or cigarettes. People had the right to vote, but could only exercise it once every few years. The trouble with political advertising, Dalton believed, was that "most of it went unread, unheard, and unnoticed." He wanted his ads to "create a sense of immediacy, of urgency, and participation," and they did. The Liberals, even John McNair, began responding to them, stung and surprised, off-guard, and starting to wobble.

In contrast to the surgical precision of Camp's ads, the Grits' broad appeals seemed akin to carpet bombing the electorate. Not just overwhelming in quantity, they conveyed a secondary message of desperation: as many as thirteen different Liberal placements sometimes appeared in a single issue of the Fredericton *Gleaner* and New Brunswick's other dailies.

———

For this 1952 election, the only other medium of mass communications was radio.

Dalton knew the powerful signal of Fredericton station CFNB made its popular newscaster Jack Fenety the best recognized and most authoritative public voice throughout the province. After Fenety read the midday news, he'd deliver five-minute commentaries on current events. Camp made arrangements to deliver five-minute philippics for him daily.

In addition to these smoothly delivered broadside attacks by Fenety on the undefended Grit machine, "radio listeners were assaulted by the dissonance of amateur voices as well." Camp lined up as many as eight private citizens each day, who "aided the Tory cause by expressing their criticisms of the McNair government." He helped with their scripts, to ensure adherence to the party line and avoid libel, but found it both easier and more effective to "allow people to speak for themselves, which they did with awkward delivery but ringing conviction."

The genius of Camp's campaign "lay in his ability to see into his opponent's campaign, to anticipate their actions," said his biographer, Geoffrey Stevens. "He could spot a foe's weakness and attack it before the foe could adjust." When any Grit made a mistake, Camp would be all over it, his most potent weapon being rapid response. "For the sake of immediacy, he always produced his radio scripts and newspaper ad copy at the last possible moment."

———

Because newspapers were the main vehicle, and since whatever was printed lingered longer than messages over the airwaves, Dalton pondered anew on how to prick the Grit balloon. He believed ridicule to be the deadliest weapon in politics.

Camp made arrangements with budding cartoonist Duncan Macpherson, with whom he had worked on a commercial account in Toronto, and within a week had a small portfolio of political art that Duncan had drawn and rushed to him, lampooning McNair and the Liberal government's secretary-treasurer, Gaspard Boucher. Flemming winced, wondering if they went beyond acceptable bounds, but "the enthusiasm of others present" dissuaded the PC leader from keeping the cartoons out of the campaign.

From one side of New Brunswick to the other, voters howled with derisive laughter. The Tories caught the friendly new wind of ridicule in their sails. McNair himself stormed into a radio station and burst over the airwaves in apoplectic anger, his rage so great he mispronounced "cartoons" as "cortooms."

The campaign was heating up, chuckled Dalton, with McNair "the warmest of all."

———

From the outset, Camp set aside a portion of his stringent budget as a contingency for the final days of his three-week campaign. He believed he must finish strong, and sensed "something would turn up."

The big turn came when Ralph Hay began complaining angrily about the appalling state of New Brunswick's polio clinic, which, as someone crippled by polio, he was especially sensitive to. He said the doctors were upset and getting increasingly annoyed with the Liberal government. "My God, I feel sorry for those kids in there. It really is a terrible place."

Hay was pointedly hostile about the existing polio clinic, and so, he told Camp, was PC candidate Dr. Jack McInerney, because Premier McNair, a couple of elections earlier, had promised to build a new facility but never had. Meanwhile, services for polio victims continued to be housed in a building hidden behind the Fredericton hospital that had been condemned as an unsafe fire hazard and health risk by public officials. The Grits had broken their promise, not once but twice, to replace it.

Camp suggested he'd drive up the next morning to see the clinic.

"Better than that," offered Hay, "I think you should talk to McInerney. There's been a hell of a row about it and the doctors are all mad at McNair."

No PCs in the legislature had been aware of the issue, safely kept out of public view for the benefit of the governing Liberals by bureaucratic underlings. Camp was dumbstruck hearing McInerney, a nominated Tory candidate, curse purple while running through a full declension of McNair's failures on the medical front and dissecting in detail the travesty at the polio clinic. The surgeon was even more scathingly profane in denouncing New Brunswick's health minister.

The next morning, Dr. McInerney arrived at Camp's hotel room and began reading the speech Dalton had drafted for him. Camp's writing always had punch, but McInerney sent this script into the stratosphere with his depthless passion. Camp immediately dipped into his contingency fund and booked time for a major radio address. The New Brunswick election campaign suddenly swerved around a sharp corner.

The newspapers, called by Camp to a press conference, got a picture of McInerney and other PC candidates, several of them also doctors, with even more doctors, also supporting the PCs, surrounding them. The headlines proclaimed DOCTORS ENTER CAMPAIGN AGAINST MCNAIR. Together, these medical men had many thousands of patients whose sympathies immediately transferred to their physicians' heartfelt cause, no matter that their votes had, up to this year, been Liberal.

———

Shaping this polio issue and helping the doctors mount their authoritative attack on the government gave the PC campaign its essential surge at the finish.

Dalton Camp and Ralph Hay, having been close witnesses of the New Brunswick Grit regime's corrupt operation, made a formidable team as self-designated crusaders to bring down McNair. As converts from Liberalism, each possessed zeal unknown to born Tories.

When someone asked Robert Tweedie how he felt about his two young protégées, Camp and Hay, leading the charge for his political competition, he sighed, "I feel like a father toward his children. I may not approve of what they are doing, but I love them all the same."

———

On the night of September 22, for the first time in years, the people of New Brunswick elected a Tory majority government. The PCs would easily dominate the legislature, with their thirty-six members to sixteen Liberals. Hugh John Flemming was New Brunswick's Progressive Conservative premier. It was a stunning breakthrough.

The next day, Camp received Flemming's heartfelt congratulations. The grateful new premier asked affably if there was anything Dalton wanted from the spoils of victory. He made only two requests: first, to reform the Elections Act; second, to keep Robert Tweedie as head of the provincial Tourism Bureau. Flemming sidestepped electoral reform, but did honour Camp's request to keep Tweedie in public harness for the good of provincial tourism.

After closing down his campaign operations, but before leaving Fredericton, Camp enjoyed a long dinner with Tweedie. As the evening progressed, Tweedie — uncertain whether he really would be left as head of the Travel Bureau — asked Camp whether his Toronto agency had any interest in the advertising account. The account had been serviced by Walsh, the Liberal agency. Walsh had served the bureau well, volunteered Tweedie, but he had "every confidence" that if Dalton were to assume the account, he "could do as well, or better."

Camp took a long drag on his cigarette and, as he exhaled, "had to tell Tweedie that the matter had never occurred to me." He added, with chagrin, "I wished I had mentioned it to Flemming earlier in the day."

Not many weeks later, Camp, back in Toronto, took a call from Tweedie, still head of the Tourism Bureau. He suggested Dalton hurry to Fredericton because it was time to settle the coming year's advertising budget. Flemming, he explained, had kept the bureau among his own responsibilities. Dalton realized the premier had seen that as his surest expedient to keep Tweedie's head from rolling. The Tourism Bureau chief worried, he told Dalton, the new premier was about to make a decision unhelpful to the province's tourism.

In the premier's office two days later, Camp and Flemming looked at one another across the same desk where Dalton had, months earlier, told McNair he no longer liked Liberal politics. The premier was distracted, conducting telephone calls while conversing with Camp. At one point, apparently recalling that Dalton was in advertising, he fished through the piles on his desk, extracting a letter on embossed stationary, and handed it over. It was from the Walsh Agency in Montreal, congratulating Flemming on his election, expressing best wishes to his new government, and looking forward to continuing their work promoting the province's tourism with the same high quality advertising they had provided in the past.

"Seems like a nice fellow," Flemming said absentmindedly as he placed another call, maddening Camp.

"Two months ago they were down here telling people you weren't good enough to be premier of New Brunswick," Camp shot back curtly.

Flemming put down his phone, the revelation and Dalton's passion jolting him to his more immediate reality. A slight smile appeared on his face.

"Well, we can't have that, can we?"

———

In the coming year, the Locke Johnson firm, as advertising agent for the New Brunswick Tourism Bureau, had billings just under $47,000. Dalton advanced from copy chief to account executive, and launched into publicity and marketing work in a new field that began to give him "a first-hand experience in the travel industry and in North American media, both Canadian and American."

Camp was not asked by the government for political advice, nor did he proffer any. "It was as if I was the new account executive from Walsh," he mused. In both cases, out-of-province ad agencies had been offered the business by a government whose election publicity campaign they'd supported. It was not a free pass to the vault, but the chance to earn money by providing service.

The important new account for Locke Johnson was a happy election aftermath for Dalton's advertising career, but his political career got a boost as well. His reputation as a brilliant campaigner who could bring down invincible Liberal regimes now reached to the most distant parts of the country.

Camp relished the awe his work inspired. As 1952 wound down, Canadian Press ranked the New Brunswick election upset one of the biggest stories of the year. Talk of Dalton Camp rippled out from Fredericton, through Tory ranks in townships and towns, into the Albany Club of Toronto and Progressive Conservative national headquarters in Ottawa. Like David slaying Goliath, adman Camp apparently had a skill and possessed a precise weapon for bringing down giants.

———

Although politicians and reporters called the September 22 upset a landslide, beneath the appearance of robust PC health was a more sobering reality. The Liberals had, in fact, slightly *more* support than the Progressive Conservatives across the province, with Grit popular support at 49.2 percent to 48.9 percent for the Tories, yet they'd won *twenty* fewer seats in the fifty-two-seat assembly than the PCs.

Dalton at least recognized the election had been "a close-run thing" and would refer with detached irony to "the myth of my own reputation" as it continued to grow. Despite this self-effacing humour, Dalton's ego had been given a gratifying lift. He felt far more confident about himself.

Because his reach now extended far and wide, Camp began to benefit from that multiplier of personal power: the increased influence of a man who is preceded by his reputation.

CHAPTER 11

BLUE MARTYRDOM BLUES

Aboard a train bound for Ottawa, Dalton was off "to give advice on advertising strategy" to the PC Party's inner circle for the coming 1953 federal election. While gazing out the coach window, he reviewed the clear lessons he wanted to share from the New Brunswick campaign.

Dalton had been called to Ottawa, he imagined, because senior people in the party's backrooms suspected he "might have some magical properties — a talisman of better luck, an augury of a renascent political party." Hugh John Flemming had won in New Brunswick when it seemed impossible. Camp had played a crucial part in his victory. "Thus," ran the logic, as Dalton extrapolated it, he "might be a part of a larger enterprise. It was as simple as that."

From his cramped room in the Lord Beaverbrook, Dalton would step, almost directly, into the backrooms of Ottawa. Nobody's image of a political backroom could have prepared him, though, for the place that opened before his eyes in the Château Laurier Hotel. Behind the bandstand at the rear of the Canadian Grill, the hotel's softly lighted restaurant, the door opened into a private dining room.

Camp stepped into an "almost baronial" setting. The maitre d' "commanded silent, efficient waiters, as we dined by flickering candles." Wine poured so no glass was ever empty, liquor replenished highball glasses. "The talk was assertive, incomprehensible, sometimes terse as a telegram, other times discursive."

He was made to feel "the stranger in the midst of this warm, intimate, mellow group of men, laughter rumbling in their throats, ritual smiles on their lips as the conversation danced over the political scene, as the candles played upon the ceiling, creating both light and shadow."

This conclave of stalwart veterans, into whose custody Progressive Conservative fortunes were entrusted, included *Ottawa Journal* publisher Grattan O'Leary; national party president and Nova Scotia MP George Nowlan; the party's national director, Richard A. Bell; its executive secretary, Cappé Kidd; adman Allister Grosart of the McKim agency; and organizer and fundraiser J.M. Macdonnell, MP for Ontario-Muskoka.

They seemed to Camp "a strange lot," men who shared filial feeling for one another, to be sure, and who seemed to have mutual tolerance for each other's opinions, however varied. As he listened to their conversation, Camp sensed they all seemed to agree, even though each offered a different view. But the differences, really, were illusory, he thought, as though each looked upon the many facets of politics and saw something different, in different light, which all agreed was there, whether it could be seen or not by anyone else.

The meal now finished, they turned to look at him.

———

"How was New Brunswick won?"

Camp cleared his throat. "It was won because Conservatives attacked Liberals on Liberal grounds, on welfare issues, and because Conservatives did not talk incessantly about taxes, government spending, and 'what-was-the-world-coming-to?' which Liberals always expected Tories would talk about."

There was interest, but some noticeable bristling.

"Go on."

"I hope the party, in the coming election, will talk to people about issues that matter to them, rather than issues that matter only to the vestigial interests of the Conservative Party."

The party elders "smiled and nodded agreeably," though one sought to remove Camp's lustre by observing that Hugh John Flemming had really been helped into office by the New Brunswick sales tax issue.

They then resumed their discourse, "hazarding guesses as to the date of the next federal election," about equally dividing between spring and fall, most seeming to much prefer the later date.

———

Camp's invitation to prepare the advertising campaign would definitely not, he realized, mean working solo as he had in New Brunswick.

This, after all, would be a Canada-wide effort, impossible for any one person to handle alone. Besides, Camp was unknown to the national party's inner circle, was untested, and word had it that the last time he'd been in Ottawa for national politics was as a voting delegate to the Liberal leadership convention that chose the man the PCs now faced as prime minister. Could he *really* be trusted?

His work would be enmeshed with this committee of Bell, Kidd, O'Leary, Macdonnell, Nowlan, and Grosart, all tested and loyal Tories. Assisting would be Kathleen Kearns, a true-blue who as principal gatekeeper at Bracken House knew just about everybody in the party and held clear opinions on most.

Dalton found the national headquarters "an aging, creaking, two-storey house," with a dusty upstairs office designated for his campaign advertising work. The optimism with which the place had been acquired by the party in the 1940s had since been degraded to a grey pessimism by the Liberals achieving another majority government in June 1949, leaving George Drew with a corps of forty battle-worn Tory MPs on the Opposition benches to face 191 Grits. Despite the bold promise that Drew might do for the party across Canada what he'd accomplished in Ontario, the party lost twenty-four seats in that election, claiming only 30 percent of the popular vote, far behind the 50 percent earned by Louis St. Laurent's Liberals.

Anticipation of yet another looming defeat cast a pall of grim resolve over the PCs, from these dingy headquarters on through the caucus members and into the country's constituencies.

———

Dalton's airless second-floor chamber had fewer amenities but more detritus than he'd known in his small Fredericton hotel room. His new campaign quarters were "overflowing with the unsorted accumulation of passing events." His allotted cubicle in the Tory structure must have seemed to Dalton like a tomb.

There were certainly plenty of ghosts, a long enough procession of past Conservative heartbreaks to have achieved the cumulative impact of anticipating defeat even before it came. For the most recent defeat, 1949's election disaster, blame had pretty much been fixed on the McKim advertising agency, Kathleen Kearns confided to Dalton.

Yet its mastermind, Allister Grosart, remained, still on the campaign advertising committee. Dalton was perplexed. He was slow to understand just how treasured a resounding defeat could be to those who felt themselves misunderstood martyrs.

For those suffering that Tory syndrome of emotions, to lose a campaign stoically was a badge of honour. Yet Tories did not, in the manner of the CCF, influenced by the inordinate number of United Church clergymen in that party's ranks, proclaim each such defeat a "moral victory." Conservatives actually harboured the hope they might win "next time," or at least in some future election once it dawned on voters that the Tories had been right all along and rewarded their patience. Meanwhile, electoral defeat was simply good training, because, as Tories knew, the strongest steel came from the hottest part of the blast furnace.

———

Dalton resolved to take control of the advertising campaign, despite the existence of a committee and the presence of Allister Grosart, "believing this to be my purpose for being in Ottawa."

He began to create his own cadre. After getting approval from Dick Bell and Cappé Kidd, Dalton lined up his respected and knowledgeable colleague, Bill Kettlewell, to create layouts for the publicity campaign. He decided that those layouts and other aspects of the campaign planning should be kept out of the hands of any single ad agency, including McKim and his own firm Locke Johnson. He did not want the PC layouts lying around in agencies' art departments where Grit-friendly eyes could study them.

He was becoming increasingly wary of Grosart, whose primary mission seemed to be retaining the Tory account for his firm. Dalton's concern was not about a rival agency getting business, however. He'd formed the view that advertising agencies in politics were "wasteful, their judgment often atrocious, and that many of their decisions were likely to be based on their interest in a profitable campaign, rather than on an effective one." He'd seen that in New Brunswick, as had Hugh John Flemming before Dalton came along.

The rivalry between Camp and Grosart sharpened when it came to the issue on which to fight the election. It was a sobering revelation about party policy-making that by the mid-twentieth century this would be a battle fought in a political back room between two admen, rather than on the convention floor in a national policy debate between voting delegates of the party, or even in the caucus of elected MPs.

Dalton had already set down his marker at the dinner meeting in the Château, by explaining the PCs won in New Brunswick by attacking Liberals. "Conservatives did not talk incessantly about taxes and government spending," he'd clarified. For the central theme of the 1953 campaign, however, "Grosart was determined that the issue in the election would be taxes; I was resolved that it should not be."

With opinion polls gaining currency in Canadian politics, Grosart sought an upper hand in this contest of wills between two admen by conducting a poll, making him appear modern, Camp the reactionary. Dalton believed parties, not the public, created issues. He'd already developed "a low opinion of political polls and a healthy respect for their cost." McKim conducted the survey itself, producing plenty of statistics from which one could deduce that taxation was the overriding concern of a large majority of Canadians. Detailed examination of the pattern of questions suggests the inevitability of such a conclusion.

Meanwhile, Grosart, who resembled a human bulldozer, seemed like one on paper, too. His proposals proliferated, outlining in "confidential" drafts a number of work plans for the 1953 general election. Some ran to thirty pages, single-spaced. They were dense, but followed an inexorable logic. Grosart expatiated at length in one on the similarities between ad campaigns for political messages and consumer products, though near the end cautioned that "the comparison should not be taken too far." On this point, too, Camp saw things differently. He thought advertising appeals in an election campaign were entirely unlike those for commercial products, as he'd already shown in New Brunswick. He believed one would fail if trying to extrapolate a campaign about the country and people's futures from the best ways of selling cars or Kleenex.

Camp and Kettlewell, despite a growing sense that their efforts were futile, continued to plan bellicose advertisements giving the Grits hell.

———

March turned to April, spring was advancing, as was another Maritime election.

Dalton happily answered a call from MP George Nowlan. He enjoyed interacting with the Nova Scotian on the election advertising committee, taking comfort in their common Maritime outlook on most things. But even more, he found the irreverent and gregarious PC Party president easy to like.

And, happily, Nowlan was more prepared to fight Grits than most Tories Dalton was encountering in Ottawa. "As a recent entrant into the House after a fiercely contested by-election," quipped Camp, "his spurs jangled when he talked."

The MP for Digby-Annapolis-Kings was on the line suggesting Camp "go to Nova Scotia and meet Bob Stanfield."

Was Nowlan seriously seeking to help his provincial counterparts, Dalton wondered, or just trying to get him off the Ottawa scene under pressure from the McKim interests? It could, of course, be both.

"Old man," Nowlan said hoarsely to Camp, "this is not going to be like New Brunswick. Nobody's going to beat Angus L. and Stanfield is not Hugh John Flemming. But I think you should go down, at least, and look around."

A couple of days later in Halifax, arriving at the law offices of McInnes & Stanfield, Dalton climbed a flight of wooden stairs, having no idea what to expect. He'd only heard that Bob Stanfield was a dull, dour man.

At the top, he found himself "standing opposite Stanfield in an austere, undistinguished room, the afternoon sun pouring through a curtainless window and falling on the plain, bare table between us." They sized each other up. Well, thought Dalton, "at least he's not pretty."

The taciturn leader of the Nova Scotia Progressive Conservative Party was seldom at ease initiating conversation. He was happier enduring long silences than speaking. If and when he did give voice, it was in single sentences. For quite a while Camp just shifted uneasily in his chair. Maritime politics could take time.

"Some of our fellows," the Nova Scotian finally croaked out, "think we could use a little help down here in the election."

"How does the election look to you?"

"Oh, I don't know, we don't expect to win, but we expect to do better." After a reflective pause, he added, "Somewhat."

"I looked at the last election returns and you could have won if less than two thousand votes had gone the other way."

"That's a lot of votes," smiled Stanfield, "in Nova Scotia."

"You're a lot closer than we were in New Brunswick last year," reassured Camp, making the Maritime connection.

"That may be true but this is not New Brunswick. The Grits are pretty strong here."

"I don't see any reason why you can't win."

"Well," smiling again, "I do."

"I don't see any sense in running to lose."

"We'll do the best we can, that's all," his smile gone. "It's not a matter of running to lose."

The two men were grating on each other's nerves. Camp was getting belligerent because here he now was, in yet another setting, meeting yet another senior Conservative who lacked all gumption for electoral battle. He'd become "so damned sick and tired of meeting Tories who can't win, don't want to win, never will win," he said of this encounter.

Stanfield, after the silence of sunlight had mellowed things a bit, said perhaps Camp could lend a hand with a few problems, getting candidates, and the publicity. "We have a fellow here who has helped us in the past. I don't know how good he is, really, but you might be able to help us there."

Dalton departed, puzzled by Stanfield's diffidence, thinking he'd never seen anybody who needed help more. Back in Toronto, he phoned Nowlan in a rueful mood, hoping the pre-defeated Nova Scotia Tories would find assistance without him, concluding he'd "only get on Stanfield's nerves."

Upbeat George Nowlan shot right back, "That's just what he needs, old boy."

Camp wanted to fight Grits. He did not want to have to do it through the enfeebling proxy of passive martyrs.

———

When April 15 arrived, so did a message cabled to Camp announcing a Nova Scotia election had been called for May 26. "Anxious to see you," signed *Stanfield*.

Nobody at national headquarters seemed reluctant for Dalton to depart. Perhaps they expected another miracle, as in New Brunswick, he thought, or perhaps they felt easier with his energies transported to other lands. He left, in low spirits but hoping to accomplish some good in a more clearly defined role, and "resignedly, but cheerfully, surrendered the federal campaign concerns to Grosart." McKim's advocate for waging the national PC campaign on the single issue of cutting taxes suddenly had a wide open field.

"Where in hell have you been?" demanded Stanfield when Camp resurfaced in Halifax.

After the confrontation, the leader departed for nominating meetings around Nova Scotia. For his part, the adman began to replay his New Brunswick scenario, moving into a small room at the Lord Nelson Hotel, contemplating his now recurring challenge: How to fight an election everyone believed lost even before the campaign had begun?

Camp's whole thrust in overcoming an entrenched Grit regime in New Brunswick had been to relentlessly attack the seemingly invincible Liberal premier, and even mock him for the government's significant shortcomings. However, because long-serving Liberal premier Angus L. Macdonald was highly revered, despite the fog of corruption wafting around the lower levels of his government, the waiting Tory victims imposed a rule of passivity, meaning that in preparing the ads Dalton "was repeatedly warned not to attack Macdonald, indeed, not even to mention his name."

To ensure Camp toed the line of polite passivity, Stanfield saddled him with a three-man "publicity committee," consisting of Halifax mayor Richard Donahue, former party leader Leonard Fraser, and leading Halifax lawyer Roland Ritchie. Encouraged by Camp's own bellicose approach, they quickly revealed themselves to be just as belligerent. Closet Tory warriors, too, they co-operated with Dalton, encouraging, rather than restraining, him.

Pleased to find that not every Nova Scotia Tory wanted to be sacrificed on the Liberal altar, Camp set up his editorial comment advertisements, similar in style to those previously signed by L.C. House. Most newspapers were happy to get the advertising revenue, but not the austere, dignified Halifax *Chronicle-Herald*. As the only paper with province-wide reach, the *Herald's* refusal to print a paid ad because it expressed robust opinions during an election campaign was a major setback.

When Dalton next sought to replicate the Jack Fenety radio commentaries, he cast around for the most popular radio voice in the province. Discovering it belonged to John Funston, he made a deal with the popular young sports announcer and his station manager at CHNS, Gerald Redmond. Soon listeners were surprised that some life, and even dissent, was issuing upon the electoral playing field. Others were simply shocked. Liberal organizers went to CHNS and retained Funston's services, too, confounding listeners who heard him support the Tories and denounce Grits, then later, as the same man, support Grits and denounce Tories. This was crazy, but it would get crazier.

When the PC candidate in Colchester County, Ike Smith, wrote a strong radio speech condemning transgressions by government employees at Inverness Mine in Cape Breton, he quoted directly from the royal commission report on the scandal. CHNS's station manager called Camp about problems with the script. Broadcasting regulations required pre-clearance of any election "free-time" talks. When he arrived, Dalton was introduced to the *Chronicle-Herald* publisher's son, Laurie Daley, lawyer for CHNS. Daley and Redmond insisted Smith could not use the airwaves for his election speech unless he deleted the offensive paragraphs, sentences directly from the public findings of an independent body the Liberal government itself had constituted. Nova Scotia's Grit fortress had thick walls of protection with deep reserves of combatants inside.

Camp was finding himself locked out. First he faced the PC hierarchy's injunction there be no criticism of the Liberal leader against whom they were, notionally, campaigning. Now he encountered media organizations seeking to steer through provincial waters without upsetting the entrenched powers of government, their readers, or their listeners.

Dalton, in despair, climbed a single flight of stairs from his room in the Lord Nelson to where the offices and broadcasting studio of station CJCH were housed, to speak with its manager. Finlay MacDonald welcomed Camp into his office and sat back to listen.

Only part way through explaining his plight, MacDonald interrupted his visitor, left the office, went down the corridor into the studio, flicked a switch, and said in confident voice over the airwaves, "On behalf of CJCH, I want to inform all politicians and all political parties that they can come to the studios of this station and say whatever they want to say, without any interference, direction, or censorship from management. The air is free, and party representatives are free to use it at CJCH." Returning to his office, MacDonald resumed his seat and asked Camp, "Now, how else may I help you?"

———

MacDonald also helped by proposing that Stanfield say something dramatic in his final speech of the campaign, to show he had beliefs and determination.

The best they could come up with, after extensive brainstorming, was a pledge from Stanfield that, as premier, he would take charge personally of industrial development to lift Nova Scotia's stagnating manufacturing operations into a new era. "Better than nothing," sighed MacDonald, "but for God's sake, have him say it with *conviction*."

A second item for "the last big speech" was to make public a fresh scandal. Harold Connolly, the minister responsible for provincial liquor stores, had secretly received a substantial gift of company shares from a Toronto distiller. Research had been ongoing and the Tories had proof.

On the rainy night of Stanfield's campaign wind-up speech, Camp and MacDonald stood at the rear of the Dartmouth hall, where about two hundred loyal PCs had gathered, to judge his impact on the audience. When the PC leader reached the part about the shocking scandal, he paused, looked out mournfully at the partisan crowd, and waited. Before proceeding, he apologized, "Now, they told me to say this ..."

Camp was dismayed. Neither he nor MacDonald could believe their ears. They were appalled by his "flat, unemotive, half-audible" reading of charges that should have exploded as a major political scandal on the eve of voting.

———

If Robert Lorne Stanfield had not the head, heart, nor stomach for politics as people knew it, he was a stark contrast to Dalton Camp's understudy, Norman Kempton Atkins, who'd been spending the summer keenly absorbing everything his political mentor was up to.

Among his many tasks for Dalton, Norman gravitated to many roles including helping with arrangements, keeping tabs on people, driving hither and yon on urgent errands, and ensuring events came together at the right time in the right place with the right people to create the desired outcome. He'd be Dalton's shadow to ensure a successful nomination, a well-delivered broadcast, an advertisement published when and where intended. He had bottles of liquor and buckets of ice on hand whenever and wherever required, which was just about all the time, everywhere. Dalton saw repeated evidence of Norman's natural capacity for close attention to administrative detail and logistics.

———

When ballots were counted the night of May 26, 1953, and recounted in several close ridings over the days that followed, Nova Scotians had elected twenty-two Liberals to form another government in the thirty-seven-seat assembly, exactly the outcome many Progressive Conservatives predicted. They were content, not in victory, but in fulfillment of their prophecy of defeat.

Anyone who made closer study of the results, however, as Dalton did, could see the PCs had done better than expected, moving up from eight to thirteen seats and standing only 5 points behind the Grits in popular support province-wide, 44 to 49 percent. Camp realized his Tory martyrdom blues might not last forever. Perhaps Conservatives could shuck off their self-fashioned defeatist syndrome. "Modern campaign techniques had come to the aid of partisan politics," he noted hopefully, believing they "offered antidote for an otherwise bland and indifferent medium which, for too long, had seemed determined to maintain the status quo."

———

In Ottawa, meanwhile, Allister Grosart had jogged unimpeded into the end zone, scoring during Dalton's absence. He'd consolidated apparent support for a PC campaign on tax cuts.

This was a different Tory affliction, Camp thought: not passive defeatism, but aggressive triumphalism in the Conservative obsession with taxes.

Grosart had won in the backrooms, but not yet with voters, and there were already three fouls against his play. Finance Minister Douglas Abbott had just brought down a budget that included a range of tax deductions, deflating the Tory's issue.

The second problem involved timing. When the Liberals did not call the election in the spring, the Tory backroom sages concluded voting would be in the fall and they'd have time to work out the details for their massive tax cut proposal. St. Laurent caught them off guard, however, adroitly calling the election for August 10. Camp rejoined national party headquarters just as a frantic meeting was in progress to finalize a PC campaign pledge for $500 million in tax cuts. On imminent deadline, Grattan O'Leary had to finish writing the speech George Drew was about to deliver in London to kick off the national campaign.

The third foul registered in the shuddering misgivings of many serious-minded senior Conservatives apprehensive about Grosart's big tax cut idea.

J.M. Macdonnell, the PC finance critic, was skeptical about the tax cut and did not see where the cuts could be made. His cautions changed nothing. Who, after all, was the party's official finance spokesman to derail an adman's plans for the national finances?

That night Drew made the announcement. The press correctly reported the $500 million tax cut as the main plank in the Progressive Conservative election platform. The effect on Tory candidates and workers was, Camp reported, "instant consternation." Most of the 248 PC candidates saw their election prospects evaporating. The party had instantly lost all flexibility and manoeuvrability, because of this one pledge. Most were dumbfounded. Where had such an astonishing policy originated?

Nobody wanted to explain that an ad agency, and in particular a single individual who was neither elected nor accountable, had such dominion over a political party. Perhaps it was because McKim had fumbled the previous election that Grosart tried so hard, for this one, to come up with a single stunning idea he'd convinced himself was the key to victory.

———

In high summer, with Ottawa sweltering in steaming heat, Dalton slipped out of town, two weeks before voting.

He headed with Linda to Robertson's Point for refuge, "uneasy and disconsolate, nursing a profound sense of personal failure, made more soulful by a feeling of inadequacy." On election day, they drove over into Nova Scotia's Annapolis Valley to sip scotch with George Nowlan and listen to the radio as voting returns were broadcast.

"Dear God," exclaimed the dismayed PC Party national president and member of the party's advertising committee along with Grosart, once the scope of the disaster became apparent, "where did we ever get that platform?"

On election night 1953, the Grits stood at 48 percent in popular vote nation wide, the tax-cutting Tories at 31 percent. Liberals won 171 seats in the Commons. The PCs, 120 seats behind, elected only fifty-one MPs.

In forming their fifth consecutive majority government, Canada's Liberal government appeared invincible for all time.

CHAPTER 12

ELEVATING POWERS

Camp's ascent into the Tory upper realms was being propelled by twin engines: his talent for devising strategies based on intuition about what the rival Grits would do, and his ability to run a publicity campaign that was focused, colourful, and dramatic.

Snapping fast onto breaking news about Liberal failures, counter-punching with memorable phrases, and doing it all on a small budget, was pure Dalton. In this, he flew solo. Others helped, of course, like Norman Atkins with operations and Bill Kettlewell with creative design. He also drew on well-informed allies like Ralph Hay, Finlay MacDonald, and Kenneth Carson at Hugh John Flemming's side. But he was a lone combatant, the happy warrior working through the night, calibrating the right trajectory for his fire, crafting the most devastating verbal bombardment to land upon Liberal forces.

Camp waged guerilla war from his typewriter, delighting in this kind of politics, charmed by his own effect marshalling and dispatching words to do battle for the forces of Progressive Conservatism, shining a merciless spotlight on Grit lapses through editorializing advertisements, radio texts for announcers, and speeches for candidates.

In addition to his normal writer's requirement of solitude for creativity, Camp disliked committees and eschewed being an "organization man." He declined to tie his identity to a larger entity, be it a university community or the army, or even a church or social club. True, he'd joined the Tory Party, but that had been on his own terms. He'd also quit the Liberal Party precisely because he disliked its operations and, by extension, his association and identity with them. Dalton was an individualist. He preferred specific information he ferreted out on his own to the vague generalizations, rumours, and theories that circulated among groups. It was how he kept his edge sharp.

Camp was a participant observer, subjectively involved, objectively detached. While never an "organization man," Camp understood all the same that "no man is an island unto himself" and knew he could only mount effective campaigns by working with a wide-ranging election organization. If possible, he'd happily leave meetings, logistics, nominations, vote rigging, and running the ground war in the hands of others. Yet, when required, he proved adept at campaign organization, and displayed instinctive talent on this front, too, a good thing because in addition to fine writing and campaign strategizing, his work as a political organizer was about to become a third engine propelling his rapid ascent.

———

In the spring of 1954, Bill Rowe asked Dalton to meet him for lunch in Toronto.

The two had shared provincial campaign activity in Nova Scotia the year before, where Camp first witnessed Rowe's devotion to the PC cause, effectiveness in aligning the diverse array of cabals and characters jousting inside the Tory ranks, and talent for scouting prospective candidates. On the basis of this "briefest acquaintance," Dalton had come to admire his contemporary, finding him ethical, intelligent, politically shrewd, and a great companion. Both loved the chess game of politics and took pleasure, together, calculating possible next moves.

Over their meal, Rowe revealed he'd been offered the daunting role of PC national director, replacing Dick Bell, who was returning to his Ottawa law practice, intent on moving from the backrooms into brighter light as an elected MP. Some who work to make politicians look good in public realize they want such a role themselves, believing they could do it even better. Dalton was not surprised by Bell's move.

Nor was he surprised that George Drew wanted Bill Rowe to be Bell's successor as national director. Bill's father, Earl, MP for Dufferin-Simcoe, was in Drew's caucus. His sister Jean was married to Clair Casselman, Tory MP for

Grenville-Dundas, whom Drew had named PC Party whip. Bill himself was an effective, respected, and pleasant party organizer. All the Rowes were major PC players, and by 1954, deeply loyal to Drew as federal leader.

Dalton believed Bill ideal for a party in desperate need of talent and, without pausing, urged his friend to accept.

Then the main course of their lunch was served. Dalton was stunned when it arrived: Rowe would *only* agree to become national director of the Progressive Conservatives if Camp went to Ottawa with him. Dalton, he elaborated, would be in charge of all party publicity and communications.

At last, so easily, here was the opening Camp had been craving.

Bill listened patiently as Dalton ran through a perfunctory catechism of reasons he couldn't join him, only to then agree, enticed by a wider avenue of public service to the Progressive Conservative Party, a chance to advance causes he believed in, a way to beat Grits. Both still in their early thirties, Rowe was to be full-time national director, and Camp part-time adviser on everything.

———

To the public, a party's internal operations, being mostly invisible and mundane, don't hold the same interest that more publicized events do, such as electing representatives, debating government programs, and handling political hot potatoes. Yet the politicians in the public eye, quoted in newspapers, interviewed for broadcasts, and enlarging their presence in all possible ways, cannot accomplish much without these unseen party functionaries, from party president through national director on to riding president and campaign manager. They'd be like soldiers in battle with no supply lines or reinforcements behind them.

A party president's activities are only newsworthy when some internal party problem, such as rebellion over the leader's performance, a divisive policy issue, errant campaign funding or voter fraud, demands resolution. When a leader resigns, a president briefly has an important public role, orchestrating a national convention to elect the successor. But in the main, party routines are conducted out of sight.

The Conservative Party in Canada, which Rowe would direct and Camp publicize, was structured differently than others, in part due to its longer history, which over time had produced a distinctive operational culture. As a national association of local associations, it was the opposite of a single national entity with a number of uniform authorized franchises in the constituencies. The high degree of local autonomy in Conservative Party affairs meant the National Association was more a coordinating body, its presiding officer closer to ceremonial head than senior executive with real powers running a responsive political apparatus with stringent lines of operational control. Tories wanted more modern methods, however, and this created impetus for two "solutions" to be more effective in contemporary conditions. The first had been appointment of a national director for the party. The second, still in embryo, would be formation of election campaign teams separate from the regular party structure.

The term *national director* was, for reasons of diplomacy, perfect. The word *national* made clear this officer would deal with the Conservative Party's *Canada-wide* interests rather than meddle in local matters. At the same time, the term *director* reinforced the idea that, as in theatre, he would work with the existing talent to present a drama someone else has scripted, perhaps only tweaking some lines, changing the costumes, or reconfiguring the set. In short, whoever filled this position was not a threat, but a facilitator; not a freelancer but someone helping the elected party leader and the elected party president oversee and advance the party's operations. A national director faced the fluctuating yet urgent and unpredictable needs of a regionalized party. Each national director would make the role into something different, a function of their individual character, the party's standing, and the times.

———

Dalton, soon called on for more than general advice or fine words suited to a particular publicity need, was becoming a "player," as he liked to identify important political operators in the country's public affairs network.

He relished being a party organizer. Commuting on the overnight train between Toronto and Ottawa, quartered at the Château Laurier Hotel for longer stays, he luxuriated in the convenient comforts of passenger trains and grand hotels. In Toronto, Linda, though having to raise their children by herself, felt rising pride in her husband's growing renown. Dalton, "so soon at the centre of things," found it astonishing to be given "so much responsibility." It sobered him to realize that the party's hierarchy had evolved through survival more than anything else, until "the elite essentially consisted of amiable and elderly mediocrities." He was shocked to discover how just "a very few at the centre, generally lacking any genuine gift in political judgment," were responsible for determining Progressive Conservative policy and strategy.

He'd already witnessed this with the 1953 advertising committee, watching Allister Grosart single-handedly engineer massive tax cuts as principal plank of the Progressive Conservative Party of Canada. And he was familiar with the disproportionate influence someone from an advertising agency, if determined enough, could wield. He'd fashioned a solo role for himself in the 1952 New Brunswick advertising campaign, and come close to it again in Nova Scotia's 1953 election after co-opting Stanfield's three "watchers" set to guard against his bellicose outbreaks when fighting Grits.

Although too few people were involved in making the party's far-reaching decisions, Dalton did not protest this state of affairs. Hierarchical structures must, after all, narrow to a point at the top. His democratic instinct still cherished the ideal of policies widely debated and openly adopted by a broad constituency of party supporters. Yet even more, he admired intelligent strategy and effective communication and believed neither was the product of committees.

If just a few good men could get it right, especially if he was one of them, why complain? There was a vacuum at the top. Dalton felt it assisting his rise.

———

Upward mobility in a broken party, however, was not to be confused with a glorious ascent to political nirvana.

Dalton climbed the creaking stairs at Bracken House, returning to the same cramped office he'd left months before. Sobered but undaunted, he and Rowe set about "to convert this dreary building into the bustling centre of party activity." The headquarters itself functioned mostly for benefit of the caucus, sometime for the leader who otherwise used his more convenient staff on Parliament Hill, and "only rarely for the party at large." There was minimal communication with the ridings. The budget was at subsistence level. Camp thought it ironic that the Tories, publicly damned as "the party of Big Business," should have so little to show for it behind the scenes.

Whatever funds could be pried loose from businessmen to support publicity campaigns and election organizing was the work of a few patient and persistent fundraisers, men like J.M. Macdonnell who suffered insults and waited in corporate anterooms for hours, trying to make collections, barely managing to keep the party alive. What irked Camp, as much as scant money for operating a national political party, was how the party's collectors "often presumed to judge how the funds could best be spent, a judgment based on their business experience, which had little or nothing to do with politics."

There were fifty-one MPs in the Progressive Conservative caucus. Close at hand in Parliament, their political imperatives extended into the operations at headquarters, consuming an inordinate share of staff time. Rowe and Camp wanted far more Tory MPs, enough to form a government, but getting them elected could not be achieved by ministering exclusively to those already in the Commons. They needed to build the party in the ridings, through the provinces, across the country.

Making a tour of the land gave Dalton his first encounter with Canada's western provinces. As he and Rowe took soundings, it became clear to both that they "could not organize the Progressive Conservative Party of Canada in the name of George Drew." He'd been known in Ontario as a strong premier, but that was only one province. Across the West and in Quebec, it registered with Dalton that the leader "was either anathema or a stranger."

Maritime Tories whom Camp and Rowe met respected Drew, but were perplexed by his failings with voters. Why had Drew been personally defeated in Ontario but his government re-elected? What had chilled Drew's relationship with his successful successor, Leslie Frost? How had he decided to campaign federally in 1953, to the detriment of virtually all Atlantic Canada's PC candidates, on tax cuts alone?

The national director and his associate also canvassed younger people in the party, finding them restrained in enthusiasm for George Drew, too.

Facing such a reality, Rowe and Camp devised a two-step, indirect strategy: they would build the national party by winning the provinces. A national Progressive Conservative government would be erected upon the building blocks of as many provincial PC governments as possible. To Camp, this seemed natural enough; winning favours to earn support was, after all, the currency of politics.

His native New Brunswick was more than just an example of the building block strategy. What had happened there was in fact the inspiration for their plan. Rowe had given $10,000 to Hugh John Flemming from the national party to get his moribund campaign moving, and Camp had waged spirited offences against New Brunswick's Grits when others wanted to concede defeat. New Brunswick proved you could knock off entrenched Grit regimes. That meant the PCs newly in office were in position to give tangible electoral support to the federal party.

This double-whammy strategy, building the national party province by province, required taking advantage of local conditions, supporting provincial Tory leaders looking for help, and taking emphatic action whenever opportunity called.

————

In March 1955, Prince Edward Island's legislature was dissolved for an election, handing Camp and Rowe "a severe test of our policy to involve the national organization in provincial elections."

The difficulty was "outsiders" appearing at election time. That's why admen from Montreal and Toronto agencies never worked from a provincial party's campaign headquarters, but secreted their operations in a hotel. For an insular island province whose population numbered about the same as the small Ontario city of Oshawa, the risk was far more pronounced. Nobody "from away," it was felt, should come onto the island and interfere with its intricate electoral mechanism. The idea that outsiders "knew better" rankled locals and caused natural resentment for Rowe's and Camp's hands-on strategy. But they were young, believed they could make a difference, and pressed on.

Rowe brought funds to get the PEI campaign rolling, reprising his role from New Brunswick when stubborn Hugh John Flemming refused to start because the provincial PCs were penniless. Camp, likewise, followed his established form. He "again resorted to the editorial column as the prime element in the advertising campaign" and, as before, his fine fighting words quickly provoked attention.

The ads were the "first thing everyone looks for in the paper," a Tory bank manager in Summerside, one of the few who knew of his presence, confided to Dalton with glee. "They've never seen anything like it around here." For entertainment value, Camp's daily blasts ranked high, but for impact on voting intentions, their effect seemed negligible. The Liberals appeared secure for re-election.

Camp's control over party publicity was "absolute." That's what he wanted, but it led to problems. Free from a restraining committee like the one Stanfield set up, perhaps after detecting something in Dalton's make-up that caused the cautious Nova Scotian to want a brake on bad impulses, he "allowed a personal sense of frustration to overcome better judgment." Unhinged, his daily editorials "became increasingly crude and acidulous." Even after he realized his columns were damaging the PC campaign, they "increased in vehemence."

To this point in his Tory career, Camp had been chagrined to find how Tories internalized their defeatism. But now he himself was launched onto an "adventure in political nihilism." When defeat came and he departed the Island, he knew it had been "the first time that a campaign I had been involved in actually weakened the party's position." It would never, he resolved, happen again.

In the larger picture, Prince Edward Island also handed the duo from head office a humbling report card of their building-block strategy. "Our assumption that Tory prospects could be measurably enhanced by the provision of reasonable funds and an aggressive publicity campaign," concluded Camp ruefully, "was not to be proven in the Island's general election."

In fact, the Island Tories would have been better left alone.

CHAPTER 13

GAINING SOME GROUND

Shortly after the PEI fiasco, Ontario premier Leslie Frost called a provincial election, presenting a different challenge for the Rowe-Camp strategy. How can you earn support by giving help that is not needed or wanted, but in fact refused?

By 1955 Ontario's Progressive Conservatives had been in office a dozen years and, after George Drew and interim leader Tom Kennedy, were now on their third leader. These factors could make re-election difficult. But the PCs, implementing major improvements under Drew's Twenty-Two Point Program, had been earning credit with pragmatic voters. The economy was strong. The budget was balanced. Government spending on highways, new schools, and hospital expansions evoked a sense of progress. And the PCs had not changed the voting system, ensuring opposition to them would continue to divide between Liberal and CCF candidates.

Advances in social justice had also been made, with new human rights laws to end discriminatory practices. In 1944, Drew's government introduced the Racial Discrimination Act, the first in Canada to prohibit publication, display, or broadcast of material involving racial or religious discrimination. In 1951, Frost's government continued this leadership, making Ontario the first province with "fair practices legislation," a new human rights initiative prohibiting racial or religious discrimination in employment, housing, and provision of services.

Frost thought a campaign based on "Progress" would be his ticket for re-election. He knew his province's history and understood how the concept of progress had become embedded in the Ontario psyche, or political culture, over decades. He tested the idea with the party's advertising executive, Allister Grosart, who in turn tested it with the creative staff at McKim and his country neighbours around his rural home. After the disastrous effort he'd engineered two years earlier, inducing George Drew to campaign nationally on massive tax cuts, Grosart had become slightly more circumspect. He reported to Frost that his excellent idea for a "Progress" re-election campaign would fly very well.

The premier had his executive assistant, Clare Westcott, who'd risen in PC ranks with Elmer Bell's support, compile data from all departments on increased spending and new programs. The PCs then printed this catalogue of progress in a blue-bound volume for all candidates, reporters, weekly newspaper offices, and libraries. The imposing volume, entitled *A Record of Accomplishment,* helped link *progress* and *Progressive* Conservative in voters' minds.

These advances, and especially the PCs' human rights initiatives, won Dalton Camp's strong personal endorsement. But apart from the good feeling these measures gave him about being a Tory, his own role in this election would again amount to no more than casting a ballot for his local PC candidate. The advertising and publicity team for the campaign, secured by Grosart and McKim and under Les Frost's own vigilant supervision, did not look for nor want any input from federal Tories.

Nor could Bill Rowe, despite knowing most of the Ontario PC ministers and members on a first-name basis, get to first base either. So long as Drew headed the national party and Frost the provincial, the gulf that separated the two men translated throughout party ranks to mean "hands-off."

Besides, the national PC office had little to add to the well-organized and fully funded Ontario Tories. Hugh Latimer, understudy of party president and chief organizer A.D. Mckenzie, travelled the ridings to find candidates and sniff out issues. Ed Bickle, the wealthy party treasurer, raised all the money needed from distillers, banks, and the Toronto head offices of northern Ontario's lumber and mining companies. These men answered directly to the premier, as did Grosart about all advertising.

Ontario's 1955 PC campaign, orchestrated by Frost, represented the apex of Canadian political organization at mid-century, and also became a baseline against which to measure campaign changes that would follow.

The concept of a leader's tour, for instance, was that the leader himself travelled the province and ran the campaign from wherever he found himself. Away from Queen's Park, Frost left his one executive assistant, Westcott, to run his tour throughout the province and get Cabinet ministers to speak wherever they could do the most good. Clare lined up ministers with events, generally on the direct suggestion of Frost, who phoned him daily. It was up to the ministers to get themselves to the meetings, and to know what to say when they got there. Each had his copy of *A Record of Accomplishment.* That provided the ammunition, but each minister and every candidate was expected to apply his own political smarts in framing the message. There could be whatever local variation in messages circumstances required. There were no "speaking modules" they had to follow.

A few standard newspaper ads were run by the party; local PC candidates ran their own ads, with a variety of messages, in their ridings. Free-time and paid radio political statements were made. Television was used, in relatively limited ways by local candidates, for the first time. The leaders did not meet face to face in debate. No spending limits applied to campaign expenditures. No restrictions applied to how much money any person, company, or other entity could donate.

There was no "centre" to the campaign. It involved Mckenzie in his downtown Toronto law office, Westcott in Frost's office at Queen's Park, and a small provincial campaign committee named by the party president, with Frost's concurrence, which met in Toronto to hear Grosart report on the placement of ads and to ensure all nominations had been completed.

When the campaign ended, Ontario's Progressive Conservatives won eighty-three seats in the expanded provincial assembly of ninety-eight members. The Liberals gained three seats, to reach eleven, and the CCF picked up one for a total of three, while the lone remaining Communist Party member, J.B. Salsberg, was defeated in Toronto by Progressive Conservative Allan Grossman.

The electoral system had again played its part in the Tory victory. The party had 49 percent of popular support, the Liberals 33 percent, and the CCF 17 percent; not very proportionate to their representation in the legislature. The two opposition parties' combined popular vote matched the number of votes won by the PCs, but the electoral system gave the PCs thirty-three more seats than the fifty they needed for a majority government.

As for their building-block strategy, the best interpretation Rowe and Camp could place on being frozen out of Ontario was that its successful Progressive

Conservative government continued to provide strength to the national party at the constituency level and among voters. Beyond that, they resigned themselves to nothing more than cordial non-engagement.

———

New Brunswick was next up. Neither Dalton nor Norman Atkins could be considered "outsiders" here, and even Bill Rowe had been on the scene four years earlier.

If the province was familiar, they could not exactly repeat their campaign roles from 1952. The difference this time was that the resources of a party in power were much greater, there was a record to defend rather than one to attack, and voters, rather than wondering what risks they might face with a PC government, had become acclimatized to Progressive Conservatives in office providing a fresher approach to provincial affairs.

When the polls closed on June 18, 1956, New Brunswick PCs were rewarded with one additional seat, the party standings in the provincial assembly now thirty-seven Tories to fifteen Grits. Behind that large PC majority, the two parties stood closer in popular support. A spread of just 6 points, 52 percent to 46 percent, separated them, with Social Credit candidates getting the rest.

The building-block strategy again looked more plausible.

———

A bigger test came with Nova Scotia when, earlier than expected, a general election was announced for October 30, 1956.

A swift series of changes, beginning two years earlier, had utterly altered the province's political complexion. When Premier Angus L. Macdonald suddenly died in April 1954, Nova Scotia's Liberal anchor was gone and a bitter feud began within drifting Grit ranks over his successor. Roman Catholic and Protestant party members divided into denominational camps and battled over an unwritten Liberal rule to alternate leaders between the two faiths.

Focused only on immediate triumph in a leadership convention, Grit denominationalists unwittingly helped the Tories by splitting their party. By the time of the by-election for Macdonald's vacant Halifax seat, a rare alignment of circumstances saw Richard Donahoe, with Dalton Camp his campaign manager, become the first Tory to claim any Halifax seat in over two decades.

In 1954, Bob Stanfield's wife, Joyce, died in a car accident. The grieving widower was left to care for their four young children. In making his excruciating decision to stay on as Progressive Conservative leader, Stanfield vowed he'd return home every night, no matter the hour or distance, so Sarah, Max, Judith, and Miriam could awaken to find their father home and helpful.

"Nova Scotians, moved by his private sorrow," said Camp, "looked again at this gaunt, homely man and discovered in him the qualities they most admired in public men. He became, for the first time, set apart from other politicians and, as Macdonald had been, above public rebuke and partisan scorn."

Henry Hicks, the strong-willed new Liberal leader, grew weary of how Bob Stanfield, increasingly perceived as a man of granite integrity, was outmanoeuvring him on a scandal involving liquor agents in the government-run stores. By 1956, the new premier called a provincial election, well ahead of his term expiring, wanting to get a fresh mandate for himself.

Camp was back, working once more on campaign advertising, again ensconced in the Lord Nelson Hotel but this time without a committee of chaperons. A second difference was that Dalton was now an agent of national headquarters, pursuing the strategy he and Rowe envisaged of winning federally by escorting provincial Grit governments, one at a time, to their political graveyards.

Norman Atkins, just ninety kilometres away at Acadia University, was a natural in the role of student provincial organizer for the Progressive Conservatives. With that title and assignment, Norman found easy hunting in Halifax. Staying with Dalton, he circulated the city's many institutions of higher learning with their voting age students. Getting to other campuses, such as St. Francis Xavier in Antigonish, was also productive. Norman found the provincial Liberals, still raw from their leadership religious wounds, fairly inactive. St. FX was already organized, its lively student PC club headed by Lowell Murray, other members including Sam Wakim and his roommate Brian Mulroney.

Atkins also began to use the telephone. "Politics," Dalton had explained, in an aside after patient Norman had waited for an interminable call to end, "is a business best conducted by telephone." Soon he discovered for himself what Dalton meant. The phone provided immediacy and efficiency, a direct one-on-one communication that obliterated distance, saved time, and enabled intimate candour if speaking with somebody you already knew. He returned to his classes, but remained in long-distance contact with his new Nova Scotia campus network.

By election night, the stunning news was that Bob Stanfield had become premier. The PCs barely eked out an edge in the popular vote, with 48.6 percent to the Liberals' 48.2 percent, but claimed twenty-four of the legislature's forty-three seats, six more than the eighteen retained by the Grits. As in New Brunswick, the Liberal machine in Nova Scotia had been broken.

Gleeful Camp and Rowe had added another building block.

———

Quebec was a long-standing challenge for the Tories, but here, too, the pair at PC headquarters devised a worthy variant of their plan to build the national party through the provinces. Without any provincial PC Party, they gravitated, instead, to the most appealing Quebec Conservative as someone around whom to galvanize support.

Léon Balcer, elected Progressive Conservative MP from Trois-Rivières in 1949, had been re-elected in 1953. A lawyer by profession, Léon was handsome and bilingual, with the confidence of a natural leader. Why not get him elected national president of the PC Party?

George Hees, also an MP, was the incumbent president. His panache and movie-star looks outclassed others in the party, but that generated more jealousy than affection. And the well-connected Torontonian's exuberant self-promotion did little to disguise his ambition to lead the party and become prime minister, fostering resentment in Tory ranks from those more discreet about their aspirations and those protecting incumbent leader Drew from usurpers.

Camp and Rowe, having discussed the party's conundrum in Quebec, hatched a plot to replace Hees with Balcer. A successful challenge seemed possible. With the PC annual meeting approaching and Hees not yet declaring interest in re-election, they met with Balcer and found him willing to stand for the presidency. He promptly announced his candidacy, with both speech and press release by Dalton.

Hees, tracked down on ski slopes by reporters, told journalists he'd not yet decided about the presidency. He was, in truth, stunned by the challenge. Hees did not offer to run again. At the general meeting, Léon Balcer by acclamation became the first French-Canadian president of a political party in Canada.

Now Camp and Rowe had an ally in Quebec with whom to work, a man with stature on the national scene.

———

Seeking to build grassroots PC support across the country, as important as toppling Liberal provincial governments, Dalton began a monthly magazine, *Progress Report*. Soon it "was finding wide acceptance within the party, even while it had its inevitable critics in the caucus," mostly because the magazine reported progress in the provinces more than it extolled the existing MPs.

Another major initiative by Dalton was something that would become a hallmark of Camp-Atkins political operations: organizing memorable events and special-occasion dinners. The patterns at Robertson's Point, where a familial group connected, relaxed, played, and interacted with a drink in hand, became their model for successful political team building. They understood the social value and communications benefits of bringing carefully selected people to a pleasing event where they would create and share a common experience.

Camp proposed a series of "Second Century Dinners" to commemorate John A. Macdonald's founding of the Conservative Party a hundred years before. His theme of a "second century" masterfully highlighted the Tories as Canada's oldest political formation while also focusing attention on the unfolding decades ahead. Four Second Century Dinners were organized, for Winnipeg, London, Trois-Rivières, and Charlottetown. The national leader and new provincial PC premiers, along with other rising Tory stars, addressed the formal and well-organized events, projecting to the public the image of a party on the rise while fusing a sense of identity and purpose within the party.

One very promising star was Manitoba's Duff Roblin, a human spark plug who'd become provincial PC leader. When Camp and Rowe first met with the diminutive Manitoban in October 1955, Roblin got right to the point: Would he get the same support and co-operation they'd given Flemming in New Brunswick and Stanfield in Nova Scotia?

Rowe assured him he would. Roblin, driven by anxiety to be even more direct, was explicit. "I want you guys to come out here and do a job for me."

No appeal like that had greeted them in Saskatchewan, Alberta, or British Columbia. They quickly assured the potential Manitoba premier, "That's talking our language!"

CHAPTER 14

FORCES OF FATE

Dalton's effort to build a national organization and knit together support in constituencies and provinces consumed him.

Busily supporting the election of provincial PC governments, launching a party newsmagazine, and organizing dinners for the party, he now paid little attention to policy. His initial New Brunswick focus on issues and programs had been shifting to an organizer's desire to seize partisan opportunities and avoid political blunders. The day he'd arrived at party headquarters with Bill Rowe, a PC press release proudly announcing Camp's role noted that someone else, Donald Eldon, would be director of policy research. Development of party policy, and advocating change in government practice and public administration, no longer drove Camp nearly so much as organizing campaigns and communicating effectively.

He felt his efforts were paying off, especially as George Drew and the Tory caucus began to turn the tide of public opinion by resolute challenges to Liberal arrogance. When the St. Laurent government treated Parliament as an inconvenient rubber stamp for major bills dealing with the renewal of a defence treaty with the United States and the construction of an energy pipeline across Canada, determined Tories valiantly challenged both measures. Camp considered George Drew to be entering his finest stage as a parliamentarian and national leader.

Then he was gone.

On September 21, 1956, Dalton was at party headquarters when Bill Rowe phoned him from Toronto, insisting he come immediately. Joining Bill in his room at the Royal York Hotel, he was dismayed to find him holding George Drew's letter of resignation as leader of the Progressive Conservative Party of Canada. Though both were stunned, neither was surprised. They'd been deeply worried about Drew's health. Dalton and Rowe sat in the darkening silence of the room, "both of us downcast and morose, reflecting on Drew's resignation." Soon after, Grattan O'Leary arrived and presented Dalton with an envelope from Drew addressed to Léon Balcer as president; Dalton's mission was to take "this sorrowful correspondence" to headquarters and get copies made for the press gallery. He crossed to Union Station and travelled overnight to Ottawa by train, thinking he'd see through the leadership race, which he expected John Diefenbaker would win, and then return to the ad agency, just as Rowe intended to go back to his farm and racehorses. It would be the end.

———

John Diefenbaker did not take long to declare his candidacy. Keen to discourage others in his third try for the leadership, the Saskatchewan MP's bid was almost as predictable as the move by the Tory establishment to stop him, also for a third time. But things were different now.

Senior Ontario Tories tried recruiting University of Toronto president Sidney Smith, a Progressive Conservative and noted academic, but a man with no political experience. They failed. They contemplated other possible candidates to stop Prairie populist Diefenbaker. They canvassed the three PC provincial premiers, Frost, Flemming, and Stanfield. None was interested.

Each of these astute leaders saw that getting individuals from outside national politics to head a Canada-wide party was a self-defeating practice. Two provincial premiers in a row, Bracken and Drew, had led Canada's Progressive Conservatives through four successive elections, each time to a resounding defeat.

As a change-up, perhaps the party's perennial leadership aspirant, a man who was already in the Commons, knew the personalities of federal friends and foes alike, and had been long immersed in national issues, might be given a turn at the helm. A growing number of party regulars, grounded in the realities of their constituencies, thought so. John Diefenbaker's dramatic, courtroom-style rhetoric and well-earned reputation as champion of the underdog made him their favourite candidate.

Diefenbaker had proven himself a stubborn true-believer. After opening a law practice in Wawka, Saskatchewan in 1919, he was elected to its municipal council the following year. In 1925, at age thirty, John ran for Parliament as a Conservative candidate in Prince Albert riding.

Losing that contest did not deter him from running again in the 1926 election, although the result was no different. Would it be easier winning election to the Saskatchewan legislature? Diefenbaker campaigned as a Conservative candidate in the 1929 provincial election. This he lost, too. Unable to win federally or provincially, he lowered his sights and ran for mayor of Prince Albert in 1933. Even this, he lost.

Diefenbaker's growing reputation as skilled defence attorney and designation in 1929 as a King's Counsel burnished the Prairie lawyer's lustre. Yet he remained, almost perversely, convinced that his future lay not in the courtroom, but in politics. In October 1936, in his early forties, John George Diefenbaker sensed his moment had finally come when he was elected leader of the Saskatchewan Conservative Party.

For two years he lived with his fantasy of becoming premier, or at least gaining a seat in the legislature at Regina and leading a respectable number of fellow Conservative members. He travelled everywhere, gave speeches to groups large and small, and patched together some semblance of a campaign organization. But as votes were tallied on June 8, 1938, John was dismayed. He'd not only presided over his party's defeat, he had nothing to show for all his ardent campaigning. Across the entire province, the Conservatives failed to win a single seat. The party leader lost his own Arm River constituency, trailing the Liberal by 190 votes.

Overall, the results documented the Conservative Party of Saskatchewan's humiliating decline. The party's popular vote had been cut in half, falling from 25 percent in the previous election to less than 12 percent. Conservatives occupied fifth place among five parties, after the Liberals, Co-Operative Commonwealth Federation, Social Credit, and Unity (communist).

Undaunted even by this adversity, Diefenbaker continued advocating his particular brand of Conservative politics, visiting many Saskatchewan communities with his wife, Edna, to build what, in his lawyer's mind, he believed was a party organization. It amounted to little more than exhorting the few who showed up at his meetings to "keep the faith."

Diefenbaker's oratory drew audiences. The issues he hit upon moved listeners. But "keeping faith" was not the same as organizing and running campaigns or assembling the votes on election day. The articulate Conservative, whose credentials as a zealous campaigner were undisputed, needed someone to bring order to his political thrusts and win his elections on the ground.

What kept him going, beyond some deep belief that his destiny lay in politics, were battles he waged as a defence lawyer for society's downtrodden and marginal individuals. In the courtroom, Diefenbaker acquired intense protective feelings for the downtrodden he represented against "the system." In the political realm, this translated into his crusade for human rights.

Keeping faith with himself, Diefenbaker was nominated in June 1939 for the next federal election, his third time as a parliamentary candidate. Even his friends shook their heads, wondering when he'd give up.

Yet when the wartime federal election that was not to happen took place in March 1940 and proved such a disaster for the Tories, Diefenbaker somehow withstood the tide and got elected in Lake Centre constituency. On the Opposition benches, this man who'd always been a keen student of Parliament's powers and traditions soon began displaying skill as a close questioner of government actions. A reputation for holding Liberal ministers to account gained him respect nationally, and assisted with re-election from Lake Centre in 1945 and again in 1949, but had not yet made him first choice for party leader.

In December 1942, when the Conservatives met in Winnipeg to select a new leader, Diefenbaker came third. When the PC leadership opened up again in 1948, Diefenbaker again lost. Both times the party picked a premier, and while they continued to lead the PCs to defeat through four more elections, Diefenbaker got himself re-elected to the Commons, the only PC member from Saskatchewan, each time. Common folk and seasoned Tories alike admired John's resolute determination.

Members of the party's establishment and guardians of traditional Conservative interests, discussing the leadership at the Albany Club following Drew's resignation, saw no obvious alternative. They resigned themselves to the Saskatchewan MP becoming head of the party, taking solace in the fact Diefenbaker would only last one election. Nobody could topple the entrenched Grits and affable Liberal prime minister "Uncle Louis" St. Laurent, they knew, least of all a radical Prairie loner. What did one more defeat matter to those with a losers' syndrome?

———

Delegates to the Progressive Conservative Party's national leadership convention from across Canada began arriving at Ottawa's Union Station in mid-December's shortened daylight, the event itself a snapshot of a country in transition.

It was the last national political gathering to which most delegates would come by train. The prosperity that settled over Canada in the 1950s saw governments building more airports and better roads, citizens buying more and bigger cars, and the skies filling with comfortable and faster passenger airplanes.

Politics was being reinvented, too, through new photographic processes and mass communication advertising. Canada's prime minister was a living embodiment of what was possible, by the mid-twentieth century, when manipulating a public persona. Camp had noted, during the federal election three years earlier, how everyone at PC headquarters kept their heads down scrutinizing Liberal press releases and speeches for fresh ammunition. Had they looked up, they'd have discovered it was no longer a campaign of words but of images, that "an austere patrician corporate lawyer of great dignity and bearing was converted into the image of 'Uncle Louis,' an achievement of public relations and advertising prowess," a made-over image that Conservative campaign planners failed to adjust to and that Camp attributed to "the modern techniques of advertising and publicity" and a process "accommodated and confirmed by a willingly helpful press."

The Grits' advertising agency had turned a seventy-year-old corporate lawyer whose natural habitat was the boardroom — not the Cabinet chamber, Commons front bench, or a podium at a political assembly — into "everyone's handsomely aging uncle" as presented by "assiduously retouched, richly coloured photographs." In this new era, Camp readily discerned, the political backrooms would increase their power through sophistication in communications manipulation.

The mid-1950s introduced, most notably, Canada's first televised leadership convention. The December 1956 PC leadership race in Ottawa would be a pioneering event in these early days of broadcasting live coverage. Most Canadians did not yet own a television set, and many were still unaware of the medium. The transformative age of "telepolitics" would be born in a combination of fresh expectation and awkwardness. Tory delegates, being first, were uncertain about how to act, but knew — and were told by media-savvy players from the backrooms — that they'd have to present a dramatic, upbeat show to convey the right impression to the watching public.

The dawning age of Canadian television was about to transform politics.

CHAPTER 15

HARDBALL POLITICS

Ottawa mayor Charlotte Whitton, an advanced feminist and ardent Tory who would soon be a parliamentary candidate for the PCs, jubilantly welcomed delegates to her city's Coliseum on December 13, 1956. As she wound up and left the stage, they were laughing with her, and cheering.

Next to the podium came Nova Scotia's newly elected premier, Robert Stanfield, to deliver the convention's keynote address. His voice was barely audible. The spare and dour leader, Canada's youngest premier, punched hard on social inequities, called for a new era of economic justice across Canada, and pledged strong Maritime support for the federal Conservatives in the coming election, all in a quiet voice.

Camp had written Stanfield's speech. When initially asked to give the opening address, the preoccupied premier had told Dalton, "I'd be glad to do it but haven't the time." Under pressure from his wordsmith, he recanted. "If you help write it, I'll give it."

The speechwriting drill between them had evolved as their different dispositions gradually reconciled. Where Stanfield had "a horror of adjectives, adverbs, and emotive words," Camp had "a passion for them, admiring the speeches of Winston Churchill more than any other." Where Stanfield would pen something "full of fact but barren of meaning," Camp sought to conjure images, communicate with all senses, and form impressions "which facts alone could not create." He may have improved Stanfield's rhetoric, he said, but acknowledged how Stanfield "in turn improved my sense of proportion" and "the value of simplicity and the discipline of restraint."

Neither of them, nor any reporter or other politician for that matter, had an ethical problem about words being spoken by a political leader that were not truly his own. Audiences enjoyed good acting, watching performers deliver the lines of a playwrite. Politics was theatre. "Speech writers" occupied a box on the organization chart, an office handy to the leader's, and a role shaping policy in speeches the way advertising men did in election publicity. In plain view, everyone lived with the ruse that, merely by speaking a speech writer's words, leaders appropriated them as their own.

"What a business it all is," mused Camp. "None can tell the illusion from the reality, or which is which. What would Stanfield have said if someone else had written it?"

———

Still a novelty, TV had been used slightly in the campaigns for the recent provincial elections, mostly by enterprising local candidates where facilities were available.

From the PC convention in the Coliseum, viewers saw scenes unlike any before, as the cavernous hall took on "a decidedly party-like tone" and performing for TV cameras became part of Canadian national politics. According to the *Ottawa Citizen*, "Over 1,300 delegates to the Conservative leadership convention discovered that politics can be fun. With pretty drum majorettes, kilted pipers, popping balloons, and an apparently inexhaustible supply of high spirits, they turned nomination night into a rollicking Mardi-Gras." TV cameras challenged speakers to address two different audiences at the same time. Delegates thought Stanfield's keynote address lacked the emotional surge needed for a clarion call to a new day in politics. PC Youth delegate Ted Rogers, who in time would understand a lot more about television, told Camp, not knowing he'd written the speech, that the Nova Scotia premier's address was "awfully quiet." Yet, Gratton O'Leary, being interviewed by CBC, was unequivocal about calling it "the best speech of the lot" because it had come over well on television. The venerable newspaperman grasped that, in this new era of television, the so-called keynote was no longer "a pep talk to a few hundred of the faithful in a hall" but an address "to perhaps a million people, roughly to the entire nation."

The three candidates were all incumbent members of Parliament, John Diefenbaker from Saskatchewan, Donald Fleming of Toronto, and British Columbia's Davie Fulton. After each was nominated and seconded, their floor demonstrations erupted, patterned on American-style showboat conventions and reflecting, Camp noted, "the pubescent demands of the new electronic media."

The delegates pranced and paraded in the aisles, grinning self-consciously, recognizing the superfluity of their unfamiliar exercise, "blindly hopeful it will somehow advance their cause." Diefenbaker's demonstration was best, by far. Camp nodded a salute to Allister Grosart, whose accomplishment as a fellow adman he recognized the show to be.

Other convention features were more familiar: wooing delegates with liquor and promises of appointments, denigrating rivals with subtlety on stage and vehemence in the corridors, and the influencing of others by powerful people announcing their own choices of candidate.

———

Camp and Bill Rowe were dismayed, as organizers of the event, when John Diefenbaker broke the tradition of acknowledging the country's French reality by having only English-speaking delegates as both nominator and seconder of his candidacy. Many other unilingual English-speaking delegates were also shocked by this deliberate snub, if for no higher reason than that it was bad politics not to show respect for a sizeable constituency of voters.

When insiders learned in advance he would exclude a French-speaking person, they appealed to Dief to change his seconder to someone who spoke French. He refused. He wanted to deliberately create a hostile undercurrent along Canada's linguistic divide. It was hardball politics of a kind not seen for years. Taking into account the entire assembly of voting delegates, a large majority of whom were English-speaking, the Prairie MP applied a brute "divide and conquer" strategy.

Camp was equally appalled by the harshness of Diefenbaker's delegates. They denigrated Drew and those who'd supported him. Although most delegates in 1956 were "eager and anxious" to elect the Saskatchewanian their new leader, the blunt and aggressive Diefenbaker loyalists, driven by memories of prior losses, brought to the convention "a particular hostility, as though they must first prove their manhood to the Tory Party in order that the prize be worthy," thought Camp.

Three Progressive Conservative MPs – Toronto's Donald Fleming, Saskatchewan's John Diefenbaker, and British Columbia's Davie Fulton – had each run for the party leadership in 1948, and in 1967 would again vie against one another for the top position, but the only one to ever win was Diefenbaker, at this 1956 Ottawa convention.

When it came time to vote, Dalton was so torn he could not cast a ballot. But others did. In the very first round, delegates convincingly elected John Diefenbaker to lead the Progressive Conservative Party of Canada.

Camp stood apart and watched "the klieg-lit dawn of the Diefenbaker age, the new leader, dazed with the sense of triumph, moist-eyed and trembling at the podium, one hand held high, at his side Olive Diefenbaker, on her face a beaming smile and in her arms the eternal bouquet." (After Diefenbaker's first wife, Edna, died, he had married Olive Palmer.)

─────

That evening, Hugh John Flemming sought out the new leader to make sure Diefenbaker was aware of Dalton Camp's role in helping him topple a well-entrenched Grit regime, the next main focus for Dief himself.

Still later that night, the New Brunswick premier succeeded in tracking down Camp. The first thing he heard was, "Rowe is quitting. And so am I. I'm going out with the people I came in with."

"Now," said Hugh John calmly, "don't talk nonsense."

He'd spoken with Diefenbaker, explained the premier. He'd urged him to see Dalton. As a result, he said, Camp was to meet the new leader. "Tomorrow morning, in his hotel room, at eight o'clock. You see him and I think you'll change your mind."

Although major Tory players occupied spacious suites at the Château Laurier, Olive and John Diefenbaker had a single room. Dalton found that "commendable in an egalitarian sense" but "awkward for the practical purposes of conversation" when, early next morning, he entered their cramped space.

Dalton remained standing, listening as Dief, stretched the length of one of the twin beds, began talking about George Drew and the aftermath of the party's convention eight years earlier, when Drew had beaten him and Diefenbaker felt humiliated. Camp puzzled to understand what message Diefenbaker was hoping to convey from the past in this early morning claustrophobic dimness.

In time Dief got around to PC Party headquarters. In light of Bill Rowe's resignation as national director, now received, Dalton heard Diefenbaker say, "I want you to take charge of headquarters for me." He also told Camp, "I have a lot of speeches to make in the next while and want your ideas." Next he told Dalton he wanted him, "personally, to show me all the incoming mail" at headquarters and "also to give me copies of all the letters you write in reply, of course. I just want to know what's going on down there, you see. Will you do that?"

Dalton felt an overpowering urge to escape the dim, stale-smelling room. "Perhaps it would be different later in the day," he thought, when the two men might be talking about all this "in an office, in the sunlight."

Camp made his escape, "hastily, clumsily, without saying yes or no." Olive graciously saw Dalton to the door. She spoke with a smile. But he "did not hear what she was saying." He was preoccupied "listening to the alarms" signalling in his own mind.

————

Through January 1957 Dalton carried on at party headquarters, having decided not to resign after all, operating in limbo, doing his best "to take charge" as Diefenbaker had asked, waiting for the leader to choose between George Hees and Gordon Churchill for the position of the party's new national director.

Diefenbaker also had to decide whether Camp or Grosart would head up election publicity, which meant determining whether Locke Johnson or

McKim would handle campaign advertising. Dalton's extended absence from his Toronto home required Linda to cope stoically, but time away from Locke Johnson was something the firm's Liberal-minded partners tolerated unevenly. He'd found them content when his departures into distant provinces to slay Grits had generated campaign work billed through the agency and, thereafter, substantial advertising accounts from the governments of New Brunswick and Nova Scotia. "Perhaps," Dalton mused, thinking ahead to the coming federal election, "they had intuitive glimpses of things to come." PC election victories had revealed their Liberal loyalty to be soluble in revenue flow.

When it was announced that Gordon Churchill would be national director, Dalton marvelled at the compromise Grosart had cooked up with Dief. Churchill, not ambitious for the leadership himself the way Hees was, would be in charge of the party machinery, while Hees would be dispatched on a cross-Canada tour for the party, giving him the publicity he craved. As for campaign advertising, Grosart and Camp would continue together, under Churchill's supervision, with the publicity budget divided between McKim and Locke Johnson. Decisions about publicity would be jointly taken by Churchill, Grosart, and Camp. The same three would, recognizing the primacy of admen in elections, have "the opportunity to discuss any policy decision" before it was communicated to the public — a ratio of two to one, admen to accountable elected representative.

Settling in under this new dispensation, Dalton resolved that he "wanted the Conservative Party to become an effective, efficient political instrument — such as could bring down a Liberal government." But building a blue machine became hard with Gordon Churchill as national director. He was a poor administrator. Dalton had Gordon's ear, but the Winnipeg MP routinely failed to take action across a range of urgent fronts. He'd smile, rub his bald head, and defer.

Hoping to force some decisions, Camp wrote Churchill a long memorandum on the state of party communication and organization. He reviewed the pros, cons, costs, and reach of advertising in daily newspapers, magazines, weeklies, and on radio and television, and discussed production of some six million copies of campaign pamphlets. Television received an extended appraisal, not only as the newest communications medium but, as Camp saw it, the most potent. His information about private stations and the CBC was detailed, his recommendations clear and specific. His early interpretations about the transformative role of television on politics would stand the test of time.

Dief named Winnipeg MP Gordon Churchill as PC national director to implement his 1957 campaign strategy of ignoring Quebec. At party headquarters Churchill frustrated Dalton Camp by failing to act on his memos about using television in campaigning.

Dalton saw television as "an intimate, personal medium, and the nearest thing to direct contact aside from personal canvass." But TV came at a price. More important even than the "heavy surcharge on publicity expenditures" that a television campaign exacts on a party, Camp made clear, was how it added "a further burden to the leader of the party."

As for campaign strategy, Camp's memo noted that, despite television now being "the most pervasive and influential medium of all," the Liberals would not use it much or well, "since it is apparent even to them that Prime Minister St. Laurent does not like the medium."

While this gave the PCs "a certain advantage," it would only be an opportunity if John Diefenbaker and the individuals handling campaign publicity realized that "the medium cannot be used to wage an argument and to win one." Instead, television created an impression. "It is always possible to leave a good impression, whereas it is difficult to leave a message. It is very nearly as simple as this." The question in a viewer's mind when watching a political television broadcast, said Camp, is: "Do I like and do I trust him?"

Speech material and technique of delivery "which answer this question affirmatively," he concluded, "are what we must seek."

———

In mid-March, Camp was stunned when Gordon Churchill unexpectedly withdrew from his role at party headquarters, leaving the party once more without a national director.

Allister Grosart, it turned out, would be in charge of everything.

Camp returned to Toronto, told his principals at Locke Johnson that his career in politics was finished, for good, and wrote a letter of resignation to John Diefenbaker. Linda looked forward to him being home more.

The phone rang. Churchill said he was puzzled. Another call came in from Grosart, pleading for Dalton to return. Both men said Diefenbaker wanted Camp helping out.

"Then why doesn't he ask me?" countered Camp, who felt he'd been led on and let down.

A few weeks later, when Dalton walked into Parliament's vast Railway Committee meeting room for the 1957 Press Gallery dinner, having accepted the coveted invitation before he'd left PC headquarters, John Diefenbaker was standing by the door. "He reached out his arm and put it around me and grabbed me by the neck and held me against his chest, and said something like 'You and I are going to be in this together, aren't we?'"

The encounter touched Dalton. He'd been hurt, but had not really wanted to forsake politics. Returning to Toronto the next day, he began preparing an advertising campaign for the 1957 election.

———

The two men had had a string of odd encounters, yet beyond the quirky skirmishes and strange interactions, something deeper suggested their lives were fated to entwine. Both were outsiders to the Central Canada power structure, each proud enough of his regional heritage to celebrate rather than sublimate this identity. Both had instinctive concern for individuals struggling at the outer edges and lower ranges of society, and felt quick disdain for men in powerful positions securing their own advantages while ignoring those in need. Raised as Baptists, both had absorbed by osmosis its Protestant creed and congregational structure that, combined, made virtues of local autonomy, egalitarian values, self-reliance, clean living, and moral uplift achieved among one's fellow adherents.

Each savoured the jousting of politics, but as accompaniment to a deeper if ineffable contest over something that mattered in the world, the country, or one's community. When it concerned Tory fortunes, the two had separately displayed a devotion to political organizing that required nothing short of a zealot's resolve, trying to rally stubborn locals out of their defeatist attitudes and indifference to Conservative interests.

Dalton, as a convert to Toryism, displayed an unrelenting need to justify the correctness of his crossover to the enemy. John's father was a Liberal, yet he too became a Tory, for obscure reasons embedded in his personal ambition to rise, and thereafter possessed the ardour of a disciple in the wilderness, pressing on for decades as a tireless Conservative to justify the correctness of his chosen party allegiance.

By temperament both were loners, happiest taking their own path without restraint or accountability — Dief never giving anyone a copy of his speech in advance or even telling organizers what he would say, Camp waiting to the very last minute to write his campaign editorials so nobody else could have time to vet them — solitary champions of worthy causes according to their own lights.

In 1953, their similar political instincts made each recoil from a PC election campaign based on a half-billion-dollar tax cut. Both knew it would be rejected by voters in their respective regions that alike depended on federal spending. Dief immediately disassociated himself with the policy and kept national party publicity about it out of Saskatchewan. Dalton "disliked the image of the Tory Party as frugal bookkeeper" and craved as an alternative a campaign "that would recognize the problems of disparity" and would benefit society's "numberless outsiders."

Instinctively, intellectually, and emotionally, the politics of both men were the same. And each envisaged a possibility of one day becoming prime minister.

They had differences. Thirty six years separated them in age. Diefenbaker had been in the army in the First World War, Camp in the Second, and neither faced battle. The former adhered to Baptist precepts about tobacco and alcohol, while the latter had fallen off that wagon. Where Camp felt at home on either side of the Canada-U.S. border, Diefenbaker lifted his eyes to Britain and upheld the Conservative Party's long-standing suspicion of American motives. Dief was a monarchist, Camp closer to a republican.

Their starkest difference was how each viewed Canada's French-speaking citizens. Diefenbaker recoiled from giving any special attention to French Canadians. Camp felt comfort in Canada's rich culture and relished, even though he did not speak the French language, how the francophone and anglophone communities cohabited in New Brunswick. But like recruits wearing a common uniform and embracing the disciplined code of soldiers' honour, none of their discordant similarities and harmonious differences mattered when the two men turned to fight their common enemy: Grits.

They'd been hardened for this battle. Each had followed different trajectories, but by the mid-1950s the politics of Dalton Camp and John Diefenbaker were aligned, drawn together for purposes beyond anything they could yet fully comprehend.

The new leader's hopeful prophecy to delegates at the Ottawa Coliseum and to television viewers across Canada had been, Camp remembered, "We have an appointment, ladies and gentlemen, with destiny."

CHAPTER 16

A DATE WITH DESTINY

Dalton listed "basic issues" around which he thought the Progressive Conservatives, in light of party stances and current events, might build a 1957 election campaign.

He had a clean slate. In John Diefenbaker's victory speech to the convention, their new leader told delegates that PC policy had been drafted "as the result of the application and thinking of every Conservative at this convention and many more not privileged to attend." It was "representative of the viewpoint of every walk of life and people from every part of this country" and dealt "with the needs and aspirations of every Canadian." Then Diefenbaker ordered the party-approved policy resolutions burned.

Thus freed, Camp began his own list of top issues for the PCs' policy agenda. First on the list were the economic problems of have-not provinces, the impasse in dominion-provincial relations, credit restrictions, fiscal policy, and inflation. Agriculture, social services, social security benefits, natural resources, and human resources, were issues he added next. Raising his eyes to the international scene, he listed the United Nations, the Commonwealth, and the United States. Back within the country, he then covered off Louis St. Laurent being "a lame duck prime minister," restoration of the two-party system, and "the rights of the people in Parliament," which, he noted, was "The Chief's expression." Already he was referring to

Diefenbaker by the handier deferential title, "The Chief." Tories liked how it rymed with "Dief."

Reviewing each issue, Dalton saw how they cancelled themselves out. An item popular or necessary in a particular region or certain segment of society would be "either rhetorical or inflammable" in others. Of all the possibilities, Camp saw only one concept that was "truly national in scope." It was what he'd identified as "the personal appeal of the leader himself."

Dalton Camp had rationalized a campaign focused exclusively on John Diefenbaker.

It was the one theme he knew The Chief, who insisted on personally approving everything, would go for: full adulation of a party that had twice denied him the mantle of leadership. It was an issue that allowed PCs to attack Grits and be positive, much better than such hoary stances as restoring a two-party system, which made Tories seem like nostalgic fogies, or cutting taxes, which made them resemble fastidious accountants. And, a focus on the leader alone would work best for impressionistic television. Camp's idea was the genesis of a cult of personality. When he'd come back to Canada, Dalton lamented how the country had no heroes the way they did in the United States. Why not make one? He'd turn Dief the Chief into a Canadian national celebrity.

In early 1957 Camp confided to Churchill, when still national director, that while it was not always possible "for a party to consider its leader as its first asset and best issue," opinion polling indicated that "the average voter appears to have an intuitive confidence and liking" for John Diefenbaker. Translating that into a strategy for campaign publicity, Camp urged that for "the greatest effect on the greatest number of people," PC advertising would have to "give the highest priority to Mr. Diefenbaker."

Certain that Churchill would share his memo with the leader, Camp summed up, "Thus, of all these issues, the one with the widest common denominator is the leadership issue."

No one would be happier to read that than The Chief.

Dalton could ascend, allied to Diefenbaker, even higher.

———

If the PC's national leader had fixed views about politics, so by this stage in his career did Camp.

When he'd become estranged from the Liberals in the late 1940s, it was because the federal party placed its corporate well-being ahead of true reform and because New Brunswick Grits circulated the benefits of office for themselves while excluding people at the margins. "They do not seek office," he said, "but the spoils of office." To preserve his integrity and uphold his beliefs, he'd left the party.

Camp never resented "the Liberal machine" as a political operation, but rather for the way it was run and what it produced. As a political organizer, in fact, he remained in awe of the Grit machinery's seamless wielding of power, conduct of public business, and election-winning record. He wanted to build a Tory version of the same thing.

To do this he emphasized concentrating focus on the leader, maximizing use of television, and designing a hard-headed plan for campaign operations. In principle, Camp favoured a decentralized campaign that would enable the party to deal as needed with various provinces and individual ridings, in keeping with the historic "local autonomy" nature, structure, and culture of the party. For pragmatic reasons, however, Camp knew the modern age had different requirements.

As a result, Camp's three-part plan not only accommodated Canada's new era of democracy, to which television was fast becoming instrinsic, but advanced it, with: (i) a national publicity campaign; (ii) a national tour by the leader; and (iii) a campaign organization that supported all campaign publicity and the leader's tour by keeping focus on the big national picture with "appreciation of the overall situation." It was a perfect "progressive" and "conservative" plan because it enabled the Progressive Conservatives to go in two opposite directions at once and yet be consistent.

There would be tight national control over what really mattered in the age of television politics — the image of the leader and a unified national publicity campaign — but beyond that, efforts would be decentralized and run locally as much as possible. "It's your show. You run it!" became the mantra from national headquarters when asked how to handle local campaign problems, a reassuringly hands-off attitude promoted even as the centre continued to hold tight reins on the campaign's most crucial elements: all advertising and the leader's tour.

To be a true political machine, Camp made clear, national publicity had to be rigidly controlled — tactically, administratively, and financially. The national tour, he envisaged, would no longer entail the leader making some speeches here and there, slamming the Grits and saying what a PC government would do in its place. Instead of that limited role, the tour would now anchor the campaign's overall strategy. Dalton stressed the need for painstaking selection of Diefenbaker's staff for this mobile operation, just as he emphasized judicious preparation of the itinerary to maximize the leader's impact for gaining winnable seats.

Camp knew from his own tour around New Brunswick in the 1948 provincial election with Liberal premier McNair the need to put in play a tightly knit cadre of savvy and versatile individuals. For Diefenbaker's tour team, Dalton's recommendations were specific. Derek Bedson, recruited from the Department of External Affairs by George Drew to the party leader's office, was chosen for the role of personal secretary and administrator. Camp had come to appreciate the Manitoban's refined political sensibilities and courteous ways. They'd also become good friends, Bedson living in the same Ottawa house as Rowe and Camp.

Allister Grosart had to handle press relations and be the TV and radio producer, said Camp. The two men had differences, but Dalton recognized the McKim's executive as someone highly knowledgeable about campaign momentum, news media, and The Chief himself, a formidable man who could get his way dealing with others. He named a research assistant to travel with Diefenbaker on tour, paired with "an opposite number" remaining in Ottawa, so the two could check any fact or chase down a new rumour while the campaign was in progress, to keep the leader accurately informed.

An "assistant on the road would prepare speech material." Camp already knew The Chief did not need or even want a set text, the way he wrote speeches for Stanfield, but merely notes that, in a pithy paragraph, covered an entire issue. These speech fragments the leader could then rearrange and select as he progressed through his remarks, in harmony with whatever response he was getting from his audience. It was how John argued his case before a jury in court, operating from the centre of a seemingly chaotic cluster of documents. Sometimes The Chief would just waive a document aloft without reading it, or jab at a newspaper clipping with his finger to make a larger point. For John Diefenbaker, speech-making was all about the dramatics.

The two other slots for the leader's tour, in Camp's blueprint, were "a detail man for local arrangements" and "regional advisers." Camp said the former would likely best be chosen by regional appointment, and for the latter recommended "caucus members, where advisable."

———

Dalton's plan for the organization itself was premised on what he knew about riding campaigns. Once the election had been called and core elements of the national campaign launched, he said, "there is no longer a federal election but rather 265 by-elections" — the number of federal constituencies in 1957 — as far as the national organization at headquarters would be concerned. For the duration, headquarters would simply "coordinate in whatever way we can the varied conduct of these constituency elections."

There was no separate facility out of which to run a national campaign. The existing party headquarters at Bracken House served as centre of operations. Two members of the party's permanent staff in Ottawa would liaise with the ad agencies for English and French language advertising. Regular employees would also handle administrative aspects for the tour itinerary. Extra staff would be hired for clerical duties and mail room work.

Camp built nothing into his plan for opinion polling during the campaign. He had little interest in pollsters' mass of detailed numbers that someone would "interpret," and only low regard for the general conclusions produced by 1950s sampling techniques. The election would be won on the ground in individual ridings and by the transcending magic of John Diefenbaker's Canada-wide appeal. Opinion samplers were useless for both. They did not know how to measure unscrupulous ground-level poll-by-poll warfare, nor could they calibrate magic.

When it came to knowing what to do next, Dalton would not look to samplings of the opinions held by sideline members of the public. He would rely instead on reports from humans directly engaged at the front lines of battle. That was how he'd written his potent political columns, seizing on the hottest reports of partisan combat and transforming them into entertaining and politically lethal messages that *turned public opinion itself* along a different direction. Camp, knowing victory resided in the raw volatility of public opinion, did not want to be distracted by polling. Besides, all polls showed the Liberals under Louis St. Laurent were a shoe-in for another majority government.

"Our campaign intelligence will be based largely on our direct relations with responsible persons in the various provinces," he instructed. In early 1957, these PC sources varied "both in degree of responsibility and in usefulness," so he urged "substantial contact" with the stronger point people and "immediate action to strengthen the weaker ones" to build the election machinery.

The two-pronged campaign strategy outlined by Dalton was a ground war fought poll by poll in the ridings combined with an aerial attack by The Chief who would roam the entire country on a well-planned and highly coordinated leader's tour. For the latter, Dief would excite voters through orchestrated interactions with reporters, radio stations, and television outlets, and raise fresh hope among party workers at well-run rallies in centres where an extra effort could defeat the Grits.

"We come closest to direct involvement in a riding," Camp said of the national campaign, "when the leader is in a candidate's area, when we assist them with regard to publicity, and when we deal with them on matters of finance." The national party would put its own money into ridings where extra cash could help. Few rules governed campaign spending in 1957, and none imposed limits on the amount of money used.

———

Camp's innovative plan was sound, but three major hurdles remained — the lacklustre party image nationally, absence of voter support and party organization in Quebec which gave a large majority of the province's many seats to Liberals by default, and lack of money to run the campaign.

It seemed the Progressive Conservative brand, despite high hopes a decade-and-a-half earlier, held little appeal for most Canadians. The ill-fated 1953 campaign, the most recent in voters' memories, had again tarnished the party's image, but it was just one more in a string of bleak defeats for the supposedly revamped Progressive Conservatives.

Why not give voters something *truly* progressive — a new style of politics? The Conservative name and all the history it evoked would be set aside. The campaign, in keeping with the strategy to highlight the one common interest in all regions, would have a single, simple message: "It's Time for a Diefenbaker Government!"

The slogan emerged when Camp, Bill Kettlewell, and Hank Loriaux brainstormed in the Toronto boardroom of Locke Johnson. Dalton knew it resonated perfectly with the "the greatest common denominator of the campaign — the belief that the Liberals had been in office too long." But there was more. A soft change to "a Diefenbaker Government" would not invoke antagonistic partisan loyalties or repel Liberal sentiments the way calling for "change to the Conservatives" would. "Diefenbaker" suggested "ethnic origins, a social order other than Toronto, and politics other than Tory." The slogan, he believed, evoked "painless change, buoyant hopes, a new order, glints of strength, and fresh promise!"

The second challenge was Quebec, a province rich in seats — most solidly Liberal. Besides their partisan traditon, voters were emotionally predisposed to support native son Louis St. Laurent, which meant voting for the Liberal prime minister's candidates. The Progressive Conservative organization existed on paper, not in the parishes. The scattering of Quebec seats held by Tories were the product of strong individual appeal and good organization in specific ridings. Léon Balcer in Trois-Rivières, for example, as a relative of Maurice Duplessis, got solid help from Union Nationale troops.

Third, being a moneyless party was like being a band without musical instruments. Though never openly acknowledging this reality, Camp's campaign strategy was crafted as a small budget operation. That's how modest circumstances had first schooled him to fight Grits in New Brunswick, proving not only that necessity can give birth to invention, but that the result can be a major improvement. He'd also concluded, watching the losing New Brunswick Liberal campaign in 1952 and hearing backroom details about the Tory national campaign of 1949, that ad agencies were inefficient, and their decisions often inept, frequently based more on making a profit than mounting an effective campaign.

———

A hardball way to confront the PC's lack of campaign funds and chronic weakness in Quebec would be to write off the province's seats.

The PCs could husband limited resources for more effective use in ridings easier to win, spending only token amounts in Quebec and having the leader's tour touch just a few safe places. Quebec Tories might appreciate running their own show anyway, not having to make apologies when parading before audiences a leader who could not speak the language and who'd slighted them at the Ottawa convention. The risk in such a blunt strategy was that it would, yet again, infuriate the *bleus* of Quebec who were being ignored by Diefenbaker. It would also provoke outcry from Conservative workers expecting to scoop money from the campaign.

Gordon Churchill would get credit for this strategy to campaign as if Quebec had somehow separated from the rest of Canada, but he never had the makings of such a brazen strategist. The malleable Manitoban's real role in this was as fall-guy in case the plan badly backfired. For this simplistic divide-and-conquer "Quebec strategy," Churchill was taking direction from John Diefenbaker, to whom he was now devoted.

Diefenbaker's hardnosed approach to winning the leadership by focusing on the majority of non-francophone voting delegates planted the seed that sprouted in this 1957 campaign decision to bypass Quebec. If it was numerically possible to form a government without winning seats in *la belle province*, why dilute the effort in other provinces where greater gains could be made? Win where you had the best chances.

Diefenbaker wanted to appeal, as the first national party leader with origins other than French or English, for "One Canada." He took smug satisfaction believing his stance helped him gain the party leadership, winning over delegates silently happy to see him pointedly exclude a French-Canadian presence. He would apply the same tactic a second time, on a national level.

Camp disliked this strategy for the election as much as he had for the convention. He'd seen Progressive Conservative victories in French-speaking communities of New Brunswick where he'd been told the party could never win. He stuck up for minorities and abhorred seeing people pushed to the margins. But nothing could change The Chief's view about French Canadians, born on the multiethnic Prairies and matured during seventeen years' witnessing the astuteness of French-Canadian political leaders in the Commons. As well, personal embarrassment about his German name, especially during the war, propelled him to advocate "un-hyphenated Canadianism." A campaign that treated all Canadians equally was fine in his books, consistent with the "melting pot" concept of a New World society and, even better, a strategy to beat the Grits.

———

As the 1957 election loomed, Diefenbaker's national campaign committee gathered early on Sunday, April 7, in the Château Laurier. The powerful group assembling that warm, quiet morning included major players in the party, all anxious to hear Camp present the advertising campaign he'd devised.

Four years earlier, after Dalton tried in vain to take charge of the 1953 campaign publicity, he had resolved "to assume control of the advertising campaign for the next election." Now that Diefenbaker had given him "important special responsibilities for creative planning of national advertising," he was where he wanted to be — in the driver's seat.

Camp told the large number present that "nearly all the promotional copy" would be not something written by Tories but extracts from "unimpeachable authority — the press of Canada." He'd collected a string of "pearls" from editorials, each one testifying to some special quality or ennobling attribute of the party's leader. Those endorsements would be evidence to support the slogan "It's Time for a Diefenbaker Government!"

There would be only two ads, both full-page. One showed a handsome photograph of John Diefenbaker. The other was an adaptation of a *Globe and Mail* political cartoon that portrayed the Peace Tower as a guillotine, reprising the national outrage when the Liberal government invoked closure on debate, the year before, to force its pipeline legislation through Parliament. At the time, the press had dubbed the fateful day "Black Friday." This full-page campaign ad carried only the stark words BLACK FRIDAY at the top. To maximize impact, the image had been reversed by Camp, so that the whole page was black with the outline of the Peace Tower/guillotine appearing in white. Both ads were clean, bold, visually commanding.

Camp's presentation done, the meeting erupted, first with applause, then a standing ovation.

Within hours, the ads were en route to *Maclean's*, *Reader's Digest*, and many other magazines, to cover everyone from farmers and veterans to anglers and Daughters of the Empire. As Camp had designed it, the advertising campaign "was a model of simplicity, efficiency, economy, and reach." The editorial testimonials with the picture of John Diefenbaker would run in every daily newspaper across Canada, and in every Canadian magazine of record.

The layout for *Reader's Digest*, a small-format publication, ran the photo on one page and the "pearls" on its facing page. This double-page spread was then also printed, in hundreds of thousands of copies, to be shipped to the ridings for local printing, on the blank side, as campaign pamphlets. The BLACK FRIDAY ad, which ran later in all daily newspapers (except those in Quebec, where use of closure to end debate had never been an issue), was similarly converted to a pamphlet.

With a single fold, the local PC candidate and his or her workers then had a four-page handout. The key message of the national campaign was thus uniform across all ridings in Canada, one of Dalton's three campaign objectives, yet each constituency had two pages of local content as well to hit points important to the riding and its Tory candidate. "It's your campaign!"

The national campaign had thus been "put to bed" even before the party leader delivered his opening speech of the election. Altogether, the 1957 PC election advertisements contained fewer than a thousand words, less than fifty of them written by Camp. There was but a single photograph, the handsome one of John Diefenbaker, and only one other illustration, the dramatic newspaper cartoon.

———

When Gordon Churchill stepped down as national director and was promptly replaced by Allister Grosart, the latter's real role, as Diefenbaker instructed, was not to direct the party but run the election campaign.

Dalton at first was dismayed, thinking he'd been beaten by an end-run, and chagrined that Grosart would not be on the leader's tour with Dief to deal with television. But Dalton mellowed when campaign manager Grosart told him to divide up the publicity budget billings, which had been set at $800,000. "It's your campaign. Take what you want, and allocate the rest."

Camp gave McKim the pamphlets and the placement of ads in the Ontario dailies. Foster Advertising got all radio ads and western dailies. To Locke Johnson he allocated all magazine advertising, Quebec English-language dailies, and all Maritime daily newspapers. The money divided pretty much equally amongst the agencies.

Camp's own agency, Locke Johnson, also got into the work of distributing materials, following the pattern of McKim, which was filling pamphlet orders coming in from riding campaigns. Dalton liked having the ad agency so closely entwined with the party's ground campaign that it became part of it at an operational level, in addition to its more traditional role in the creative work and placement of ads with broadcasters and publications. What McKim and Locke Johnson were doing was much faster and far more efficient, since it eliminated an intermediary step of getting the materials to party headquarters in Ottawa for redistribution from there.

———

Camp considered becoming a candidate in New Brunswick.

The campaign structure he designed did not depend on his presence in Ottawa to operate it. He knew at some point he'd make the transition from backroom to front bench. It was not a question of if, only of when, to make his move.

He exchanged correspondence with political friends in New Brunswick, who sought to enlist him. While he did "not quite find the idea impossible," he concluded it was "rather unlikely." Although frequently in New Brunswick for work and vacations, his home with Linda was now in Toronto, where their children were in school and, when he intermittently returned to Locke Johnson, where he also worked.

What really ended his thoughts about running, though, was that Diefenbaker and Grosart suggested Dalton take responsibility for the entire campaign in the four Atlantic provinces. Camp believed he'd be far better off, at this stage in his political career, getting more Tory MPs elected than becoming one himself. At thirty-seven years of age, his ambition for high public office had plenty of time for fulfillment. Elections came along as regularly as commuter trains.

Already he occupied a unique role in public affairs and party politics, wielding influence in PC backrooms in Fredericton, Halifax, and Ottawa, increasingly renowned for prowess in campaign publicity and prescience in electoral strategy. It would be smarter to see just how far this could take him.

Of the thirty-three seats in the four Atlantic provinces, Grits held twenty-seven, and because the region was still a two-party enclave, each loss by a Liberal counted twice in the simple arithmetic of gaining an advantage over Liberals in Commons seats. Dalton realized the key to a possible win by Diefenbaker, and thus his best role in the campaign, lay in his own corner of Canada.

CHAPTER 17

RAW CAMPAIGN REALITIES

Relocating to Halifax for the duration, with the title "campaign coordinator for Atlantic Canada," Dalton was on familiar ground and felt confident about running the four-province campaign.

Norman Atkins, preparing to graduate from Acadia, was also happy to be in campaign harness again, as Dalton's assistant campaign coordinator. Camp's colleague in battle and at the bars, broadcaster Finlay MacDonald, now president of the Canadian Association of Broadcasters and owner of Halifax's station CJCH, was equally ready, willing, and more than able to collaborate.

Dalton's opening move was to amass a special fund for extra campaign advertising in the eastern provinces, by applying his building block strategy. With $10,000 he'd extracted from national headquarters, he got Stanfield in Nova Scotia and Flemming in New Brunswick to each match the amount, giving a $30,000 publicity budget he alone controlled, for special ads he himself would devise as needed.

Another Atlantic campaign benefit from the building block strategy he and Bill Rowe had pursued was that, now with Tory regimes in the two largest provinces, Camp was able to get strong organizational support from the provincial Progressive Conservative foot soldiers of Stanfield and Flemming. Even in PEI, the Island's Tories remembered Dalton's valiant, if intemperate, battle against the Grits and happily reciprocated with all the support they could muster for the campaign he was organizing.

Regional policy was also important to fill a gap in the national campaign. Dalton's own campaign structure, developed in Ottawa, was decentralized. Now he took advantage himself of the latitude afforded by the "It's your campaign, you run it!" concept to reinforce the centralized messaging with a detailed program that spoke directly to Atlantic Canadian voters.

Dalton happily revived the idea he'd worked on with other Atlantic Liberals at the 1948 national convention to create concrete policy proposals for hard Maritime realities. Camp invited all PC candidates from Newfoundland, Prince Edward Island, Nova Scotia, and New Brunswick to meet in Moncton and hammer out a manifesto for action. MP George Nowlan chaired proceedings in the main hall of the Brunswick Hotel, while upstairs Camp and Kenneth Carson, from the premier's office, began composing the "Atlantic Resolutions" and relaying them to Nowlan.

After a few hours, the unanimous vote of Tory candidates downstairs gave John Diefenbaker and the eastern-Canadian PC candidates a solid program. They had fleshed out the national campaign with programs addressing needs in all corners of Atlantic Canada.

When Dief said he couldn't accept the package of policies and programs, Hugh John Flemming, desperate because the manifesto included federal funding for a vast hydro project he'd launched in New Brunswick despite lacking the money to pay for it, stood up to The Chief.

"Come on, John. You wouldn't talk like that to Les Frost in Ontario."

A couple of hours later, having reflected on the help he'd need to reach his date with destiny, Dief said in a television interview he thought the Atlantic Resolutions excellent, supported such constructive measures, and as prime minister would work with Atlantic Canada's provincial premiers to implement them.

———

For the leader's tour in the East, Dalton was hands-on, greeting the Diefenbaker train as it arrived in Moncton and remaining with the party for a week of Maritime campaigning.

Accompanying Dief aboard his special train, which had "survived two harrowing days in Quebec" at campaign stops on its way through the province to the Maritimes, was Olive Diefenbaker, George Hogan as "train manager," secretaries Marion Wagner and Connie Irving, and Fred Davis, a professional photographer who also tended to the needs of the eight journalists covering this swing of the leader's national tour.

John and Olive enjoyed the leisurely pace of campaigning by train. So did the reporters, one of whom had been in the army with Dalton. Fred Davis ran a bar that never closed. The kitchen had available, on request at any time, cold chicken, ham and roast beef, fresh milk, hot coffee, fresh fruit, and rich cheddar cheese. There was sleeping accommodation, ever changing scenery, and a calm sense of being directly engaged in something major while buffered in remote comfort. Gathering for conversation was easy, but so was finding solitude to reflect, read, or regain perspective. On one run aboard the train, Dalton, "tieless and shoeless — and mindless," savoured "the slow ebbing of tension and fatigue."

As both organizer and tour assistant, he travelled with Dief not only on his special train, but on a bumpy early morning flight to PEI aboard a Maritime Central Airways DC-3, and by car over winding mainland roads. Along the way, Camp reviewed the day's itinerary, providing The Chief with briefing notes that supplemented each day's schedule, fed him the names of locals, arranged media interviews, and highlighted regional issues. He also hurriedly wrote text for Diefenbaker's speeches, on yellow paper, pulled ragged from his portable typewriter, heavy with overtyping and corrections, which The Chief then overwrote with his own revisions.

In these opening days of the 1957 election, John Diefenbaker appeared to Camp as a man "uncertain and vulnerable, and needing help." People everywhere seemed eager to provide it. The local halls for campaign meetings filled up, and Diefenbaker connected in these assemblies, as he did on the streets or in restaurants, with the life-worn and weary who found cheer in his concern for them. The Progressive Conservatives were becoming respectable. It was alright to be seen at the party's gatherings, to come and learn why it was "Time for a Diefenbaker Government!"

What had seemed perfect as a slogan in a Toronto ad agency's boardroom during brain storming, and been cheered by party officials at Camp's slick presentation in a comfortable Ottawa hotel, still had potential to backfire when unveiled to voters. But when Maritimers heard how John Diefenbaker understood their plight and stood up for their rights to a better deal, the slogan "It's Time for a Diefenbaker Government!" became an anthem in their hearts.

The program outlined in the Atlantic Resolutions further underscored sense that John Diefenbaker really understood and had a solid plan.

"There was no public man in Canada," concluded Camp after listening to more of his speeches, "so capable of airing another's grievance and injustice as John Diefenbaker."

The Maritime tour was the first time Camp had seen Diefenbaker campaign among people in public places. "He shook hands firmly, not aggressively," Dalton observed. "He did not invite constituents to touch or embrace him, but kept his distance by playing his role — the leader, a little taller than the rest, the one dressed in black, with the hard black hat, black coat, subdued tie. He smiled and frequently said things that made people laugh, even though they were not that funny."

Camp would henceforth model his grip and expression, when greeting someone with a handshake, on that of this veteran, professional campaigner.

———

Dalton sensed, as the week progressed, that the audiences coming out to hear Diefenbaker were growing larger, that interest was passing from curiosity to something bordering on conversion. This was the sort of intelligence he liked to absorb in the raw immediacy of a campaign's front lines, a reading he trusted, unlike the abstracted numbers from pollsters quantifying random samples of the public's opinion.

As Dief and Camp travelled together, their currency of exchange was a steady supply of names of those about to be encountered, speech notes, and political gossip. The warmth of their working relationship strengthened. Away from the train, travelling in automobiles supplied and driven by local Tories, keeping up a steady pace, The Chief became drained of energy and had to draw on deep reserves to present one of his dramatic sixty to ninety minute performances. The more Dalton caught on to his style and the sorts of issues he wanted to hit, the more his speech notes became the actual texts Diefenbaker used, helping him husband energy by not having to present another original show at every meeting hall.

Camp found it miraculous how everything came suddenly into place, "a hundred separate energies now working as one to change the course of history." Nobody yet believed victory possible, but, "like the promise of summer on the land outside the window," Dalton "felt the faint, uncertain pulse of change."

Dalton Camp was national PC organizer for Atlantic Canada in 1957, advancing John and Olive Diefenbaker's East Coast tour. When they headed west, Dief spotted him on the station platform. "Wave goodbye to Dalton, Olive!" Camp waved back, tears in his eyes, beginning to think Dief just might win.

Taking stock, he realized how the new Tory machines in Nova Scotia and New Brunswick had "the sleek, shining allure" of the latest-model vehicle, and how "word was out" after their victorious elections in the two principal provinces that Tories now treated folks to drinks and "the fellows around Liberal headquarters weren't quite as friendly as they used to be." Times were changing, power was shifting, and "the first to sense these currents are the luckless and the poor who must always know where their best chances may be found, where the distant job prospects are, and where the possibility of favours are likeliest."

In tandem with that, Camp saw the "competitive lust" of these newly triumphant Maritime Tories. Pride would not let them lose. The taste of winning was still as fresh as their memory of defeat, "each made keener by recent, exhilarating experience." These powerful forces in the Maritimes were now Diefenbaker's: an "unexpected inheritance" that came to him by accident, the unscripted timing of a date with destiny.

There was yet another force, a deeper psychological mystery. "Men who hardly knew him," Camp saw, including some who even vaguely mistrusted Diefenbaker, were beginning to "now commit themselves entirely to his success." Dalton, to his own amazement, was one of them. He'd become "caught in the fastness of another man's driving ambition, swept along in the tidal flood of all the hopes and urgent desires which powered his campaign."

Although he remained uncertain about the election and still had doubts about the leader, Camp nevertheless had "come to serve this strangely compelling, puzzling man with a fierce and unrelenting concentration" he found difficult to explain, even to himself.

The emotion, though inexplicable, was real. As Dalton stood on the Moncton station platform, watching the railway cars begin to move west carrying the Diefenbakers onto the next leg of the leader's national tour, he spotted Olive and John standing observant at the back of the last car. "There's Dalton," he heard Diefenbaker yell, "wave goodbye to Dalton!"

The beaming couple waved. Dalton returned the salute, his arm waving high as the train pulled away, his eyes stinging with tears.

———

A month after that first Maritime campaign tour in early May, John Diefenbaker returned. Camp found him changed — more imperious, his temper quicker, his patience shorter.

At Liverpool, The Chief launched into an attack on the government for granting the Liberal Party access to the voters' list of military personnel, which had been denied to the Opposition. Reporters immediately dispatched this news across the country, but when they pressed Diefenbaker to prove his allegation, he could not. He'd been relying on a letter Dalton had shown him from Prime Minister St. Laurent to members of the Armed Forces, coupled with Dalton's complaint that when he'd tried some months earlier to get the military voters' list from National Defence headquarters, he'd been told such lists were not available.

From then on, Dief would not speak with Camp. His name was banned on the campaign train. If the leader had to refer to the man running his Atlantic Canada campaign and in charge of all national campaign advertising, he'd allude to "that Toronto advertising fellow," as if he'd forgotten the name of Dalton Camp.

In terms of electoral politics, the second coming of John Diefenbaker to the Maritimes, in these wind-up days of the campaign, was a "complete political success" in Camp's appraisal, though it was marred by the fact that Dief departed "full of complaint and abuse for most of those who had helped him."

Nearing the end of an intense forty-three-day national campaign tour, part of the difference was no doubt the leader's fatigue. The absence of an equally weary Olive Diefenbaker, who'd not accompanied her husband on his return to the Maritimes, was also a factor, because he was never the same if she was not around. In Nova Scotia, Diefenbaker argued vehemently with George Nowlan. Everywhere, he commanded supporters to do this, to fetch that.

On the last night, for The Chief's final event, in an overflow high-school auditorium near Kentville, Dalton sat high in the galleries and listened as Premier Bob Stanfield paid tribute to Diefenbaker, reading a speech Camp had written. Then he heard The Chief return the tribute to Stanfield and Nowlan, using text he'd also written. When the night ended and the crowd began to slowly scatter, Norman Atkins slipped out to bring the car around. Dalton climbed into the back seat. Norman drove him back to Halifax, through the darkness, in silence.

————

Meanwhile, the Liberal's lacklustre campaign was the poor effort of organizers confident of re-election no matter what they did, disdain for the rag-tag Progressive Conservatives and the party's unusual leader — a wounded loner from small-town Saskatchewan — and their relaxed anticipation of smooth transition, a year or so after the election, to a new leader.

During the campaign, St. Laurent made few television appearances, as Camp had predicted. When he did enter a TV studio, "Uncle Louis" refused to wear makeup, seeing no need for it on a man. Uncomfortable with the medium, the Liberal prime minister read his speeches from a script, trying to make an argument; it was a boring and unmemorable performance in its own right, made worse when contrasted to fiery John Diefenbaker's strong impressistic impact on television audiences.

———

Back in Toronto for election day, Dalton's work to influence voters and help Diefenbaker now done, he left home early to vote for Frank McGee, PC candidate in his York-Scarborough riding.

If one wanted to vote Tory, McGee had the full pedigree — grand-nephew of Father of Confederation and Conservative MP D'Arcy McGee, grandson of both Clerk of the Privy Council John Joseph McGee and Conservative MP Charles McCool, and son-in-law of Tory luminary Grattan O'Leary. Dalton hoped he'd win.

By evening, with polls closed in Atlantic Canada but results unknown further west, the result of time zone differences and broadcasting blackout rules designed to preserve voting integrity for those yet to cast ballots, anxious Dalton phoned Finlay MacDonald in Halifax.

The PCs had miraculously taken all four seats in PEI! Even Grit-solid Newfoundland had yielded two of its seven Liberal seats. Results in the two mainland provinces indicated a Liberal rout. Ralph Hay called in from Fredericton, telling Camp with enthusiasm, "We've licked Gregg!" The Victoria Cross war hero and Liberal Cabinet minister had been defeated. Dalton knew he had to be glad — "defeated Cabinet ministers count for more" — yet he felt "a twinge of regret, deeply buried in a dimly remembered past." As quickly as he experienced this feeling, he buried it.

Only late into the night would final results come from British Columbia. By then, Liberal-minded Blair Fraser's column in *Maclean's* was already printed, the publication's influential Ottawa editor comforting his national readers that Canada would continue under the steady command of Prime Minister Louis St. Laurent. It was a journalistic gaffe on a par with the premature headline DEWEY DEFEATS TRUMAN across the *Chicago Tribune's* front page confirming in 1948 that Republican challenger Thomas Dewy had trounced President Harry Truman. Blair's red face and *Maclean's* impaired credibility were a measure of the expectations of Canada's self-satisfied political and media establishments for the invincibility of Liberal government, all reinforced by opinion polls. Nobody had predicted the upset.

Most news reporters missed how, especially in the Maritimes where the Rowe-Camp building-block strategy had paid off handsomely with Flemming and Stanfield, and in Ontario where the blue machine under Frost helped elect many MPs — including Frank McGee in York-Scarborough with the highest vote in the entire country — folks accepted that it really was "Time for a Diefenbaker Government!"

Few covering Canadian politics could yet know that Diefenbaker's win was even more than a major election upset, the felling a Liberal dynasty, and a change of government for Canada.

It was, indeed, to be "a date with destiny."

CHAPTER 18

ONE WIN GOOD, TWO BETTER

Prime Minister John Diefenbaker sat with his minority government of 112 Progressive Conservative MPs facing, across the Commons aisle, the shocked ranks of 105 Liberals and the combined 44 Social Credit and CCF members.

Among the CCF MPs was Douglas Fisher, who'd entered the House dubbed a "giant killer" because he'd handily defeated the Liberal's most powerful minister, C.D. Howe. Nobody had thought it possible, including the PCs, which is why no effort had been made to run a strong Tory candidate in his Port Arthur riding, a factor contributing to the hulking librarian winning the seat.

Other prominent Cabinet ministers had gone down, too, oblivious to their crumbling support, thinking the immense crowds flocking to John Diefenbaker's rallies were merely curious folk going to watch a freak show, not a political phenomenon manifesting historic change.

Tory representation in Atlantic Canada rose from five to twenty-one members. In Quebec, the PC ranks remained about as slim as when major campaign spending took place: nine seats out of the province's seventy-five. In Ontario, the number of PC representatives climbed from thirty-three to sixty-one. On the Prairies, PCs edged up from six to fourteen seats, while in British Columbia, the three became seven. Diefenbaker won where the party already had strength and Progressive Conservative provincial governments were in power. In his own home province of Saskatchewan, and in neighbouring

Alberta, the Diefenbaker-led PCs still came third in popular vote and claimed only a few scattered constituencies.

———

With Dief shaping Canada's first Conservative government since 1935, Norman Atkins wound up his campaign duties with Dalton and, a fresh university grad, began a new stage in his own career.

Working in Montreal for one of Canada's most powerful companies, twenty-one-year-old Norman had landed a position in the accounting department of Canadian Pacific Railway. From his small desk he began to see the grand workings of a vast, interconnected system that depended for operational success on careful attention to detail in schedules, bookings, rates, maintenance, supplies, revenues, records, payments, and logistics.

The accounting department, though removed from the front lines of CP's integrated transportation, accommodation, and communications businesses, opened a window for Norman onto the company's agglomeration of freight trains, passenger trains, national and international airline operations, coastal and inland ships, prestigious hotels, and telegraph services. He could also see at CPR how, by 1957, the individual freedom offered by private automobiles and the increasing speed and comfort covering wide distances with airplanes were combining to eclipse the golden age of passenger trains.

Norman was just getting into a new groove, working in CPR's impressive bustle and enjoying a young bachelor's life in Canada's most cosmopolitan city, when he was called to sign for a special delivery letter.

Norman Kempton Atkins stared in stunned disbelief at his U.S. Army draft orders. Though fitting in as a Canadian, he was American. Two years compulsory military service was now demanded of him by the Land of the Free.

Instinctively, he turned to Dalton for advice. After thrashing out such alternatives as getting a deferral by attending law school at UNB, Norman decided, reluctantly, that he should benefit from the army's training and get paid to "see something of the world." To reassure fretful Norman that his future would be secure, Dalton said, "I don't know what I'll be doing in two years, but whatever it is, you can be part of it."

On September 9, 1957, Atkins dutifully reported to Fort Dix. Two weeks later, after completing a battery of aptitude tests, he was transferred to Fort Benning in

Georgia for basic and advanced training as a quartermaster. His test results disclosed a natural talent for planning and supply that would not have surprised his fellow students back at Acadia. They'd seen him gravitate to the students' union management board, volunteer to help organize the catering services, run student events, and become chairman of their management board.

Training to be a quartermaster, Norman's time alternated between classroom instruction and field training. He was taught leadership skills and schooled in operational tactics. He was repeatedly drilled in how to maintain and operate the weapons and vehicles used by a quartermaster platoon. When this round of training was complete, Norman was elevated to acting lance corporal, appointed supply clerk in Mortar Battery 30 in the army's 3rd Infantry Division, and sent to Germany's

Lance Corporal Norman Atkins was quartermaster in 1958, organizing and running supply operations at a U.S. Army base near Koblenz, West Germany, training that later helped him run Canadian political campaigns "like a military operation."

Rhineland where he reported for duty at the U.S. Army base near Koblenz.

———

In Ottawa, meanwhile, the Diefenbaker government, pumped with energy and excitement, was kept on its toes because across the Commons aisle sat enough MPs to defeat them and trigger a new election at any moment.

At first this risk was low because the Liberals were preoccupied choosing a new leader. But once Lester Pearson replaced Louis St. Laurent in January 1958, the new matchup could come any time. Amazing though it seemed, the Grits had lost none of their arrogance. The fresh Liberal leader rose in the House and asked Diefenbaker to resign and hand over the national government to him. No defeat in the Commons, no election in the country, would be required for a Liberal return to office as Canada's natural governing party.

John Diefenbaker was in his element campaigning along any main street in Canada. The Chief himself is credited today for coining the still-popular term "mainstreeting" to describe his populist form of electioneering.

The preposterous stance — based on the limp ground that a Liberal restoration was essential because an unexpected economic downturn was showing the Conservatives incompetent to govern — flouted the people's verdict in the recent election, centuries of parliamentary precedent, and the Grits' own credibility.

John Diefenbaker replied by calling another election. Let the people decide!

———

Allister Grosart would again be campaign chairman. The Diefenbakers would once more tour the country by special train with a similar entourage of staff and reporters. Dalton Camp would run national advertising for the Progressive Conservative campaign and, as in 1957, also direct the campaign in Atlantic Canada. It was as if the first election had been a dress rehearsal.

Two elements in the 1958 campaign that *were* different from the earlier election reflected a political realignment underway in Canada. One was the reversal of the prior year's Quebec strategy to ignore unwinnable seats. The second entailed regaining ground on the PC Party's conservative flank, which some simplistically dubbed its "right wing."

For the first, voters in Quebec, savvy about political positioning, had no trouble discerning the popular trend flowing toward the Diefenbaker government and knew they'd be better off with those in power than sticking with the increasingly unappealing Liberals. Moreover, in 1957 *les rouges* had been led by proud Quebecer Louis-Étienne St. Laurent. His replacement, Ontario's Lester Bowles Pearson, removed that tug of kindred loyalty.

Another part of this shifting Quebec configuration unfolded behind the scenes. In the precincts and parishes where campaigns are fought and won, the Union Nationale political machine of Premier Maurice Duplessis was being deployed in full support of the federal *bleus*. The plan Duplessis first devised with Robert Manion back in 1939 would finally be implemented for Diefenbaker, almost two decades later.

On the second front, to the west, the Social Credit Party's support eroded as the 1958 campaign advanced. Before the 1957 election, some Canadians predicted Social Credit, having ditched its radical monetary policies and opted for basic conservatism running Alberta's provincial government, might in time displace the Tory Party. Others wanted more immediate action, lamenting how Socred and Tory candidates were splitting the vote, weakening each other's chances in many ridings and helping CCF and Liberal candidates. It was time to realign conservatives who were dividing themselves, they said, and "unite the right."

None of these landscape architects, in reimagining the political terrain, had envisaged how the popularity of John Diefenbaker would pull most Social Crediters away from their party. Instead of a party merger, what a simple, unexpected solution!

John Diefenbaker arrayed speaking notes, clippings, and letters on a podium the way an artist spreads colours on a pallet, ready to dip into whatever seemed needed next. His speeches were a dramatic art form. Dalton Camp, in charge of party publicity, helped with notes for Dief, and made sure photographers got shots like this one of The Chief performing for Hamilton Tories.

With these changes in Quebec and western Canada, Les Frost's support in Ontario, and Dalton's efforts in the Atlantic provinces, where Stanfield and Flemming were going all-out, it seemed the PCs might even win a majority of seats this time.

"It was one of those extraordinary campaigns," said Camp, "when it was almost criminal to do anything."

———

On the electrifying night of March 31, 1958, just nine months after the last election, as vote counts flowed in province by province, John Diefenbaker's minority government was transformed. The Progressive Conservatives had the largest majority government in Canadian history.

Enthusiasm for Dief the Chief was high. Eighty percent of all eligible voters cast ballots. The Tories climbed to 54 percent in popular support across the country. The gain of ninety-seven more seats pushed the PCs to a total of 208 in the 265-member Commons. Overall, the Grits had foty-eight seats, the CCF just eight.

In four provinces — Prince Edward Island, Nova Scotia, Manitoba, and Alberta — the Diefenbaker forces claimed every available seat. In Diefenbaker's once begrudging home province, his candidates won all Saskatchewan seats but one. Social Credit voters, numbering 437,000 in 1957, dwindled to 189,000 over nine months, going from 7 percent of total popular vote to 3 percent, not huge numbers but enough to make a difference in ridings where vote splitting was a determinant. This realignment enabled the PCs to pick up all nineteen seats Socreds had won in 1957, including Alberta's seventeen, and also claim many more seats previously held by Liberals or CCF members, by reducing vote splitting between Tories and Social Credit.

Across battleground Ontario, the Tories won sixty-seven ridings and held the Liberals to a meagre fourteen. Emerging from Quebec's political earthquake, the PCs had doubled the Liberals, taking fifty seats to their twenty-five.

Dief's first election win had come as a stunning surprise. The second was one for the record books.

CHAPTER 19

ADVANCE OF THE ADMEN

John Diefenbaker formed his majority government. The Progressive Conservatives were solidly entrenched, with adman Allister Grosart running the party organization. Dalton travelled to Ottawa often, but not for campaign or political work. There was little point trying to call on The Chief, because Diefenbaker was hardly seeing anybody.

Camp was in the capital, instead, handling a great deal of new advertising work from the Government of Canada, including the tourist bureau account. After the Liberals lost power in 1957, the Grit-enmeshed Cockfield Brown agency soon lost its lucrative federal advertising contracts, too. With a change in government also came change in the ad agencies servicing the government.

Advertising agencies had been incrementally reversing the client-supplier relationship, no longer taking a subservient role under direction from the party, but instead directing the party themselves. Camp had been part of this realignment. His tightly focused political texts for campaign ads had helped turn the tide of elections in New Brunswick, then Nova Scotia. His partisan blasts failed abysmally in Prince Edward Island, but there was no escaping the larger point that he was the one creating and issuing those political messages for the PC campaign. Advertising executives were at the helm, for better and for worse.

The advance of the ad guys was slowed by performances that fizzled. Dalton's effort in PEI's 1955 election had demonstrably been counterproductive.

Allister Grosart of McKim Advertising handled the agency's account with the Progressive Conservatives, ran the convention demonstrations for John Diefenbaker's leadership win in 1956, and battled rival adman Dalton Camp over party policy.

McKim's orchestration of the 1949 debacle, for George Drew's first campaign as national PC leader, was an ineffectual but extravagant advertising effort culminating in a solid, full-page ad of illegible type in all Canada's daily newspapers. The party's national director, Dick Bell, saw it for the first time when he'd opened his newspaper. He gasped, broke down, and wept. In 1953, for Drew's next election, Grosart outdid McKim's 1949 performance with his single-issue tax-cut campaign, helping the PCs lose even more seats.

The point was not how good or bad the policy or its presentation, but that the battle to determine the message — in 1953 advanced relentlessly by one adman, Grosart, and strongly opposed by another, Camp — was being fought by admen rather than by the party members themselves. Dief's order to burn all policy resolutions approved by delegates at the national convention was a dramatic, undisclosed step in this transition, giving Camp the green light to devise the PC's complete campaign marketing strategy for the 1957 general election himself.

———

If the admen were on the ascendant in politics, it was because by the late 1950s advertising had come to impart an aura of potency to its practitioners in all realms.

"Style" was important.

Following the dress code of New York's Madison Avenue agencies and the mannerisms projected on screen by Hollywood, account executives like Dalton got ribbed by Finlay MacDonald for his "grey flannel suit and nightly pilgrimages to the Martini Belt." Admen were edgy, opinionated, zany, constantly rotating between brainstorming sessions and client boardroom presentations, long lunch meetings in good restaurants, and even, occasionally, their own homes.

But the "message" was everything.

Dalton had been reading a raft of ground-breaking books from the United States on psychology, politics, advertising, mass communication, and techniques for altering patterns of human behaviour. Vance Packard's 1957 book *The Hidden Persuaders,* with its exploration of "subliminal" messaging, provoked a debate about the distinctions between persuasion and manipulation, which became integral to the rapidly changing world in which Dalton operated. New theories, experiments, and practices altered traditional ways of advertising and political communication. The adman held the key to powers that could, across great distances and through a variety of communications media, change the thinking and alter the behaviour of complete strangers who, among other things, voted in elections.

A transformation in party campaign advertising was also underway on the business side, in the shift from use of a single agency to several. In the 1940s, when parties began turning things over to advertising firms, they tended to have one preferred agency. MacLaren Advertising had a steady relationship with the Liberal Party of Canada until ousted by Cockfield Brown, which then became the Grit agency of preference. The Liberals in New Brunswick stuck with Walsh Advertising. McKim had a lock on work for the federal and Ontario Progressive Conservatives. With each election, this nexus between adman and politician became more intimate.

But a crack opened once Dalton and his Locke Johnson agency were rewarded with New Brunswick's account for tourism publicity, then opened wider when Dalton was invited in 1953 to help the federal PCs with campaign advertising, even though the party's work at the time was in McKim's hands with Allister Grosart. Two agencies might share the same party's work.

By April 1957, when Dalton, in full charge of Progressive Conservative election publicity made his presentation to the National Campaign Committee, he was astonished by the presence of so many admen. Allister Grosart, who chaired the meeting and was overall campaign chairman, was the solid link with McKim. Arthur Burns was present for his own agency, Burns Advertising, as was Mickey O'Brien of O'Brien Advertising from British Columbia. Camp was accompanied from Locke Johnson by Bill Kettlewell, Hank Loriaux, and Jim Mumford, the agency's media director. "It occurred to me," quipped Camp, after surveying them all, "that Diefenbaker had more advertising agencies than General Motors."

John Diefenbaker invented this all-inclusive National Campaign Committee. In addition to those whose party office or high standing required they be included, The Chief had further populated the unwieldy sixty-two-member body with his own trusted supporters and many admen. Just as he would never entrust his fate to a single person, he refused to place his fortunes in the hands of one advertising agency.

The Chief liked to divide, in order to gain and maintain control. If he could not divide a single ad agency, he could achieve the same result by multiplying them. This example of many agencies getting a share of the publicity work planted an idea with Dalton. What if, instead, the best and brightest from a number of different agencies were pulled together in a separate, ad hoc entity to handle all aspects of campaign advertising and publicity? It might be something to try, someday.

Halifax broadcaster Finlay MacDonald and wife, Ann, with Linda Camp and her adman and backroom organizer husband, Dalton, vacationing together in the Bahamas, basking in the afterglow of the historic 1958 Progressive Conservative election win.

Dalton also observed something else. The ad agencies had taken a hands-on role in 1957 campaign: filling orders for pamphlets, sending out photos of The Chief, and ordering further printings of brochures to meet the rising demand. Such tasks might, in a future election, be pulled together into a single-purpose campaign operation of the party, rather than handled exclusively out of party headquarters or by advertising agencies. A dedicated off-site campaign organization, in harmony with the rest of the party's election operations, would provide greater control and assurance that everything was being done right by whoever was responsible for running the campaign.

The campaigns he'd seen were run from a premier's office, or party headquarters, or an ad agency's facilities. All had other things to do, as well. Why not a free-standing operation, allied with the party, whose only purpose was to run the election campaign?

———

By summer 1959 Dalton was convinced he had to advance in his personal advertising career. He was now thirty-seven. He and Linda had a growing family. Dalton's daily fare provided scope for writing, both as a leading copywriter in Toronto's advertising universe and in PC campaigns, but he wanted to do more "serious" work, writing for magazine and book publishers, perhaps even try his hand at a novel.

He'd learned much about the craft of commercial advertising and had honed some unique skills in political advertising's rarified realm. It was time to rise as a partner in Locke Johnson. He could use more money, wanted the prestige, and believed he'd earned an ownership interest in the firm based on the lucrative accounts he'd brought in during his seven years with the agency.

He arrived with confidence and made his pitch to Willard Locke. He did not even glance around the offices on Davenport Road for a last look as, moments later, he stormed out.

The shock of being turned down was the jolt Camp needed to realize that, if he was bold enough, he had even better future prospects than becoming a Locke Johnson partner. With his own promising political career, and the rising prospects for Progressive Conservatives on many fronts, Dalton Camp would launch his own advertising agency.

As quickly as he found midtown Toronto office space at 600 Eglinton Avenue East, he had a sign painter imprint DALTON K. CAMP & ASSOCIATES on the door. The place was far enough from the city's downtown's congestion to be calm, yet close enough to the action to be mentally stimulating.

He invited his talented friend Bill Kettlewell, who'd worked closely on the Maritime and Diefenbaker campaigns, to join him as a business partner. Before the two linked up at Locke Johnson, Bill had been artistic director at J. Walter Thompson. Dalton also enticed Fred Boyer, another skilled veteran at Locke Johnson, to join them as a third partner. They hired staff and set themselves up for a fresh start in a business they all relished, with greater freedom, more money, and a stronger focus than ever on Tory interests.

Dalton's departure not only deprived Locke Johnson of three of its most talented admen. He also took with him a number of his revenue-producing advertising accounts, including the tourism work for New Brunswick, Nova Scotia, and the Government of Canada, a solid foundation to launch his new agency, provided he and his team could keep Tories in office.

———

Hardly had his lawyers completed the incorporation of Dalton K. Camp and Associates Limited in September 1959 when Norman Atkins, having served his country, was back in Canada, discharge papers in hand, to take up Dalton's pledge of work.

Atkins was a novice to the advertising business. Kettlewell and Boyer were skeptical. But Dalton knew his brother-in-law's abilities. "He was confident I could do the job," said Norman. "I worked hard, people took me under their wings, and in six months I was okay."

Camp himself laughed about his brother-in-law's baptism of fire. "He had a tough apprenticeship and then made his own way. It was a great endorsement for nepotism."

The firm handled ad campaigns for such corporate clients as Clairtone electronics and Labatt's breweries, and expanded its rarified promotional expertise in the tourism industry. As Norman mastered more aspects of the business, he was given greater responsibility as Dalton's alter ego. He oversaw office operations, handled clients on his own, got commercial spots produced and booked onto television and radio, and administered production of advertisements, whether for billboards or the pages of newspapers and magazines.

With Dalton becoming more involved in politics as the 1960s progressed, any vacuum his absence created at the agency Norman handily filled. Even when working together, they complemented rather than overlapped one another, with Norman increasingly absorbed in operational practicalities that held less interest for Dalton.

Two years of national service had convinced Norman that a rigid organization such as the military was no place for him. He never again worked in a structured environment. Instead, he thrived in the demanding world of an advertising agency, not far removed in nature from the pulsating dramas of a political party's campaign backroom.

With hard work and long hours, Norman proved adept at running the office, dealing with clients, completing media buys, and keeping track of every pencil.

———

Most advertising agencies focused on traditional accounts for major corporations, some occasionally handling election work when that aligned with the partisan leanings of the firm's senior partners or a particular in-house aptitude.

In this constellation, the Camp agency stood apart. Dalton had more than "partisan leanings." Driven by two fundamental imperatives, he was vindicating his decision to quit the Liberals and join the Progressive Conservatives, and making a viable business of the firm that now bore his name. Advertising provided a robust revenue flow, which helped attract top talent, develop pioneering techniques, and gave him the financial resources to be a player in the political arena. The agency, not a seat in Parliament, was still his power base for now. Advertising was a wiring system connecting all parts of the increasingly sophisticated apparatus Dalton was creating, one he dreamed might carry him all the way to 24 Sussex Drive.

Tourism was the ideal kind of account for an agency whose highest specialty was an election campaign. The tourism "product" was a destination, an experience, a personal encounter with the good life. Selling somebody on a destination was, at heart, an appeal to emotions about finding something better than they had ever experienced before. If Camp and his admen could persuade more folks to vote for John Diefenbaker, or for the Tories in New Brunswick and Nova Scotia, they could sway them to enjoy touring Canada and spending their vacation dollars for the benefit of Canadians in the process.

The kind of advertising that interested Camp and his hand-picked business partners was not the narrow hard-sell promotion to boost consumption of a particular brand of toothpaste, automobile, cigarette, or soft drink. Because he'd come to the world of advertising through politics, and had not changed, Dalton only found resonance in the higher latitudes of persuasion, the space where one connects with real people over things that matter in their lives, showing them a pathway into a more promising future.

In the bargain, the advantage for the Progressive Conservative Party was having a true blue advertising agency reliably standing by to provide politically astute messaging, buy space in newspapers and air-time on radio and television in elections, while more or less working for free.

CHAPTER 20

COLD WAR POLITICS

Political history made clear to all Canadian Tories that, by mid-twentieth century, seat-rich Ontario was the party's last redoubt, and its most important base for any fresh sortie nationally.

In December 1956, when federal Progressive Conservatives gathered to elect a new leader, Ontario's respected premier, Les Frost, influenced hundreds by speaking openly in support of Diefenbaker. In the 1957 general election, Frost put his potent blue machine into gear across Ontario and helped the federal party's candidates win sixty-one seats, almost doubling the thirty-three that Tories got in 1953. For the 1958 election, Frost's organization waged battle again, bringing six more Ontario seats into the PC column, although Dief's own political uplift in that election likely counted for more than the ground war at breaking ever deeper into Grit-held ridings.

With his friend finally in the rare position of heading a strong Progressive Conservative government, Frost wrote the PM, after reflecting on Dief's whirlwind of scattered activity, to make a single point.

The PM had been riding a political merry-go-round non-stop for three years, under intense pressure with unprecedented personal demands that would exhaust any mortal. It would be wise, Frost urged Dief, with time on his side at last, to pause, restore his personal reserves, and focus. Because Diefenbaker now held unprecedented sway across the nation and through most sectors of society, he should bring together leading experts and, in calm retreat, explore Canada's future prospects and plan effective long-term programs for his government. Frost was not asking for anything, personally or for his province. He was offering wise, selfless counsel. As a seasoned head of government, and given the roles he'd played in making Dief the chief, he had good reason to think he might be heeded. Dalton could have told Frost, had he been asked, to not even bother writing the letter.

Anyone who knew John Diefenbaker, the way Camp now did, understood The Chief did not want other people's advice. He had not laboured so many years on barren fields to share his harvest banquet with others. The vindicated loner would continue along his own path. If Dief burnt the policy resolutions approved by his own party's grass-roots delegates, he was hardly going to replace them with recommendations by people from the country's various establishments who'd long disdained him. When he wanted significant recommendations on a specific issue, the PM could appoint a royal commission and pick all the commissioners himself.

Instead of following Frost's advice, Diefenbaker busied himself with legislation and appointments, and worked on relations with the United States. He delivered a major speech on Canadian-American relations at Dartmouth College in New Hampshire, invited U.S. president Dwight Eisenhower to address Parliament and, with Eisenhower, inaugurated a joint U.S.-Canada Cabinet-level committee on defence.

In tandem, the military side of North American air defence was rapidly maturing, in response to the Cold War threat from a possible Soviet attack over the Arctic. As part of the North American Aerospace Defense Command (NORAD), Diefenbaker agreed to arrangements for shared aerospace warning, air sovereignty, and defence for North America. In late 1958, Canada and the United States integrated their continental air defences and began constructing a costly air defence network, with missile bases in Ontario and Quebec and radar installations across the Far North to detect and destroy incoming Soviet bombers.

With these crucial developments in play, and other major matters looming, Canada's prime minister astonishingly departed for a frenetic world tour of most of the Commonwealth countries throughout November and December.

Canadians, still enchanted by the Northern Vision Diefenbaker foresaw for Canada, were amazed to see a parade of front-page pictures of their prime minister — atop an elephant in India, sipping tea with the prime minister of Pakistan, dining with Sri Lanka's prime minister, strolling Singapore's crowded streets, angling for fish with Australia's prime minister. Was this part of Canada's rendezvous with destiny?

Les Frost gazed in stunned disbelief at the front pages of Toronto's three dailies. He could not comprehend why his friend was frittering away the unique chance to build a strong and enduring Progressive Conservative dynasty, and was, instead, almost taunting Canadians who had so recently entrusted him with so much.

———

John Diefenbaker, however, believed he was doing well.

His PC majority government had taken strides on many fronts since 1958 to realign international relations and introduce within Canada a new sense of equality. To deal with the economic downturn and rising unemployment, the government introduced a novel Winter Works program to construct infrastructure. To resolve the dilemma of overproduction of Prairie wheat, the Diefenbaker government began multi-million dollar bulk sales to China, where food shortages kept millions close to starvation. This initiative helped western farmers and benefitted the Canadian economy, but shocked Cold War hardliners who believed that, because China had gone Communist, Dief should "Let the Commies starve!"

A champion of those at society's margins or who faced discrimination, Diefenbaker appointed Louis Rasminsky governor of the Bank of Canada, a lone Jew atop a Canadian banking system exclusively controlled by Gentiles. He named Helen Fairclough, one of the 1942 Port Hopefuls, to Cabinet when before only men had been ministers of the Crown. He extended the right to vote to Aboriginal Canadians in 1960, when Canada's only First Nations voters before then had been in the army during war. He proudly enacted into law the Canadian Bill of Rights, precursor of the Canadian Charter of Rights and Freedoms that a later prime minister, Pierre Trudeau, would sponsor as a constitutionally entrenched version of the same thing. In the Commonwealth, Diefenbaker led the challenge to racial segregation programs of the white South African government that effectively made prisoners of the country's suppressed majority black population.

Yet something negative can trump many positives.

For John Diefenbaker, it was the politics of Cold War defence.

Upon returning from his world tour, the pumped PM picked up one of the most problematic files he'd left smouldering on his desk in his absence. Dief knew a great deal of public money had already gone into development of the sleek Arrow warplane by A.V. Roe Canada Limited, a subsidiary of a British corporation. A briefing note in the file confirmed no other NATO countries would buy the Avro Arrow. Repeated efforts to land advance orders and recoup funds for the aircraft's costly development had all failed.

The government was being asked for vast additional public spending on a private company's jet aircraft that the United States, Britain, France, and every other NATO country pointedly refused to buy, the result of high-level U.S. government political pressure being exerted on these allies, for the benefit of American competitor companies making fighter aircraft and missiles. John Diefenbaker balked. Although the Canadian-built military aircraft would operate with advanced capabilities, the PM felt Canadian taxpayers should not foot the bill for it, first through subsidies to A.V. Roe to develop the Arrow and, second, through the Department of National Defence being the sole purchaser of the fighter jet. Committing billions of dollars for a weapon of war did not seem to John Diefenbaker an appropriate balancing of Canadian values.

On February 20, 1959, the prime minister announced cancellation of further financial support. The futuristic Avro Arrow was suddenly history. The project's abrupt demise shocked the country. Outrage was intense across Canada, but the storm centre was Ontario, where the Arrow's development employed thousands of highly skilled workers and where protests erupted in support of the war plane.

Leslie Frost, irrevocably on track to call a provincial election, was livid.

Had Diefenbaker taken time to review the larger picture and future prospects of Canada, as a "rendezvous with destiny" invited and as Frost had urged, wouldn't the PM have gained a deeper grasp of the country's vital assets and advancing prowess in space and aeronautics? The country's future development of science and technology depended on more than finding buyers for the Arrow. As part of the fallout, Canadian scientists and engineers who'd lost their jobs at A.V. Roe headed south to join the Americans putting a man on the moon. But before they left, they made sure to vote against the next Tory who put his head into the line of fire.

As the Ontario election campaign got underway, one of Frost's new candidates, young Brampton lawyer William G. Davis, took a heavy battering in Peel, a riding deeply impacted by the Arrow's cancellation. Wherever he canvassed, Davis met irate people vowing to never vote Progressive Conservative again in their lives. In what had been a safe Tory seat, Progressive Conservative support was melting.

By voting day on June 11, 1959, popular support for Tories had plummeted 15 percent across Ontario. A dozen PC members were defeated. Far more would have tumbled had not the anti-PC vote divided between Liberals and CCF candidates. Somehow, with only a few votes to spare, Bill Davis managed to squeak into Queen's Park, a twenty-nine-year-old MPP.

When John Diefenbaker came calling again, there was no way Ontario's blue machine would be in gear working for him the way it had in 1957 and 1958.

CHAPTER 21

PROVINCES RED, PROVINCES BLUE

The provincial scene was where Dalton, with Norman, had launched into Canadian political campaigns, and the fate of provincial parties remained an enduring determinant for their electoral operation and their advertising firm.

When Dalton wore his national organizer's hat, working with Bill Rowe, their building-block strategy was all about winning nationally through PC strength in the provinces. When Dalton unexpectedly landed New Brunswick's tourism advertising, creating a precedent he thereafter followed while wearing his ad firm's hat, winning in the provinces was also good for business.

In 1960, Dalton and Norman became engaged in two Maritime campaigns at the same time. Nova Scotians would vote June 7, New Brunswickers on June 27. Atkins was glad the two events had even three weeks between them, since he was communications and production coordinator for both, entailing daily supervision and constant action in two separate theatres of political battle.

Norman now had far more responsibility as Dalton's assistant than in earlier Maritime campaigns and applied the organizational drills he'd honed to near perfection in the U.S. Army, blended with newer skills acquired at the Camp agency. He was hardly starting from scratch. Familiarity with Maritime provincial politics enhanced his confidence. Norman's little black book, as constant a companion as his wrist watch, contained names and numbers for hundreds of friends and contacts throughout both provinces.

Writing speeches for Bob Stanfield, Dalton had become indispensable to the Nova Scotian, who'd remarked, in a typically languid endorsement, that he'd "rather not go into an election without him." With the party controlling government, aggressive constituency-level organizers like Halifax's militant Rod Black now taking province-wide roles, and smooth Finlay MacDonald coordinating broadcasts and other media outreach with Norman, Dalton's focus narrowed to the government keeping power and his agency retaining the tourism account.

The results were good. Robert L. Stanfield was now as entrenched in power as Angus L. Macdonald and his Liberal machine had once been. When the votes were tallied on election night, the Stanfield-led PCs claimed twenty-seven seats in the House of Assembly, where they'd face fifteen Liberals.

———

Over in New Brunswick, the campaign was not going nearly so well.

For a couple of terms after Hugh John Flemming's PCs came to power in 1952, marking Dalton Camp's own arrival in the backrooms of power, everything had been good. But as the 1960 campaign unfolded, the Grits succeeded in turning a hospital tax into a scalding issue. No words Dalton could write for Hugh John to speak, no advertisements about the exceptional record of Flemming's progressive government, no blandishment of benefits to voters in close ridings, could stem the emotional force of Grit outrage over a hospital tax, a single negative trumping all else.

The Liberals won with thirty-one members elected, putting the PCs back in Opposition with twenty-one. With only two parties, the electoral system had mirrored the popular vote across New Brunswick accurately, since the Liberals had a modest majority of all votes cast, slightly over 53 percent, and the Tories slightly less, at just over 46 percent.

Following the defeat of the Hugh John Flemming government, the Camp agency lost the New Brunswick tourism account, giving Dalton renewed impetus to get advertising work from Ontario's PC government. As for the defeated premier, John Diefenbaker named Flemming his forestry minister, a portfolio for which the lumberman from Juniper, who soon entered the Commons in a by-election that Dalton helped him win, was eminently qualified.

———

Two other provinces gave Dalton a chance to see if the building block strategy, by which New Brunswick and Nova Scotia helped Diefenbaker edge narrowly past the Grits in 1957 to provide a launching pad for 1958's historic victory, could work in reverse. Forthcoming elections in Manitoba and Prince Edward Island could test whether a strong PC government in Ottawa would help raise non-Tory provinces into the blue.

In Manitoba, peppery Duff Roblin had already made a strong appeal for help to Dalton Camp and Bill Rowe when, at age thirty-seven, he'd just become Manitoba's provincial Tory leader in 1954.

Roblin faced a complete rebuilding job of the provincial party, and "rebuilding" wrongly suggests there was even a structure to work with. For decades the provincial Tories and Grits shared a governing coalition that had operated under different names, most recently Liberal-Progressive. By the early 1950s, many Progressive Conservatives had become restive in the stale coalition. Under the leadership of Errick Willis and then Roblin, this group broke away and became a new Progressive Conservative force in Manitoba's political arena. With a $5,000 cheque from the Ontario Progressive Conservative chief fundraiser Beverley Matthews, Roblin was able to get started. With an office provided by Rowe and Camp, he established a base of operations.

To this point, Manitobans could only choose between two parties, the CCF on the left and the Liberal-Progressives on the right, with little in between. Duff staked out the political centre by emphasizing a Progressive Conservatism akin to Diefenbaker's. With a provincial election looming for 1958, Dalton flew to Winnipeg and reported for duty.

He was not surprised that the proud provincials craved the benefits distant professionals could provide, but were loath to let anyone know about their outside help. Bringing in a "foreigner, that is, non-Manitoban, for a provincial election was anathema," sniffed high-minded Roblin, "you just didn't do that." Roblin had his team "go to some pains to conceal Dalton's whereabouts. He was not advertised as being among those present."

His "secret weapon" in the campaign, as Roblin called this phantom, brought to Manitoba techniques he'd honed for provincial campaign advertising in the Maritimes. What Camp called his "editorial column," Roblin dubbed "Dalton's daily paid minitorial." However identified, it was his same unpatented invention: a series of punchy editorials, run as advertisements, in this case carrying the Manitoba PC party logo, each written in his unique blend of edgy criticism, humour, and political savvy.

Roblin did not want Camp in public places, or anywhere political rivals or reporters might spot him, yet craved the good ideas and political insights Dalton could toss off with rapid-fire ease. In private, he also wanted Camp's complete candour. So he took him fishing in northern Manitoba.

Dalton had earlier recommended Duff advance his organization by creating a cohesive sense of purpose among candidates and a common focus for their campaign operations. The meeting he'd orchestrated at Moncton when running the Atlantic Canada campaign, Camp explained, brought together nominated candidates from the four provinces, as well as their campaign managers. The candidates had known little about the PC Party, but a great deal about their ridings, and they'd bonded in the presence of such major Tory personages as Premier Flemming and MP George Nowlan while discussing and adopting the Atlantic Resolutions, PC policy they could advocate in common. The same thing, he proposed, could work for the Manitoba PC candidates and campaign managers.

As for the operational side in the ridings, Camp continued, he'd had tough and talented organizer Rod Black from Halifax in Moncton to coach

Duff Roblin (left) took Dalton Camp fishing in northern Manitoba to snag good campaign advice while avoiding public attention. The provincial PC leader used bug dope to keep insects at bay. Dalton wisely preferred a good cigar.

the campaign managers. Huge credit for Stanfield's wins belonged to hard-core political operations on the ground in Nova Scotia by Black's dedicated shock troops.

Duff followed through. Ahead of the 1958 Manitoba election, a two-day meeting of all PC candidates discussed the party's election booklets and speaking notes. As in Moncton, this Winnipeg gathering brought together candidates who were strangers to one another, unfamiliar about what to do as politicians, and unsure what they would do if the Progressive Conservatives formed a government. The session "was a deliberate effort to make them feel comfortable in their political skins," as Roblin put it, "and to give them know-ledge of the platform they would support." A further benefit was psychological, making the candidates feel part of a team and boosting their confidence in the larger campaign and the public purposes of Manitoba's PCs.

This model was then replicated in a second meeting for the candidates' agents and other key constituency organizers. In the field of campaign organ-ization, said Roblin, "We were transforming amateurs into professionals." Over a couple of days, seasoned campaigners and experts in new approaches instructed attendees about organization, publicity, canvassing, raising money, brochures, different programs and methods for dealing with the electorate, and how to get every last voter who'd indicated support out to the poll to mark his or her ballot on election day. As he observed them, Roblin became satisfied each was gaining a new sense of purpose as part of an integrated, province-wide team, "members of an intelligent, organized, focused approach to the business of getting elected."

The Progressive Conservatives under Duff's leadership straddled a signif-icant transition point, not only in campaigning, but in the realignment of Canadian politics. What especially made Manitobans more open to support the PCs had been John Diefenbaker's advent as a national party leader and Canadian prime minister. Diefenbaker's background, personality, and political sensitivity reoriented the national Progressive Conservative Party, and its new openness extended into provincial politics and especially Manitoba, home to First Nations, Anglo-Saxon, French, Ukrainian, German, Mennonite, Jewish, Icelandic, and other diverse peoples. The new prime minister, said Roblin, made the Progressive Conservatives "attractive and welcoming to so-called ethnic Canadians" so that "Manitobans of every origin began to see themselves as part of everything we did."

In the Diefenbaker sweep of 1958, all fourteen Manitoba federal ridings elected PC candidates. Three months later, in June 1958, Roblin's PCs won enough seats to form a minority government, twenty-six out of fifty-seven, with 40 percent of the popular vote. The Liberal-Progressives became Official Opposition with nineteen members. The CCF elected eleven.

Soon a slogan began circulating in Manitoba, "Duff'll do what Dief did." Roblin liked how the sentiment conveyed his association with Diefenbaker's alchemist powers, and encouraged his candidates and those introducing him at meetings to use Dalton's line as a prophecy.

For Manitoba's May 14, 1959, general election, fully two-thirds of the province's voters showed up at their polling stations, a level of participation not seen since the 1936 election, when, in the depths of the Depression, people also sought to realign politics. This time, the turnout was to finish the provincial realignment begun the year before when election of a PC government ousted a long-running political coalition from office. The Roblin-led PCs climbed to 46 percent in popular support, which translated into thirty-six seats in the fifty-seven-member legislature, a comfortable majority. The Liberal-Progressive coalition still held 30 percent support, the CCF, 22 percent, but ended up with eleven and ten members, respectively. The polarization of Manitoba between "left" and "right" had, for now, come to an end.

The Progressive Conservative wins in Manitoba's 1958 and 1959 were part of a larger political transformation, emergence of a *Progressive* Conservative party as envisaged earlier when the Port Hopefuls sparked a change in the national Tory Party at its Winnipeg convention. In slow-moving Canadian politics, everything takes time and delayed reactions are the norm. The Roblin Progressive Conservatives, elected a decade and a half later, made good on the early vision, trebling public spending, mostly on health care, social welfare, and education, including construction of 225 new schools.

In the bargain, and with his continuing help in the 1959 campaign, the Camp agency continued to handle tourism advertising for the Manitoba government.

———

Amidst this mood of political realignment in Canada, the Liberals in Prince Edward Island called a general election for September 1, 1959.

The Island had a traditional two-party system. As the political tides rose and fell, Tories and Grits would alternately be washed into or out of office. The question was not about when the next tide would be, because elections came up every four years or so, but just how long before a tide high enough to change things reached the steps of the legislature? The last time the Conservatives had been pushed into office by an electoral wave had been 1931. Since then, at each of six successive elections, up to and including the one in 1955, Liberals had found themselves stranded in office, unable to do anything but exercise power and enjoy the perquisites of government.

Unlike Manitoba, with a socialist party that drove Liberals and Conservatives into a coalition, the calmer Island province had only Grits and Tories. Relatively few voters needed to switch sides to alter which would govern.

By the time of this 1959 election, it had been four years since Camp had last tried to help dislodge the Island's Liberal government. His interest in seeing PCs reach office remained as strong as ever. Continuation of a Grit regime in the Maritimes was his unfinished business, even a blot on his reputation. Having learned some kind of lesson, Dalton did all his campaign work at a safe remove from PEI, orchestrating everything through his partner Fred Boyer, who'd snuck into Charlottetown to run the PC advertising while staying out of sight.

Doubtless with most credit to Dief's overarching presence, which federally had accounted for all four MPs representing PEI in the Commons being Progressive Conservatives, the tide came in high and Walter Shaw, a farmer and civil servant who'd become provincial PC leader two years before, led the Tories to victory, forming a majority government with twenty-two seats to eight for the Liberals. Dalton K. Camp & Associates received, from the new PC government, the advertising account for Prince Edward Island tourism.

John Diefenbaker's big impact on provincial politics seemed highly beneficial, except in Ontario.

CHAPTER 22

UNSCRIPTED POLITICS

For what came next, nobody had a script.

The Diefenbaker Cabinet was uneasily grappling with a controversial military agreement that, given the nature of Cold War politics, could not be disentangled from people's surging emotions around the political, economic, scientific, industrial, and military dimensions of the now-hallowed Avro Arrow that hung like a trophy of shame around John Diefenbaker's neck and tainted Progressive Conservatives in Ontario.

In the fall of 1958, while the PM was planning his extended world tour, John Diefenbaker's government agreed with the U.S. government to deploy in Canada two squadrons of the American ramjet-powered anti-aircraft missiles, known as Bomarc-Bs. This defence decision flowed from the NORAD agreement between Canada and the United States, which also created a joint command structure, resulting in the two countries operating as one for air defence.

The Americans argued at the time that Bomarc surface-to-air guided missiles, having a range of 640 kilometres, would be better than the manned interceptor Avro Arrow warplane, a point they underscored by refusing to order any of the Canadian-built aircraft. That had left Diefenbaker no option but to scrap the Arrows and buy the Bomarcs, which he did.

Some fifty-six Bomarcs were procured and deployed at North Bay in Ontario and La Macaza in Quebec, under ultimate control of NORAD's commander in chief, an American. In theory, the missiles would intercept any Soviet airborne attacks before they reached the industrial and populated heartland of Canada and the United States. But now, arising to reconfigure Canadian politics and Canada-U.S. relations, an explosive new political issue appeared: the Diefenbaker government had never made public that the Bomarcs would carry *nuclear* warheads.

When this became known in 1960, Canadians were plunged into intense dispute about nuclear weapons. Protests erupted throughout the country in strong opposition to arming the Bomarcs. The prime minister seemed politically paralyzed.

The missiles as a weapons delivery system were one thing, the kind of warhead they delivered, another. Some felt it crazy to separate the issue this way. Why have Bomarcs if you weren't going to arm them with deadly warheads? Others felt it national folly to embrace nuclear weapons when Canada had already officially repudiated them at the end of the Second World War. No public debate or decision had reversed this fundamental national policy.

As the nuclear warheads crisis erupted around Diefenbaker's Cabinet table, its explosive effects spread out to the Progressive Conservative government, the caucus, and PC Party ranks from the Women's Association through the youth and student wings. They, like the ministers of Canada's government, despite being united in the same party, were divided by Cold War differences over defence against Soviet aggression and the role of nuclear weaponry.

Diefenbaker was caught between the sides. His minister of national defence, Douglas Harkness, wanted to complete the Bomarc project to "honour our commitment" and be ready to shoot down inbound Soviet bombers. His minister of external affairs, Howard Green, deplored nuclear war and had vowed, after Hiroshima and Nagasaki, to work for abolition, not expansion, of nuclear weapons.

———

The man who headed a government with the highest number of MPs ever elected should have been on track for confident re-election in 1962.

When Prime Minister Diefenbaker called the election for June 18, his support had sagged greatly. In a private poll Dalton Camp conducted to test how stormy the campaign might be, The Chief's ratings stood lower than those for the Progressive Conservative Party itself, a complete reversal from four years earlier. It wasn't that the PCs had risen, but that Dief had fallen. With the Avro Arrow and the Bomarc missile crisis, he'd been damned when decisive and condemned when delaying.

Allister Grosart, in charge of the campaign, asked Dalton to run the same plays he had in the past two elections, taking charge of national publicity and managing the campaign in Atlantic Canada. Camp considered the prospect. His deep loyalty to the PC Party translated into support for its leader. His serious misgivings about the leader in 1956 had been cancelled out by seeing him in 1957 display compassion, humour, and concern that, if such qualities could again be brought to the surface, would surely help him reconnect with voters. And so Camp went, around and around, dizzy in a maze of pros and cons.

He often made decisions by drawing up a list of drawbacks and advantages, though it seemed a truly perverse exercise because he'd invariably pick the less attractive option. Dalton had deep motivations, impossible to add to a point-form list. Also, Dalton's ego prevailed over any list; nobody else, he believed, could do what he did. Moreover, his sometimes unpredictable decisions sprang from undeclared ambition to someday be prime minister. Dalton agreed to run all campaign publicity for the 1962 national PC campaign.

As biographer Geoffrey Stevens said: "If he positioned himself carefully, loyal to the leader but not part of his circle, he might one day have a shot at the leadership himself."

———

This time, television would play a bigger role than ever.

In 1958 the CBC inaugurated a coast-to-coast live television network. In 1961, a rival private sector network joined the communications landscape, CTV Television Network. Also opening the television sluiceway wider was a loosening of broadcasting rules. Movement and filmed action could now be part of campaign television advertising.

The Liberal TV ads showed a campaign bus rolling up and candidates climbing off. Not bad, thought Camp. But he was significantly more inspired. He hired a camera crew to follow Dief around and film him giving speeches. Brief segments, taken from otherwise long and winding discourses, were extracted from the raw footage, packaged at Film House in Toronto, and swiftly dispatched to broadcasters across the country. Its emotional impact was dramatic and captivating. Camp understood the medium was meant to convey an impression, not win a debate.

Another image for the campaign, produced for magazines and newspapers, was the antithesis of what Camp produced in 1957. Forsaking the personality cult, which initially helped win the election but ever since facilitated focusing all blame for the government's shortcomings on Dief alone, Dalton ran a photograph of the PM surrounded by his entire Cabinet, communicating the impression of a "team" and "unity," even if that was less and less the reality.

All this work Dalton carried out in Toronto at the Camp agency, with Norman as production coordinator for the campaign. Atkins had surrendered his U.S. citizenship, at Dalton's request, as a condition for joining him on this contentious campaign. Camp was sensitive to their vulnerability if it appeared an American, or any American influence, was at play in the PC backrooms when Dief was so strongly campaigning against U.S. influence and interference in Canada over the Bomarc issue. Norman complied. If he'd made this change earlier in life, he'd never have been drafted, but then he'd never have learned the advanced quartermaster skills that already were setting him apart in organizing campaigns.

The line-and-staff system in vogue with the U.S. Army when Norman served demanded he set objectives, design all tasks required to achieve them, assign individuals with requisite abilities to perform each one, allocate resources, create an effective communications system, keep track of all details, and establish a hierarchy of command. Nobody else running election campaigns in Canada did all that. Norman wedded this methodology to an organization chart, boxes with titles, each filled with names of carefully selected individuals and connected by reporting lines.

The brothers-in-law operated out of Toronto, not only for convenience but because Dalton wanted to steer clear of Grosart's cluster of campaign workers at national headquarters. He felt they meekly agreed with whatever Diefenbaker wanted, unable and unwilling to direct the leader the way those running a campaign ought.

———

For the leader's Atlantic tour, Dalton and the PM made the rounds of a campaign circuit now increasingly routine to both.

He found Dief irrational, the campaign dreadful. "He was unable to respond to the challenge," Stevens quotes Camp saying of Diefenbaker, "He was out of touch with the country. He could no longer reach people. He wasn't credible."

By mid-June, Camp expected a minority Liberal government would take office. In 1956, party insiders at the Albany Club, unable to find a challenger for the leadership, conceded it to Dief, confident he'd only last one election anyway. It turned out to be two, but they seemed about to be vindicated.

On election night, Dalton and Linda settled in at the Camp agency, with Norman and his wife, Anna Ruth, and Bill Kettlewell and his wife, to watch the curtain come down on the Diefenbaker years. But the results reaching them over national television were not as dire as Dalton feared. In Atlantic Canada, his own campaign bailiwick, the PC s won eighteen seats to fourteen for the Liberals. Then Quebec presented a stunning outcome nobody had seen coming — twenty-seven seats for Social Credit — ensuring the Liberals could not gain enough seats to form a government.

The New Democratic Party, evolved from the CCF and now affiliated with organized labour and led by former Saskatchewan premier T.C. Douglas, expected a major breakthrough. The buoyant New Democrats were held to a modest nineteen seats. Another party had taken its turn to show that provincial premiers couldn't cut it with voters as national leaders.

———

Winning the 1962 election kept the PCs in government, but with more than a million voters deserting the Tories, John Diefenbaker would have to govern without majority support in the Commons. His government faced defeat at any time.

To lose ninety-two seats, almost as many as the ninety-seven the party had gained in its historic 1958 "landslide," brought swift recriminations from those who'd lost, rekindling ambitions among leadership rivals, nourishing editorial writers and pundits with rich political fodder. If the glory for the 1958 win had been claimed by Diefenbaker, it seemed fitting that credit for the party's diminished standings should flow to him as well. In the party backrooms, Eddie Goodman of Toronto, vice-president of the Progressive Conservative Party, tried to get John Diefenbaker to agree to a retirement date, only to be angrily sloughed off.

Canadians looked at the number of Commons seats each party had, because that after all determines which party governs, and politicians and journalists used this same seat count for their resolute opinions, reinforcing public consciousness that the Diefenbaker regime was crumbling. Trend lines were clear, weren't they? Another election and the Liberals would be back in power.

But Tory backroom strategists, looking deeper than a seat differential between the PC and Liberal parties, perceived a different reality, and hence a different scenario going forward. The Liberals were stagnant under Lester Pearson. In 1958, with his fresh leadership and new lustre as a Nobel Peace Prize–winner, the Grits earned 34 percent of the popular vote nationwide. In 1962, after Pearson's four-year effort to make a better public impression, and with all the issues plaguing the Diefenbaker government, from economic recession and the declining value of the Canadian dollar to the Avro Arrow conundrum and Bomarc missile crisis, Liberal popular support across Canada had risen only a paltry 3 percent.

In the 1958 election, a rare alignment of forces raised Diefenbaker's support to 54 percent of voters nationwide, helping the PCs pick up those ninety-seven additional seats. Now the two parties were all but tied at 37 percent of the popular vote, PC candidates altogether receiving 2,865,000 votes to 2,846,000 for the Liberals. That had worked out in the ridings with the Grits regaining fifty-one of the fifty-six seats they'd lost four years earlier, while the Tories, with slightly more votes than the Liberals overall, dropped ninety-two seats.

The future for the Progressive Conservatives, as any discerning political strategist could see, lay in the ranks of those supporting *other* parties, most notably the Social Credit and NDP. The former now had thirty seats (with 12 percent popular vote), the latter nineteen (with 14 percent support). Voters attracted to Dief in 1958 but disenchanted after their first date, had pointedly *not* gone back to the smug Liberals waiting confidently for them. Instead, they'd either been seduced by the better prospects political conservatism offered with Social Credit as proclaimed by Robert Thompson, or enticed by the new-era democracy of political socialism as preached by Tommy Douglas.

More than one in four voting Canadians had opted for either Socred or socialist candidates. Those voters represented the best route back to majority government. The Progressive Conservatives should not try winning over immovable Grits by being more Liberal than the Liberals. They should campaign to draw the disenchanted and the hopeful back for a second date with destiny. And, if they could not do that, the best option still lay along this path with stronger third parties, especially the NDP who could split the Liberal vote and produce Progressive Conservative wins, the way it had been happening in Ontario since 1943.

Camp strongly favoured this plan. Having managed much of the 1962 campaign — all the publicity, and the election operation in the four Atlantic provinces — he found himself drawn into the spinning vortex of the party's internal rivalries. He tried to calm estranged dissenters. He embraced an all-consuming drive to find balance points for the sake of party unity. He'd have no party to lead, in the future, if it split apart now. Having embraced Toryism as fully as any man could, Camp's immediate cause was to keep its life force intact, helping the party revive its relationship with a million Canadians or, at least, develop issues that would help the NDP take support from the Grits.

His plan depended on John Diefenbaker being astute in all his stances, and masterful when taking new initiatives. There was no guarantee a scenario envisaged in the backroom, though, would unfold as performance on Canada's public stage. Already it seemed this political drama in progress was closer to a display of improv theatre.

CHAPTER 23

JOB OPENINGS IN ONTARIO

Dalton Camp's easy entry into PC backrooms of the Maritimes, the federal party, and Manitoba, where Progressive Conservatives in opposition were eager for his help, was a taunting contrast to his failure to break through the serried ranks of Tory Ontario. Here the party had been restored to power when he was still in Camp Utopia writing love letters to Linda.

Ontario Progressive Conservatives formed the government, at the pinnacle of which towered Leslie Frost, hard as nails behind closed doors, pleasingly avuncular in public. McKim and Allister Grosart had a solid lock on the government's publicity business. Frost was no more looking for lavish spending on admen than Hugh John Flemming had been in New Brunswick.

Dalton, seeking to expand his advertising operations and looking for a political role in the province where he lived, could not find even a mouse-hole sized entrance to Queen's Park. He had only one contact in Ontario's government. He'd met Clare Westcott, executive assistant to Premier Frost, over lunch with some mutual PC contacts. Sharing a party connection and common interest in the political game, they stayed in touch. A few months later, Westcott was dispatched from Frost's office to work for Robert Macaulay, Ontario's dynamic minister of energy resources. When Frost retired in 1961 after twelve years at Ontario's helm, triggering a race to succeed him, Westcott and Russ Ramsey, a student working for the minister, organized Macaulay's leadership race.

During the campaign, which Dalton joined, he happily met and worked with the candidate's brother, Hugh Macaulay, another Queen's Park insider. Camp also met Bill Davis, the MPP for Peel riding who was chairing Macaulay's campaign. They got along in the friendly way of two men thriving on politics and sharing a common endeavour.

Bob Macaulay was not a politician in need of much direction; he knew the business and had a strong mind. He did not require others to write his speeches so that he'd know what he believed. With little scope for Dalton in the Macaulay campaign, he yielded to Westcott's pressure to run the candidate's campaign letters through his Pitney-Bowes postal machine at the Camp agency, helping keep postage costs off the books and under the $75,000 campaign spending limit the party had imposed.

When PC delegates from across Ontario convened in Toronto to choose Les Frost's successor, it took six ballots to choose between seven candidates. As the rounds of voting progressed, not one of the contenders dropped out to swing his support to another, or even to shorten the process when it was clear he could not win.

The outcome was unclear until the fifth ballot, and even then there was doubt. Only three candidates were left by then: John Robarts, Kelso Roberts, and Bob Macaulay. Macaulay could not win, but if he wanted to be kingmaker, his withdrawal in support of either Roberts or Robarts could determine Ontario's next premier. He remained neutral. In the end, of course, Robarts won.

———

Upon taking office, John Robarts promoted Macaulay to minister of economics and development, where he soon decided Ontario needed a "trade crusade."

A survey showed 55 percent of all Canada's manufactured goods were made in Ontario, but the only trade vehicle to support their sale outside the country was the federal government. Because it was doing little overseas promotion, the province had a problem. "Let us get into the trade business," decided Macaulay. His goal was jobs in Ontario and prosperity across the province.

Westcott brought in Camp, reminding Macaulay that he'd helped in his leadership race, thinking Camp's ad agency might promote the campaign to boost sales of Ontario's manufactured products abroad. It was not the easy meeting Westcott expected. A clash erupted between the smart Maritimer who respected the indispensable role of the federal government and the smart Ontarian who saw Ottawa as a stumbling block to Ontario's best interests. Camp protested Macaulay's concept of sending salesmen on trade missions, arguing Ontario could not do so because trade was a federal, not provincial, jurisdiction.

But Dalton was not running, nor even influencing, Ontario's government. Robarts agreed with Macaulay's recommendation to set up foreign offices, and Westcott was dispatched to Europe, opening Ontario trade offices in Milan and Dusseldorf, adding others later in Paris, Tokyo, and Hong Kong.

"Dalton was pretty sour, until he found out how much our advertising budget was," observed Westcott. Business was business, but Camp believed strongly in two principles. The first was constitutional: Ontario should stay out of overseas operations, exclusive purview of the national government.The second was pragmatic: Ontario's market economy should be supported by Ontarians in their own self-interest. He persuaded Macaulay that the biggest market for Ontario goods was also the closest. Millions of Ontarians needed to stop buying the imported products of foreign competitors and start purchasing items made down the street or across town.

The Camp agency came up with what Westcott viewed as "an odd kind of advertising" campaign about a hippopotamus. Still rooted in small-town Ontario values, the ministerial assistant expected nothing more than a full page ad commanding consumers to "Buy Ontario!" or "Buy Canadian!" He, Macaulay, and just about everybody else were stunned when the clever campaign "just took off like you would not believe, with billboards and newspaper advertising." Camp's marketing concept was that some things just had to be imported, like a hippo, because Ontario didn't have any of its own. But apart from exotic things like that, Ontario produced just about everything else and Ontarians should give themselves an economic boost by buying Ontario-made goods. The more prosperous Ontario's economy, the better it would be for all who lived in the province.

Dalton found effective ways to spend the entire budget of several hundred thousand dollars. Decades later, people who'd been exposed to the hippo campaign would still remember the image and its essential message about buying Ontario-made products. The Camp agency was paid for its creative work and production, plus a commission on buying billboard and newspaper advertising space and airtime on radio and television. Dalton prevailed in a campaign that was constitutional, which mattered to him on principle. The rest, he simply could not change.

Westcott took sales missions to Britain, Germany and Italy, but whatever benefit they created for Ontario's economy and employment wasn't doing much politically for the Progressive Conservative government. As Westcott said, "word wasn't getting back." So Dalton, adept at getting big results with little money, at least helped the overseas operations by outlining a "this-for-that" scenario. Westcott accordingly phoned Canadian Pacific Airline's president, Grant McConaghy. "Look, we are going to buy a lot of tickets from you for our overseas sales missions. For every twelve tickets, I would like one free so I can take a newspaper man." McConaghy immediately saw the benefit for Canadian Pacific and the deed was done.

The first reporter to fly was David Grenier, respected financial editor of the Conservative-supporting *Toronto Telegram*. The second was rich-voiced Jack Dennett from Toronto's wide-reaching CFRB Radio, owned by Ted Rogers, a Conservative. A steady succession of friendly or impressionable newspapermen working for city dailies around the province, from the *Kitchener Record* to the *North Bay Nugget*, would follow.

"All of a sudden their reports back here in Canada, especially by the influential Jack Dennett at CFRB, began to give us great publicity," said a gleeful Westcott. "This effort, with Dalton Camp helping Robert Macaulay and the trade crusade, created a great image for Robarts across Ontario."

Although Robarts himself thought highly of these efforts, his close friend and political organizer, fellow MPP from London Ernie Jackson, could not forget that Camp had backed a strong rival of John Robarts for the leadership. Jackson, given power by the new leader to carry through the transition from one premier to the next, including party organization and campaign operations, hired new staff at Progressive Conservative headquarters and brought in an advertising agency that had been friendly to Robarts in the leadership race and had helped him keep his campaign costs below the spending limit, too.

Norman Atkins, miffed about any loss of business, was greatly agitated over cancellation of the Ontario government's advertising business that the Camp agency had only recently begun to acquire.

The Camp agency at least kept the provincial government's trade crusade account. Dalton had been so successful with the hippopotamus it would have seemed petty and spiteful for Robarts and Jackson to pull that business, and politically stupid, too, since Camp had an expanding circle of friends in Tory ranks.

It was hard in Ontario, whether on the factory floor, at an ad agency, or in a political backroom, to get the jobs.

CHAPTER 24

CONFRONTATION AND TURMOIL

On the morning of October 22, 1962, Livingston Merchant, a former American ambassador to Canada, flew to Ottawa as special envoy of President Kennedy to give Prime Minister Diefenbaker a top-secret briefing on what the CIA had discovered in Cuba and provide advance notice to America's continental military ally to ensure no surprise and full support for a high-stakes confrontation only hours away.

In a galvanizing television broadcast that evening, the American president revealed to the world that the Soviet Union had been caught secretly installing missiles in Cuba. Viewers were shown high-altitude spy photographs substantiating the alarming claim and making real the deadly threat.

The Soviet Union's nuclear warheads would reach major North American cities with unstoppable swiftness and accuracy. Forget about those manned bombers the Bomarcs were intended to take out. This threat was closer and more imminent. President Kennedy had United States Navy ships set up a blockade around the island to prevent Soviet ships bringing further military supplies to Cuba. He issued Soviet leader Nikita Krushchev an ultimatum to remove the missiles and destroy the launching sites.

The world held its collective breath, gazing into the stark face of nuclear war that had been everyone's worst nightmare since the Cold War began. For thirteen days, a tense world would wait on the brink of global annihilation.

Prime Minister Diefenbaker did not respond right away with Canadian support for the American president's stance. Nor did he put Canadian forces on full alert, as expected. The government's "procrastination" was criticized by Liberal leader Lester Pearson and infuriated Kennedy, making them political allies.

Some attributed the PM's handling of the Cuban missile crisis to poor personal relations between the two North American leaders, or to Diefenbaker's innate suspicion of American governments, or even "anti-Americanism," an enduring animus among segments of the Conservative Party. While those reasons may have contributed slightly to Ottawa's delay in supporting Washington, the main reason was grounded in domestic politics about Communism and the Bomarc missiles.

Earlier in the year, during the 1962 election, Diefenbaker had positioned himself as an ardent foe of Russian expansionism. As Canada's prime minister, he'd presented a resolution at the United Nations calling on the U.S.S.R. "to give its subject-peoples the right to decide their own future by a free vote." The Tories were staking out political turf, hoping to corner Liberal leader Lester Pearson as soft on Communism, ready to lavishly quote the former diplomat's assertion, "I'd rather be Red than dead."

According to Diefenbaker's closest advisers, Cabinet minister David Walker and Allister Grosart, Diefenbaker's strategy was to "suck in" Pearson and get him to reaffirm his anti-nuclear arms policy, which, as Walker explained in confidence to Henry Jackman, his predecessor in Toronto's Rosedale riding, "would then give Diefenbaker the opportunity to accept nuclear weapons and go to the people in an election on a strong anti-Communist platform."

But the Cuban missile crisis unexpectedly intersected this manoeuvre.

At a time when most Canadians strongly supported President Kennedy and felt visceral urgency about standing with the Americans, continuing to hold onto an unexplained partisan stratagem was not astute on Dief's part. Canadians lived the Cold War like few others, occupying the only country directly between the Soviet Union and the United States and now feeling extra vulnerability from Cuba's offensive missiles aimed north. After two days delay and under intense pressure, Diefenbaker expressed Canada's support for the American action, but not in time to arrest the dissipation of more of his support among Canadians or prevent emergence of a belligerent antagonism from Kennedy.

When Soviet chairman Khrushchev withdrew his missiles, removal of the immediate threat of war between East and West allowed people a sigh of anxious relief. But the larger issue of Cold War unity with the Americans remained, and was of great strategic importance. Canada was a treaty partner with the United States for shared North American defence. Missiles had been installed in Canada and, because of the Cuban missile crisis, arming the Bomarcs had now been catapulted to even greater prominence.

Taking a serious political toll on the Diefenbaker government were the cumulative effects of cancelling the Avro Arrow, buying Bomarc missiles and fighter aircraft (the CF-101 Voodoo interceptors based in Canada and the CF-104 Starfighters with Canada's forces in Europe), dithering over acquiring nuclear warheads to arm them all, and hesitating to support America's ultimatum that the Soviet Union remove its Cuban-based offensive missiles. Many Canadians feared their government too feeble for Cold War engagement, their prime minister too paralyzed by choices to make up his mind.

———

John Diefenbaker's plot to impale Lester Pearson on the nuclear weapons issue, and to win back a majority government by fighting an election over it, was nullified in January 1963 when the Liberal leader reversed his own position.

Pearson said Canada was "honour-bound" to accept nuclear warheads for the rockets under the NORAD agreements. This shocking about-face caused widespread public demonstrations. It drove a number of Liberals away from their party, at least for a while, and provoked Pierre Elliot Trudeau, a professor in Montreal supporting the NDP, to write a scathing analysis of Nobel Prize–winner Pearson's embrace of atomic weapons, calling the Liberal leader "the defrocked prince of peace."

Dief could not trigger an election over the issue, as he'd once envisaged, because his Cabinet was split down the middle, as was the PC Party itself, over whether to accept nuclear warheads for the Bomarcs. The government's indecision continued to strain Canadian-American relations.

Political divisions within the PCs continued to threaten the party, and Camp tried deliberate and diplomatic ways to maintain some unity by paving the way for an eventual leadership transition. But Cabinet ministers pressed on with their blunter method, a political coup. Defense Minister Doug Harkness, disgusted by what he deemed the PM's shameful failure to honour Canada's commitment to acquire U.S. nuclear weapons, resigned. George Hees led a number of irate Cabinet members into the PM's office where they angrily insisted he step down. Overcome by their vehemence in this showdown, Diefenbaker wobbled out of the room muttering, as he pointed to Fleming, "I'll resign. I'll resign. I appoint you, Donald, my successor."

But as word that Canada's prime minister had been toppled began spreading through the Parliament Buildings, Alvin Hamilton, a deeply loyal Cabinet minister from Saskatchewan, rushed about to rally Dief's allies in caucus. They pulled off a scheduling switch so The Chief would meet national caucus before his next Cabinet meeting, rather than after. At caucus, deftly orchestrated support for the leader boosted Dief and sent him into the Cabinet meeting resolved to recant his statement of resignation, beat down the political insurgents, and defiantly retain his position as leader.

With the Cabinet revolt disintegrating in failure, Hees resigned. Others in the plot to topple The Chief included Richard Bell, Wallace McCutcheon, and Eddie Goodman. Senior ministers and party figures Roland Michener, Pierre Sevigny, J.M. Macdonnell, Davie Fulton, and Donald Fleming also resigned or retired from politics, expressing lack of confidence in the prime minister as they left Ottawa.

Against this tide, Dalton Camp defended John Diefenbaker. He angrily opposed the Cabinet revolt, and tried to prevent it, on the basis "It would take years for the party to recover."

––––––

The government was defeated in the Commons. A general election would take place on April 8, 1963. It would not be fought over Lester Pearson's nuclear arms policy, but on John Diefenbaker's leadership. Dalton's plan to reclaim voters from the NDP and Social Credit parties had evaporated.

Camp agreed, in response to Diefenbaker's request, to replace Allister Grosart as manager of the entire national campaign for the April election, with Norman Atkins at his side as the campaign's production coordinator.

Dalton proposed, and The Chief agreed, to reprise an election "whistle stop" campaign aboard a train. He tried everything he could to revive the magic of 1957 and 1958, working with a leader equally determined to stop the Grits at the gates. Camp called on his friend Finlay MacDonald to run, who dutifully became a candidate in Halifax.

But the Pearson-led Liberals, who benefitted from support of Kennedy in Washington and their behind-the-scenes emissaries in Canada, managed to win enough ridings to form a minority government. Liberals had 128 seats to the PCs' ninety-five. Social Credit went back up to twenty-four MPs, regaining supporters in western Canada who'd last time gone to Dief, and holding onto most of its representation in Quebec with twenty Socred members. The New Democrats slipped to seventeen MPs, which is where the Liberals made their gains. With the Liberals at 41 percent in overall popular support and the New Democrats at 13, some suggested the two parties should merge. With the Progressive Conservatives at 33 percent and the Social Credit at 12 percent, proposals were advanced for these two parties to get together, too. Nobody talked about just reforming the electoral system.

Camp blamed George Hees for costing the party the election. Part of the defeat could certainly be attributed to the Bomarc issue — the way the crisis had been handled, not only by the PM but also by his ministers. Either decision would have been defensible. Either would have lost the PCs some of their public support. It was the indecision that created the debilitating political turmoil that exacted a far greater price.

The new Liberal government of Prime Minister Pearson accepted nuclear warheads for Canada's nuclear-capable forces, which were delivered from the United States to their North Bay and La Macaza sites on the last day of December, 1963, virtually unnoticed, as intended, because Canadians were preoccupied getting ready to celebrate New Year's Eve.

CHAPTER 25

PROVINCIAL CONSEQUENCES

Political life in a two-tier federal state meant a campaign machine like the one Dalton and Norman now operated for Progressive Conservatives was seldom idle long. In 1962 two provincial elections rolled around to keep them busy.

Norman found his first election campaign in western Canada a refreshing contrast to battling for votes in the Maritimes. In Manitoba he carried the title "communications and production coordinator," by now his reserved box on the organization chart, a designation giving plenty of scope as well as desired obscurity.

When voting took place on December 16, Premier Duff Roblin's PC government was re-elected, his second straight majority. The number of PC MLAs remained unchanged, at thirty-six members. The Tories claimed 45 percent of the popular vote, while the Opposition split between Liberals at 36 percent with thirteen seats, and the NDP at 15 percent with seven. A lone Social Credit member entered the legislature. Manitoba remained blue, showing no real fallout provincially from the federal PC difficulties.

—————

A December election in Newfoundland held little prospect for a Progressive Conservative win, however. The province was tightly controlled by the political machine of Liberal premier Joey Smallwood.

Even so, Dalton Camp and Cape Breton Tory Flora MacDonald headed to St. John's to do what they could for provincial PC leader James Greene.

Coming by a fluke into possession of a copy of the Liberal platform prior to its release, they reviewed the specific list of everything Smallwood was going to promise, item by item. Private television broadcaster Don Jamieson had offered his station to both parties for free-time campaign broadcasts. Greene went on TV and promised *one more* of everything in each category, be it a new school or fishing trawler, before the annoyed Liberals had a chance to unveil their now second-rate program.

With Camp at his mischievous best, the PCs also used the TV station to expose a corrupt Liberal scheme to buy votes in exchange for groceries. The PCs climbed from three to seven seats, better than expected, all wins coming in St. John's, where voters received the television signal and followed the public exposure of Grit corruption. Province-wide, the Tories had a popular vote of 37 percent. The Smallwood Liberals, back in government, had thirty-four members. Newfoundland remained red.

————

A couple of weeks after Liberals won the 1963 federal election, New Brunswick voters went to the polls again, this time for a provincial election that came as a surprise to just about everyone.

The puzzling timing of the election, called by Liberal premier Louis Robichaud only two and a half years into his mandate, was justified publicly over a seemingly small issue: a Tory accusation of Grit corruption involving a paper mill in Newcastle. Several much-touted Liberal projects, including tax reform and overhaul of post-secondary education, died in the legislature when the election was triggered. Robichaud confided to insiders that he'd instituted the election because his popularity was high and the Conservatives weak.

The campaign overlapped with the federal election held two weeks earlier. When the Liberals won in Ottawa, Robichaud sought to use his party's national victory for provincial leverage, saying New Brunswick would receive better treatment from the federal government with the same party in power. The New Brunswick Liberals were re-elected, but Robichaud's opportunistic gambit resulted only in the Liberals gaining a single seat. The Grits, with 52 percent of the popular vote, took thirty-two seats; the "weak" Tories at 48 percent got twenty. New Brunswick remained red.

———

The same year, John Robarts called an Ontario election for September 25, to get his own mandate after taking over the Progressive Conservative leadership and provincial government from Les Frost in 1961.

Ten more seats had been added to the legislature, bringing to 108 the number of members at Queen's Park. The PCs won seventy-seven of them, another strong majority. The Liberals and NDP each added two seats, edging up to twenty-four and seven MPPs, respectively.

Ontario's PCs had now won seven consecutive terms in office; the province was still deep blue.

———

To round out 1963's roster of Canadian elections, Nova Scotians showed up at their polling stations on October 8 to record their approval of Bob Stanfield, yet again.

When the ballots were tallied, the PCs were rewarded by a 44 percent increase in their province-wide popular support over the 1960 standings, raising their popular vote to 56 percent of the provincial total. That increased their number of seats from twenty-seven to thirty-nine in the forty-three-member Assembly. The Liberals under leader E.W. Urquart had a solid 40 percent of popular support, which disappointingly gave them only four members. The New Democrats lost the only riding the party held. The province continued blue.

Taking these 1962 and 1963 provincial elections into account, Camp could see how provincial political systems really did operate on their own timetables and sway to their own rhythms. The resilience of Progressive Conservatives, even under dispiriting pressures at the national level, reassured him there was still hope.

———

At Ottawa's Château Laurier Hotel, where the party held its annual meeting in February 1964, Dalton ran to become president of the Progressive Conservatives. He was ready to step into a slightly more public role.

Elected unopposed, he emphasized in his acceptance speech, as well as by informal remarks, that he could and would hold the party together. A united

Progressive Conservative Party would stymie the Grits, which for Camp was a worthy end in itself. A united party would be there for him to lead someday when John Diefenbaker was ready to retire, another desireable goal. Having journeyed through the PC's desolate wasteland of defeated, despondent, embittered souls, Camp resolved to use old methods or invent new ones to save Conservatives from themselves.

But the 1964 meeting was alive with exploding firecrackers. The PC Student Federation, led by Joe Clark, called for a secret ballot on the leadership. Some delegates even tried to get a leadership convention so John Diefenbaker could be replaced. A number present accused Camp of "playing both sides of the street."

In response, the high-wire balancer who was now national PC president explained that he was trying to avert a confrontation and that his motive was to "discourage the plotters without giving any encouragement to Dief to stay on." Camp expressed support for John Diefenbaker as leader, saying the former prime minister had "earned his right to another election." Before the Ottawa meeting adjourned, Camp ensured that delegates passed a resolution endorsing John Diefenbaker as leader.

As the party's new president, Dalton began to travel the country's far reaches, where different factions of Tories dwelt, interacting with the PC national executive members and others to assuage local party supporters and assist journalists in Canada's regions better interpret the positive state of Tory affairs.

CHAPTER 26

POLITICS REIMAGINED

Even at the best of times, the relationship between a party's president and its leader requires a delicate touch, often tricky to achieve, usually difficult to maintain.

If the relationship clicks and each recognizes an appropriate division of labour, the partnership can be productive for all concerned. The mid-1960s, however, were not the best of times for Canada's federal Progressive Conservatives. Harmony had given way to rivalry.

Dief was still "The Chief," but he was an embattled leader. His long years suspecting the presence of plotters, saboteurs, and knavish rivals now had a basis in reality as ambitious contenders plotted to replace him.

Dalton, though ambitious himself, occupied a unique position. He knew John and Olive better than most Tories. He'd travelled with the Diefenbakers for a decade and weathered a great deal with them. Camp also had deeper connections than anyone else, as a result of his numerous provincial and federal election campaigns, to most of the PC apparatus: the campaign backrooms, individual caucus members, party headquarters staff, provincial leaders and their advisers, and those who set policies, ran party publicity, and worked as partisan troops in widely scattered ridings. In ways both practical and emotional, the party was his as much as anyone's.

He feared the fractious Tories were on the verge of disintegrating. Its elected members in Parliament, and its senators, were either deeply loyal to

Diefenbaker, or adamant that it was time for the old coot to go. Few were neutral. This fault line divided members of caucus and extended throughout the party membership across Canada.

Added to the sense of division arising from these intense feelings about The Chief was a second challenge for "party unity." It arose from the lack of cohesion amongst many of the separate centres of organized Progressive Conservative activity, and from individuals who believed themselves more important than the party as a whole: the leader and those supporting him; the parliamentary caucus; the party's elected national executive; and the riding association executives and members. There was also the women's PC association, the PC Youth, and the campus clubs. All were part of the same party's national structure, but each had a different role, and not only were at odds with the others but also divided within by the internecine splits over Dief.

There were still other centres of power in the party. The PCs' bagmen knew they were irreplaceable, a real if largely anonymous presence in the party, because without the money they raised nothing else could happen. The admen in charge of campaign publicity knew they occupied positions as indispensable persuaders, because without them campaigns to win political power would be ineffectual. The national director and staff at party headquarters knew they held things together, because the administrative structure supported all other parts of the operation.

Each of these rings of operation needed to be joined, or balanced, or assuaged. Each had to be enlisted to support the leader, and the efforts of each other. If not, the work of one or other of them could become counterproductive to the efforts of the rest. Unity required coordination of all party components.

Camp's immediate duty as president was to save the party from exploding. Dalton envisaged his role as a bridge between the pro- and con-Diefenbaker factions, as he'd signalled at the annual meeting that elected him, to mollify the dissidents while giving the leader time to adjust to reality and retire with dignity. He needed, for this strategy, an activity all factions could focus on, other than themselves. Convening a conference on something utterly different, replacing stale and churning arguments about Diefenbaker by something that looked toward the future might help Tories advance together and find a fresh rallying point. In the process, Camp could show the news media and Canadians generally that the party over which he presided was progressive and relevant.

But what kind of conference? Camp wanted Progressive Conservatives to be in phase with the '60s, with the decade's exhilarating, in-your-face humanism and counter-culture upheaval, and the era's new issues. One option was a policy conference, such as Liberals had organized at Kingston in 1960 to develop specific proposals and refurbish their party after its humiliating 1958 electoral crushing. Conservatives at Port Hope in 1942 had achieved something similar, at a time when their party was in a political wilderness. Special-purpose party gatherings, clearly, could play a constructive role as counterpoint to a generally bleak situation.

Yet when Camp assembled a planning group, it became clear that deep divisions existed even in this aspect of party affairs. Some strongly favoured a policy conference. Others were just as adamant about avoiding debate over policies, fearing it would degenerate into a proxy battle between the two sides contending over Dief's leadership.

This group consisted of Camp and Atkins, George Hogan, Eddie Goodman, Hal Jackman, Patrick Vernon, and David Meynell. They met several times at the Camp agency. Hogan and Goodman favoured what Eddie called a "yahoo" event, a "feel good conference to build party esprit." Meynell, an earnest intellectual type, held out for a "thinkers' conference" but was in a minority. Asking a Jesuit friend how to turn the line of argument his way, he was told, "That is not difficult. What you say, when asked for your opinion, is, 'It's got to be a thinkers' conference because it is useless.' Say nothing else, just leave it at that." Puzzled, he nevertheless delivered these lines at the next meeting. "The effect was electric," he said. Meynell did not understand the line, but "Goodman did a 180-degree turn on the spot, as if I'd punched a button. With Eddie turned, the battle was won."

For the Progressive Conservative thinkers' conference, designated a "National Conference on Canadian Goals," there'd be four day-long sessions, each covering a different "basket" of issues. The gathering had to be "big picture" if it was to work at all. Camp wanted participants to think about Canadian problems that were not yet well framed in the public discourse. He hoped new thinking about culture and communications could help Progressive Conservatives imagine Canadian politics differently. Dalton wanted speakers who could see the horizon, even if unclear about how to reach it.

Meynell was assigned the crucial opening day, about "the future," to highlight education, medicine, computerization, and the future generally. With few "futurists" around, Meynell contacted a laureate friend at California Tech, who said he'd be happy to come, "but you want the leading guy in the field and he's right there at the University of Toronto. His name is Marshall McLuhan." Meynell immediately bought and read McLuhan's most recent book. "It set my hair on end. I had found my way to the future."

A McLuhanesque view of communications would not be the only demanding new frontier the thinkers would confront. The Front de libération du Québec had begun detonating bombs and claiming lives, and Camp knew Canada's parties had to come to grips with terrorist activity linked to political aims. In 1963 the FLQ had proclaimed that "suicide commandos" would "completely destroy by systematic sabotage" colonial institutions, English-language media that held French Canadians and the FLQ in contempt, and businesses that discriminated against Quebecers or did not use French as their primary language. Wanting Conservatives to understand why these events were occurring, Dalton enlisted as speakers Claude Ryan, editor of Montreal's *Le Devoir*; Montreal lawyer Marc Lalonde, who'd worked in Ottawa as assistant to Progressive Conservative justice minister Davie Fulton; and Montreal financier and constitutional authority Marcel Faribault. Joining them, to present the long view of French-Canadian grievances and how containing separatism in Quebec might require military force, he recruited Manitoba historian W.L. Morton. Someone Dalton did not invite was a Montreal professor he'd met. They had a preliminary discussion over dinner, but Camp found Pierre Trudeau "too superficial."

———

Dalton's recalibration of the Progressive Conservative Party though a broadening intellectual experience required a different pace in a distinctive place. Few were surprised he chose Fredericton. The best person for on-site organization in Fredericton was the party president's brother-in-law. Norman quickly took charge of organizing the September 9–12, 1964 event.

He and Dalton liaised with Flora MacDonald, who was preparing background papers at party headquarters in Ottawa and distributing them, along with other conference materials, to attendees in advance of the conference. Joe Clark, an Albertan active with student Progressive Conservatives, helped Norman invite participants, confirm travel arrangements, and collect fees. Nova Scotian

Lowell Murray, who'd been president of the campus PCs at St. Francis Xavier and had since tried to win office as PC candidate in Cape Breton, was to ensure that reporters got copies of speeches, access to telephones, and enough to drink.

———

Opening the conference on September 9, the PC national president expressed intent, "so far as lies within our power, to purge from Conservatism that which is doctrinaire, obsolescent, and irrational." Camp added that, while clichés are comfortable, "they do not really provide a refuge from facts, and while shibboleths can be worn and waved by partisans, they provide no defence against reality."

Then Marshall McLuhan spoke.

Progressive Conservatives listened as the professor amalgamated concepts, twisted old homilies to give them new meaning, extracted lessons from cultural anthropology, and viewed through time's long lens how innovations in technology produce transformations in humans and society.

The 1964 Fredericton Conference was one of the early attempts to come to grips politically with Quebec's Quiet Revolution. McLuhan had been asked by Meynell and Camp to address the issue, which he did in his unique way. Marshall talked of the electronic age "reviving tribal modes," and said "dialects are re-emerging as a result of electronics," although, on the other hand, "the world is homogenizing because of advances in communications." Despite the paradox, the French Canadians present were intrigued. "They were thinking they were being submerged," said Meynell, "but here was McLuhan saying they would become stronger. He was talking about why we were not going to turn into vanilla ice cream."

Some thought everything Marshall said was a bit dippy, while others kept listening and began to nod in acknowledgement, if only for fear of not wanting to miss the boat, or appear like they weren't getting it. Still others whispered, "McLuhan is really onto something here."

Meynell was accosted by the *Globe and Mail*'s George Bain and other newsmen from the Ottawa Press Gallery for "foisting a charlatan like McLuhan on the press, the people of Canada, and the party." Yet before long, their reports seemed to embrace ideas McLuhan had advanced at Fredericton.

"Dalton showed great courage to go with these ideas at the time when very little was known or understood about them," concluded Meynell. "One thing for sure is that McLuhan's speech and paper at Fredericton changed the rhetoric for a generation of Canadians."

The Progressive Conservative Party could not be made over at a four-day stand in New Brunswick, but if some of those present caught hold of a new way to engage experience and understand what was happening around them, that could be enough, over time, to result in real transformation.

———

Those who believed political parties needed practical policies more than conceptual stimulation were nonplussed, however. Hal Jackman, who'd not only shared in the planning but was a nominated PC candidate who attended the panels and participated in discussions, was "frustrated that no specific policy issues were discussed." Jackman diarized his belief "that Camp's rhetoric, although more cerebral, had no more substance than Diefenbaker's." He remained convinced that "the overriding matter of leadership was the paramount issue" and that Dalton was ducking it.

Hal was not alone in panning the Fredericton Conference. Looking on the same event, Jackman's nemesis, John Diefenbaker, also saw the gathering of "intellectuals" as an affront to his vision for the party. He also did not like the timing because Dalton's conference detracted attention from the extended filibuster he was conducting in Parliament to prevent the Grits' new Canadian flag with its Liberal-red maple leaf, the so-called "Pearson Pennant," from being adopted to officially replace the Red Ensign. In the end, John Diefenbaker did go to Fredericton, but gave an address to the delegates that did little to awaken fresh patterns of thinking. The event, intended by Dalton to bridge the gap between those supporting and opposing Diefenbaker's continuation as leader, or at least achieve a truce in their fighting while binding the party and buying The Chief time, had the ironic effect of deeply damaging Diefenbaker's relationship with Camp.

If a party called both "Progressive" and "Conservative" was able to go in opposite directions at the same time, it was certainly living up to its name. The president wanted to bridge the gulf, to notionally reinsert the dropped hyphen that once bound both halves as one. The leader not only was "opposed to hyphenated Canadianism" in sociological terms but even, in terms of this broadened nature of his party, it seemed, in politics as well.

CHAPTER 27

DAYS OF RECKONING

Dalton Camp could see, from his presidential vantage point, that his conference at Fredericton and similar efforts to bind Tories in even fragile unity were insufficient responses to the core conundrum of John Diefenbaker's continuing leadership. The Progressive Conservatives were in an end-game, with no end in sight.

Throughout the party's many centres of power, feelings were high, but acceptable solutions few. The earlier botched Cabinet coup, led by Hees and Harkness but countered by Hamilton, proved how messy this fight over Dief's leadership could be, and how high the cost: losing the power to govern the country.

On February 3, 1965, Dalton presided at a meeting of the Progressive Conservative national executive. It passed a motion that rebuffed John Diefenbaker, a formal sign of how serious the elected party officers and representatives from across Canada felt about the leadership crisis. Their motion, intended to pressure Diefenbaker to quit, might have worked in normal times with most people, but was counterproductive with The Chief. It only provoked him to keep on fighting. He would not relent. Dief relished battle, became focused with a foe. The exhilaration he derived when giving hell to the Grits was the same rush he'd felt, over nearly three decades, fighting other Tories within the party.

Party president Dalton Camp tried valiantly to figure out what John Diefenbaker would do when under assault from within the Progressive Conservative Party after losing the power to govern. Here, in a hotel room with other backroom blue machinists, he watches Dief declare on national television his intent to soldier on as leader.

Dalton was drawn inexorably into the centre of this political family firefight, trying to identify and hold a patch of authority and power in the uncertain no man's land between hundreds of thousands of Tory militants engaging in a civil war.

———

Amidst these battles, looking for any happy presidential duty, Dalton wrote Peter Lougheed to congratulate him on becoming leader of the Alberta Progressive Conservative Party.

The party's inaugural meeting, on March 20, 1965, marked the sprouting of a Progressive Conservative presence at the provincial level in Alberta, a significant point of departure in Canadian politics. Dalton had encouraging words about the new leader one day ousting the long-entrenched Social Credit Party.

Lougheed was heading up a different kind of Progressive Conservative Party, in a province with a political culture as alien to Camp as he was to Albertans. Conservatives had never held power here, and Lougheed, the handsome Calgary lawyer and former professional football player, was building his party from the ground up. It was natural to look for help. Duff Roblin had gone to Toronto for start-up funds from Ontario's Tories when he'd begun rebuilding the Manitoba PC Party. In the same way, Joe Clark, twenty-six years old and helping Lougheed organize, visited Toronto to meet wiry Hugh Latimer, Ontario PC organizer, for tips, contacts, and support. Hugh was courteous, and gave some limited information, but was certainly not as forthcoming as normal when helping a fellow Tory. As Joe left, Latimer wished him well, but pointed out that Ontario's PCs worked well with Alberta's Socreds and both governments considered the other as "friendly."

Despite the national president's encouraging words, fledgling Alberta PC operatives could only feel resentment toward the Easterners manning Ontario's Tory bastion who worked in tacit partnership with their Social Credit rivals.

Such strains between Progressive Conservative encampments across Canada remained mostly unseen by the public. Yet they were part of the reality Camp as the party's president had to navigate for survival. Lack of Ontario PC support for Lougheed's new Alberta PCs, due to cozy relations with Social Credit, would in time crest publicly in sharp political differences in Ottawa and at the highest political levels between the governments of Alberta and Ontario over energy, constitutional amendments, and the national party leadership.

———

One way to be aware of dangers lurking beneath the political surface of Torydom was to frequent the Albany Club of Toronto.

Camp, to his disadvantage, was not a member. At heart a loner who happily bypassed established structures, he did not mind. But most Tory players just assumed their national president would belong. One was Senator David Walker, who invited Dalton to join him and others at the club for lunch in the spring of 1965.

Following the meal, Walker made a strong plea for all present to help resuscitate the Albany, with "new blood, so it can survive and grow." Dalton quickly saw how the club "would be convenient and convivial for a number of purposes related to my political activities," and told Walker he'd join the board of directors, as requested, except he was not a member. The senator, one of John Diefenbaker's most trusted advisers, promptly fixed that deficiency by sponsoring Dalton.

On June 1 Camp became both a member of the club and a director of it simultaneously, "an anomaly unique in the club's history," he smiled to recall. Soon his friend Pat Patterson became the club's membership secretary, sparking "an appreciable increase in new members," including, as Dalton wanted, "many of those closely associated with me in the politics of the day," such as Eric Ford, Ross DeGeer, and Norman Atkins. This regeneration of the club "was something of a miracle," he wrote, transforming it from a place "with few members" to one "where almost everyone I knew had become a member." That was a diplomatic way of saying he and Norman had launched a takeover of the Albany Club.

Dalton believed the Albany's networks would facilitate his bridging effort as national president. They did that, and more: he discovered, at last, that the entrance to Queen's Park was actually downtown at 91 King Street East. At the club he developed a warm relationship with Premier John Robarts.

His work as bridge-builder seemed unending, though. New rifts kept opening. The national PC caucus, one of the most visible centres of organized power in the party, itself had many subsections, such as regional caucuses of MPs and senators divided according to provincial boundaries. Quebec PC parliamentarians met separately, as did those from the Prairies and Ontario and Atlantic Canada. In mid-1965, Trois-Rivières MP Léon Balcer, a former president of the national party and Tory Cabinet minister and the man designated by Diefenbaker his deputy leader in Quebec, had had enough. He convinced Quebec Tories at their caucus to support a motion calling on the party's national executive to meet and set a date for a leadership convention.

Balcer's ultimatum to the national executive forced Dalton to figure out his next move to keep his fighting partisans from each other's throats. Balcer was seeking a date and place for the awaited duel. Camp saw other combatants on the field, however. The Liberals were waiting for the PCs to be gravely wounded or even leaderless so they could call a quick election and add the few seats needed for their majority government.

As a solution to this immediate conundrum, Dalton devised a questionnaire, which he put to the national executive in hopes of disposing of the Balcer ultimatum while giving Dief yet another opportunity to step down gracefully. He feared voting on a motion to hold a leadership convention would not carry because most national executive members would worry, as he did, that with Tories in the protracted process of changing leaders, the opportunistic Liberals would call a snap election. On the other hand, if the motion did not carry, Diefenbaker would take it as an endorsement to continue as leader. As debate continued at the national executive meeting, the hardliners on both sides resolved to push all the way, without compromise.

When the afternoon session resumed, the issue came to a head in a deadlocked vote on the motion about Dief and the convention. Camp as president had to cast the tie-breaking vote. He did not do the deed. Eddie Goodman, who, like Hal Jackman, was doing everything possible to move Diefenbaker out of the leadership, left in angry exasperation. "We had them beat," he criticized, "until Dalton ducked."

Camp was unwilling to take a public stance against The Chief. He did not want the party caught holding a leadership convention when the Liberals launched an election. Dief, feeling gleeful that he and his loyalists on the national executive had outmanoeuvred both Camp and Balcer, not to mention Goodman, would not step down. Soon Léon Balcer left the Progressive Conservatives to sit in the Commons as a political independent, declaring, "There is no place for a French Canadian in the party of Mr. Diefenbaker."

For his part, Camp was finally convinced there was no way The Chief would go peacefully, ever.

––––––

The awkward struggle was unlike anything before in Canadian politics: a protracted public embarrassment involving a raw contest of human wills. Even when Ontario's premier Mitch Hepburn squared off against Prime Minister Mackenzie King, the two men and their Liberal supporters were separated by distance and different levels of government, and kept the worst of it private.

This Tory feud had an epic quality, but was the protagonist a vanquished man refusing to withdraw in dignity, or a valiant man fighting on nobly against meanest fortune? Either way, John Diefenbaker needed an opposite, and so

Dalton Camp became that foil, entering the period of his celebrity, as news reporters covered the drama's twists with incredulity and the public looked on with fascination, alarm, or disgust.

Through 1965 Dalton accepted a growing number of invitations to speak, the PC president intent on refreshing his party with a contemporary image. The Fredericton Conference had heightened his reputation as an intellectual, adding to his established credentials as a successful campaign organizer, talented speech writer, and brilliant adman. This made him more suspect to certain Tory MPs, who disdained "intellectuals" and pronounced the word with a sneer. Others, however, had become increasingly attracted to Dalton's plans for the party. Rising interest in Camp convinced The Chief more than ever that his party's president was his personal rival.

In fact, despite his wish to avoid a party crisis by directly challenging Dief to resign, Dalton had begun to feel that that the time had come for him to finally find a place for himself in Parliament. It was time to extend his power base into the national caucus. A general election loomed.

Bill Davis urged him to run in Peel, northwest of Toronto, where the Brampton MPP's own political organization could help him win a Commons seat by taking the strong Tory riding. In 1962, capitalizing on the anti-Diefenbaker anger over the Avro Arrow, Liberal Bruce Beer won the seat — "It's time for Beer!" — the first Grit in the twentieth century to do so. Davis believed conditions had changed by 1965. Yet Dalton took a pass.

He wanted to enter the Commons, not by a side door but through the main entrance, defeating a leading Liberal. Also, it was more practical and credible to run where he lived and operated his business. To make Progressive Conservatives appealing to contemporary Canadians, representing a city riding was the right fit. A breakthrough was needed. Dief and his supporters might appeal in outlying and rural areas, but Dalton wanted the PCs to be contemporary and stronger in urban Canada.

He could lead this reformation by example, retaking Eglinton from Liberal Cabinet minister Mitchell Sharp, the sitting MP. Chad Bark, president of the Eglinton PC association, was urging Camp to run in the riding and, to "test the waters," speaking engagements were lined up.

When Dalton addressed the Eglinton Young PCs, Brian Armstrong was in the room. Recruited by Bill Saunderson to the PCs three years earlier, when a law student at University of Toronto, Brian had displayed intense interest in politics, working in Eglinton's 1963 federal and provincial election campaigns. Now, however, he wanted to join the Liberals. "The party under Mr. Diefenbaker was something most young people could not associate with," he explained, adding it was "an object of ridicule on university campuses across the country."

At this lowest point, he heard the party's president speak. "Dalton absolutely blew me away," he said, "because he was a thoroughly modern Conservative — intelligent, urbane, thoughtful, progressive, incredibly articulate, charismatic, and someone who really wanted the party to open itself to young people." Armstrong would stay with the PCs, a disciple of Dalton Camp.

When Dalton addressed the Downtown Toronto Kiwanis Club, Roy McMurtry was in the audience. The 1965 federal election had just been called, and it was rumoured Camp might run. As a resident of Eglinton riding, McMurtry had voted for Sharp in 1963 but was impressed by Camp's "rational and moderate approach to federal political issues." He heard "a refreshing departure from the pointless partisan bickering that had for too long dominated the national political discourse." Roy volunteered to assist Camp, if he became a candidate.

Two days later, Dalton declared. Norman, who'd attended all his brother-in-law's speeches recording names and numbers of those interested in helping him, began working the phones. Among those assigned campaign roles for the Camp campaign were Armstrong and McMurtry.

The campaign headquarters on Eglinton Avenue, a block east of Yonge Street, directly across from the Dalton K. Camp & Associates offices, was convenient because the two operations functioned as one. In the headquarters basement, campaign manager Atkins convened an organizational meeting. Norman had already produced VOTE CAMP bumper stickers to provide mobile visibility for the candidate. He double-checked that everyone attending got their supply.

McMurtry, "despite lack of experience in political organizing," accepted responsibility for putting together a political team. Armstrong became area organizer for six polls, recruiting a team of canvassers, making sure each poll was canvassed, and identifying all who would vote for Camp. On election day he was to ensure the PCs had poll clerks in each voting station, PC volunteers working the lists and phones, and drivers getting all identified Camp voters out to cast their ballots.

Around the table at this first organization meeting, both new recruits and veteran campaigners were fascinated when Eglinton's provincial PC member, Leonard Reilly, turned over for Dalton's campaign his "entire campaign organization," which he tracked on a system of file cards. "Every person with whom Len had ever come into contact in the riding had a file card," said Armstrong. "They were in metal recipe boxes: everybody whom he'd helped, who had put up a sign for him, who'd made a financial contribution." For a starting candidate, this information was a political gold mine.

When they climbed the stairs to leave, each with his or her supply of voters' lists, brochures, buttons, campaign contact numbers, and other paraphernalia issued by the quarter master, Brian reassured Norman, "I have my sticker and will be putting it on my car."

––––––

Intent on getting into Parliament, Dalton concentrated on Eglinton. Norman took no role in the national campaign either, totally focused on Dalton winning Eglinton to better position his run for the leadership.

In place of Dalton, who in 1963 had run the federal campaign, this time Eddie Goodman was national campaign chairman. He began by persuading his friend George Hees to return to the fold in a show of unity, and in doing so, flamboyant George helped other Tory dissidents rally to the PC cause. That was positive. Dief was ecstatic.

The Eglinton campaign was civil, even urbane. Camp and Sharp were well matched in the personal campaigning department: both were very poor at it. Neither the adman from the campaign backrooms, nor the civil service mandarin from Ottawa, was at ease meeting strangers. Camp could not glad-hand nor make easy chat, despite having studied carefully John Diefenbaker's mastery of the art; he seemed, instead, to emulate the style of reluctant Bob Stanfield. For his part, Sharp looked especially awkward at all-candidates' debates, seemingly miffed if someone in the audience didn't know the deep implications of policy the way his civil service interlocutors in Ottawa would have. Each candidate could only seem happy, and be fun in a socially outgoing way, with a circle of his own chosen friends, musical Mitchell at a piano, Dalton entertaining with stories over drinks and cigarettes in a bar.

By election night, Camp had failed to attract enough votes. His 16,777 ballots could not trump Sharp's 18,719. Nor, over in Rosedale riding, had Hal Jackman quite succeeded in his repeated effort to get into Parliament. City seats were hard for Tories in the 1960s. Even in Peel, Bruce Beer got re-elected.

Progressive Conservatives across the country, campaigning on the slogan "Policies for People, Policies for Progress," did manage to win ninety-seven seats, however. Diefenbaker, to everyone's astonishment, again held Pearson's Liberals to a minority. The Liberals remained in government but with only 131 MPs they were still two short of a majority. NDP candidates were elected in twenty-one ridings, the breakaway Social Credit Rally in Quebec, nine, and Social Credit itself, in five. This time the seat allocation was a reasonable reflection of popular support. The Liberals with a minority of votes (40 percent) got a minority of seats; the PCs had 32 percent of the popular vote; NDP, 18 percent, and the two Social Credit groups together, 8 percent.

———

John Diefenbaker interpreted keeping the Liberals to a minority government as a victory.

Feeling vindicated by this outcome, he refused to resign the leadership, although many continued clamouring for him to go. He knew how the Tories' long years in the political wilderness had not improved party fortunes by changing leaders in the past. He reminded people about political leaders, in Britain and elsewhere, who'd carried on into advanced old age. He purged those he considered threats. When he fired Flora MacDonald as party secretary at national PC headquarters, her extensive network of friends and allies throughout the party were incensed.

With a Liberal minority, another election could come at any time, making a leadership convention problematic, had it even been possible. John Diefenbaker's continuation as leader left few Tories with the stomach for a battle they saw themselves preordained to lose.

Having led his party into five elections, many Tories and a majority of Canadians felt The Chief had enjoyed all the outings any one man was entitled to. His virtue of resilient determination, which rank-and-file Tories so admired when electing him leader in 1956, now seemed a vice. Resolution of the "leadership issue" would be neither clean, nor quick.

John Diefenbaker was ardent about remaining leader; Dalton Camp was equally resolved to end the conundrum.

The time of reckoning was at hand.

CHAPTER 28

SHOWDOWN AT THE CHÂTEAU

In the Albany Club's wood-panelled main dining hall, members gathered on the spring evening of May 19, 1966, heard master of ceremonies Hal Jackman remind them, following dinner, that Dalton Camp's address was "off the record."

The PC national president outlined, to the hushed attention of some two hundred, his proposition that "leadership of any great political party should be made subject to review." He said "the party is not the embodiment of the leader but rather the other way around; the leader is transient, the party permanent." He added, if "the leader does not know the limits to his power, he must be taught and, when he is indifferent to the interests of his party, he must be reminded."

He spoke eloquently, with care, and dealt with principles. His concept was novel in Canadian politics at the time, certainly not yet a provision in any party's constitution. While a leadership review clearly applied to the incumbent PC leader, Camp framed the issue in generic terms, advocating a democratic process, a principle rather than anything personal.

Jackman's father, Henry, among the scores of prominent Tories present, correctly heard the speech "as a direct challenge to Diefenbaker" all the same. He surmised, because Senator David Walker was at the head table, that "Diefenbaker must have known about the speech in very short order."

Dalton certainly expected word would spread. Next day he began sending out copies. With the one mailed to Finlay MacDonald in Halifax, he wrote, "This was an off-the-record thing to just the party members, but now, I suppose, the balloon will go up." It didn't. He'd not imagined club members would dutifully honour his remarks as privileged. No mention was made in the press about the content of Camp's speech.

Among those present that night was Ross DeGeer, chairman of Toronto's Junior Board of Trade. As Diefenbaker's leadership continued to plague Conservatives through the summer, Ross suggested Dalton use the Junior Board's podium to repeat his message, "this time for public consumption."

When Camp delivered the identical speech four months later on September 20, the young business-minded members of the Junior Board were attracted by his eloquence and determination. Being intense competitors, they relished a contest for power, a high-stakes game; raw politics, not the canned stuff. Camp, having awakened it, drew on that reservoir of latent support in his non-party audience. Had he been addressing a meeting of Progressive Conservatives, he'd have heard some boos and seen a few stomp out to denounce their president to reporters for treachery and disloyalty to the leader.

Toronto Telegram publisher John Bassett, a major power in the Tory Party, thought Camp and his little group supporting leadership review were hopelessly out of their league and would be shredded by Diefenbaker's hardened forces. He dismissed them in his newspaper as "the Eglinton Amateurs."

———

"The cat was truly out of the bag," said DeGeer, as the speech gained immediate and wide coverage.

"From that time on, Norman and the organization he and Dalton had assembled from across the country as a result of the Fredericton Conference were assessed for their take on this issue, to identify supporters of the leadership review process." Those they could reliably identify as favouring review, said DeGeer, "quickly became part of the organization needed at the Ottawa annual meeting."

After the Junior Board speech, Dalton and Norman began what they called a "pilgrimage" to campuses and editorial offices across Canada. Dalton spoke at PC meetings and in television studios, advancing the cause through September and October, taking political temperatures, calculating how to proceed. It was hard to get a good reading. Feelings varied, from supportive to hostile. Dalton's own emotions swung between buoyant and deflated. Norman couldn't stabilize things because he took his signals from Dalton, who was sending mixed ones, and tended easily to nervous fretting himself.

As party president and issuer of an unprecedented challenge to the leader, Camp was now the public face of an organized challenge to John Diefenbaker. Camp was not only its leader but the lightning rod attracting bolts from Dief loyalists, who described Camp as filled with ambition, a "slick front man for Bay Street interests."

Yet he was hardly alone. Behind the scenes others were developing scenarios to outmanoeuvre Diefenbaker, too. Davie Fulton, who'd returned to Ottawa in the 1965 election after his quixotic tilt at B.C. politics, was an impatient candidate-in-waiting. In July Fulton told Hal Jackman, who'd been raising money for his leadership bid, that he was "seriously considering going it alone in an attempt to dump Diefenbaker prior to or at the November annual meeting." Davie knew this would kill his leadership hopes, but was "prepared to do so, for the good of the party."

Another scenario was Fulton's plan, suggested by Lowell Murray, to have "the six leading men in the party — Robarts, Roblin, Stanfield, himself, Hees, and Camp — give The Chief an ultimatum." Davie complained to Hal that he'd suggested this to Dalton but had no response, and was critical of Camp for going public on leadership before lining up this heavy-duty support. Jackman discussed this at length with Atkins on September 27, 1966, then reported back to Fulton that Camp had decided to deal with the leadership issue "completely on his own," without any assurances of support from the premiers or other leadership candidates, and though aware of Fulton's proposal for getting five or six leading figures in the party to come forward, "had earlier dismissed the idea as being impossible to organize."

Atkins also told Jackman that Dalton planned a motion at the annual meeting calling for a leadership convention but, realizing the difficulties in presenting such a motion, he might, as an alternative, "focus the entire battle on his own re-election." It would be clear by November "that a vote for Camp is a vote against Diefenbaker."

In the past, Conservative leaders had been changed many ways, initially with Tory MPs and senators performing the task as a caucus, sometimes with the governor general taking a role in Confederation's early years. Then the task of choosing a party leader passed to a national convention of voting delegates from all constituencies. Sometimes the national caucus chose an interim leader. No matter which of these methods was in play, the selection and replacement of the leader always saw power-brokers in the party's back-rooms pull strings and move others so that leadership transitions could be reasonably swift.

But the rocky, decade-long ride of the Progressive Conservatives under John Diefenbaker was not progressing according to any known pattern. Camp felt Diefenbaker had alienated Quebec, most provincial premiers, and broken unwritten rules. He believed Dief incapable of moderation and saw no smooth end or happy transition. It had only been when he was convinced Dief would not leave until forced out that, as party president, he resolved to establish a new principle of "leadership review."

———

Dalton faced unprecedented conditions as president, entering no man's land, challenging the leader's unaccountable decade at the helm. For what lay ahead, he needed a tightly knit, highly reliable group that could work secretly with machine-like effectiveness to achieve tactical goals.

He already had well-placed political operatives across Canada. Norman, working almost full-time on Dalton's political activities though keeping tabs on Camp agency projects, did far more than record everybody's names and numbers. He'd become a proactive organizer. He stayed in constant contact by long-distance telephone with this network of progressives. Though both extensive and reliable, this organization was not enough.

Several hundred Torontonians had come forward to actively support Camp's bid for a Commons seat in Eglinton the year before. They remained an effective, diverse, and talented squad, anxious for the next election's rematch. But these Eglinton constituency supporters, the "amateurs" identified by John Bassett, were an unwieldy group ill-suited for the national hardball politics now polarizing Progressive Conservatives.

The power struggle in which Camp was engaged demanded a clandestine cadre within the PC Party itself, a "special operations team" in play for him the way covert squads advance unique missions for military, espionage, and religious organizations.

Dalton and Norman formed a secret group to strategize, plot, and carry out projects. From their vast talent pool, they hand-picked seasoned men who'd already performed exceptionally well in campaign operations. Dalton was the group's magnetic centre, Norman its organizer. Eglinton PC riding president Chad Bark was in, as were downtown Toronto lawyers Patrick Vernon, Don Guthrie, Pat Patterson, and Roy McMurtry. The others in the brotherhood were Bill Saunderson, Eric Ford, Ross DeGeer, and Paul Weed. Saunderson, a chartered accountant, looking around at their first gathering, recognized in his fellow members "interesting, intelligent, active people who all loved poli-

The clandestine blue machine group the "Spades" knew each other by their playing card identities. Camp was the "Ace" of spades, his brother-in-law Atkins, the "Five." Three others were "Six," Eglinton riding PC president Chad Bark; "Seven," McCarthy lawyer and PC bagman Patrick Vernon; and "Nine," lawyer Donald Guthrie.

tics." Each came with his own network. None depended on politics for their livelihood.

Saunderson came up with their code name, "Spades," which initially had the connotation of "doing spadework" to prepare Dalton Camp's way in national politics, even a loose association with "digging" deep in the party's grassroots for support. But once Saunderson produced a deck of miniature playing cards and handed the ace of spades to Dalton, that design and identity stuck. From that day on, their code name for Camp was Ace.

Most carried their card, like membership ID in a secret fraternal society, alongside money and driver's licences in their wallets. But the Spades were men of diverse personalities. McMurtry evinced little interest in this juvenile, "secret-society" feature of the group, while Atkins so venerated his five of spades card he hung it, framed, on his inner office wall. As part of keeping their work hidden, Norman and others referred to one another, in cases requiring ambiguity, by their playing card number alone.

Bark knew a lot of people in Eglinton riding and most old-time Tories around Toronto as well. Saunderson, a chartered accountant in the financial business, thrived on politics as had two of his grandfathers. Ford, a strong and positive man, was a chartered accountant with Clarkson Gordon, a dedicated supporter of his church and community organizations, and Albany Club director and president. Patterson, a partner in the Toronto law firm Stapells & Sewell, was a good fundraiser and recruiter of many younger people at the Albany Club where the Camp forces were marshalling. Guthrie, a bright lawyer of patrician manner who acquired sure knowledge of any topic that engaged him, inherited his political gene from an uncle who'd served in Prime Minister Bennett's Conservative government. McMurtry was a lawyer, artist, and front-line worker for people's equality and dignity, a former football player who remained athletic. Vernon was a partner in the prestigious McCarthy law firm and enjoyed a deserved reputation as one of the PC Party's most reliable and productive fundraisers. DeGeer, an investment dealer who chaired Toronto's Junior Board of Trade, was ambitious to get into politics, liking policy but also excelling as a hands-on event organizer of Grey Cup parades and international conferences. Weed owned and operated a collection agency and, carrying his no-nonsense ways into politics, was a veteran trench worker for the Tories, adept at getting results, especially when he did not have to explain how he'd achieved them.

The Spades met, usually at the Albany Club but also in their private homes, whenever Dalton needed a sounding board for an idea or tactical action for a political manoeuvre. They frequently discussed how he should proceed, using his role as party president, to braid John Diefenbaker without damaging his own eventual run for the leadership. Camp also consulted individual Spades about specific projects.

As a group, the Spades planned in detail everything for the crucial 1966 annual meeting showdown, which, DeGeer noted, included organizing attendance, debating changes to the party constitution, running candidates for the party's offices, and recruiting pro-Camp voting delegates in ridings across the country.

They believed history was on their side, seeing John Diefenbaker, as Bark put it, "increasingly anachronistic and authoritarian." With their Ace as national president, the Spades wielded considerable influence and unseen power in the Progressive Conservative Party.

———

Roy McMurtry, among the Albany Club members hearing "Camp's principled eloquence" at the May dinner earlier that year, knew many in the party "would regard his challenge as disloyal and unacceptable." He feared the speech "might affect Camp's political future," tacitly understood to include becoming leader himself. Even so, Roy undertook to support Dalton, alongside the other Spades, "in his battle to establish the democratic principle of leadership review."

As the PC general meeting approached, bringing closer its challenge to Diefenbaker in the form of Camp standing for re-election as president, McMurtry and his friend and mentor Arthur Maloney, a former PC MP and leading criminal lawyer, discussed the leadership conundrum. Maloney was not one of The Chief's most ardent supporters, though McMurtry "detected that he was uncomfortable with the growing challenges to Diefenbaker's leadership." Arthur contended a leader should be able to choose his own time of departure. Roy countered, in a jocular manner to render his serious point to the devout Catholic less confrontational, "The leader should not enjoy papal-like prerogatives."

A few weeks later, McMurtry took a phone call that stunned him. "Brother McMurtry, get out the Maloney signs. I'm going to challenge Dalton Camp for the presidency of the federal PC Party."

Arthur Maloney's candidacy was an inspired stroke by the Diefenbaker forces. He'd distinguished himself in difficult cases for hard-pressed clients. As a member of Parliament from 1957 to 1962, he had impeccable Tory credentials, and worked with Dief on the Bill of Rights. Maloney was well-known and broadly respected by members of the press. And as an enthusiastic and successful campaigner, Maloney was better than reticent Dalton at meeting and greeting others.

His surprise entry into this high-stakes battle caused consternation for many Tories, including McMurtry and Brian Mulroney: each supporting Dalton Camp on leadership review, yet both devoted friends of Maloney, who had been their inspiration as young lawyers.

———

Nobody expected a national meeting electing the president, a proxy fight over continuance of John Diefenbaker as leader, to be pleasant.

Arthur Maloney, leading criminal lawyer and Progressive Conservative MP from 1957 to 1962, waves to delegates at the confrontational 1966 annual general meeting in Ottawa while shaking hands with Party president Dalton Camp, whom he's challenging. A vote for Maloney was support for Dief; for Camp, an endorsement of "leadership review."

Grown men, who had public careers as MPs only because they'd been carried into office by The Chief, openly wept at the prospect of him going down. They would do anything, and everything, to keep him. Yet others were possessed of steely resolve that he must depart. MP Gordon Fairweather of New Brunswick contended that, for the sake of overriding national interest, Diefenbaker must never again be prime minister, "even if removing him required destroying the party."

Knowing fireworks would explode in Ottawa's Château Laurier Hotel at the November meeting, the Spades prepared to limit the damage.

The issue of a secret ballot would be central to the showdown. While many PCs had strong feelings about Diefenbaker's leadership and roared like bears about it in private, they'd clam up in the presence of other party members who might not share their views.

Already the party's national executive had divided sharply, in several meetings, with angry disagreement over holding a secret vote on matters pertaining to John Diefenbaker, leadership review, or the calling of a convention. Whenever one section of the party mounted a challenge, The Chief's loyalists promptly engineered an offset response in another section.

As each side's move in one venue was countered by another elsewhere, the inconclusive political chess match dragged on, wearing people's patience thin, boring and annoying the public. Reporters spread "news" of the latest move. Pieces fell, but the end-game never came. November's meeting was intended to change that, but required strategic sequencing of the meeting's events, from when Diefenbaker would address the gathering in relation to the vote for president, to when secret voting by delegates would occur and the real showdown take place.

Because "leadership review" had become a euphemism for the leadership convention to replace Dief, his loyalists would insist any motion on the subject be decided by open vote, not secret ballot, believing they could publicly intimidate enough delegates to defeat it.

But once Dalton knew he would be challenged for the presidency by Maloney, he realized the all-important secrecy in voting could be achieved by shifting to his backup plan: unequivocally staking his own candidacy on leadership review. Because contested elections were always held by secret ballot, this would circumvent any need to get agreement for a secret ballot on a direct confidence motion about Dief as leader. Voting for Camp, not by a public show of hands but through the privacy of one's marked ballot, would be endorsement for a leadership convention. It seemed, nodded Hal Jackman approvingly in his diary, "a good strategy," the deft sort of manoeuvre one expected of Dalton.

Camp remembered, as Diefenbaker's Maritimes advance man for the 1957 leader's tour, how The Chief insisted nobody speak after he'd finished, so the impact of his message would be strong, the last thing people remembered. The sequence of events at the Château, the timing of Dief's speech in relation to voting, was crucial. Because the national executive controlled the meeting's agenda, Dalton knew that before there was any showdown on the floor with delegates, one had to take place in the boardroom with party officers. It did. A change in the order of proceedings was orchestrated, ensuring that Dief would be unable to unduly sway delegates just prior to voting.

———

Dalton's campaign for re-election was entrusted to Norman.

None of the Spades wanted big "demonstrations" at the meeting, fearing such shows could escalate the event from an orderly meeting to elect officers and approve an eventual leadership convention into something resembling a leadership race itself. Having floor demonstrations to sway delegates would telescope the two events, complicating an already complex matter. But others, believing in the importance of demonstrations to move people in their moment of decision, did not agree.

Hal Jackman, an active player as candidate, participant in the Fredericton Conference, financial contributor, fundraiser, and leading light at the Albany Club, had campaigned hard as the PC candidate for Rosedale riding in 1963, and again in 1965, despite his increasing determination to oust Dief. He now teamed with Alex McBain, chief coordinator of federal PC fundraising in Ontario, and prominent Toronto barrister Joe Sedgewick, "to pay for the travelling expenses of student and YPC members of the national executive who could not otherwise afford to attend the 1966 meeting and register their vote against The Chief."

As the showdown approached, Jackman remained anxious about the vote and met on November 6 with Camp to review detailed plans. That night he wrote in his diary that Dalton "seems to be light on organizers as far as the actual convention is concerned and, unless he is prepared to counter the emotional pitch which the Diefenbaker people will undoubtedly throw at him, he runs the risks of being snowed."

Hal pressed for a stronger effort, taking measures to supplement the plans of Camp and Atkins. Because he envisaged the coming event more like a leadership convention than a regular annual meeting, Jackman contacted Eddie Goodman and Del O'Brien about his desire to stage a big demonstration. Goodman, who'd chaired the national campaign in 1965, and O'Brien, president of the PC Party's youth wing, had to remain officially neutral. But, as Jackman himself noted, "their co-operation in facilitating the anti-Diefenbaker youth delegates to attend the annual meeting reflected their true feelings." The plan the three agreed to was for fifty students to be bussed in from Toronto, Trenton, and Kingston and kept on standby at Ottawa's Eastview Motel for events at the Château. "Camp and Atkins have some reservations about demonstrators, but, as I am underwriting the cost with Goodman and O'Brien's approval, there is nothing much they can say," recorded Hal. "I feel these things are very important."

————

Once Dalton and Norman realized this escalation would occur, they decided it could not be a half-measure. They made calls for more money to support and expand the effort. Three student delegates opposed to Diefenbaker would be brought to Ottawa from Saskatchewan, the leader's home province, not only for their votes but as a symbolic gesture. Norman booked a series of suites in the east wing of the Château Laurier's fifth floor from which to run Camp's re-election campaign. Every room in the hotel, and all available spaces elsewhere in the nation's capital, were filling up with Tories come to make Canadian political history.

On Monday afternoon, the day Diefenbaker was to speak, Roy McMurtry collared Brian Armstrong crossing the Château lobby. "Listen, we have a bunch of young people out in a motel in the east end of Ottawa and a couple of buses to bring them to the convention. Can you help?"

McMurtry and Armstrong took a taxi to the Eastview Motel. "We got all these young people who were YPCers and bused them downtown and got them into the front twenty rows of seats," said Armstrong. They arrived early, ahead of others delegates, who later had to take seats further back in the hall, around the walls, or at the rear entranceway. The place was so jammed many could not get into the room.

Dief's speech showed how far he and the party had drifted apart since February 1958. Then, at an emotionally charged rally in this very same hall, a thousand jubilant PC partisans gave him a twenty-minute standing ovation when, as prime minister, he'd called a general election. Now, eight years later, the room, though again filled beyond capacity, was silent as he spoke, except for interruptions of jeers, and even boos.

"Is this a Conservative meeting?" demanded the old warrior, now at bay.

"Yes, yes it is!" arose strident youthful voices in reply, directly in front of him.

John Diefenbaker, who had come to the convention hall to subdue yet another wave of discontent about his leadership, stood impotent and humiliated, his head shaking uncontrollably from side to side. He had lost control of his party.

A well-orchestrated campaign that left nothing to chance had displaced voting delegates by students who remained seated when Diefenbaker made his grand entrance, and sat on their hands when he delivered lines expecting applause. Seated behind them, the majority of delegates, at least two-thirds of the total, watched the spectacle in mute apathy, on edge yet sickened by this fight.

Having failed in rallying the partisans, Diefenbaker turned to attack expressionless Dalton Camp, sitting on the stage, his arms gripped tightly around him, only feet away. Next to Camp sat Bob Stanfield, the other Tory premiers, and the senior party officials. "A leader cannot lead when he has to turn around to see who is tripping him from behind," exploded Dief, pointing his outstretched arm and boney index finger at Dalton, making perfectly clear who the villain was.

"A leader cannot lead when he has to turn around to see who is tripping him from behind," charged John Diefenbaker, pointing public accusation at party president Dalton Camp, on stage at Ottawa's Château Laurier Hotel. The November 1966 drama, dubbed "the night of the knives," was a galvanizing moment in Canadian political history.

When Diefenbaker's troubling spectacle at last ended, Camp quickly sought private refuge in his fifth-floor room. "I felt sad. I wanted to get out of there. I'd never have believed it would be as bad as it was," he explained later that night to the *Toronto Telegram*'s Ottawa bureau chief, Ron Collister. Dalton lamented how costly the "shattering experience" was going to be for Progressive Conservatives. Dief's own speech, he said, had been "the turning point."

John Bassett had gone directly to his hotel room, too, after Diefenbaker spoke, to dictate the editorial for Tuesday's *Telegram*, proclaiming that the Conservative Party's "Diefenbaker Years" were over. "They ended here tonight when the former prime minister's appeal for continued support fell on deaf ears and was greeted time and again with boos and jeers."

Privately, Bassett also revised his taunting assessment, made earlier in the year, about "the Eglinton Amateurs." Seeing how Camp's forces outmanoeuvred The Chief's troops, the impressed Toronto publisher renamed them "the Eglinton Political Mafia."

———

Meanwhile, the night surged with electric viciousness.

Not one of the party's most seasoned veterans had experienced such a highly charged political meeting before. Many felt limp and hollow. Fights broke out. Diefenbaker grappled with agitated Quebec MP Heward Grafftey, who'd confronted him. Several women loyal to Dief used canes and umbrellas to batter James Johnson, the national director and Diefenbaker functionary who physically resembled his nemesis Dalton Camp.

Jack Horner and his brother, Hugh, both Alberta Tory MPs militant for Diefenbaker, roamed the Château Laurier's hallways looking for trouble in the form of Dalton Camp or anyone remotely connected with him. The Horners, hard men with an even harder edge to their defence of Dief, saw PEI Tory MP Rev. David MacDonald and threatened to knock the Camp-backer's teeth down his throat. Jack Horner took a swing at McMurtry, inspiring Roy to punch out the Albertan. Somebody landed a fist on Brian Mulroney's face and, though not breaking his jaw, bloodied his nose. A university student referring to Dief as "the old S.O.B." took a quick lesson in Tory Feuding 101, in the form of a blow to his head. The deeper wounds could not be so readily seen, nor would they heal as quickly as bruised and bloodied body parts.

Dief, outmanoeuvred and humiliated by Camp's organization, did not for an instant contemplate resigning. Instead, he stood defiantly in a corridor by the main lobby and told reporters, slightly paraphrasing the "Ballad of Sir Andrew Barton," with eyes flashing: "I am wounded, but I am not slain / I'll lay me down to bleed awhile, / then rise, and fight again."

The Chief then exited into the darkness of the November night, where wet snow on the ground was turning to slush. Fighting overwhelming odds had never daunted John Diefenbaker. Combat was his elixir. The more desperate the battle, the stronger he grew.

———

Next morning, McMurtry and Camp left the Château suite they shared with Atkins and, stepping out of the hotel for a brisk walk, hoped that exercise and fresh air might refresh them after the long night of heavy drinking, hard fighting, and deep feelings.

"What you are doing is right," Roy said about Camp's challenge to Diefenbaker's leadership. "You should have an outstanding political future. But if you are successful today, you will likely never be forgiven by the Conservative Party."

"The leadership of any great political party should be made subject to review," asserted party president Camp, addressing Progressive Conservative delegates, because "no one has a right to continue as leader indefinitely and without accountability." The backdrop sign is for his rival, former MP Arthur Maloney.

Despite delivering a speech that was far less dramatic than his opponent's, after the secret voting was over and all ballots counted, Dalton was re-elected president of the Progressive Conservative Party. His edge was narrower than expected, 566 votes to Maloney's 506. The jurors' verdict reflected the backlash from delegates saddened by Diefenbaker's shabby treatment, which Maloney brilliantly capitalized on in his speech: "When the Right Honourable John George Diefenbaker, sometime prime minister of Canada, enters a room, Arthur Maloney *stands up*!"

But with Camp reconfirmed as president, many Dief loyalists and Maloney supporters left Ottawa in disgust, or despondency, or disillusionment about party politics altogether. The more militant made a point of boycotting the rest of the proceedings. Given this change in the mix of delegates, the next agenda item, a motion to trigger a leadership convention, passed by a majority of almost a three-to-one. By secret ballot, delegates also adopted a resolution, 563 to 186 votes, expressing "wholehearted appreciation" for John Diefenbaker's "universally recognized services to the party," yet simultaneously directing the PC national executive to consult with the leader and then "call a leadership convention at a suitable time before January 1, 1968."

––––––

Dalton Camp's campaign cost between $20,000 and $22,000 and was paid by donations from a wide number of individual donors, most raised by Sinclair Stevens who'd also pulled together Camp's Eglinton campaign war-chest, and Toronto lawyer Pat Patterson, Q.C., a Spade.

They'd limited contributions to $100 from any one donor so that, if required to disclose their sources, it would be clear Camp was in nobody's pocket, and that he was certainly not a "front for Bay Street" as alleged by Dief spokesmen like Erik Nielsen. By contrast, all costs for Arthur Maloney's campaign to support Diefenbaker were paid by the PC Party itself, using funds raised from oil companies, banks, and big corporations.

"There were so many ways to win that thing, so many arguments to be made," Camp said about handling the leadership issue at the November meeting. "They just never made them." Instead, as his biographer Geoffrey Stevens quotes Camp saying, "They just had their yahoos around. They were drunk, obscene, and they offended people."

But the loyalists put their spin on events, too. A legend was born that the whole plot by Camp was engineered by James Coyne, former governor of the Bank of Canada, who'd left office under censure from the Diefenbaker government and become head of the Bank of Western Canada, in alliance with Sinclair Stevens. The loyalists took specific actions, too. Camp-supporting MPs were removed from Commons committees. A loyalty oath was circulated for all Tory MPs to sign. By the time it reached MP Heward Grafftey's small Centre Block office, it carried the signatures of most PC MPs, both the willing and the intimidated. When handed to Heward, he tore the document to shreds. Alvin Hamilton convened a policy conference of loyal Dief MPs to make his point that the annual meeting had not dealt with any policy at all. Dief and his devout loyalists would be relentless in ensuring that anyone associated politically with the fiendish traitor Camp would, henceforth, be tainted goods themselves.

———

Three weeks after the tumultuous annual meeting, back in Toronto, Spade Chad Bark and Hal Jackman discussed Camp's political future.

Bark wanted to raise a substantial fund and open a safe Tory seat for Dalton, either in rural Ontario or New Brunswick. The plan was to get Camp into the Commons where he'd be better poised to run for the leadership. Chad sought $100,000 for a substantial lump payment to entice a sitting PC member to give up his seat, salary, and pension.

In the months that followed, the project to create a by-election was aborted. The gambit proved a non-starter as 1967 progressed, because nobody could raise $100,000 for such an untoward purpose when PC fundraisers and donors were already draining themselves for the federal leadership candidates and to support Ontario's PCs for an expected provincial campaign. Moreover, back-channel soundings with top Liberals indicated they saw no benefit to them in advancing Dalton Camp's political career by calling a by-election. A deliberately vacated Tory seat could sit unoccupied a long time, damaging only the PCs. On top of all that, naked hostility to Camp in the Conservative caucus, from those who supported Dief, made the whole plan unappealing to Dalton. A by-election win would be easier to orchestrate once he was party leader.

———

Spade Ross DeGeer considered the 1966 Progressive Conservative meeting and Camp's role in it "truly a watershed for the party and its membership, since it represented the democratization of the party."

Dalton, after discussion with the Spades, understood he could no longer continue in the normal manner of president. On January 28 he met the party's executive committee and senior officers in Toronto, explaining that his "unique involvement in the matter" meant he would not chair the convention committee or proceedings at the convention itself. Next day, two co-chairs were chosen instead, lawyer Eddie Goodman and Quebec MP Roger Régimbal. Another MP, Eugène Rhéaume, was named convention executive secretary. The co-chairs met with Diefenbaker in February and settled the convention date and venue: early September 1967 at Maple Leaf Gardens.

CHAPTER 29

AMBITIONS IN PLAY

After the November showdown, John Diefenbaker remained the tenacious leader of a party adrift. He did not announce his retirement from public life. He watched for opportunities, tantalizing anxious friend and nervous foe alike about whether he might even be a candidate himself at the coming leadership convention. The Chief's most recent statement of personal ambition, after all, had been that he'd "rise and fight again."

Dalton Camp had not come this far to see Canada's Centennial Year end with John Diefenbaker still at the helm, nor had the Progressive Conservative Party. But with so many ambitions in play, anything was possible. Behind the scenes in Tory backrooms, and increasingly in public, the dance of rival ambitions became the movements of a political party in turmoil.

Davie Fulton, the former justice minister, had been well into the leadership race even before there was one, burning through money and attracting such organizers as Hal Jackman, Lowell Murray, Joe Clark, Alan Eagleson, and Brian Mulroney. Fulton was intelligent, and carried himself with the bearing of a prime minister, but expected others would devote themselves to his career and raise a lot of money to support him personally and politically.

Moreover, as Camp had witnessed firsthand, Fulton was like many urbane sophisticates, a lion adept at demeaning Dief who morphed into a lamb if he stood before him. When Davie's time had come to stand up to Dief, he'd resigned and scurried behind the Rockies to safety. Lowell Murray counselled Fulton to sidestep the Ottawa fray, which was only going to get messier, lead the defunct British Columbia PCs to power provincially, and then, as victorious hero, return in triumph when Dief was gone to claim his prize as Canada's prime minister. But Fulton led the B.C. Tories into a provincial election only to emerge with the same number of seats: zero. And he'd already run for the leadership against John Diefenbaker in 1948 and 1956, without success. In a two-way fight against Dief in 1967, if that's what it came to on the last ballot, Dalton believed he'd lose a third time.

Dalton knew George Hees would enter the fray. His ambition to lead had been apparent for years and he had major backers like Tory powerhouse Eddie Goodman and publisher John Bassett. George had boxed heavyweight, played pro football and won a Grey Cup, taken a sniper's bullet leading his men into a Second World War battle, and as Dief's trade and commerce minister, tackled his tasks with enthusiasm and performed end-runs around stubbornly entrenched Grit-sympathetic civil servants. But his shrewdness and efficiency were overshadowed by the reputation that dogged him as a man who must have sustained a permanent head injury on the playing field, spread by those who envied his millions, handsome good looks, and gregarious nature.

Moreover, as Camp had witnessed directly, Hees had criticized Dief, then led a failed Cabinet revolt, then resigned, then reconciled with Dief, then run away from Toronto where he lived to the safe Northumberland seat in eastern Ontario's Tory belt where he owned a weekend farm to get elected there as MP in 1965. Nothing in that showed leadership qualities of courageous resolve. By February 16, 1967, a month after Fulton declared, Hees opened his campaign for leader.

To Camp, neither seemed strong enough, nor sufficiently in tune with the new phase of national life Canadians had entered, to be an effective leader and eventual prime minister, or, in the shorter run, even capable of besting Diefenbaker at the Toronto convention, should the wily Chief run.

Dalton's concern about that became palpable a week later. Michael Starr, one of Diefenbaker's most loyal former ministers, announced his own candidacy on February 27. Mike had been Dief's go-between lining up Arthur Maloney to run against Camp for the party presidency. Now his candidacy for the leadership, like a perplexing wild card, convinced half the observers in the party, press, and public that that Dief *would not* be a candidate. Starr was so loyal to The Chief he'd be the last man in Canada to run against him. But the other half was just as firmly persuaded Diefenbaker *would* be a candidate. Mike, who obviously could not win, was just a stalking horse, a man whose presence on the field would reveal the state of play, keep others out, and hold a place for Dief to later occupy himself.

For the next ten weeks, no other candidates entered the race, giving Dalton nightmares about the outcome of a leadership convention he and so many others had sacrificed so much to bring about. The only three contenders were "old guard" Diefenbaker ministers, not candidates with fresh faces or new ideas to rejuvenate the Progressive Conservative Party. Dalton foresaw that if only they ran, Dief himself could be a successful candidate, beat them, retain the leader's ring, and pass in the hardest possible way the "leadership review" Camp had insisted on. What vindication for a man so often written off before!

The party's president was not alone in such fears. Many Tories reverted to form and, looking at provincial premiers to be their national saviour, saw as potential candidates Roblin in Manitoba, Robarts in Ontario, and even, as a distant third, Stanfield in Nova Scotia. Dalton decided, with stronger motives than mere due diligence, to reappraise their prospects and determine their willingness to run.

————

As the leadership race took uneasy shape, Dalton's dawning realization was that if he was ever going to become leader himself, perhaps the time for his big move was at hand. Certainly he could not remain passive. He'd seek a worthy candidate who could defeat John Diefenbaker, starting with the provincial premiers, if only to rule them out and be better certain of his own chances. Or, in the process, if he should be able to persuade one of the premiers to run, that would get him out of his current conundrum and still leave open his own turn another day. At forty-seven, he might yet have time.

The problem was that Dalton had become politically toxic.

He'd served the best interests of his country and Tories by introducing leadership accountability to a political party whose vitality was essential for Canada to function as a parliamentary democracy. Camp's "solution," the concept of leadership review by party delegates following an election the party had lost, was unprecedented in Canada. He'd invented the missing piece.

Yet Dalton was suffering from the impulse of many people to over-simplify a complex, multi-layered problem by personifying it. A wide swath of individuals and groups within the Tory Party had wanted John Diefenbaker replaced. Many ministers around Diefenbaker's Cabinet table had repeatedly plotted his removal. Men who ran party operations in the backrooms were also part of this extensive and intricate process. By 1967, however, the entire challenge to Dief's leadership had become synonymous with one man, summed up in hostile utterance of the single word: "Camp!"

His own strategy for implementing leadership review contributed directly to this tainting. As Atkins told Jackman the summer before, "It will be clear by November that a vote for Camp is a vote against Diefenbaker."

Dalton had facilitated the cult of personality around an all-too-willing John Diefenbaker, with his advertising campaign for the 1957 general election, and since then had been trying to cope with the consequences. He'd brilliantly created his own predicament.

———

To overcome this dilemma, he hoped to find a suitable candidate to become next leader of the PCs. Recruiting a premier for the job had not proven successful in the past and it was not something Dalton put much faith in now.

He saw the irony in how Tories, though making a virtue of heritage, often ignored their own history. No premier had ever become prime minister. Yet because many were importuning Robarts, Roblin, and Stanfield to take up the national leadership, Dalton would start by reconfirming their intentions. People could change their minds.

Stanfield had already quipped, when asked by reporters, that he'd no more interest in running for leader than taking up ski-jumping at his stage of life, a clear dismissal of national political ambition. Dalton knew his Nova Scotia friend was content where he was. Robarts said "no" when Camp asked him directly about it, and Dalton believed, unlike others, that when Ontario's premier said no he meant it. The premier did not speak French. He preferred being in charge of Canada's most populous province to leading the fractious Opposition in Ottawa. "I'd rather govern than be governed," he'd once said, and that is what John Robarts was happily doing.

Both premiers reinforced their irrevocable stance by calling provincial elections, conveniently renewing their provincial mandate while eliminating pressure on them to enter the federal race. In May Stanfield was handily returned to office with a big majority, forty seats to six for the Liberals, and comfortably over 50 percent in province-wide popular support. During the campaign, he'd again confirmed to opposition parties and reporters, who sought understandable reassurance on the point, that he'd stay put in Nova Scotia. Robarts, using the same expedient, even scheduled Ontario's provincial campaign to overlap the September leadership convention, with voting in October. He could hardly run for the leadership while actively seeking re-election as premier.

If one wanted a premier as national leader, this left only Roblin.

Dalton listed reasons why Duff might, in fact, be good. A western Canadian, he could hold the Prairie support that had aligned with Diefenbaker since 1958. Along a different salient, Roblin's record of support for French-speaking Canadians could be parlayed into a new West-Quebec axis of PC voter support. He had energy. He'd followed Dalton's recommendations in rebuilding the Manitoba PCs, and engaged him behind the scenes in his winning campaigns. He was experienced running a government.

Camp and Roblin enjoyed a productive relationship through campaigning, advertising, and fishing. There were other considerations, however, more personal in nature. Dalton disliked how Duff kept him out of sight and referred to non-Manitobans as "foreigners." Did Roblin's reticence to engage openly reveal a lack of courage on his part? Where had Duff been when Dalton needed public support on leadership review? Stanfield and Robarts had more or less aligned themselves, in their particular ways, with Camp.

Dalton was mulling all this over when he took a call from Roblin's senior adviser. Could he come to Winnipeg and discuss the premier's interest in the federal leadership?

On the flight west, he'd already decided to urge Roblin to run for the leadership. Talking things over with Norman en route, he decided to sweeten the deal by making the Manitoban an offer he couldn't refuse.

Although he'd come to Winnipeg at the premier's invitation, Camp was chagrined to discover they would meet, not in his office at the legislature, but at the suburban home of Wally Fox-Decent, a Roblin insider, where the premier was secreted waiting for Dalton. The rendezvous was unfolding like a clandestine meeting with a foreign agent.

Duff did not even discuss the situation; he just abruptly asked what help he could get for strategy, speeches, and campaign organization. Dalton, at least encouraged that Roblin seemed ready to run, pledged he'd provide everything a major campaign needed, short of being a speechwriter himself. Then, so determined the process of renewal not fail, he even said he'd resign as PC national president and campaign for Roblin.

Yet, instead of welcoming the offer, Dalton's "sweetener," Roblin stunned him further. He told Camp that, *if* he did run, he'd want Dief's endorsement. He even added that he believed he'd get it.

Numb, Camp stared at him in dismay. Where had Duff been? Dalton slowly extracted a cigarette and took all the time he could in lighting it, then inhaling, then exhaling, to gain composure. He quietly explained that, if this was the case, he could not himself also support Roblin.

When the perplexing session ended, an unhappy Camp returned to the International Inn where Atkins waited for news, ready to take action. It appeared, he told his brother-in-law, that the Manitoban, like the Ontarian and Nova Scotian, would not venture into federal politics.

———

Others contenders, meanwhile, had resumed jumping in.

On May 11, Senator Wallace McCutcheon, Diefenbaker's trade minister and, before that, vice-president of Canada's most powerful conglomerate, Argus Corporation, declared his candidacy.

On May 26, so did Saskatchewan MP Alvin Hamilton, Diefenbaker's agricultural minister and a vigilant combatant against the plotters trying to overthrow The Chief. As with Mike Starr, Hamilton's entry was read by many as a signal The Chief *would not* be running, while just as many saw this as confirmation he *would* and that Hamilton, alongside Starr, now made a team of stalking horses for a foxy leader resolved to somehow retain his title.

On June 7, Donald Fleming entered the race with the slogan, "Only Fleming is Ready Now!" although he did not say ready for *what*? Don had lost his bid for the leadership to Diefenbaker in 1956, and before that lost in 1948 when Tory delegates chose George Drew instead of him. Courteous, exceedingly hard working, an evangelical Christian, he'd been a solid performer in Diefenbaker's government as minister of finance. But when Cabinet split and the government fell over the nuclear weapons crisis, Flemming just stepped away, washing his hands.

With a half-dozen aspirants in the race, all of them "old guard" Diefenbaker ministers, Dalton wanted more than ever "a good cross section of candidates with some alternatives other than those persons still in Parliament."

———

Roblin had told Dalton he'd wrestle with his decision and give an answer by the end of June.

Time was getting short. Duff dithered. It began looking like Dalton would have to run for the leadership himself because no other options remained. Starting to warm to the idea, he sent word to the Spades to not commit to anyone in the leadership race, that he was expecting to support Roblin although, as Geoffrey Stevens notes, the Spades themselves "had in mind a candidate they liked far better: Dalton Camp."

Camp telephoned Flora MacDonald and requested she not take on the running of any party functions for the Toronto convention, but instead keep clear for leadership campaign action.

During June, Camp and Atkins convened the key organizers in Toronto to review their organizational status. They were in great shape, lacking only a designated candidate to make leader of the party. The enterprise could be deployed for any one of several candidates. All contingencies had been thought through and covered off for whichever one of the various candidates they'd support.

A final appeal to Stanfield seemed in order, just to reconfirm he'd not decided to take up ski jumping. When Dalton reached Nova Scotia to test the prospect, Stanfield reliably balked at becoming a candidate. He'd only move if finance minister Ike Smith replaced him, since nobody else was up to the task, but Ike was leaving public life for health reasons.

The meeting at Stanfield's home dragged on, going in circles, Stanfield's stubborn resistance only broken when Smith relented and, despite believing it a mistake, agreed to be interim premier and free Stanfield for a run for at the national leadership.

Back in his Lord Nelson hotel room, Camp phoned key Spades and Flora to say Stanfield was their candidate. He wanted Flora to come to Halifax and work with him for Stanfield's announcement. He felt an exhilarating rush. He had still not heard from Roblin, who'd only been in touch once, indirectly, just to let Dalton know he needed more time than the end of June to decide, but now promised to let him know by mid-July. Camp was glad Stanfield had committed. It was doubtful Roblin would ever know his own mind.

Next morning, still in his room, Dalton was awakened by a phone call from Stanfield. He had changed *his* mind.

There were new excuses, nothing to do with Ike Smith being unavailable, but the need to fire an alcoholic Cabinet minister, an urgent budget crisis, the need to prune his rose gardens, whatever he could think up. Stanfield suffered even more misgivings than Roblin, without even trying to calibrate, as the Manitoban was doing, the tradeoffs involved in getting controversial Camp's support.

Dalton's spirits sank. He lay quietly on the bed after recradling the phone. Some time passed. Gradually, he felt a new surge of energy come over him. He picked up the phone and called Norman.

Atkins in turn reached Flora, explaining Stanfield had backed out and she should forget about going to Halifax and come instead to Robertson's Point. "This," Norman pronounced excitedly, "has cleared the way for Dalton."

Dalton sped his car towards Robertson's Point. It was time to accept his own date with destiny.

———

With the missing candidate now supplied, Atkins at last had a top-to-bottom organization chart showing boxes with names, committee structures, and lines of reporting.

What his plan for Dalton's campaign also represented was how, since his return to Canada in 1959, Norman had amassed a depth of campaign experience working closely with his brother-in-law federally and in many provinces, seeing the big picture yet never failing to attend to telling details and keep in touch with the exceptional campaign troopers he encountered.

For this run to replace Diefenbaker, Camp and Atkins had in place a substantial national organization, superior to those of the declared candidates. Although he'd announce his resignation as president when declaring his candidacy, Dalton still effectively controlled or influenced much of the party apparatus, from the national executive on through the party's far-flung players whom he knew well. From Fredericton in 1964, to Ottawa in 1966, and now to Toronto in 1967, the blue machine's organization kept getting deeper, stronger, and more innovative.

"Norman was outstanding at putting that sort of thing together," observed fellow organizer Ross DeGeer, "developing personal relationships with people across the country, which was probably his strongest suit." With the Spades, Dalton also had a disciplined, covert cadre ready to spearhead his leadership drive.

As a leadership candidate he "was progressive, a reformer, a modern man for the new age ushered in by Centennial Year and Expo '67," said Stevens. "He connected with young people. He had ideas, and he was certainly bright enough for the job." He'd also figured out that most PC Party members at this stage embraced the progressive side of the dichotomized party, wanting fresh approaches in international relations and economic development.

At Robertson's Point over the late July weekend, joining Dalton and Linda, Norman and Anna Ruth, were Flora MacDonald and an impressive roster of other key PC politicians and party members. Dalton grinned as he looked around at the deeply loyal group, lighting a fresh cigarette while Norman pulled out more of his documents. He'd already drawn up "a battle plan."

As they talked over strategy and the rollout of the campaign, Dalton was clear that, with so many candidates in the race, nobody would have victory sewn up before the convention. The outcome would depend on ground performance in Toronto. For that, Norman unveiled his extensive organization chart with committees for reception of delegates, demonstrations, advertising, media relations, communication with other leadership campaigns, delegate management and tracking, convention floor operations, scrutineers to watch over voting, each reporting directly to him. All positions were filled by the very best operators he and Dalton had recruited during their years running campaigns. Norman explained how their candidate's every move in Toronto for convention week demanded meticulous care and timing. For two exhilarating days, the Robertson's Point planners worked through grand strategy and critical details, considering all possibilities. They felt the surge of what would be a dramatic campaign building to a crescendo at the convention.

Given everything that had happened over the past years, and all that was now at stake, Camp was ready. Linda was fully supportive. As the group wound up its session Sunday night, Flora drove into the neighbouring town of Jemseg to telephone Finlay MacDonald and make arrangements for Dalton's declaration of candidacy from his television studio in Halifax.

"My God," said MacDonald, relieved to finally have contact with the Camp group. "I've been trying to get in touch with you people all weekend, to let you know that Stanfield has changed his mind."

––––––

Bob Stanfield did not have ambition to be prime minister; he only felt duty.

While tending his roses, he'd reflected on what would happen if neither he nor Roblin ran. When he'd learned from Dalton that his fellow premier had extended his self-imposed deadline for making up his mind, Stanfield decided he'd speak directly with Duff about the leadership when the two met in early July. All premiers were to be entertained by Queen Elizabeth and Prince Philip aboard the royal yacht *Britannia* at Kingston on Lake Ontario, following the July 1 Centennial ceremonies in Ottawa. Stanfield knew he'd have opportunity to speak directly with Roblin, so each would know the other's true intentions.

The rendezvous never occurred, however. Bob stayed in Nova Scotia for the funeral of his brother Frank, who'd died on the July 1 weekend. Forced to miss the ceremonies in Ontario, Stanfield also lost his chance to discover Roblin's plans face to face. Had they met, the laconic Nova Scotian would have found the peppery Manitoban intending to enter the race, merely heeding advice from Ontario's Les Frost to enter late "for maximum impact." He never bothered to pick up the telephone and call Roblin. So much Canadian history turned on a brief conversation that never took place.

Stanfield did not want to run. Only for the sake of his province had Stanfield entered politics against all odds. Only for the sake of his country would he now do the same and stand for leader of the PCs. He harboured deep concern for the party if George Hees should win, a probable outcome in the absence of either Roblin or himself being available to the voting delegates. He felt nothing personal against Hees, just believed George not to be the calibre required for leader and prime minister. Stanfield also knew Camp well enough to understand that his own sense of duty and indeed his personal ambitions could lead him to be a candidate, and was convinced a contest in which Dalton was a candidate would split the party irreparably, and risk significant physical danger to Camp himself.

If Roblin was selfishly pondering his run in terms of Camp's involvement, wanting Dalton's considerable help yet wary lest association with the man should trash his own acceptability to Diefenbaker loyalists, Stanfield had considered Camp's new pariah-like quality from a selfless perspective.

He'd run as a duty. He'd save the party from imploding, and spare Dalton from further abrasive assault by members of their party. Stanfield saw plenty of choices, all of them bad. But after his own on, off, then on-again vacillation, he'd now quickly make public his resolve to forsake the mandate just given him by Nova Scotians, renege on his commitment to provincial voters, and venture into the federal political arena.

Why not become prime minister? Nobody had ever thought he'd even be premier.

———

The news devastated Dalton.

Excited and starting to plan the campaign, Dalton had begun to prepare his organization for take-off, only to be suddenly grounded. Linda, steadfast and proud of Dalton and his works, beside herself with anger over how her husband was being treated, disappeared into the woods for a very long time. Over the next two days, Dalton slipped into depression. He found that he could scarcely utter a word. Stanfield's reversal, he thought as he mulled over it, had thrown a huge obstacle into his plans to become leader. It would also, he realized, leave Duff Roblin on the sidelines, too.

When Stanfield sent word he expected Camp to hightail it to Halifax and draft his declaration of candidacy, it reminded his reliable speechwriter how the same man had commanded his performance at the start of the 1956 provincial election and been annoyed when Dalton failed to immediately materialize.

Camp remained quiet at Robertson's Point, wrote out some text that Flora phoned in, and stayed glum.

———

After the July 20 weekend, Norman and Flora went to Halifax to review the plan with Stanfield and his provincial organizers, only to be shocked discovering how they, still flush from their May 30 election win, intended to mount the entire national campaign themselves.

Already the problems of working with a premier were showing up: minor leaguers who thought that play in the majors would be the same. Flora succeeded in persuading Dalton to join them. In Halifax, managing to mask his sullenness, he tried to convince the Maritimers of their advantage partnering with the full-scale toughened team he and Norman already had in place in Toronto and across Canada waiting for action.

The advantage for the Stanfield campaign, Dalton emphasized, was that Toronto, where the PC convention was to be held, was also base of the Camp-Atkins organization. But the fusion of both organizations, it became clear through testy talks, would only be acceptable if there were *co-chairs* for all committees. Fortunately for Stanfield, the two halves wanting to support him had a history of collaboration. Whenever an election took place in Nova Scotia, Camp, Atkins, and crew arrived and fitted in like close cousins. When Dalton needed support in Ottawa at the 1966 annual meeting, the Nova Scotians showed up in strength and delivered.

Stanfield's compromise plan was that Camp would be in charge of overall strategy and messaging, but had to stay far out of site. The campaign structure had three parts: regional representatives organizing in all parts of Canada, a pre-convention tour group handling Stanfield's itinerary throughout the country, and the convention committee itself. Stanfield's right-hand organizer in Nova Scotia, Maurice Flemming, was campaign chairman responsible for the first, Finlay MacDonald headed the national tour, while Norman Atkins would run the third component as convention chairman.

With so many candidates, none had victory assured. The win would be fashioned on the ground in Toronto. Camp would work with Stanfield on his convention speeches while Norman took complete charge of the final week at Maple Leaf Gardens.

———

The reports Finlay, accompanying Stanfield on his tour, began telephoning to Norman did nothing to lift morale. Stanfield underwhelmed any audiences he did manage to draw. He himself made deprecating remarks about his candidacy. Those covering the various campaigns placed Stanfield fourth, after Davie Fulton, George Hees, and Duff Roblin.

That Manitoba's premier had finally entered the race further stunned Dalton. He first got word on July 26 that Roblin, without support from the Camp-Atkins organization, lacking his coveted endorsement from John Diefenbaker, and now with another premier already in the race, was still going to declare his own candidacy for the leadership anyway. It finally happened on August 3.

In the frenzied days that followed, Roblin's "abiding impression" of the leadership race was "the way in which my campaign committee organized itself out of thin air."

Camp coped with his depression as the summer progressed, his spirits lifting by re-engaging with a major campaign. He was in constant telephone contact from Robertson's Point with Norman and others, although he shared his wife still-smouldering anger at being treated like a political yoyo by both Roblin and Stanfield.

From his detached position, Dalton was intimately engaged by events that seemed a climax of his years of work with and for the Progressive Conservatives. At the convention in Toronto, he believed, Stanfield's long-shot entry had the possibility of being won on the ground. Yet the danger of Diefenbaker rupturing the party, destroying everything, continued to give him nightmares.

No matter how bad it got, Dalton knew he had to see it through to the end.

CHAPTER 30

THE REMAKING OF BOB STANFIELD

At the Westbury Hotel headquarters in Toronto, beginning Monday, August 3, Norman gathered his entire convention committee, just as he would begin each week until the convention started. Then they'd shift to daily breakfast meetings starting at 8.45 a.m. sharp.

"We had spectacular meetings," enthused Bill Saunderson. Chairing them, Norman asked each person around the table, one by one, to update everybody on how their division was progressing. "It was exciting to see such good organization. It made us feel that we could win," Saunderson said. Atkins was "teaching us how to run a campaign." He not only had clearly defined systems, but "demanded everybody do things a certain way. It was the first time I had ever seen that kind of discipline in politics, where it was run like a war — real planning, uncompromising execution."

They faced a large field of rivals, with Stanfield trailing well behind the other major contenders. Atkins stressed, "We not only have to be good at the convention, we have to be the best." He, and they, repeated "be the best" like a mantra.

———

In August, as a run-up to the convention and implementing a proposal by party president Camp, who still kept his eyes on the larger picture of fashioning a contemporary Progressive Conservative Party, a thinkers conference to discuss and frame policy statements convened at scenic Montmorency Falls, downriver from Quebec City.

Some two hundred individuals began crafting statements of principle on matters vital to Canada's future. These statements would in turn be considered at Toronto in September by four hundred policy delegates selected from every constituency, a status additional to being voting delegates at the convention. As the final step, the policy statements would be ratified by the full assembly at Maple Leaf Gardens. The PCs would not just have a new leader but a fresh approach for a revitalizing nation heading into its second century.

The Progressive Conservative "thinkers" comprised an impressive cross-section of party officials, federal and provincial elected representatives, senators, university professors, and key players from private sector organizations. Canada's French-speaking and English-speaking communities were represented by articulate, contemporary individuals. Thick binders of background readings on all topics were distributed early in the summer to all participants. The leadership candidates dropped in to make themselves part of the scene. An education minister, Ontario's Bill Davis, chaired the policy sessions.

Quebec itself was astir on the political front. Across the province, the abstract notion of political separation was becoming a specific project, dramatized by visiting French president Charles de Gaulle's provocative open support for separatism. Just as Camp had this tension-fraught subject of Quebec nationalism broached at the 1964 Fredericton Conference, the PCs at Montmorency Falls discussed ways to embrace its sobering new expression. The Montmorency Conference adopted a straightforward statement: "Canada is composed of two founding peoples (*deux nations*) with historical rights who have been joined by people from many lands."

That simple statement would have been objectionable only to Aboriginal Canadians trying to figure out where they fitted in their own country.

Montreal businessman and Union Nationale member of Quebec's legislative council Marcel Faribault said the statement was a reasonable accommodation of all interests. Pressed by a throng of journalists, Marcel did his best to coolly explain how, in the French language, the sociologist's word *nation* best expressed the contemporary reality of Quebecers. It corresponded with "people" when used in a sociological context — two peoples, *deux nations*.

At this juncture in the 1960s, English-speaking Canadians tended to view the quest of French-speaking citizens to preserve their culture and govern themselves according to the country's Constitution in one of three ways: sympathetic understanding, mute indifference, or hostile resistance. John Diefenbaker was not only in that third category, but one of its leading exponents. From Ottawa, he thundered in outrage.

Dief did not use the words "founding peoples" adopted at Montmorency, but substituted his own translation of *deux nations* as "two nations," meaning countries not peoples, deliberately changing the express wording of the statement. He then intimated that the PC Party was supporting, either through a surreptitious plot or by innocents duped by Quebec nationalists, separation of Canada into two countries. Marcel Faribault was the antithesis of a Quebec separatist. There was no "plot." But for Dief, reality was not relevant.

He was vindictive. He was scornful. He was untruthful. He played with semantics in opposing the simple Montmorency statement of conciliation and clarity because The Chief, finally, saw a glimmer of hope for himself. Still leader of the Progressive Conservative Party, he would identify himself in a new role, warning Canadians about the peril of separation, leading the country back from the brink, and identifying that national quest with the necessity of his own continued leadership.

John Diefenbaker would foment a crisis about "One Canada."

———

Stanfield, on the other hand, did not have a strong presence. Nor did he even have the sort of compelling looks that attract attention, a problem his own supporters had to contend with. Bob Stanfield was "not the most photogenic of people," one blue machine insider lamented to another. Camp himself had said, after first meeting the Nova Scotian and evaluating his attributes as a candidate, "at least he's not handsome."

But something strong had to be projected for the premier's image if he was to stand apart from, and surpass, almost a dozen other candidates in the increasingly crowded race. Atkins asked a creative artist at the agency to make a line drawing of Stanfield's face. "By using the line drawing," he said, "you could give Stanfield's character strength that did not come through in a photograph."

The result was more abstract, and dramatic, presenting not Stanfield's human limitations but his symbolic essence, the way popular posters in the '60s celebrated the *look* of Che Guevara, Marilyn Monroe, Bob Dylan, and others who personified something larger than themselves.

Bob Stanfield had been a direct, simple man who answered his own telephone in the premier's office, strolled out to meet visitors, and liked gardening "because flowers are beautiful and don't talk back." Now he was Robert L. Stanfield, whose features were as strong as rocky Nova Scotia itself. His essence distilled by abstraction, he was no longer a person but a persona, his social distance and apolitical nature no longer liabilities but qualities placing him above the jostling fray, the rare phenomenon of a true leader emerging from among the people.

The line drawing image was used for all the campaign graphics, on posters and pamphlets, buttons and bags. "At the appropriate time during the floor demonstration," beamed Ross DeGeer about the convention show he was running, "a huge banner will drop from the ceiling of the Gardens, with the Stanfield drawing on it — very dramatic!" That kind of imagery and use of graphics, an integral aspect of Atkins's plan for winning, became an essential part of the blue machine's complete make-over of Bob Stanfield.

The machinists, knowing that political events do not unfold like a natural blossoming flower on a woodland hillside, but are the product of deliberate grafting and forced growth in a hothouse atmosphere, were planning to seize the high ground and convert their improbable candidate into a front runner in a variety of ways.

Camp, whose strategy proceeded from his belief that the convention had to be won in Toronto, insisted Nova Scotia and other pro-Stanfield Maritime delegates arrive early and register right away, to have plenty of dedicated workers in play from the outset. Supplementing these focused forces were knowledgeable locals, Atkins's "Eglinton Mafia." When delegates began arriving at Toronto's downtown hotels, they landed unmistakeably on Stanfield turf.

Other campaigns had noted the convention's starting date, so their teams could start putting up signs then. But by the time volunteers for Hees, Fulton, Roblin, and Fleming appeared at the Royal York and other convention venues, they encountered a profusion of Stanfield posters and signs. There was little space, if any, for them to affix their slogans, banners, and candidate photos. Certainly, all the best spots, with long sight-lines and good elevation above the crowds, were taken. It was a clever blow, making these supporters feel behind even before things got started.

This opening psychological victory was then followed by triumph over the competition in another dimension. All lobbies and corridors of the convention hotels were populated with delegates committed to Stanfield who, after checking in early and being issued Stanfield buttons, had been requested, on Atkins's instructions, to cluster around any television cameras they saw.

Reporters with the national TV networks, incorporating interviews of voting delegates in their early convention coverage, revealed from day one that Robert Stanfield had overwhelming support. Voting delegates were the ones who mattered, after all, and they preponderantly supported him. It was as if the reporters had tapped into an undiscovered groundswell.

This was real news. It quickly spread with its own momentum. The Nova Scotian was the powerhouse candidate nobody had previously realized.

———

At the first convention campaign meeting Atkins convened in Toronto, he took up Ross DeGeer on his offer "to bring some people together to run the floor demonstrations at Maple Leaf Gardens."

Able to draw on his extensive network in the Toronto Junior Board of Trade, DeGeer had readily available a group of some three hundred young Toronto businessmen and entrepreneurs. This potent force of energetic, talented individuals in their late twenties and early thirties was ready, willing, and exceedingly able. Looking for new adventure, they were a campaign organizer's dream.

DeGeer was responsible, too, for a huge competitive advantage he and Atkins quickly added to the Stanfield campaign. Ross, just returned from a Junior Chamber of Commerce convention in the United States, had been awed by "the effective use of telephones on the floor of the convention and in delegate tracking."

He and Atkins acquired the new technology for their operations. This, said DeGeer, "gave us a leg up because we could follow the activities of certain key opponents and their staff and their supporters and flag that information immediately back to Atkins and Camp and others who needed to know." The Stanfield campaign not only made unprecedented use of two-way telephones at the Gardens, but applied this innovation "to every aspect of the campaign."

Nothing was left to chance when it came to communications. Norman's emphasis, in every campaign, was "people and communication."

Stanfield organizers were issued light-blue jackets, making them readily identifiable to each other across a crowded room, on the street, and in the Gardens. This further intimidated the competition, who saw a couple of hundred such blue-clad individuals sprinkled everywhere, passing information and instructions to one other by mobile telephones; they realized, yet again, that they were up against superior force. By the same token, as the former soldier Atkins understood, members of his political machine wearing their pale-blue uniforms became united in bond of identity and elevated in status. The women were also issued black top hats, which Norman felt added panache and helped shorter females stand out more readily in the crowds.

A campaign song was written and performed in many venues; fitted to the well-known tune "This Land is Our Land," the lyrics extolled "Stanfield, the man with the winning way." A press trailer was set up at the northwest entrance to the Gardens; manned by press-savvy spokespersons it provided reporters any information they wanted about Stanfield or his campaign, morning, afternoon, and evening. A lively tabloid newspaper was also published every night of the convention by the Stanfield team. It was filled with engaging pictures taken by a team of four photographers, news written by three reporters, all edited by Jack Wilcox and printed at 4:00 a.m. in Brampton and distributed by 7:30 a.m. under the doors of delegates in all twenty-four hotels where they were staying. Everyone would see the PC event through Stanfield eyes and understand the week's complex activities according to pro-Stanfield interpretations.

Even "spontaneous" activities — a placard-waving demonstration, a cluster of delegates in a hotel lobby breaking into the Stanfield song, a throng forming around Bob and Mary Stanfield as they moved from one place to another — were planned in detail, in advance. Every hour of each day was accounted for with purposeful performance by the Stanfield organization, but reviewed daily to be changed as required in response to new circumstances.

The four main hotels — the Royal York, King Eddie, Lord Simcoe, and Westbury — had popular Stanfield "hospitality suites," manned by Stanfield-voting delegates as greeters who pushed their candidate in friendly ways and offered an extensive bar, food, and non-alcoholic beverages. These busy venues were closed whenever official convention proceedings got underway, to ensure

Stanfield's campaign was never blamed for keeping delegates from formal sessions of important business.

Selling Bob Stanfield was the business at hand, because the Nova Scotia premier stood third, perhaps fourth. The large squadron of pro-Stanfield delegates, circulating to woo undecided voters and calmly seek the eventual support of delegates committed to other candidates, were under strict orders from Atkins, relayed from Dalton, to remain low-key. They must only talk up Stanfield's personal qualities and his track record as a winner. The Maritimers were, as reporter Fraser Kelly noted, "infectious and convincing persuaders" when talking about the worth of Bob Stanfield, true believers in "his sincerity and political integrity."

There was to be no pressure, though. There would be no mention of another delegate's candidate being eliminated as the rounds of balloting advanced. Stanfield was just to be the respectable, easy choice when the time came.

———

The most important communication of all would be Stanfield's own.

By the summer of 1967, Bob Stanfield and Dalton Camp had honed their speechwriting regime to a high art that essentially had two dimensions. First was their shared outlook on most major issues: the legitimate aspirations of French-speaking Canadians, the need for governments to take an active role in economic development, the scandal of people lacking work and money in a prosperous country. The second was Stanfield's ready acknowledgement that Camp could express ideas with a potency he was incapable of, balanced by Dalton's knowledge that craggy, unemotional Bob could convey his words with a public authority he lacked. An odd couple, they were ideally matched.

Camp, ruefully accepting his status as a villain nobody wanted to be seen with, continued operating through the summer from Robertson's Point, a setting conducive to the personal restoration he needed anyway. In addition to the strategy and plans he and Norman discussed daily by telephone, Dalton's main role would be to write speeches for Stanfield that set him apart by catapulting him to the forefront as the only candidate with a true leader's vision for the country's future.

Camp's apparent recovery from his deep emotional bruising took the form of sublimating his own quest for the PC leadership into Stanfield's. He had, after all, made a sustained effort to persuade the premier to run, despite knowing he felt uncomfortable at the prospect. And Stanfield's heart-wrenching change of mind, in some measure, turned on what could happen to the national PCs, and hence the country, if Dalton ran: at best becoming leader of an irreparably divided party, at worst dividing the party while becoming more politically crippled himself in the process, perhaps even being physically harmed because feelings against him were so intense. Dalton got this. He'd do his uttermost to help Stanfield, despite his unresolved deeper emotions. Writing some of the best speeches of his life, Dalton would now gift his candidate with the words he'd have spoken himself, had he been the one at the podium.

Because Atkins insisted on complete, accurate, and timely information about *everything*, he learned, as soon as it had been decided, that an opening evening in the convention would feature policy presentations by each candidate to the four hundred policy delegates. Dalton was informed, and began preliminary work on a concise, hard-hitting, forward-looking outline of Robert Stanfield's political philosophy, policies, and programs.

When Roy McMurtry observed that "Stanfield was clearly not prepared for the aggressive central Canada media," Norman discussed the problem with Dalton, who crafted a self-effacing and humorous speech for the candidate to deliver to a luncheon organized by the Stanfield campaign for the news corps and help win them over.

Most important of all would be the main convention speech each candidate delivered to the full assembly and a national television audience at the Gardens. For this one, Camp would expend extraordinary effort, because it also had to confront the inflammatory spectacle his nemesis John Diefenbaker was making of "two nations."

———

On Labour Day, Bob and Mary Stanfield arrived at the weekend farm of Don and Ann Guthrie, near Moonstone north of Toronto, where they were to stay for the next three nights, before heading down to the convention on September 4. The Stanfield's whereabouts was kept strictly secret, making the news media more interested and the other candidates more apprehensive.

The candidate was being refreshed, after travelling twenty-seven thousand miles to meet PC delegates all August, and getting focused on the intense week

ahead. For two days he and Mary relaxed. Then they were joined by Camp
and Atkins, who had come to prepare them for the crucial days to come, one
discussing the content of the speeches, the other the nature of the organized
events. Sunday evening and Monday morning were consumed with discussion.
Then Dalton and Norman headed south to Toronto, into the rising tempo of
the Tory convention and Atkins's third-floor suite at the Westbury, the party's
president camouflaged by sunglasses and hat.

That evening, still secluded in the suite, Camp drafted the speech, with the help,
as prearranged, of Quebec's Bernard Flynn and Queen's University political scientist George Perlin. Bernard guided the writing of the section dealing with French
Canadians, and also translated the passages Stanfield would speak in French. Next
morning, Tuesday, Camp was taken by one of the Spades unnoticed up a service elevator to Stanfield's sixth-floor suite at the Royal York, where the two men
revised the text. After those changes were made, Stanfield again tweaked a few
words, marking the pages on his hotel room's small desk with his fountain pen.

That evening, having rehearsed repeatedly, Stanfield went downstairs relaxed
and fully prepared. He entered, with a small entourage, the Royal York's concert
hall where a long table had been set up for the candidates to face the many rows
of seated policy delegates and some three hundred pro-Stanfield supporters
whom Camp and Atkins had urged to arrive early and occupy all available space.
For Stanfield himself, this was the moment to make a strong first impression.

Bob edged his way along the riser behind the other candidate's chairs to
his seat. He paused to greet ebullient and well-tanned George Hees, quietly
commenting, "You look a little pale, George. Are you feeling alright?" As he
continued down the line, Hees visibly deflated.

When he passed Duff, the first time they had seen each other in months, he
first just nodded a greeting, but then added, "This is a pretty important night
for all of us, I guess." Roblin was shaken. He'd been wrongly informed by his
campaign team that he was only to make a brief opening statement, friendly
and easy, then field specific questions from the policy delegates — no sweat
because he knew his stuff. Roblin looked with alarm across the crowded rows
of delegates waiting to narrow their choices for leader, the first time they'd see
and hear the candidates in a common setting, each delivering his major policy
statement to the national PC convention. Whereas Stanfield practically knew
his thoroughly debated and well-crafted speech by heart, Roblin began hastily
scribbling a few top-of-mind notes on a pad.

PC leadership candidate George Hees, left, hears John Bassett tell him he's switching his influential support as Tory publisher of the *Toronto Telegram* to Robert Stanfield. The newspaper carried front-page editorials by Bassett that helped sway many delegates and build momentum for the blue machine's campaign to elect Nova Scotia's premier.

By the time the session was over Roblin, with his rough improvisation, had offered a bunt that rolled foul. Stanfield, with Dalton's finely honed message, had hit a homerun. Camp, enjoined to keep out of sight and unable to witness the candidate's stellar moment, happily chose instead a quiet dinner at a posh Yorkville restaurant with Linda.

The galvanizing impact of Stanfield's brief speech could not be exaggerated. Its resounding triumph made all other contenders pale in comparison, establishing him as front runner. With the heavily pro-Stanfield audience, he'd been warmly applauded when he stood to speak, been interrupted by applause throughout his brief remarks, and was the only one given a standing ovation at the end.

The media were impressed, both with his speech and the response to it.

Roblin's campaign team, which had not yet gelled, became rattled. They'd thought their main competitor was George Hees, not realizing, as the *Toronto Telegram*'s Fraser Kelly wrote, "the impressive power of the Stanfield organization." But they were beginning to appreciate, at last, the threat posed by "a supercharged, smooth-running machine with Dalton Kingsley Camp oiling the gears."

Just how smooth was demonstrated overnight. *Telegram* publisher John Bassett wrote a front-page editorial switching support from Hees to Stanfield after their policy speeches. By 7:00 a.m. next morning, Atkins's Eglinton Mafia had slipped a copy of the *Tely*'s early edition under the hotel doors of every PC delegate, in all twenty-four hotels.

Said Winnipeg South MP Bud Sherman with the Roblin campaign, "We didn't wake up in time to the fact we were working against a tremendously polished, sophisticated, intuitively intelligent organization." Privately, Sherman rued the fact the blue machine could have been backing his candidate, had Duff not dithered.

———

Stanfield's second speech, to the media, was just part of busy Wednesday's "fun day" of campaign activity, when he earned laughs with Dalton's lines at a noon-hour press luncheon consisting of cocktails, clam chowder, and conviviality.

Stanfield was at ease through Wednesday, realizing, as did Atkins and Camp, that their campaign was taking off. That night, the blue machine pulled a coup entertaining and wooing delegates by booking the Royal York's massive Canadian Room for a party that started at 10:05 p.m., just five minutes after a reception hosted by convention co-chairs Eddie Goodman and Roger Régimbal ended *at the same location*. More than two thousand delegates simply re-entered the hall for upbeat down-home music performed live by Don Messer and His Islanders, alternating with vibrant sets by the Quebec band Les Cailloux, all accompanied by free drinks instead of the one's they'd been paying a dollar for at the prior reception. Bob and Mary circulated the room twice, before the party wound up at 1:00 a.m.

———

John and Oliver Diefenbaker arrived at the Royal York Wednesday morning, September 6, and ensconced themselves in the vice-regal suite. The party's leader wasted no time creating a crisis atmosphere for the convention, commenting on "two nations" to the reporters who swarmed him.

He challenged the concept of the Montmorency policy statement, but pointedly left unclear whether he'd come to town to bust up the PC convention or be a candidate to succeed himself as leader. Thursday he'd address the convention, and the country via television, from Maple Leaf Gardens.

By Thursday, the Roblin troops, noted Ron Collister of the *Telegram*, "were reeling under the impact of the Camp-Stanfield machine." They vowed to fight back with a lot of hoopla and noise. By contrast, Norman and his team decided to make Thursday "a quiet day," since a blatant Stanfield demonstration on this trying day for Dief could provoke an antagonistic response from his sympathizers, who understood that Stanfield was backed by Camp, the ultimate villain of the piece.

"The convention is essentially a serious business," said Atkins, "and that will be our theme today." Atkins felt tactically that a shift in tone would be appropriate. Intelligence reported at his breakfast session indicated that Roblin's supporters "would be trying to plan some extra demonstrations to gain back lost ground." So, Atkins decided, "a change of pace by us will confuse them."

On this day for tributes to John Diefenbaker, followed by his long-awaited speech, the Roblin forces busily stirred up all the action they could, while Stanfield and Camp stayed out of sight and quietly worked on his speech for Friday. Stanfield's main campaign activity, in accordance with this day's tactic of deliberate quietude, was to be first candidate to appear at Maple Leaf Gardens that evening, calm and dignified, and then to sit impassively for television cameras in his reserved seat, and quietly witness John Diefenbaker's performance.

When at last he spoke, The Chief took strength from the huge assembly of fifteen thousand people in the Gardens and intense heat, made hotter by glaring television lights. Whatever he said to the massed delegates would also be carried in this moment of drama to millions viewing their TV screens or tuning in on their radios. John Diefenbaker delivered one of his best addresses, almost a textbook classic. It was designed to divide the Progressive Conservative Party by asserting that its "two nations" policy would split the nation in two. "I couldn't accept any leadership that carries with it this policy that denies everything that I stood for throughout my life."

He'd said his piece, erecting "two nations" as an artificial issue. It was "the desperate attempt of an old man trying to keep from being fired," said one reporter, with bleak realism.

It might have been credible for a politician to champion "One Canada" if he evinced a sympathetic understanding about the importance to the country of Quebecers and French-speaking Canadians generally. Leading

French-Canadian nationalist Henri Bourassa, early in the twentieth century, had defined such a view of national unity when he expansively declared, "All Canada is my home," refusing to be sequestered in a cultural ghetto and rightly laying claim, as every Canadian should, to the whole country, while respecting inescapable, valuable differences between the diverse peoples who dwell in it. John Diefenbaker's "One Canada," however, did not embrace Bourassa's optimistic realism. Dief campaigned for his party's leadership in 1956, and won it by snubbing French Canadians. The following year, he campaigned in a general election, and won it by writing off Quebec as a Tory wasteland not worth the effort or expense. The year after that, fifty MPs from Quebec joined his Progressive Conservative national caucus only to find a prime minister uninterested in their talents and unresponsive to their political demands. By 1965, his own dispirited deputy leader in Quebec, Léon Balcer, asserting "the Conservative Party of John Diefenbaker has no room for French Canadians," had quit.

The early steps Diefenbaker had taken as PM, appointing Georges Vanier Canada's first French-Canadian governor general, introducing simultaneous translation in the House of Commons so French-speaking and English-speaking

For months John Diefenbaker had held his party and the country in suspense about his future, while trumping up a divisive issue about "two nations." Delivering his major address to the convention, the leader ramped up more dramatic tension but still left his options open.

representatives could understand one another, and printing bilingual family allowance cheques were constructive, for their times, though limited. Even these initiatives were politically nullified by the overarching battle he'd begun to wage: rallying those mutely indifferent or hostile to French-speaking Canadians, fomenting a fearsome political storm among their English-speaking compatriots by fabricating a shoddy issue out of his politically mischievous linguistic distinction.

John Diefenbaker's attack on "two nations," when coupled with his lofty-sounding appeal for "One Canada," especially in Centennial Year, imparted specious nobility to old bigotries. But it was his best shot, as he imagined the scenario, for remaining party leader and returning to the prime minister's office.

John and Olive Diefenbaker at the Gardens in September 1967, with convention co-chair Eddie Goodman guiding them unhappily off stage. Behind Olive is Ontario premier John Robarts, holding his hands but not applauding, and behind him, former premier and prior national leader George Drew, looking on with his hands at his side. The arena was jammed with delegates, Tory observers, and news media perplexed about Dief's next play.

The next day, just moments before the 10:00 a.m. Friday deadline for filing candidate nominations, television personality Joel Aldred, who'd been working in support of Dief, rushed with the signed papers and presented them to Lincoln Alexander, the convention's chief election officer.

The unyielding Chief was a candidate for his own job.

————

For the crucial floor events at the Gardens, DeGeer had pulled together "a very powerful organization," whose core group included Bill McAleer, Hal Huff, Gordon Petursson, and Tom MacMillan.

Stanfield's campaign was the only one with phone communication. Roblin's "thin air" campaign, like the others, hadn't acquired such capability. Fulton's campaign had specifically rejected new technology for networking, instead relying on floor workers' personal contact, Lowell Murray having ruled against walkie-talkies because "they could be jammed."

The DeGeer-Atkins mobile communication system had facilitated a precision arrival of Bob and Mary Stanfield at the Gardens on voting day. The couple walked up one street, with a large marching band, toward the arena at the corner of Carlton and Church; their arrival was smoothly synchronized to coincide with the arrival of a second large marching band coming along an adjacent street — each group pulling their own crowd of onlookers, both troupes meshing seamlessly into a jubilant large force heading on into the building and its waiting throng of cheering Stanfield supporters.

Meanwhile, Duff and Mary Roblin found themselves left standing in the Westbury's parking lot when their small band, on predetermined schedule but not cued for last minute changes, left while the busloads of their supporters mistakenly went directly to the Gardens. The Roblin campaign had plenty of activity, but lacked the exquisite coordination of Atkins's machine.

In the Gardens, the Stanfield team's competitive advantage included the two telephone-type lines, installed by advanced-electronics technician Jim Pearce. DeGeer ascended to Foster Hewitt's broadcasting gondola, high above the Garden's floor. Holding a pair of binoculars to his eyes with his left hand while speaking into his mobile phone in his right, he was able to transmit intelligence instantly to eight key operatives at four locations around the voting section. A second high-altitude spotter in the press box added to this flow

Roy McMurtry, equipped with the blue machine's two-way communications gear, and Norman Atkins, wearing a rose, are ready for action on the convention floor at Maple Leaf Gardens. All the Spades had key roles in the campaign to make distant-choice Stanfield the new PC leader.

of timely updates on the movement of key personnel from all campaigns, critical when candidates were defeated and their delegates came free to vote for Stanfield. Stanfield poll chairmen wore black top hats with large white numbers, on top and four sides, so the spotters could direct the Stanfield floor men with headsets to relay information to one or another of them specifically. These phone lines also connected to Stanfield's private room at the Gardens, where Flora MacDonald received calls, screened info, and via her "hot line" relayed key updates to Dalton Camp and Finlay MacDonald in the Stanfield war room at the Westbury.

———

The party compiled lists of voting delegates and provided them to candidates, but the ability of each contender's organization to use the information varied.

For Dalton's 1965 campaign in Eglinton, Norman quickly saw the usefulness of Len Reilly's tracking system when he unveiled it and turned over his recipe boxes of index cards. The MPP's painstaking method of recording details on every voter with whom he interacted, and codes to indicate key information unique to that person, became the basis for organizing and tracking Dalton's campaign support. The same method had been adapted by Atkins and Flora MacDonald for a nationwide tracking system of PC delegates and their voting preferences, identifying undecided voters to help Stanfield workers focus attention on the most fertile possibilities for expanding his support, and also identifying which delegates were backing candidates who'd have to drop out and thus warranted special missionary attention.

Flora spent the summer in Halifax organizing an extensive system of file cards: one for each delegate. In September, she transported her priceless records to Toronto and, with Norman's collaboration, set up her delegate tracking system in the Westbury. As the week progressed and undecided delegates began to narrow their choices, their cards had been updated. Other campaigns marked up the original party lists as best they could, but their intelligence was haphazard and follow-up more sporadic. The delegate-tracking committee of Stanfield's team narrowed its gaze to winning the convention, one voter at a time.

A week before voting day, Flora had determined with precision at which of the twenty voting machines each of the 2,256 delegates would make their choice. Roy McMurtry, who with Parry Sound-Muskoka MP Gordon Aiken was running the extensive Stanfield floor operations, had this list days in advance. "As a result," he said, "my poll chairmen and scrutineers were able to have the best persons available at each machine to help persuade support."

———

Anyone thinking John Diefenbaker would not continue to fight, as he always had over many decades against great odds, did not know him.

A battle at the Gardens was the drama Dief craved. Since his flailing humiliation at the Château Laurier in November, he'd kept everyone on edge about his intentions. Camp was far from alone in his apprehension that The Chief would be a candidate and, somehow, remain leader. So many candidates might split the opposition to Diefenbaker and, in one of those crazy convention outcomes, allow him to hold on.

Dief's dream, fostered by advisers like Gordon Churchill and David Walker, was that on the first ballot he'd get upwards of 1,000 votes from the 2,256 delegates, a mixture of The Chief's loyalists and others wanting to express a final "thank you" with their first ballot, before getting down to selecting his successor in subsequent rounds of voting. Their fantasy was that getting close to a thousand votes could translate into a surge to return to John George Diefenbaker.

The hard edge to this plan, and Dief's justification for trying to withstand the greatest challenge any incumbent Canadian party leader had ever faced, was the anti-Quebec, anti–French-Canadian undercurrent he sought to foment, and then exploit, with his "two nations" ploy. On Friday, the crisis was escalating, but nobody knew how grave it might become.

Diefenbaker told reporters, "I remain unchanged and unswerving in my opposition to the two nations concept." Gordon Churchill stirred around, building up tensions. It was imperative, he asserted, to reject the policy committee's recommendation to adopt the two founding peoples (*deux nations*) statement, to have it "openly debated and voted on at the Gardens by the full convention," or it would provoke "the crisis to top all crises" because Diefenbaker would lead a massive walkout.

The work of politicians is to solve a crisis, and because Toronto was awash in Tory politicians, a plan to appease Diefenbaker was desperately hammered out behind closed doors. The policy would be tabled, rather than adopted. Bill Davis as policy chair, ready to address the convention about the importance of the "two founding peoples (*deux nations*)" statement, had to delete those paragraphs and use his ten minutes to say, essentially, nothing.

With Dief appeased, the convention could get on with the candidate's final speeches. Roblin was convinced The Chief would make a short speech then withdraw as a candidate. He tried to bet on it with reporters.

———

In his convention address at the Gardens, Stanfield said English Canadians must accept that French-speaking Canadians "have the right to enjoy their cultural and linguistic distinctiveness. This right was clearly accepted by the founding fathers as a basic principle of Confederation," he continued, "and it is our responsibility to see that it is given meaningful expression."

Behind that reference to a principle of Confederation, which resonated profoundly in the year when Canada was celebrating its hundredth anniversary, was the fact that during the Second World War the Government of Canada had temporarily, as part of the war effort, entered provincial jurisdictions of authority and acquired provincial fields of taxation. After the war, the new sense of nationhood across English-speaking Canada did not impel a return to the earlier state of affairs. Indeed, the governments of English-speaking provinces agreeably acquiesced in Ottawa's drive to expand its programs and introduce new services in fields of provincial jurisdiction. Quebec's government stood apart, resisting federal intrusions into its areas of responsibility. The "new demands" of Quebec nationalists in the 1960s were the most conservative of voices in the land, insisting that Ottawa respect the Constitution of 1867.

That is what Stanfield understood and sympathized with, as did Camp. It was what Dief misconstrued and opposed.

John Diefenbaker sought to convey his special affinity with Canada's first prime minister, John A. Macdonald. But the links were more coincidental than substantial. On fundamentals of nationhood, Dief never adhered to Macdonald's teaching about, or shared his sympathetic understanding of, French Canadians. "Treat the French Canadians as a nation," Macdonald preached in 1856, enunciating his core principle, "and they will act as a free people generally do, generously." Macdonald knew harmony between French- and English-speaking Canadians was vital for everything else, from constitutional stability to political success of nationhood. He believed building a strong Canadian "nation" while simultaneously treating French Canadians as a "nation" did not create a conundrum, the way Dief pretended, because Canada's Constitution never required uniformity but it did protect minority rights.

The Montmorency statement, entirely consistent with Macdonald's formula for nationhood, was misconstrued by Dief, who equally ignored Sir John A.'s admonition that politics required "an utter abnegation of prejudice and personal feeling."

———

In Saturday's first round of balloting, only 271 diehards supported The Chief.

He ranked fifth, after Stanfield, Roblin, Fulton, and Hees. With the second ballot, he fell to a paltry 172 votes. Dazed by the disaster, with Olive weeping, he huddled in shock with David Walker and Gordon Churchill, then blurted, "That's it. It's over." He wanted to withdraw, but by now the third ballot was underway, in which his support dropped to 114 votes.

The leader's humiliation, devastating in scope, provided a precise measure of the large bubble of unreality in which the former prime minister had been living. Dalton's earlier memos and conversations with him, diplomatically aimed at guiding the old man to accept that it was time to depart with dignity, had never worked. When it had dawned on Camp that the leader would never step down peacefully of his own volition, he'd shifted, in light of his larger responsibility to the party as its president, to press for leadership review, which had brought them inexorably to this September showdown in a hockey arena.

In the important opening round of balloting, when relative positions were established, Stanfield gained the advantage because Diefenbaker's candidacy drained votes from Roblin. His 519 votes placed him measurably ahead of Duff's 347, while the Manitoban and Davie Fulton were in a virtual toss-up for crucial second spot. The British Columbian was chagrined, after his long and costly campaign, to land just five votes behind late-starter Roblin. Those close to him saw Fulton's face turn white.

Of the other major contenders, George Hees stood fourth with 295 votes. As the rounds of voting continued, and the lowest candidates dropped out, Stanfield stayed ahead. Once Dief was out, with his prominent supporters Gordon Churchill, David Walker, and Joel Aldred moving over to visibly support Roblin against Camp-backed Stanfield, Roblin closed the gap, with just ninety-four votes separating the two premiers. Fulton's and Alvin Hamilton's delegates would now be forced to choose one of them. Both were western Canadians, and their delegate base might reasonably be expected to have greater affinity with Roblin.

But back in July, when the field of candidates was shaping up, Camp had concluded that though Fulton could not win he would be a significant player in the end-game. A key part of his campaign strategy, as a result, had been to patiently woo British Columbia delegates. He dispatched J. Patrick Nowlan, son of George and now a PC MP from Nova Scotia, to the West Coast to spend weeks quietly attracting support for Stanfield. It was an inspired choice, because Patrick had lived in British Columbia, practising law, running as a provincial PC candidate for Fulton, and establishing a network of Tory friends. At the convention, McMurtry remained in close contact with Fulton organizer Brian Mulroney. Outreach to those around Fulton also included organizers Joe Clark and Lowell Murray. With constant attention from Atkins, an understanding had been established that, if Fulton couldn't win, he'd come to Stanfield.

Stanfield, Nova Scotia's taciturn premier, when announced as winner of the PC leadership convention, raises his eyebrows in a slight expression of surprised apprehension. The deluge of balloons offered an apt touch to the blue machine's remarkable campaign.

Back in his Royal York Hotel room after being elected Progressive Conservative national leader, Robert Stanfield had a caller sometime after 2:00 a.m. Dalton Camp, who'd been kept in hiding, arrived via a service elevator to congratulate Stanfield and heave a sigh of relief over the outcome.

Yet when Davie was forced out and the final ballot loomed, he was too dispirited to make the traditional walk over to Stanfield. After conferring with his top organizers while Duff and his key political assistant, Joe Martin, waited nearby to meet with him, Fulton said he would personally support Stanfield but freed his delegates to go where they wished.

Alvin Hamilton chose to not openly support either man.

All the while, Stanfield's floor workers had been seeking out Fulton delegates and handing them Stanfield badges. The space between the seats for Fulton and Stanfield was jammed with swarming delegates and pressing reporters. McMurtry relayed the message that Fulton would support Stanfield, but he'd have to come to him. Walking the fifty feet to Fulton's box, Stanfield raised his hand, claimed his delegates, and got 54 percent of the votes on the final ballot to Duff's 46 percent, a ballot count of 1,150 to 969.

The Conservative Party had often been led by federal parliamentarians who'd become prime minister, and it had twice been led by premiers whom national victory eluded. Now, for a third time, the Tories had chosen a provincial politician, thanks to a come-from-behind campaign that astonished just about everyone.

Back at his Royal York suite in the wee hours of the morning, sitting on a sofa in shirt sleeves and sock feet talking over his win, Stanfield heard a knock on his door. Looking up, he saw coming in the man who'd orchestrated his campaign from Robertson's Point, a farm at Moonstone, and a room in the Westbury Hotel.

Stanfield rose and in two strides was shaking Dalton's hand.

"Congratulations," beamed his strategist and speechwriter. "It was great!"

CHAPTER 31

POLITICAL TRANSITIONS

Bob Stanfield, Dalton Camp, Norman Atkins, and countless other politically active Canadians had landed in unfamiliar territory. What came next was a period of transition.

First, three elections quickly engaged some Progressive Conservatives. New Brunswick's PCs, led by Charlie Van Horne, gained more seats on October 13 but the Liberals still held onto government. Ontario's PCs fought the election John Robarts had instituted to sidestep the federal leadership race and, despite drifting unfocused through a campaign lacking a defining issue, were re-elected on October 17. The third vote, in November, was a federal by-election in Nova Scotia's Colchester-Hants riding, enabling the new PC leader to enter the Commons. Dalton and Norman engaged in none of these contests. They were not supporters of Van Horne, the blue machine remained locked out of Ontario campaigns, and Stanfield's by-election required no effort on their part.

In Ottawa, the transitions were anything but smooth. The new Opposition leader kept Diefenbaker's staff but, for comfort, added as principal secretary Lowell Murray — a fellow Nova Scotian, who'd run unsuccessfully, despite a province-wide PC victory, in the 1960 Nova Scotia election, and who'd since been helping Davie Fulton lose elections. In his maiden speech to the Commons, Stanfield boldly moved a vote of no confidence in the Pearson government, the gambit's effectiveness nullified when he couldn't even vote on his own motion because he'd ineptly agreed to be "paired" with the absent prime minister. Who, insiders asked, was advising him?

The PC leadership change triggered, in turn, a Liberal shift. Prime Minister Pearson watched 1967 close out with his nemesis, John Diefenbaker, no longer leading the Tories, and on December 14 announced he'd retire in April, asking the Liberal Party to hold a convention to choose his successor. The PM and chief Grit organizer Keith Davey hoped a convention could boost the Liberals, now trailing the Stanfield-led PCs in public opinion. Camp ran through the permutations, imagining an election that pitted Stanfield against Paul Martin, Mitchell Sharp, Paul Hellyer, Eric Kierans, or, if the Liberals alternated according to party practice, either Jean Marchand or Gérard Pelletier. Against any of them, he envisaged a Stanfield win.

The PC caucus wanted to give their new leader a win also, and Mike Starr, House leader for the Tories, saw an opening in mid-February. The prime minister was vacationing in the Caribbean, Cabinet ministers in the running to replace him were away from Ottawa campaigning, and third reading of an Income Tax Act amendment was coming to a vote. If the government could be defeated on a tax measure, it would be deemed to have lost the confidence of the Commons and be forced to resign. The governor general would either have to ask Stanfield to form a government or dissolve Parliament for a general election with Pearson still leading the Grits. Either way, the Tories would be sitting pretty.

Starr surreptitiously arranged for all PC MPs to get into Ottawa and secreted them in the Parliament buildings so as not to alert the complacent Grits. One Tory MP was even transported from hospital by ambulance and smuggled in behind the curtain of the Opposition lobby. When the vote was called, the Tories entered the House in full strength. The speaker had no option but to call the vote. The government was defeated, eighty-four to eighty-two.

Mike Starr, sitting beside Stanfield, saw him "turn white" as the vote was announced and the government defeated. "That's when I knew he did not really want to be PM," said Mike in despair.

Pearson telephoned the Opposition leader from his tropical retreat, resolved to avoid the constitutional requirements, save his government, and prevent the PCs from taking power. The veteran diplomat knew the first rule at a time like this: *Buy time to defuse the crisis.* He also applied a second rule: *spread some fog.* The Nobel Peace Prize–winner asked Stanfield for forty-eight hours to rush home to see what *they* should do. He cautioned Stanfield that the government's defeat would cause a run on the dollar and precipitate a financial disaster. The prime minister then had Bank of Canada governor Louis Rasminsky call Stanfield to reiterate his "sky will fall" scenario, an unprecedented step into partisan manoeuvring for a senior civil servant.

On the brink of gaining government, Stanfield allowed himself to be co-opted, and he acquiesced. Starr was furious at the new leader for letting the Grits off the hook. Many Tory MPs saw a spooked provincial politician, clearly out of his depth; he was labelled "gutless," a "jellyfish," and just plain "not a man."

After the delay, with all Liberals back in their seats, a new motion was introduced for a direct vote of confidence, which carried, keeping the PCs on the Opposition benches. The Liberals could get on with their change of leader.

On April 6, 1968, at the Ottawa Coliseum, Pierre Trudeau, who'd entered the Commons only three years before, won the leadership and, after just three days in office as prime minister, called a general election for June.

When Stanfield first won the leadership, said Ross DeGeer, "the big blue machine made a seamless transition into the national campaign, with Dalton and Norman very much involved in developing the strategy." But those had been early days, before the Liberals changed from Pearson to Trudeau.

––––––

Camp's interest in his party's leadership, or even getting into the Commons, had diminished with the emotional pummelling he'd sustained from the time of his Albany Club speech on leadership review to the principle's raw application at Maple Leaf Gardens in autumn 1967. He had no stomach to run for Parliament. Yet having been instrumental making Stanfield leader, Dalton was torn between personal impulses and a sense of duty.

Over the preceeding decade, tourism advertising work had been introducing him to places he found a salutary counterpoint to Canadian public affairs. True to form, now facing this personal crisis, he fled to the West Indies island of Antigua, where white sand beaches and beguiling blue waters offered a pacifying perspective on his troubles. Camp called Atkins and McMurtry to the Caribbean to help sort out his dilemma.

He was still president of the Progressive Conservative Party. He was credited with having helped make Stanfield leader. His ad agency had run all the publicity for Stanfield. He and Norman were largely responsible for how the public persona of the new PC leader had been imprinted on people's minds. It was credibly expected by most that this support would continue. But at the same time it was also imperative, others believed, for Dalton to recalibrate his own political career. His role in the party had altered permanently. Symbolic of this shifting ground, his home riding of Eglinton, where he'd run in 1965, had been absorbed by redistribution into surrounding electoral districts, no longer existing as a place for him to run.

McMurtry found Dalton "very pessimistic about his chance of winning in any of the available constituencies in Metropolitan Toronto, given the growing level of support for Trudeau in urban Canada." After hashing everything out with the two Spades most intimately connected to him, Camp expressed the verdict: "I cannot walk away from the fight, regardless of how slim my chances are."

The vote was set for June 25. With the Trudeau tide now flowing even stronger, Dalton's strategy was to get elected as a nationally known person in his own right, not as a PC or even a Stanfield man. He was nominated in Don Valley. His slogan on lawn signs and in brochures was DALTON CAMP: THE MAN WE NEED IN PARLIAMENT Liberal candidate Bob Kaplan was unknown, but use of an early photo of him taken with Pierre Trudeau in Africa was exotic enough for Don Valley residents to support him amidst the euphoria of Trudeaumania.

Brian Armstrong volunteered with devotion seven days a week for Camp's election. Brian had worked closely with Atkins for several years, and been initiated into the Spades early in 1968, on Norman's recommendation. Norman initially had him organizing the YPCs of Don Valley, but with volunteers being drained from Tory campaign rooms by Trudeaumania, he responded by putting Brian in charge of Camp's campaign into apartment buildings, too.

"Don Valley had a forest of apartment buildings," said Armstrong, "following a building spree that started in the mid-1950s." To reach the large number of high-rise voters, he orchestrated a "variation of the neighbourhood coffee party" with a "particular technique for campaigning in these apartment buildings." He'd book the event in the meeting room, lay on coffee and cookies or wine and cheese depending on the time of day, send in his team to canvass the building from top to bottom by sliding flyers under everyone's doors inviting them to hear Dalton speak, just an elevator ride away. Then he'd conduct the meetings, introduce Camp himself, and the candidate would make his remarks and answer questions. "We blitzed the entire riding with these meetings."

———

Norman bounced between managing Dalton's campaign in Don Valley and overseeing the national publicity he was directing out of PC campaign headquarters on Toronto's Church Street. For the 1968 election, he implemented an idea Dalton had been contemplating for some time. Both Camp and Atkins understood advertising as a business, its fee structure, and its creative communications processes, so knew how to get better results for less money. Rather than parcelling out the election advertising work to various agencies, as in the past, Norman created a secret ad hoc advertising agency to handle all aspects of the Stanfield election campaign. The consortium of exceptionally talented admen, all hand-picked, would disband once the campaign ended.

"He recruited the top people from a variety of agencies," said DeGeer, "the best people for specific roles, the first time this had been done." This saved the 15 percent commission paid to agencies for placing ads, a significant saving on all television, radio, newspaper, billboard, and magazine placements, which meant extra money to plough back into more advertising. As the campaign developed, this secret advertising unit received analysis of polling research, planned the "party line" on issues, and developed messages. Atkins, DeGeer, and others would review the material, merging the roles of client and focus group.

The television ads were always key. In one of the early PC free-time TV messages, Bob Stanfield's voice was heard over the images. Screening it, DeGeer hesitated. Something struck him as wrong. "It is in black and white," he said.

"You are quite right," one of the advertising specialists finally said, after a deathly hush. "We have to go to colour." The PC campaign changed the look of its commercials.

Normally, such improvements in details would, cumulatively, give an advantage. And indeed, as the campaign progressed, for a number of reasons, the Stanfield-led PCs did narrow the gap on the Trudeau Liberals, reducing what was initially a twenty-two-point lead to a fourteen-point spread.

But the Liberals, shameless in exploiting John Diefenbaker's unrelenting roguery with "two nations," deliberately misled voters about Stanfield's position on French-Canadian aspirations, running full page ads in Alberta "The Honourable Robert Stanfield says two nations — special status." The PCs never did adopt the wording from Montmorency. Trudeau himself, though apologizing for that particular example of overreaching when called on it by Stanfield, played the same "One Canada" political card as Dief, saying with clever sophistry that he'd "put French Canadians in their place," which French-speaking people understood to mean places of power and influence, but those opposed to Quebec's aspirations took to mean he'd swat down separatists and nationalists.

By election night, the Liberals had a majority, 154 seats to 72 for the PCs. Dalton Camp lost by more than five thousand votes in Don Valley. Nationally, the party had twenty-five fewer seats under Stanfield than Diefenbaker had won three years earlier. Although city ridings did not elect PCs, Lincoln Alexander in Hamilton was an exception. Quebec, Ontario, and British Columbia were a PC wasteland as far as elected MPs was concerned, leaving only the Maritimes and Prairies with any real Tory strength. John Diefenbaker, again MP for Prince Albert, gleefully chortled, "The Conservative Party has suffered a calamitous disaster."

Dalton didn't mind his own disaster in Don Valley, which he, Norman, and Roy had anticipated, although Brian Armstrong's "political baptism" brought tears to his eyes by "driving home the reality of what electoral politics in Canada is all about." Dalton's daughter, Connie, sad for her dad as were the other Camp kids, became puzzled by his relaxed smile and "genuine relief." He evinced a happiness not seen in a long time. Linda was sad for his loss but hopeful for their gain as a couple.

Camp realized if he'd made it into the Commons he'd have been confronted by the hostility of Diefenbaker and his hardened caucus warriors. Even Stanfield himself increasingly distanced himself from Dalton, as he patiently sought to reconcile the Diefenbaker forces still dominating the party he ostensibly led.

None of the transitions, so far, had been according to anybody's established playbook.

———

After John Diefenbaker had vacated the leader's office, James Johnson was shown the door as national director at headquarters, replaced by Malcolm Wickson.

Dalton and Norman first got to know Malcolm, president of the B.C. Progressive Conservative Party, during the battle for leadership review. He shared their belief in the need for change. With the fresh-thinking Vancouver developer now at the helm of the party's national organization and relocated to Ottawa, their focus was on building a better team.

Wickson relied heavily on Atkins as they began to design an organization superior to the amalgam cobbled together for the 1968 election. The only hope, as Norman saw it, would be a campaign team able to outclass and out-perform all rivals, no matter what. They would not try to revamp a defeated Tory organization, the way the Port Hopefuls had at Winnipeg in 1942 with new policies for a platform and new name on the party. Their effort would focus exclusively on campaign organization.

They would innovate and win. They would adopt and adapt top proven methods from other disciplines and other countries. They especially looked for anything fresh from the United States because it was a convenient laboratory for new campaign methods, was more like Canada because of sharing a North American culture, and because the thinking and methodology was instinctive for Norman Atkins from New Jersey.

Atkins and Wickson vowed to create an integrated, professional operation that could drive winning elections regardless of policy or leader. The experience of getting reluctant, dour Bob Stanfield elected at Maple Leaf Gardens proved that a strong organization with a brilliant strategy could prevail. Atkins and Wickson were true believers in the potency of a sophisticated campaign machine.

———

Meanwhile, the ongoing transition required other realignments.

With his term as national president expiring with the PC annual meeting in March 1969, Dalton was more than ready for change on this front. He'd exhausted his personal influence within the Tory Party structure and, besides, was weary of internal party struggles. This did not mean the big blue machine would loosen its grip on the PC Party, however. Certainly Camp did not want to abandon the tight cross-country network he'd developed as president.

A potential replacement was Frank Moores. Elected an MP from Newfoundland in 1968, the playboy millionaire had been a supporter of leadership review in 1966 and was onside. Norman met Frank to propose he become Dalton's successor. Moores agreed to run, provided Norman conducted the campaign. Atkins was pleased to have this control, though made clear he would conduct a largely covert operation due to lingering feelings about Dalton within party ranks. He booked suites at the Château Laurier for the campaign and had all Moore's literature and signs designed at the agency in Toronto.

The PCs not only elected Moores their new president, but with support from the Camp-Atkins team, also made Spade "Pat" Patterson PC national treasurer and Winnipeg lawyer and Camp-Atkins friend Nathan Nurgitz party vice-president. These seamless moves ensured the blue machine would remain a force within the Progressive Conservative Party of Canada.

In tandem with the rippling spread of these changes, more was happening with Dalton than relinquishing the presidency. The most curious and significant part of these larger political transitions was how he began to disassociate, even while retaining an unbreakable hold over his followers.

CHAPTER 32

NORMAN ATKINS TAKES THE CONTROLS

Dalton Camp craved fewer meetings and more solitude, and resolved to experience both.

He especially wanted more time for writing. Free of party duties, he could direct his intelligent creativity into books, newspaper columns, and on-air commentaries. He might even salve his wounds from the political arena through the healing power of reinterpreting the narrative of his life. He wanted to write about public affairs "free of cant," he said, and "with candour about the lives of those seeking and exercising power" who were impacted by politics' "darker forces." A manuscript he'd begun earlier, but put aside on advice from Spades Donald Guthrie and Patrick Vernon, he now retrieved and resumed, choosing as a title *Gentlemen, Players & Politicians*. Yet his diminishing personal ambitions in politics did not mean Dalton's many other drives had died, or that his lifelong enchantment with public affairs had evaporated. There was still a future. He would transition out of the agency, just as he had left behind the presidency of the party, but ensure that his unique creation, the big blue machine, kept operating. One just never knew what might happen.

———

For so many years Dalton had delegated activities to his brother-in-law that by now it was instinctive. He'd next hand off to Norman their interlocked advertising and campaign enterprise. Norman had created neither yet had become integral to both. In the pattern of entrusting the family business to an up-and-coming younger member, Dalton made Norman president of the agency.

Acting quickly, keen to display his worthiness, he streamlined the agency's name, changing it to Camp Associates Advertising. As in musical chairs, he moved into the president's large office at the Eglinton Avenue premises while Dalton relocated to a smaller space down the hall. Dalton would still appear intermittently, for instance if needed to impress a new client, but otherwise Norman could readily keep the existing stable of clients happy, attentively maintaining the high level of service they'd come to expect.

Despite his small office, Dalton retained a big interest in the agency's wellbeing, because he still got half the profits. He'd earlier bought out Bill Kettlewell and Fred Boyer's interests, so he and Norman shared the operation 50-50, a division consistent with how the two men had come to function as one. Their different yet complementary temperaments, and their dissimilar but meshing skills, were unified in advertising work and election campaigns, embodiments of an entwined personal relationship that had endured and triumphed across forty-seven years.

––––––

Now it was like Dalton was leaving, without ever going away.

Norman felt fulfilled running the operation, handling commercial advertising accounts for an impressive roster of clients and conducting the blue machine's campaigns. Camp Associates had plenty of remunerative work that appealed to him for its diversity of contacts and broadening range of activity. He appreciated, as Dalton had, that income from commercial work enabled their political activities. If the Albany Club was unofficial head office for the Tories, the Camp agency operated like the party's permanent campaign headquarters.

Norman saw commercial campaigns and election campaigns as much the same, a generic operation. The effort to mobilize resources and to persuade gifted individuals to accomplish a goal, whether commercial or political, required meshing diverse areas of business life, government, politics, and communications with effective timing and error-free logistics. Although creativity in advertising was vital, it was just one component among many, whether the campaign was to sell Clairtone stereos or Progressive Conservative candidates. By now Norman had a well-honed approach to managing campaigns. Because they required deliberate planning and integration of so many elements, he'd begin with an approved budget and a detailed organization chart. In fact, his reliance on clearly established methods, a legacy from his days in the U.S. Army, became legendary. "Norman was big on organization, structure, and job descriptions," said Dianne Axmith, who worked with him at the agency and in political campaigns. "He lived with flow charts."

He defined "organization" simply as "people and communication." Seeking "the right people for the responsibilities" on his organization chart, he'd pick people he knew were "responsible and respected my approach to organization." After vetting volunteers with great care, he felt confident in his choices.

"I always knew if I gave them an assignment they would get it done," he said, "and I would only involve myself if they were looking for assistance or direction."

In fact, the volunteers knew Norman was incapable of restraining his curiosity about how a particular project was proceeding. "You were around Norman because he trusted you," said Tom MacMillan, "but he couldn't help himself. He would check on how things were progressing."

Because a campaign must do many things through a variety of different roles, from raising money and printing brochures to putting up signs and organizing events, it seemed as logical for Norman to have a plan of organization as for a contractor to have a blueprint for the building he was constructing.

But his chart of boxes with connecting lines, a neat graphic representation on the wall to help people conceptualize roles and relationships, was never the reality on the street. So, off the chart, Norman always kept three things in mind: the man (virtually all his campaigns were run for men), the money, and the message. The candidate might be an asset or liability, so good organizers and constituency associations had to take care recruiting a worthy standard-bearer as the face of the campaign.

The amount of money raised, and the thoughtful development of a campaign budget that prioritized allocation of funds and enforced spending controls, would directly impact what he as campaign manager could really do. So a campaign budget for Norman was not just a series of spending categories with allocated amounts, but a tool to drive performance. In this era before election finance laws imposed limits and required proper accounting, he had seen too many free-spending electoral adventures. Thus, having a strict budget, and volunteers clearly responsible for their section of it, was key to his tightly run operation.

The "message" part entailed a broad mix: compelling statements about issues of the day, visually arresting brochures and signs, slogans and songs, pins and publicity, and every other component by which the campaign would be perceived by others. The entire campaign was a medium, and the medium itself was the message.

Once Norman discovered the benefits of in-depth polling, his budget always included money for a market research firm to conduct an initial base study. Astute polling analysis would guide his campaign's overall strategy. Norman, in contrast to Dalton, studied polling data at length and valued its analysis. This helped balance what organizers believed and hoped with what those they sought to influence were actually thinking. He insisted the polling firm's principal report directly to him as campaign chairman, to the leader, and to any others the two of them designated. "This provided information to the senior people in charge," he said, "so that whatever intelligence is important for implementing the campaign can be shared."

These sophisticated private polls were not the same ones news media publicized. Norman exhorted his campaign organization to never rely on the media's opinion reports, or be influenced by them to change election strategy. He did not want his well-planned effort thrown off course. He saw thoughtful, deliberate pre-writ planning as "critical for a successful campaign." Once that plan was settled, he knew that other important elements to implement the overall strategy, such as point-of-purchase materials, logo, and music, "seemed to just fall into place for the campaign."

His campaign's secretive war room monitored what opposition parties were saying and doing, to determine if he "needed to respond to some issue that was surfacing" or that "might be important in preparation for a leadership debate." Yet, while Norman acknowledged the value of tracking activities of the opposition, he "always believed the most successful campaigns were those put together in a way that we had our own game plan and stuck to it."

———

An Atkins campaign operation required plenty of meetings. Though he'd talk at length with individuals one on one, he insisted on regular gatherings where every senior person in the campaign reported on progress.

Such frequently recurring deadlines put an onus on everyone to complete something new for their update. With each report, a sense of excitement was imparted around the table about how the larger campaign was building. The process also enabled Norman to evaluate individual and collective progress.

"While those meetings could be long and tedious," he said, "they refined the organization in preparation for the writ period" when the official campaign got underway. "At these meetings each person would describe their responsibility and how they were going to implement the work to be done, so that all other members of the committee knew what he or she was doing." Dubbing this his "shakedown" for a campaign, Atkins's goal was to "iron out all the areas of difficulty that an individual might have" and "avoid any overlap." He wanted "everybody singing from the same hymn book."

Norman devised slogans to embrace this ethos. He'd plaster headquarters with posters, hand out special campaign pins, and issue volunteers coffee mugs imprinted with the slogan "Let's have fun while getting the job done." There'd be humorous awards for offbeat campaign accomplishments. He'd ensure regular delivery of piping hot pizzas to headquarters, and host intermitent social events to maintain his team's cohesiveness for a successful campaign. He wanted all volunteers to experience his approach and "feel good about the campaign and believe their contribution truly important to the ultimate success on election day."

———

Such was the operational approach of the man now solo at the controls, but on the higher level of Norman's activities, Dalton's presence continued to be real.

For one thing, Dalton, although more in the background, remained the senior strategist, and when it came to writing speeches and pithy campaign messages, a role he continued to enjoy, nobody was his equal. For another, Dalton had been his mentor. His eclectic pattern, which encompassed most dimensions known to politics, had become the model Norman followed and applied to himself. Any differences in their ways of practising politics were due merely to dissimilarities in character, interests, and talents. Camp's entry into political life had, from the beginning, incorporated a healthy mixture of public policy and campaign strategizing. His instincts and efforts were not abstract, but practical, because he lived in and absorbed the experiences of a real world. He might one moment be advancing or criticizing specific programs, but the next, writing inspiring speeches for candidates or getting voters to the polls.

At the highest levels of electoral politics, Norman had witnessed Dalton fusing brilliant strategy, writing cogent messages, and intelligently pressing the combative edge of partisan attack. Camp kept abreast of advertising's changing nature, from his first glimpse of the business in 1948 looking over the shoulders of admen from Montreal in a Fredericton hotel suite, to his triumphant experience with Norman in the Bob Stanfield makeover of 1967.

Dalton had come to understand advertising as sophisticated social engineering. French social scientist and philosopher Jacques Ellul offered a radical interpretation of the nature and role of political propaganda, and when an English-language edition of his book appeared in 1965, Dalton devoured it. The goal of contemporary propaganda, discerned Ellul, was not to modify ideas but to provoke action, an insight Dalton had instinctively embraced for years, displayed in his first editorial advertisements in the 1952 New Brunswick election. Of abiding interest to Dalton were the writings of Vance Packard on how economic behaviour and social patterns were influenced by advertising, B.F. Skinner on his methods of conditioning human behaviour, and Marshall McLuhan on how media and humans interact in ways that transform people even though they are not aware of it.

Camp stayed in contact with political and journalist friends in the United States who were absorbing these ideas, and relished discussing the nature of campaigns of persuasion with them. Election campaigns in the United States had never been clean, but these deeper theologies of persuasion and newer practices of propaganda were now escalating fear and smear to greater prominence, aided by television.

Dalton and Norman alike monitored the distasteful effectiveness of "negative advertising" in campaigns, aimed at destroying one's rival more than promoting one's own principles and plans. Dalton mused about his sharp "editorial ads" in election campaigns, and the Duncan Macpherson political cartoons he'd initiated, seeing them as somehow part of this escalating trend from lampoon to ridicule to hard negative personal attack.

In the 1950s and 1960s, their blue machine grew ever more potent through application of new technologies to fight political rivals, the domestic political equivalent of an arms race between nations. Most of their new approaches came from the United States, not only because they were convenient imports but because Dalton and Norman, and the like-minded Canadians who gravitated into their orbit, were open to doing so. Camp and Atkins each cherished America's vibrant diversity and celebrated the country's dynamic democratic nature. That set them apart from many Conservatives whose traditional disdain for the United States and sense of "Britishness" kept them looking for inspiration to the so-called Mother Country and made them less open to American innovation.

Dalton and Norman happily accepted invitations to events in the United States from a number that country's political luminaries. Through the casual conversations these opportunities provided, they absorbed large principles and specific details about campaign developments that were proving effective in the United States. The republic next door was a convenient laboratory for experiments in political persuasion. With their open minds, free from anti-American filters, they unhesitatingly imported new U.S. practices into Canadian campaigns.

———

The reason they so complemented each other, all their lives, was that each cherished the field in which he excelled without competing against the other. The political machine they created for PC campaigns embodied their separate attributes.

Dalton was happiest waging guerrilla warfare from a cramped hotel room, chain-smoking cigarettes and gulping tar-black coffee, crouched for attack at his typewriter through the dark silence of night: a maestro's stunning solo performance. Norman thrived on meetings, drawing up and filling in organization charts, long telephone conversations, inventory control, talent scouting, order, and careful attention to all details of planning: the exemplary quartermaster of political campaigns.

Some who tried to differentiate between them focused on physical attributes, such as manner of speaking. Political observer Ron Graham, in an article for *Saturday Night*, noted how Atkins apologized to others "for not being very articulate" and admitting "that speeches, policy discussions, and big ideas" were not his strengths. Dalton, on the other hand, was a persuasive public speaker. Brian Armstrong was about to quit the PCs and join the Liberals when he heard Dalton speak, and immediately changed his mind. Roy McMurtry, who felt unease about the acrimonious and petty nature of national politics in the 1960s and had voted Liberal, heard Dalton speak in 1965 and right away volunteered to help in his election campaign. Camp exherted this same power over hundreds more, including the vast number of recruits from Toronto's Junior Board of Trade.

Norman's great ability, instead, noted the journalist, "is organization: putting together events, keeping an eye on the details, establishing contexts in which the best people available can do whatever they do best."

The more Graham sought to explain "the great symbiotic partnership" between Camp and Atkins, the more he drew heavily on characteristics extrapolated from their physical dissimilarities, almost to the point of parody: "Camp is natty in a tweed jacket and cravat. His bald head bespeaks power and intelligence. He radiates toughness and self-assurance." Then, "Next to him Atkins appears rather oafish. He's heavy and ill at ease, though there's a grace to his step that explains why the former high-school quarterback is still a terror on the tennis courts. His face is as big as a harvest moon, his three-piece suit looks more utilitarian than senatorial, and he exudes sheepishness."

Graham would continue in this vein. Norman "has a grin as wide and heartwarming as a Halloween pumpkin's, and his soft, woeful voice has a slight lisp of vulnerability." The writer invoked Nancy McLean, who'd produced TV commercials for the big blue machine, to support his psychological portrait of Atkins. She told Graham, "He's extremely sensitive and easily hurt."

———

If Dalton was an essential loner who cared little for meetings and could be ill at ease and out of sorts at social events, Norman was a social creature who thrived on getting people together and being part of a closely bonded group.

Given his nature, it seemed as if the Albany Club was a place Sir John A. Macdonald and his wily partisan organizers had created just for Norman. A convenient subway ride downtown from Eglinton Avenue, he'd be "at home" easily and often at 91 King Street East. Dalton's admission as a member began an infiltration, and then effectively a takeover, of the club by the blue machine. Although Camp remained a frequent attendee, as in other realms it was Atkins who took organizational control.

By the time the two arrived on the scene in the 1960s, the club had functioned as the out-of-Ottawa headquarters of Canada's Tories for generations, its extensive connections running from well-tended precincts in the heart of downtown Toronto to all parts of Canada. As a hub of Canadian Toryism, the country's only enduring political club played a role in Canadian public affairs much greater than most people realize. Over many decades, the Albany's members had been active in producing provincial Tory governments, sending the bulwark of Conservative MPs to Ottawa, and funding party operations across the country. Whatever the issue, no matter whose career, regardless of the year, the Albany Club threaded, as Ross DeGeer observed, "its steady blue line" through Canadian politics.

Increasingly, Dalton and Norman organized their blue machine through the club, at the club, and with members of the club. Everyone in the Albany was already Progressive Conservative, so this was like the egg and the chicken creating each other. For the quarter century between 1971 and 1996, the club's presidents included Eric Ford, Ross DeGeer, Norman Atkins, Brian Armstrong, Tom MacMillan, Bill Saunderson, Dianne Axmith, Bill McAleer, and Paul Curley, all senior blue machinists, many of them Spades. The Albany's board of directors and committees were even more generously populated with Norman's loyal allies and organizers. Unending gatherings in a building honeycombed with private meeting rooms, and a continuous parade of formal dinners in the club's grand dining room to commemorate Tory milestones and celebrate PC achievements, all acquired gravitas from the high-toned setting. The club fostered the camaraderie and communication Norman believed essential for bonding effective political campaigns and supporting friends.

The clandestine Spades were themselves a central part of the Albany Club. At intervals, a half-dozen of them held the presidency. Once a year, at Norman's instigation, the Spades would seek even greater privacy in the countryside. The retreats for this band of brothers became anticipated, one said, as "marvellous weekends away together, a group of men who loved politics, enjoyed extended philosophical discussions, lots of laughs, and sport."

By getting, dissecting, and evaluating good intelligence in this manner, the Spades decided who in the party warranted their support to advance, who should be sidelined, and where money should be seeded to ensure that "bright people" got elected, whether the office was in municipal politics or on the national executive of the Progressive Conservative Party.

Norman knew money was essential to implement actions the Spades felt desirable. They raised the cash among themselves and from an expanded trustworthy group, their discreet wealthy friends. Accountant Saunderson was treasurer, managing the Spades' bank account, keeping all financial records, and acting as lead fundraiser, ensuring plenty of oil to keep the blue machine running smoothly.

"It was money we would use to help people," he explained. "There was no tax receipting in those days." If somebody was running for office at a party annual meeting, either nationally or provincially, Norman would just say, "We are going to need some money for the annual meeting." The Spades wanted "to make sure the right people, some of the bright people, got elected. We would always cough up money for a good cause." Such backing helped Michael Meighen, grandson of Conservative prime minister Arthur Meighen, become president of the Progressive Conservative Party of Canada, and David Crombie to become mayor of Toronto, then later an MP and Cabinet minister.

For the blue machine, primarily a backroom operation, secrecy had been the order of the day ever since Dalton became master and commander, initially because admen had to operate separate from the rest of the campaign team, then because he'd become *persona non grata* within much of the Tory party when he confronted the Diefenbaker conundrum. With his understudy co-pilot Norman taking over the controls, secrecy continued to prevail, thanks to Norman's innate shyness, his military instinct to keep battle plans from the enemy, and his preference to speak through actions rather than words.

The day of campaign organizers holding press conferences had yet to arrive. Besides, in 1969 there was still too much to do in Tory campaign backrooms to become distracted.

CHAPTER 33

UPGRADING THE MACHINE

The 1968 election had left the PCs defeated, diminished, and dispirited.

Even though the upgraded political machine Norman Atkins and Malcolm Wickson were creating was intended to work regardless of party platform, the PCs' yawning policy deficit could not be ignored. Diefenbaker's focus on rearguard actions over retaining the red ensign flag and other British symbols, and his preoccupation in fighting plotters, had produced aimless drift. From 1963 to 1965, the Opposition PCs held no policy meetings to seriously address programs the party might advocate. The 1964 gathering in Fredericton had been a "useless" thinkers' conference. The 1966 annual meeting, embroiled with the leadership issue, failed to deal with any policy at all. The national convention in 1967, despite extensive efforts by two hundred people at the Montmorency Conference and by four hundred policy delegates at the Toronto convention, failed to adopt any policy statements, a consequence of the backstage deal to placate Diefenbaker's fomented crisis over "two nations." By the time Stanfield campaigned in the 1968 election, he had so little to choose from he just made up policy as he went: a tunnel to Newfoundland; tariffs to shield fruit farmers; quotas to protect vegetable producers; tax deductibility of mortgage interest payments; a guaranteed annual income, perhaps?

With parties seeking power to implement programs reflective of their political philosophy, policy conferences should be routine. Stanfield certainly thought so. He initiated a national policy conference at Niagara Falls, hoping to see a policy adopted for a guaranteed annual income. He also wanted regional policy conferences, on a regular basis.

In this period, the lack of coherent Tory policy and the predations of the Diefenbaker faction caused many individuals to give up trying to rebuild the PC campaign organization. Yet a few spirited individuals remained keen. Phillip Lind, long ardent in his Tory Party involvements, was one of them.

Attending Ridley College, a high school in St. Catharines, Ontario, Lind and another young Conservative, Bob Amaron, started a "campus" Conservative club by playing on the word *college* in their high school's name. Thus qualifying as voting delegates to a 1960s PC annual meeting in Ottawa, the young teens received their political baptism in debate about nuclear weapons for Canada's Bomarc missiles, and found the creative possibilities of politics exhilerating.

When Lind was later studying political science at the University of British Columbia, West Coast PCs were neither plentiful nor strong at either the provincial or federal level. Any enthusiastic young Tory had wide-open opportunities simply by showing up and taking a role. When Malcolm Wickson decided to seek the presidency of the provincial PCs, Phil agreed to run his campaign. The two got to know each other well, and appreciated the compatibility of their respective strengths.

On the federal side, B.C. Tories had representatives in Cabinet, with Davie Fulton the justice minister and George Pearkes in defence. Other MPs included John Fraser, in Vancouver South. Lind was drawn to the intelligence, modernity, and political attractiveness of Fulton and Fraser. He worked in Fulton's re-election campaigns and after graduating from UBC in 1966 was offered a job as Fulton's executive assistant in Ottawa. Although he thrived on politics, Lind wanted to learn more about political sociology so instead pursued a master's degree at University of Rochester in New York. His political and academic worlds again collided when he returned to Toronto in 1967 to continue studies at York University, but this time he opted to join Fulton's leadership campaign. After Stanfield won the contest, with Fulton's end-game support, the new leader asked Malcom Wickson to become national PC director, who in turn hired Lind as his special assistant in Ottawa.

Malcolm knew that Lind thrived on creative political work, and that he had as big an interest as Camp and Atkins in American politics and its constantly evolving methods. Lind's mission was to be chief Tory scout south of the border, seeking out new parts for a better blue machine.

Lind already had many connections through attending American presidential nominating conventions, and he closely followed the personalities of national and state campaigns. One of the people he'd met and befriended, Ray Bliss, was chairman of the Republican National Committee during the lean years of Lyndon Johnson's presidency, when Republicans languished in a political wilderness.

Republicans vanquished by Johnson's lopsided victory over Barry Goldwater in 1964, and Progressive Conservatives devastated by Pierre Trudeau's big win in 1968, may have shared common electoral humiliation, but they also had the same advantage: a clean slate for building a better, fully contemporary electoral organization.

Chairman Bliss had been unusually resourceful, perfecting a technique for direct mail fundraising, applying more sophisticated practices in public opinion research, and devising a simple method for developing comprehensive campaign policies. With these components, he laid the foundation for the modern Republican Party. Lind believed imitating Bliss's example would be the best way to flatter him. Atkins could not have agreed more. All Lind had to do was spend time with his boss, Wickson, sojourning around the United States soaking up ideas and deciding which ones could become components of an improved Progressive Conservative campaign machine.

Lind was on such good terms with Republican organizers that in 1968, after the election of Richard Nixon, he was invited to Washington for the inauguration. Bliss was not a Nixon man, so, despite his indispensible role building a winning campaign organization, he was about to be dispensed with. On his way out, Bliss eagerly provided Lind with his key contacts.

One was a young public opinion researcher named Robert Teeter, a principal of the Detroit-based firm Market Opinion Research. Already Teeter was on his way to becoming one of the truly respected American political pollsters, whom David Broder of the *Washington Post* would praise as "the most consistently insightful." Lind and Wickson, meeting with Teeter in Detroit, were not only surprised to see his resemblance to Norman Atkins but happy to find him keen to do a poll in Canada. The two Canadians believed Teeter held the key to a new era in Canadian political campaigning, but had no money to pay for his polling. Heading out the door, they cheerfully said they'd be back in touch to finalize arrangements.

Wickson had a developer's talent for operating with little or no money, leveraging deals using somebody else's funds. He and Lind went to see Ernie

Jackson, the Ontario PC MPP who'd become legendary as Ontario's director of political organization for Premier John Robarts, to discuss sharing the costs of a poll.

By the time of their second meeting, Robarts himself, who was pondering his political future, joined them. Recognizing his vulnerability, Lind and Wickson lathered on the persuasion and Robarts agreed to split the costs of a Teeter poll with the national PC Party. The research, to be conducted in Ontario, would ascertain what Ontarians thought about the provincial party and its leader and about the national party and the leadership of Robert Stanfield.

Few thought Robarts needed any poll to tell him it was time to pass his gavel to someone younger, leaner, and keener to be Ontario's politically engaged premier. Yet because sampling Ontarians' views helped gain the necessary money, Wickson had solemnly confided that a Teeter poll about Robarts was, well, essential.

It was the first public opinion research the PCs had conducted in a *very* long time. The national party under Dief had reverted to a pre-polling political era. But thanks to this time warp and the advances by Robert Teeter, the blue machine clicked back into the scene by leapfrogging to the latest methods in sophisticated *political* public opinion research. The Tories embraced a technique that would become the new Canadian standard for masterminding election campaigns.

Conducted in autumn 1969, the Teeter poll proved instrumental in John Robarts's decision to step down as premier. As for the federal side, the American's polling information enabled Atkins, Wickson, and Lind to calibrate a new approach for selling Bob Stanfield. All communications from the PCs would now *contrast his values* to those of Pierre Trudeau — values that the PC leader personified and that, as Ontarians told Teeter, they honoured.

The senior players in the PC Party's campaign organization were both shocked and impressed by how their new understanding invited them to translate research into campaign themes. Even though money was scarce, they resolved to keep on polling. They now saw it as indispensible. Every campaign budget Norman would henceforth draw up included, as a priority, money for polling.

———

Lind was bringing significant new components to the blue machine, with no doubt more to come, when late in 1969 he walked into Wickson's office at headquarters to resign as the national director's assistant. Ted Rogers in Toronto had made him an offer he could not refuse.

Rogers and Lind shared strong interest in Tory politics, where they'd first met as students debating on opposite sides about nuclear weapons, but the rapid evolution of communications technologies fascinated them even more. If they played it right, they could build a communications empire. Lind had agreed to spearhead Rogers' media drive into the United States.

Wickson asked Atkins's help to find a replacement. Soon Norman suggested Brian Armstrong, not only for his natural talent in organizing and running projects, shaping events, and operating with discretion in the presence of power, but because Armstrong could also pass for a "neutral," despite being close to Camp and Atkins. He'd not been at Maple Leaf Gardens nor worked in anybody's leadership campaign in 1967, since he'd instead been organizing and hosting an international conference for his fraternity.

A Spade, Armstrong became Norman's surrogate at national headquarters, abetting his surreptitious efforts to build a campaign team that might make Stanfield prime minister, even though Stanfield was giving Atkins cause to abandon the whole effort by the way he was treating Dalton. It was normal to keep campaign development from the Grits, but in this abnormal phase of the PC Party, with Stanfield unwilling to challenge the Diefenbaker faction who continued gunning for Camp and his brother-in-law, the blue machine had to keep secrets *from Tories*.

Armstrong and Atkins "worked really closely together." Whenever he went to Toronto, Brian would spend a half day at the Camp agency with Norman. After touring the facility, reviewing progress on current projects together, the two enjoyed lunch or dinner while exchanging reports and evaluating political rumours. "Although nobody else knew it," said Armstrong, "the agency was doing all of the work for the party's communications. We developed a Progressive Conservative newsmagazine. The agency did all the design work, and a lot of the editorial work, for that publication. But it was all sub rosa."

The components of the upgraded political operations for the national PCs were being patiently assembled through party headquarters in Ottawa and the Camp agency in Toronto, Norman Atkins spearheading all stages of development, Brian Armstrong working as facilitator and middleman, and Malcolm

Wickson painstakingly introducing these new techniques into the federal PC organization. Each had resolved that the next election against Trudeau's Liberals would not be a repeat of 1968.

"I went to work for Malcolm Wickson and Robert Stanfield at one of the lowest points in the history of the Progressive Conservative Party," said Armstrong. "Little did I know it was going to get even worse."

———

The PC national headquarters, relocated from Bracken House, occupied several floors of a modest office building on Queen Street, short blocks from Parliament Hill. Its skeletal staff interacted with the small staff working with the leader on Parliament Hill.

The party was deeply in debt. Money was essential to run the improving blue machine, but there was not cash enough even to maintain routine operations. With the party's national office living hand to mouth, Wickson was a magician juggling the bills, keeping the PC Party operating when it was insolvent.

The traditional methods of fundraising were being pushed to the limit. Bagmen like Patrick Vernon were joined by Jean Casselman Wadds, Bill Rowe's sister. She found it "very discouraging." Perhaps, Jean thought, the direct mail solicitations pioneered by the Republicans, which Phil Lind and Malcolm Wickson had been exploring, might be a better way to end PC poverty.

Teeter put Wickson in contact with the expert running the Republican direct mail fundraising system. By far the blue machine's best import from the United States, direct mail solicitation would, within a half-decade, prove lucrative enough for the Tories to keep their new market research system in place, make many other upgrades to the campaign machinery, and emerge as Canada's best funded political organization, one with its own "guaranteed annual income."

———

Yet, for now, the party was still broke in another way.

Stanfield desperately needed the talent of the campaign organization that first helped him become premier and later national leader, but was paralyzed in dealing with the blue machine because he lived in fear of Dief and his squad of loyal MPs who prowled daily for Camp's scent.

Paul Weed, a Spade who operated a collection agency and played politics just as hard, shakes the hand of leader Stanfield, whom he'd worked with persuasive force to elect as national leader.

From 1968 on, these backroom strains were taking their toll on the effort to build a better PC campaign organization as Wickson worked intimately with Atkins to develop an organization that could successfully fight the next federal election. This effort should have been straightforward, making best use of limited resources as everyone in the party collaborated to make Robert Stanfield Canada's prime minister.

But the relationship between Camp and Stanfield deteriorated because of the Diefenbaker maelstrom. By extension, this caused cracks in the relationship between Atkins and Stanfield.

The ghost of John Diefenbaker haunted the party still, but the problem was that Dief's was no phantom presence. The man himself lurked everywhere. He sat in a front-row Commons seat, beside Stanfield, often upstaging him. Behind them perched rows of Dief-loyal MPs.

If Bob Stanfield ever wanted to be prime minister, this was the fight he needed to take on; however, it would be several more years before his stoic patience broke. For now, he took the pacifist's path, waiting, avoiding confrontation. Rather than facing down Diefenbaker, he distanced himself from those who'd devotedly advanced his career in Nova Scotia, and still sought to do the same nationally.

———

There was another major problem to be dealt with, too: television.

The broadcasting of images had been transforming politics since the late 1950s, and unless one mastered the new medium, it could kill a campaign. Terry McCartney-Filgate, an acclaimed television producer whom Dalton introduced to improve the national campaign and upgrade Stanfield's on-camera performance, knew Stanfield not only needed him as a producer, but also as a media coach.

McCartney-Filgate worked patiently with awkward Bob Stanfield on his delivery — an embarrassing relationship, as if he was training an adult who'd never learned to articulate. He was "trying to get Mr. Stanfield to the point," said Armstrong, "where he could do a fifteen-second clip and present effectively to a camera."

While this was underway, Armstrong worked directly with Bob Teeter on the research side, to determine how best to present the PC leader, and with McCartney-Filgate on the television production side, filming shows for *The Nation's Business* on CBC that incorporated the key message.

This television upgrade initiative was vital for a successful election campaign, expected in 1972. None of the TV activity took place in the leader's parliamentary offices, but was conducted out of party headquarters. Wickson was committed to the whole program of polling, direct mail fundraising, enhancing television performance, and everything else the blue machine was creating for the campaign, but it was against his nature to bother getting approvals from "the Parliament Hill gang," as he called the leader's staff and caucus. "This way Mr. Stanfield had a little separation between what these guys from headquarters were doing with Norman Atkins," explained Armstrong. It was also another example of how the Nova Scotian distanced himself from those associated with Dalton who were trying to help him, hoping to keep peace with Diefenbaker's faction who sought his demise.

The CBC Sunday night free-time broadcast *The Nation's Business* followed the main newscast, and those who stayed tuned were avid followers of Canadian public affairs. Mostly what viewers saw, on their black-and-white screens, was a man in a suit behind a desk with a speaking text he held and read. In an era before colour, tele-prompters, or much heed for production values, Terry McCartney-Filgate changed everything he could, to the extent technology of the day allowed. The shift from black-and-white TV had begun in 1966 in Canada, but full-time colour transmission would only become universal in 1974.

Instead of using the CBC studio and doing the show live, as was the pattern, McCartney-Filgate and his crew headed out with Stanfield to film on their own, in venues Canadians could identify with. They invested time and care, editing the footage, professionally producing the five-minute segment, then handing over the completed film to the CBC producers in advance of the Sunday evening broadcast.

"I can remember driving all around, doing location shots with McCartney-Filgate for a *Nation's Business* program," said Armstrong, "and then sitting in a hotel room for the better part of a day while we did about twenty-three takes in order to get one good one from Mr. Stanfield." The PC leader stuck with it, apparently as determined as McCartney-Filgate and Armstrong to get it right. "It was hard work for us and for him, but eventually it paid off because he became much more proficient and effective at it."

Yet it was never easy. An underlying reluctance on Bob Stanfield's part to be an innovative player accentuated his natural inability to be a performer. When MP Heward Grafftey, who had travelled the country on Stanfield's behalf to deal with housing and urban affairs issues, sought to get the leader to a location in Hull and film him outlining the need for federal action against a backdrop of desperately inadequate housing where people lived in sight of Canada's Parliament buildings, the effort was akin to dragging an unwilling child to the doctor's office.

Marshall McLuhan, however, proclaimed Stanfield "cool," according to the professor's twinned categories of "cool" and "hot" to explain how a person's image projected through television. A cool person, said McLuhan, left plenty of room for a viewer to "plug in meaning" and interpret according to their own beliefs what the ill-defined individual meant or represented. Being vague, even silent, helped.

This pronouncement by Dalton's friend was greeted favourably by members of the blue machine. They interpreted it as freedom to convey, through the ill-defined or cool image of Bob Stanfield, a wide variety of messages according to what analysis of polling research indicated would connect with Canadians.

———

On the provincial level, elections continued to roll around like clockwork, with 1970 producing a trio in the Maritimes.

In Prince Edward Island, as communications and organization adviser, Norman performed a steady backroom role, in charge of campaign advertising and distribution of campaign materials. Taking a team with him to work for provincial Progressive Conservative leader George Key, they developed the slogan "Key Clicks" for the campaign. Only a few insiders knew all the PC election material was printed in Ottawa at national headquarters and shipped to Norman in Charlottetown. National director Wickson was also in PEI working with closely with Atkins, leaving Armstrong in Ottawa to coordinate production of materials, while in Toronto the Camp agency wrote all copy. On the Island, the campaign gave every appearance of being a local effort.

The election itself did not click for the Tories, however. In a two-way fight with the Liberals, the PCs lost 8 percent of their popular support from 1966 and dropped ten seats, winning only five of thirty-two. PC leader George Key did not even "click" with voters in his own riding.

Deeply discouraged, Norman fretted. "Almost no one would talk to me," he lamented. "I thought my days in politics were over."

In Nova Scotia, where people did speak to him as communications coordinator for the October 13 provincial election, Norman was local go-between for operations at campaign headquarters in Halifax and Dalton at the agency in Toronto. Just three years earlier, Stanfield's wide esteem had ensured a strong electoral mandate for the PCs, who'd taken forty seats to six for Gerald Regan's Liberals.

Despite assurances he'd remain in Nova Scotia, the premier then departed for national politics. His successor, Ike Smith, faced a long filibuster in 1969 by Regan's Liberals who opposed a hike of the sales tax. At the end of the hard-hitting 1970 campaign, the PCs still had a marginally higher popular vote than the Liberals, 46.9 percent to 46.1 percent across Nova Scotia, but forfeited the government as the Liberals took twenty-three seats to their twenty-one.

Despondent over the second loss, and now missing the advertising account of another Maritime government, Norman crossed back into New Brunswick, where he'd also been active during the previous weeks, juggling two campaigns at once, as PC organization adviser for an October 26 election. It had been called unexpectedly by Premier Louis Robichaud, hoping to catch new Tory leader, Richard Hatfield, ill-prepared for a snap election. But Hatfield immediately announced the PC platform, well ahead of the Liberals making their program public.

Now victims of their own snap election, the Liberals rushed to complete their platform, but missed the newspaper deadlines for which they'd hurriedly booked advertising space. The papers printed blank pages, which they had held to insert the Liberal program. Hatfield, Camp, and Atkins pounced on the gaffe, pointing out that the Liberals, after ten years in office, could think of nothing more to do. Because there was no Liberal program, it was time to turn them out. The Liberal blunder became a campaign turning point.

The blue machine had more ready for New Brunswick. Next it took the wraps off its pioneering campaign effort at rapid and frequent campaign appearances by the leader: travel by helicopter. Young Hatfield dropped in everywhere around New Brunswick for his campaign, growing increasingly confident, touching down in the province's French-speaking and English-speaking communities, impressing everyone with his easy communication in both languages.

By the end of it all, the Liberals stayed slightly higher in popular vote, but the Conservatives won a majority of seats in the provincial legislature, thirty-two to twenty-six, and formed a majority government.

The Camp agency regained the province's tourism advertising business, a happy note for Norman since New Brunswick first established the precedent that inspired Dalton to go after other tourism accounts when the government was one he'd helped elect.

———

Back on the national front, meanwhile, autumn 1970 brought a shuddering halt to the work-in-progress of improving the PC campaign machine.

Malcolm Wickson, who did not always master his moody periods, announced he was stepping down as national director to return to British Columbia. He was restless to resume a more satisfying full-time life on the West Coast. He was wealthy. He did not need to put himself through battle after battle in what seemed a forlorn cause.

Eddie Goodman, well-connected and still the party's director of organization in the fall of 1970, moved to replace Wickson, even though he did not have Norman Atkins's aptitude for spotting and vetting top organizers. Liam O'Brien would be the PCs new national director. Hollywood handsome, "Liam was just a terrific guy," observed Brian Armstrong, "but he had no experience in national politics and very little experience in political organization." Both were, primarily, what his new job entailed.

National headquarters put together a Canada-wide tour for O'Brien to introduce him to the organization. On the day he and Armstrong started, Prime Minister Trudeau proclaimed the War Measures Act as a response to FLQ terrorist actions in Quebec. This precipitated a crisis atmosphere across Canada. In the nation's capital, armed troops occupied and patrolled Parliament Hill. The two Tory organizers proceeded on their tour as this galvanizing drama unfolded.

At each city, from Toronto to Winnipeg to Calgary, every news report from Ottawa and Quebec seemed grimmer. The FLQ crisis was the only topic anyone cared about. O'Brien and Armstrong reached Vancouver and were having dinner with Wickson when news spread that Quebec's labour minister, Pierre Laporte, who had been kidnapped by the FLQ, had been murdered, his body found in the trunk of an abandoned car.

Public sentiment swept across party lines in support of Prime Minister Trudeau's handling of the crisis. Ontario Tory premier Robarts declared, in support of the PM, "This is war!" In coming days pollsters would track how the PCs sank to an all-time low of just 18 percent support after the harsh War Measures Act was proclaimed in force, while ratings for the Trudeau-led Liberals soared to their highest point ever, exceeding even the crest of Trudeaumania.

Not all Progressive Conservatives fell in line with the prime minister, or Ontario's premier. The party's civil libertarians grew agitated. Dalton Camp became distraught over how things were playing out, and met with the executive assistant to Ontario's attorney general to express his dismay and discuss possible responses they could take. At Queen's Park, Education minister Bill Davis disagreed with Robarts, but kept silent.

For members of the blue machine, where someone stood on the War Measures Act became a litmus test. "Virtually to a person," said Armstrong, "we were all against it." Nate Nurgitz wrote "a brilliant and passionate pamphlet we distributed nationally," showing how the War Measures Act was unnecessary because the national government had all the powers it needed under the Criminal Code to deal with the events occurring in Quebec. Camp was strongly opposed, as was Atkins. Roy McMurtry published a strong critique.

Stanfield was also against using the War Measures Act, with its heavy-handed powers of arrest and other state actions that disregarded due process of law, but in the end he and the PC caucus voted support when the Commons was asked to endorse the government's action. Only one Progressive Conservative, David MacDonald, displayed the courage to stand against the measure in the Commons. The NDP was opposed on principle. Quebecers saw how old scores were being settled under the act's harsh emergency provisions; Canadians elsewhere saw a prime minister taking the hardest line anybody ever had with separatists.

In the weeks that followed, spirits in senior Tory circles and at national headquarters sank so low as to register negative. Liam O'Brien began chain-smoking. Time was bringing the next federal election inexorably closer. The huge shift in public support to the Liberals made it clear who would win.

———

Wickson, though no longer national director, was considered by core blue machinists as essential to whatever success the upgraded campaign organization might achieve in the election. Atkins, Armstrong, and others implored Stanfield to name Wickson successor to Eddie Goodman as chair of party organization. Although this required repeated appeals, Stanfield finally appointed the British Columbian to the post.

Being national chair of the party, an entirely voluntary position, usually entailed doing the leader's bidding at the most senior level to intervene in party operations, including the delicate tasks of recruiting, promoting, sidelining, or dismissing individuals. With Wickson, matters were different.

Having invested so much effort in revamping the campaign machinery, he instinctively remained attentive to its operation, even though Liam O'Brien was, officially, now directing it.

At the time, it was impossible, and in retrospect it is still hard, to say who fooled whom in this game of musical chairs at Progressive Conservative head-quarters. But at the end of the day, Wickson's job was not to tweak the party on orders from its leader, the way Goodman had, but to continue what he'd been doing for three years already, getting ready for the next election, building a campaign structure, developing political technology, working on electoral readiness, and getting Progressive Conservatives set for round two of the Stanfield-Trudeau matchup.

CHAPTER 34

CAMPAIGNING AGAINST BILL DAVIS

Well before John Robarts announced his retirement as Ontario's premier in December 1970, triggering battle for the securest Tory crown in Canada, the most significant event in the race to replace him, a bizarre twist on the poisoned relationship between John Diefenbaker and Dalton Camp, was already over.

It was clear William G. Davis, leadership heir apparent, only awaited his coronation as King Billy. The Tory establishment felt comfortable with Bill. His deep blue Tory credentials, his record atop Ontario's burgeoning and costly education empire, even his seasoning in national politics as policy chairman at the Montmorency Conference and Maple Leaf Gardens leadership convention, assured continuance of a Progressive Conservative regime unbroken since 1943.

In fact, Robarts was so sure Davis would succeed him he'd gruffly tell people, near the end of his premiership, "Don't talk to me about it. See Davis. He's going to be premier." The education minister's undeclared campaign was top-heavy with supporters.

———

All the same, some Conservatives thrashing out political scenarios at the Albany Club concluded that if the provincial Tories just yawned and continued as before, if the convention was merely a predictable elevation of the

MPP from Brampton, the PCs would not excite media attention or attract voter interest. The essential rejuvenation in party ranks that a hotly contested convention invariably generates would simply not occur.

A hard-fought contest was desirable, if only to shake up Davis and spark more political energy in him and the party.

But who would serve as a challenger? It had to be someone liked and respected but who, in the end, would not beat Davis. Several candidates were already sniffing around, but none fitted the criteria this Albany Club cabal desired.

As soon as talk began circulating of Robarts stepping down, Camp contacted Clare Westcott, who'd become Davis's executive assistant after Bob Macaulay retired from Cabinet, about a role for himself in the leadership race. "Dalton wanted to support Davis," stated Westcott.

Camp kept calling, but to his annoyance, got nowhere. "I'm not sure what he thought," shrugged Westcott. "Dalton wanted to get into the action. He was phoning me, wanting to see Davis, and I was phoning back, saying, 'No.'"

Davis had erected a protective wall of silence around the leadership question. Robarts and he had become close, politically and personally. Loyal and courteous, Davis firmly instructed Westcott, "I am not going to meet anybody or do anything, or even *say* anything, until John Robarts officially resigns."

That had not yet happened.

———

Downtown at the Albany Club, meanwhile, it took a couple more lunches before the Tory firecrackers agreed on Charles MacNaughton as their challenger of choice.

Charlie represented small-town and rural Ontario. He was popular in caucus, feisty yet fun as a speaker, representative of bedrock Tory Ontario values. Experienced in business, he was a successful seed merchant; he had also served as one of Les Frost's Tory appointees to the newly created Ontario Water Resources Commission in the 1950s. After election to the legislature, he became highways minister and cut ribbons to officially open better bridges and new highways all over Ontario, broadening his support among gratified Progressive Conservative MPPs in the process. He was so loyal to Robarts that he'd never, in the end-game, upset the premier's plan to have Davis replace him, they believed.

The cabal of political engineers convened a dinner meeting at the Albany Club, in one of the large private upstairs rooms, and invited Charlie. He looked around at some of the party's best-known faces, many of them his influential friends, and was overwhelmed. When he responded to their request that he agree to them laying leadership race groundwork, for when the time came that he might run, the choked-up Cabinet minister told them he'd seriously consider it. By the time he left the club, Charlie had begun envisaging himself as premier.

November's days passed. MacNaughton was increasingly charmed by the fantasy, even though, as he told his son John, "the issues a premier must deal with are beyond the scope of my experience." The Tories importuning Charlie to run realized more pressure was needed. Their invitation-only lunch at the Albany Club drew an even larger number of ranking Conservatives, almost twice as many as before. Their putative candidate again listened to impassioned pitches. Money would not be a problem.

Later that same day, after work, his son John went to the Frost Building at Queen's Park to see what his father had decided, hoping he'd run.

"They were very persuasive," Charles told him. "If I don't decisively take myself out of the race right away, with all these good people who want me to run and my own foolish thoughts starting to make it seem like a good thing to do, I'm about one day away from saying yes."

"Now, you can't stay long," he continued, moving John toward the door of his top floor minister's office. "I've asked Bill Davis to come over. I've got to tell him I am not running, because, if I don't take myself out of play, the next time they ask I'll not be able to say no."

Ontario's treasurer was as desperate as he was determined.

The next day, Bill Davis, having no official campaign, announced that Hon. Charles S. MacNaughton would chair it.

———

Dalton was irate.

He tracked down Westcott at the Ontario Institute for Studies in Education and insisted he be pulled from a top-level, do-not-disturb meeting. As Davis's executive assistant put it, "He was *quite* angry."

Camp wanted to support Bill Davis because the MPP from Brampton had supported him in the 1965 general election by trying to persuade him to run in Peel, where he'd almost certainly have won a seat in the Commons, and had supported him in the 1966 quest for a review of John Diefenbaker's leadership. Even more, Dalton believed Bill the best prospect for premier.

For years, moreover, Camp had been longing to get involved in Ontario provincial politics. Now his best chance for doing so had just been foreclosed. A leadership campaign Davis would not even discuss in private had a public chairman, self-appointed Charlie MacNaughton, who had been ardent and influential on the pro-Dief side in the Tory Party's acid test of leadership review. Westcott succinctly stated Davis's dilemma: Camp and MacNaughton "hated each other over a dispute going back to the ousting of Diefenbaker."

"Dalton thought that Davis did not want him, had been refusing to even speak with him because he'd been trying to line up Charlie MacNaughton. That was not true. Davis would have loved to have had both," Westcott said.

Supporting Bill had been Charlie's bold expedient to thwart his own growing temptation to run for premier. What could Davis do but agree?

But MacNaughton's head-over-heart move had sidelined and profoundly frustrated Camp.

———

In early December, Robarts arrived at a suite of private rooms in the Albany Club to confer over drinks and dinner with four of his political cronies. In the room next door, executive members of Ontario's PC Party were holding a dinner meeting. After a time, the door between the rooms opened and Robarts joined the top-level PC Party gathering. He announced to party president Alan Eagleson and the rest of the provincial PC executive that he'd be asking them to call a leadership convention.

Many wondered how the Tories could manage without Robarts. "We needed someone of his stature to win," said Ross DeGeer, now a member of the provincial executive. Regardless of his "stature," the premier knew he must not face another election. For him to retain his dignity and the Progressive Conservatives their lock on Ontario's government, it was time to depart. Bob Teeter's poll showed he could not win again. Others would seek his mantle, such as his ministers Darcy McKeough, Bert Lawrence, Bob Welch, and Allan Lawrence. But Robarts was sure the prize was destined for Bill Davis.

———

All this time Norman Atkins and the Spades were busy contemplating Ontario's political scene, knowing Ontario's Progressive Conservative Party would soon be choosing a new leader who'd automatically be premier.

The Spades met, explained DeGeer, "to come to some determination as to whom we were going to support." After quite a bit of discussion, they decided by a show of hands to support Davis. It was not unanimous. A number felt Allan Lawrence presented a better face and was more electable. Chad Bark was designated to contact Clare Westcott with an offer of significant campaign support.

When the Spades regrouped a few days later, Bark reported that their offer had been rebuffed. "The silence in the room was deafening," said DeGeer. "We could have all found a way to help."

Bill Davis felt awkward, ever after. He would spread fog over the reason the blue machine had been rejected. "Two or three people came to see me.... They either came to see me or got the message to me that they wanted to support me in the campaign. I either told them or got word to them that I was not starting any campaign while Mr. Robarts was still there." That stunningly ambiguous "recollection" was a convenient shield for a harder truth.

The Davis insiders were becoming wary of the risk that their candidate was already looking like too much of a shoe in. Besides, his organizers were convinced they had victory locked up, and neither needed the help of newcomers nor wanted to share with others the power they would have once Davis became premier.

Both those reasons were normal, but the exceptional reason for Atkins and his team being rejected was Dalton's enduring toxicity. Across Ontario, many PCs harboured distaste for how Diefenbaker had, in their eyes, been brought down by Camp. On top of all that was the intense dislike of Camp by Ontario's treasurer, Charlie MacNaughton, chairman of the "Davis For Leader" campaign.

"I don't think Charlie could organize himself out of a phone booth," opined Westcott, "but to have his name associated with you as campaign chair meant you would get half the caucus." Embracing Atkins, and with him the aura of Camp, would lead to the highly damaging public departure of Charles S. MacNaughton.

———

Norman was stunned.

Other Spades were angry and humiliated by their stinging rebuff. They loved campaigns so much they did not want to miss out on a good one. They were Ontarians and this race was about their own province and its political future. They knew constant involvement in elections was necessary to stay current with latest methods. There was always a fresh angle in the struggle for power, so they had to stay in the game to remain players. Being sidelined would damage the team's reputation, after its now legendary accomplishment at Maple Leaf Gardens in 1967.

A couple of days later, Paul Weed called Atkins and DeGeer, suggesting lunch. "Look, we can at best be marginal helpers in a Davis campaign," Weed explained over their meal, "or we can have our own campaign. We can find a candidate and play a pretty important role in this race."

"We don't have to look very hard," replied DeGeer, after a brief pause. "Al Lawrence is a fellow some of us already think would make a better leader."

Lawrence was not only a Toronto MPP they frequently encountered but also a fellow director of the Albany Club. When the Spades first met at Guthrie's home to settle on the leadership, several had expressed clear preference for him.

Weed proposed that, rather than sitting on the sidelines, the blue machine continue to hone its skills, have some fun, and teach a lesson to the smug bastards around Davis who'd ungraciously turned them down.

In Ottawa, when Brian Armstrong heard that his fellow Spades seemed to be agreeing on Allan Lawrence as their candidate of second choice, he found the news "really disturbing" and left immediately for Toronto.

Atkins and Weed met with Armstrong, trying to decide on the best course for the Spades. They listened while Brian laid out his concerns. First, he thought Davis was going to win, and would be a good premier, so what benefit could come from being part of the group to oppose him for the leadership? Second, Armstrong looked ahead and believed Dalton would likely want to be a candidate in the next federal election. Even if the party did not win, he hoped and believed Dalton would get elected. "That will position him to run for the leadership of the party," explained Brian. Atkins was paying solemn, close attention. "If that is the future we want for Dalton, why would we want to alienate the entire Ontario organization by fighting against the guy who is likely to become premier?"

Weed, as hardball a player as politics could produce, had devoted his tough talents to Camp's ascendancy. He responded to Armstrong, "You know, all the other arguments don't really cut it. But your argument about Dalton and his future does."

Norman demurred. He said he'd think about it. He knew Dalton's life was changing. The man who'd wanted to be prime minister was now disinclined to contest the next election. Camp's estrangement from Stanfield, who was being cool to him in hopes of warming relations with Diefenbaker's faction, had diminished his ardour for being a candidate.

"That is the only reason Norman persisted with Allan Lawrence," said Armstrong, looking back. Atkins did indeed think about it further, but remained undeterred. A few days later, he confirmed with the Spades his decision to back Lawrence, Ontario's minister of mines and northern development.

———

Alan Eagleson, Ontario Progressive Conservative Party president, set in motion steps for a provincial leadership convention. The race began a couple of weeks later, on December 21, with Bill Davis officially declaring his candidacy. He was so far in the lead it was impossible even to count by how many lengths. His romp would be an easy contest between the Brampton MPP and "the rest."

As minister of education and minister of colleges and universities, he'd criss-crossed Ontario for a decade, opening new schools, addressing gatherings of educators, and building his network of Tory supporters in every riding. A feature of Davis's campaign was a map of Ontario, with flag-pins on all the places Bill had visited as minister. Except for a few remote moose pastures, the entire province was plugged with pins, a visual message saying nobody knew Ontario like Bill Davis.

When Charles MacNaughton hosted a dinner for PC MPPs at Sutton Place Hotel, a couple of blocks east of Queen's Park, they all came over, many pledging fealty to Davis on the spot. Ministers not themselves in the running anxiously crowded to support Davis, joining the throng of backbenchers coming forward to openly declare their faith in the presence of others.

Davis himself later acknowledged that he would have been seen as "the establishment candidate because of the large number of people from Cabinet and caucus" supporting him. The leadership, observed DeGeer, "was his to lose, which made everybody in the Davis campaign so nervous about not making a mistake that it had a paralyzing effect."

The Spades held meetings in Ross DeGeer's boardroom at St. Lawrence Securities, away from the Albany Club's eyes and ears, "busily putting an organization together, at least in our minds, if not yet as an organizational chart."

Within a couple of days, Atkins, DeGeer, Weed, and several other Spades met Allan Lawrence in the same boardroom and proposed that, if he'd run for the leadership, they'd provide a powerful vehicle to carry him toward the finish line. "Al was very appealing because he was young and attractive," explained DeGeer, summarizing a common Spade view of their candidate. "He spoke with conviction and looked the ideal leader."

They met a second time with Lawrence a couple of days later.

"Well," he announced crisply, "I have decided I am not going to do it."

The Spades were stunned, again. This was their second rejection.

It took time, special efforts of persuasion, and back channels to influence the reluctant candidate. Paul Weed's conversations with Moira Lawrence, Allan's politically savvy wife, helped turn the tide. Ultimately, Allan agreed that, "on further reflection," he really should become Ontario's premier.

The Spades had their campaign, at last. Atkins chaired the organization, DeGeer was campaign manager, and together they finalized the detailed organization, worked the phones, and pulled together a tightly disciplined operation. DeGeer invited his flotilla of colleagues from the Board of Trade to meet Lawrence, ask questions, test his mettle, and make up their own minds individually about signing on. Most did, and "became integral to the success."

They set up the Lawrence campaign headquarters in the Westbury Hotel near Maple Leaf Gardens, site of the Ontario PC convention, where they'd pulled off an unpredicted victory for Stanfield in 1967 and would now try to perform similar magic for Lawrence. DeGeer got a penthouse apartment not far from the Westbury where he and Norman "camped out for what seemed like months. It was a full time job."

With the vote slated for February, they worked through the holiday season. Atkins wanted to prove he was best, teach the Davis organizers a lesson about smug complacency, apply the top methods from his repertoire to further refine them through fresh battle, and prove to Dalton he could fly solo. With all that motivation, Norman plotted one of his most brilliant campaigns.

His slogan for Allan's campaign was "Winning is Only the Beginning," which made clear a big future lay ahead. Winning the leadership would only be the start of what the Ontario PCs would do in revamping their party and refreshing its programs. Winning meant the start of an exciting new era, together with Premier Allan Lawrence, in Ontario's growth. It was a campaign energized by implicit promise.

————

For the first time, Dalton and Norman diverged on political choices.

Atkins's decision to back Lawrence was made without Camp's support, at least initially. Camp, who could withdraw into himself and not share thinking with others, especially when depressed, had not told his brother-in-law he'd be backing Bill Davis. Dalton's thinking ran along the same line as Brian Armstrong's.

Dalton would not play a public role in his support, and was clearly no part of the official Davis campaign organization, but he intended to go to the convention and vote for Bill, unless something happened.

Something did. A few Davis supporters, seeing Atkins supporting Lawrence, reasonably figured, given the nexus between the blue machine brothers-in-law, that Dalton must be supporting their rival, too. The Davis backrooms plotted how to turn this "news" to their advantage by winning over the Diefenbaker wing of the party across Ontario rural ridings and small towns.

In developing this strategy, a member of the Davis team, prudently wanting to be sure of the core fact, called Camp's residence in the evening on some pretext. Finding neither of the parents at home, he spoke with one of the Camp children. The child answered the caller's question about whether it was true his father was supporting Allan Lawrence. When Dalton discovered this and ascertained the caller was with Davis's campaign, "it so incensed him," said Armstrong, "that he was no longer prepared to support Davis at the convention."

Dalton's resumption of his accustomed presence with the other Spades served the Atkins-run Lawrence campaign well because, like his brother-in-law, Dalton now had a score to settle. He began to help Norman and the campaign team assembled for Lawrence, most importantly writing a powerhouse speech the candidate would deliver with stellar force at the convention, in contrast to Bill Davis's lacklustre address.

———

"You can't really understand the significance of Norman's role and the Lawrence campaign," said DeGeer, "without some sense of the organization and the people supporting Bill Davis. The leadership campaign being run for him was a disaster. It was, from its beginnings, a mismanaged mess. They were lovely people, but their idea of campaigning was just too casual and lacked creativity. It was hopelessly outdated."

DeGeer, choosing a military metaphor, described the Davis campaign organizers as "wanting to fight the war using the old rules — make two lines to shoot at each other. Well, sorry, we were into guerilla warfare, a different kind of campaign."

Lawrence was critical of establishment ways. He portrayed Bill Davis as the candidate of the party establishment. An articulate urbanite, Allan expressed a confident future for Progressive Conservatism as a relevant and contemporary political philosophy. In contrast, Bill Davis played to the party's rural and small-town base by pointedly emphasizing he was *not* from Toronto but the town of Brampton. Lawrence was the reform candidate. Atkins positioned him as the one taking the party forward, in contrast to "status quo" Bill Davis.

Much of Lawrence's support came from northern Ontario, where people felt Queen's Park remote. Northerners were disaffected with the party's southern orientation, typified by how Robarts had named a Torontonian his minister of mines and northern affairs, even if Lawrence "had some connection and was able to persuade them he understood some of their issues." At least he wasn't "the establishment," which is how they saw Davis.

Allan had slim pickings in caucus, with most elected Tories elbowing ahead in the lineup behind Davis. The only Cabinet minister supporting him was the health minister, Tom Wells, a friend since their days together in the YPC; the lone private member, Eglinton MPP Leonard Reilly, was territorially entwined with the Camp-Atkins Eglinton Mafia.

———

The first lap of a leadership race extends from the announcement there will be a convention to choose a new leader, through the build-up phase of travelling to meet delegates, distributing campaign information, advancing policies, and making plans for the second lap, which begins when everyone arrives at the convention itself.

In telling respects, Lawrence's challenge to Davis in 1970 bore close resemblance to the Stanfield leadership campaign three years earlier. Atkins, with no reason to depart from that winning formula, followed the same strategy for Allan: dominate convention week, and dominate Maple Leaf Gardens for the vote.

The Camp agency designed a visually bold logo for the Lawrence campaign, consisting of three basic forms (a circle, a square, and a triangle) in three solid basic colours (red, yellow, blue) that was unmistakable, bold, and simple. It also wrote and produced all the materials necessary to create the impression of a winner. The Royal York was the convention hotel. "We had that place covered with signs before the others even arrived," beamed DeGeer. "We had every location." No matter where a television camera pointed or a voting delegate looked, "the Lawrence logo and the Lawrence campaign was front and centre."

Atkins and DeGeer assembled a special operations unit of on-site advance men to ensure the Lawrence campaign "dominated events taking place at the hotel, dominated sessions in the breakout rooms." These operatives, connected by walkie-talkies, were on the lookout for television crews hunting for delegates in the hotel, and "made sure that our delegates were the ones being interviewed. We did not get 100 percent of the interviews, but at least 75 percent." Every newscast reported on Allan Lawrence and the strong impression he was creating.

Atkins was an enthusiastic believer in the necessity of a campaign tune. When he and DeGeer agreed they "wanted something different," Ross signed up a lively and loud West Indian band, fronted by Dick Smith, while Norman got music and words written for "Winning is Only the Beginning," probably the catchiest campaign song in Canadian history.

"The convention itself went very well for us," said DeGeer. Atkins had it organized into a number of components, with a team responsible for the floor demonstration, other people tracking delegates, and DeGeer and his team running candidate liaison. Lawrence supporters working the Gardens floor were easily spotted by one another, all of them decked out in bright green jackets, each connecting by mobile phones.

Alan Eagleson boasted that the convention was going to be "fast and smooth, because we have voting machines." When one voting machine broke down, however, that disabled the whole set-up. The convention entered a freeze-frame state of suspended drama while party officials printed paper ballots. Hours passed as time stood still. As the extended, agonizing delay stretched into the night, the mood shifted. Delegates got word from those who'd ventured outside onto College Street that "a bloody great snowstorm" was raging. Some left, others hunkered deeper into the Garden's surrealistic cocoon.

"What we're trying to do here," repeated Atkins to all his campaign organizers, "is keep our people together. Lock them in so they don't go and get on the train." Sheila Willis, a key member of the Eglinton Mafia, realized, "We need to chant." She got it organized and going, up in the stands. "This is what we are going to do, chant: 'Allan Lawrence, Allan Lawrence, Allan, Allan, Allan Lawrence!' It just rocked the place."

"That chanting built momentum," recalled DeGeer, "whereas others had a Dixieland band and straw boater hats right out of the 1950s American-style conventions."

Norman Atkins and Allan Lawrence dazzled Ontario's Tory political establishment with a surprising 1971 Ontario PC leadership campaign that, if just twenty-three votes had switched, would have made him premier instead of Bill Davis. Watching on with cigar, at a garden party for Lawrence campaign supporters the following spring, is Spade Brian Armstrong and Moira Lawrence, Allan's politically astute wife.

Bill Davis, knowing his rudderless campaign was adrift, could only hope the dead weight of his ship would drift him safely into harbour. Anyone observing him becoming quietly traumatized, standing stoically in the seats amidst his becalmed supporters in Maple Leaf Gardens, waiting and watching his promising political future melt away, would understand that he was vowing, if somehow he did manage to survive, to make big changes.

By night's end, Davis eked out a meagre forty-four-vote win over late-starting challenger Lawrence.

For the blue machine, *losing* was only the beginning.

———

If some freelancing PC strategists at the Albany Club had not craved an exciting convention and sought out Charlie MacNaughton as their candidate, *if* MacNaughton had not impulsively taken himself out of play by forcing himself on Bill Davis as campaign chairman, *if* John Diefenbaker's refusal to step down had not caused Dalton Camp to launch a leadership review that made him so hated by many Tories, *if* the Atkins-Camp organization had not been driven to orchestrate a rival campaign to challenge Bill Davis, and *if* a galvanized Davis had not resolved to replace his amateur organizers with the superior blue machine, then Canadian political history in Ontario in the 1970s and nationally in the 1980s would have been unrecognizable from what transpired.

The first step in the transformation that did take place was Bill Davis's resolve to tie his future to the Camp-Atkins blue machine.

After almost forfeiting his long-sought prize because his rival had better organizers than he'd spent years acquiring, Davis was now rightly wary of the looming provincial election he'd soon have to call. If he could all but lose a sure bet within his own party, the risk of Liberals pulling off an upset with the general public was genuine. Would he be the Tory premier to ignominiously flame out and end Ontario's PC dynasty?

Davis and Roy McMurtry, who'd first become friends when playing football together at University of Toronto, had remained on good terms. Roy, one of the Spades, was also close to Camp and Atkins. This already made him a trusted go-between, but his standing was even further improved by the fact that back surgery had painfully sidelined McMurtry during the leadership race, making him something of a "neutral." Though incapacitated, he'd relentlessly kept in constant contact with his friends on both sides by telephone during the race, and the rival campaigns had each named McMurtry one of their special six delegates at large. Was there a more ideal person to broker the meeting Bill Davis wanted and the blue machine needed?

The outcome at the Gardens boiled down to Allan Lawrence getting a lot of votes *because* of his organization, Bill Davis a lot of votes *despite* his organization. As Westcott explained, "We had a lot of guys like Charlie MacNaughton and others who meant well but really did not have a refined approach to conducting a leadership campaign, which Dalton and Norman did. Davis had leadership skill, and Dalton and Norman organization talent." Westcott, pleased to hear what McMurtry was proposing, described it as "sort of a 'Let's bury the hatchet in the back of the Liberals, not in each other' type of meeting."

After the campaign, added DeGeer, the party's new leader "knew he had to find a way to heal the rift that inevitably results from such a battle, and did not have a lot of time to do it."

The phone lines bridged Hugh Macaulay and McMurtry, McMurtry and Norman Atkins. Bill Davis wanted a meeting between the key players from Lawrence's campaign and members of his inner circle. The Albany Club, too much in the lens of high-placed Tories, was not a suitable venue. The National Club, at the corner of King and Bay Streets, was just as convenient but politically detached. McMurtry asked DeGeer to have one of his partners book dinner under his name in a private room. Nobody could know about this secret, top-level meeting Ontario's new premier was having with rival combatants for power in the province.

At the appointed time and place came Bill Davis, Hugh Macaulay, Clare Westcott, Roy McMurtry, Dalton Camp, Norman Atkins, Paul Weed, Bill Saunderson, and Ross DeGeer. Allan Lawrence was not invited. It was the organization, not the candidate who fronted it, that was the prize.

"It wasn't as easy as it may sound," said Westcott, to turn up for a dinner with men who for many weeks had been arch-rivals for the power to govern Canada's keystone province. "After a leadership campaign, feelings are pretty hard within the party, often more volatile than between parties."

"What Mr. Davis wanted out of the meeting," said DeGeer, "was to bring our group, and Norman Atkins in particular, into the mainstream preparations for an election. This was an incredibly important, and courageous, thing for him to do."

Such fusion was a high-risk challenge for Ontario PCs; there were very real divisions within the party, exemplified by the intense animosity of Charlie MacNaughton toward Camp. "There were a lot of old-fashioned Tories who did not like Camp and the knifing of Diefenbaker stuff," said Westcott. "Except Davis was smart enough to recognize a deep need in his political organization for something far better than what had existed in Ontario before, and that is how it got started."

Atkins and Weed were surprised to find Davis conciliatory, expecting the victor to reward those who supported him and punish those who had not. But the premier had been awed by their talent and wanted to work with them going forward. Discreet and even-tempered when interacting with others, Davis seldom revealed his feelings, and this night displayed no hint of belligerence. At the dinner, this man who'd almost forfeited the premiership made a most pacifacatory speech.

Afterward, as the conclave disbanded, Bill Davis, Norman Atkins, and Roy McMurtry headed north to Sutton Place Hotel, took the elevator to the top floor bar, and, over drinks, kept talking so Davis and Atkins could "get to know each other and see if they were comfortable with one another," said DeGeer. The career of each was riding on the promise and pitfalls of their politically awkward relationship.

In discussing political issues, Ontario's premier for some reason revealed that he had never agreed with proclamation of the War Measures Act, despite Robarts's support of it. That crystallized their connection in Norman's mind. Even though not given to the policy side of politics, Atkins had absorbed from Camp, McMurtry, Nurgitz, and other blue machinists their strong opposition to use of such draconian powers against the FLQ when Criminal Code provisions sufficed. This common cause about a transcending issue was another bonding agent, but McMurtry already knew the much bigger pull for Norman was the fact Bill Davis was premier of Ontario.

Davis succeeded in recruiting the entire blue machine: Norman Atkins, Dalton Camp, Ross DeGeer, Paul Weed, Bill Saunderson, the rest of the Spades, and their extended legion of devoted political players. Many organizers who'd ridden with Davis to the top of the party and government would be sidelined. That, DeGeer rightly noted, was "very, very difficult to do. Davis and Macaulay, to their everlasting credit, just were ruthless in establishing a new team and new, more relevant faces to the party organization."

Within days, Davis asked Atkins to be Ontario Progressive Conservative campaign manager.

Norman had been vindicated. Dalton's long quest to get into Ontario Tory campaigns had finally been accomplished, by proxy.

CHAPTER 35

CAMPAIGNING WITH BILL DAVIS

Norman Atkins's rule of etiquette for the proper starting of an electoral engagement had been observed when leader Bill Davis personally asked him to manage his campaign and he'd agreed. Only this ensured both men knew their political marriage was real, a two-way committment.

Norman advanced to the next two steps, filling in names on the obligatory organization chart, and developing a campaign budget. Next he turned to broad strategy, envisaging a campaign focused entirely on Davis, a new premier with a fresh approach. It would be the antithesis of his recent campaign for Allan Lawrence, which portrayed Davis as a "status quo" voice of the Tory Party establishment. To implement his strategy, the campaign would centre on a province-wide leader's tour in which Bill Davis would star as the election's constant focal point.

Back in 1957, Camp's plan for the national PC campaign included much greater emphasis on the leader's tour and primary focus on John Diefenbaker. By 1968, public fascination with Liberal leader Pierre Trudeau meant his campaign travels, and Bob Stanfield's for journalistic balance, were being heavily covered by television news. From this emerging pattern, Atkins's idea was to consolidate the practice, support it in novel ways, add new technology and more resources, and feature the leader's tour as the very campaign itself.

Because the tour would be the most crucial component for PC election plannning, Norman turned to fellow Spade Ross DeGeer and John Thompson, a disciplined, resourceful, and independent-thinking entrepreneur who'd impressively run Darcy McKeough's convention activity at Maple Leaf Gardens. DeGeer and Thompson devised a tour concept with detailed components and mapped out a rudimentary itinerary for places Davis should visit, mainly priority ridings for PCs. The route would be fine-tuned when Bob Teeter's research identified "winnable" ridings with more precision.

Now having "some sense of what it was we wanted to do when the time came," said DeGeer, Atkins invited the best performing individuals from the various provincial leadership campaigns to the Albany Club early in February 1971 to "put together some workers and get ready for the provincial election in the fall." This was the genesis of a self-reliant and innovative squad of advance men. Soon dubbed "the Dirty Dozen" by other blue machinists, their label was inspired by the title of a then-popular film about a team of hardcore convicts selected for covert commando operations during the Second World War who depended on the separate skills of each to work as a lethally effective unit. Many of these young men had been recruited from Toronto's Junior Board of Trade. Most had no prior political experience. All were volunteers.

Up to this time, a party's leader visited as many locales and public events as possible during an election, according to a schedule blending such variables as the leader's personal nature, modes of available transportation, amount of money, time, weather, and readiness of party workers to plan and produce events along the way. Travels by the leader had not been a campaign's *exclusive* focus, because parties traditionally drew on a number of major spokespersons, such as Cabinet ministers and celebrity candidates, during a campaign. But with television news cameras turning increasingly onto the leader to the exclusion of other figures, the blue machine would get ahead of the curve in Ontario for the 1971 campaign by reconfiguring the fundamental nature of the tour into a media showpiece. The touring ensemble would include extensive facilities and resources for working journalists, as close to a mobile newsroom and studio as technology could provide.

To prepare the locales, in place of one or two individuals who'd go ahead to check things out and then accompany the leader themselves, the way Dalton "advanced" for Diefenbaker in the Maritimes, Atkins, DeGeer and Thompson would now deploy their stop-at-nothing Dirty Dozen. This team's objective would be to get every detail nailed down in advance, create conditions for success, maximize positive publicity, anticipate and avoid problems (be they logistical, human, or policy), and generate overall political momentum for the campaign. Because good advance work should be invisible to the public, few were aware of the advance men's background preparations that allowed touring Davis and his extensive entourage to arrive at the right place, on time, and do something worthy of media attention. One gaffe might ruin the whole day; a serious one could cast a cloud over the entire campaign.

The tour's new importance as central pillar of the campaign made DeGeer and Thompson resolve never to screw up. They'd ensure talented people were always in position to execute the operation. The professional nature of their manoeuvres would be a stark contrast to the pattern of leaders being accompanied by just one or two helpers and folksy local amateurs.

"I did not have a clue what an advance man was, what he did, or how he did it," said Tom MacMillan, one of those chosen by Atkins, DeGeer, and Thompson at the Albany Club audition dinner. He found answers in a manual "basically ripped off the Democratic Party in the United States."

DeGeer had a document from Bob Teeter, used by Democrat Jerry Bruno, a former labour organizer who'd advanced John Kennedy's campaigns and worked on tour plans in the JFK White House. "I revised the document to suit our circumstance," said DeGeer, "and it formed the basis for the methodology we'd use during the campaign." Numbered copies were signed out to each advanceman.

To the PC advance men, hard-bitten Bruno was a hero they sought to emulate. The Dirty Dozen invited him to Toronto, and learned much from his experiences over dinner at the Albany Club. In addition to studying DeGeer's revamp of Bruno's instruction manual, the Dirty Dozen devoured the American's new 1971 book, *The Advance Man*, with key tips and tough rules based on how he'd advanced Kennedy's successful 1960 presidential campaign.

One major difference from the American practice, though, was the PCs' decision to not go overboard playing hardball with the locals. In the United States an advance man went into an area, organized for the leader, and moved on, never expected to return because he'd make so many enemies doing his job. The blue machine's view, more Canadian, was that the art of advancing a leader was not to burn bridges, but build them. Unlike their U.S. counterparts, confirmed MacMillan, "We were expected to be able to go back to that same area later in the campaign." It made sense.

"They really developed the art of event management in the campaign context beyond anything we had ever seen before," said Brian Armstrong about the team's work. The way the Dirty Dozen advanced the 1971 leader's tour in Ontario was so novel, compared to prior Canadian campaigns, that it became another blue machine innovation to be emulated by other parties.

MacMillan and fellow Junior Boarder Peter Groschel were designated to advance eastern Ontario, covering the Ottawa Valley, down through Ottawa to Kingston. Other areas of the province were similarly divided up and assigned to advance teams. "We were expected," noted John Slade, who with Gord Petursson got southwestern Ontario, "to go out and organize things for Premier Davis in advance of the election, and then in the election itself." They went into their assigned territories, met with constituency folk, worked on "centralizing the messaging in terms of where the media would go" and what the leader could say and do that was most appropriate for both the overall campaign and the local setting. On the day Bill Davis appeared, they'd return, run the event, and be responsible for news media logistics.

"They were aware in the ridings that we were from Toronto, from the central campaign office," noted MacMillan. "It had never been done this way before."

The advance men encountered blowback, even when not playing hardball. "Well, you know," one man told MacMillan, "this is Smiths Falls. We do things differently here." Near Kingston, when reviewing the program and the ten minutes allocated for Bill Davis to speak, Tom was again upbraided. "You don't understand eastern Ontario, son. We expect our leaders to give speeches for forty-five minutes."

Such traditionalists would be disappointed now, for the new-style tour would no longer be leisurely outings for the pleasure of local partisans, but rapid-paced events with short speeches that contained only the day's news hit for the accompanying reporters filing to deadline.

Being on the road with the power to orchestrate how and where the premier of Ontario would appear was heady stuff for these young men. MacMillan at age twenty-six took his duties seriously. "I had more responsibility on the road as a volunteer advance man than in my paid job at Abitibi Paper Company." He put in "long, long, long days." After working in Toronto all week, on Friday at four o'clock he'd begin driving many hours to reach a riding and work all weekend before returning late Sunday night. For that, "It had to be fun. I had to be getting something out of it, like learning a lot about the province, about people, and about politics. And I had to believe in the cause. Bill Davis was a very easy guy to believe in."

The others were just as talented and dedicated. In 1971, the Ontario PC election campaign would deploy close to twenty such operatives. No matter their ever-growing number, the advance team still proudly counted themselves a "Dozen."

———

Shortly after the blue machine began working *for* Bill Davis, it also began integrating its political operations at Queen's Park.

In May, when Brian Armstrong answered his phone at party headquarters in Ottawa, Roy McMurtry asked, "How would you like to come back and work for Bill Davis? We need somebody in his office."

Both Brian and Roy enjoyed a certain diplomatic immunity in Tory ranks that allowed them special freedom. For the divisive 1971 Ontario leadership convention, when McMurtry had been sidelined by his back injuries, Armstrong adroitly sat in the stands behind John Robarts, basking in the outgoing premier's neutrality so nobody present would think the PC national director's office was aligned with any particular candidate. Roy's special status had enabled him to orchestrate the National Club dinner that fused the Camp-Atkins blue machine with the Davis-led provincial PCs, and continued to make him the all-purpose go-between in getting a potent campaign organization together for his friend the premier. Roy contacted Brian because a call from Atkins would have been perceived as the Ontario campaign manager raiding the national organization. Roy and Norman were carefully assembling more talent around the leader, playing from their hidden hand of Spades.

Upon reaching Toronto, Armstrong went straight to the premier's large corner office at Queen's Park and met with Davis and his deputy minister, Dr. Keith Reynolds, who offered him the position of special assistant. None of them seemed clear about what Brian was supposed to do. "But implicitly," said the recruit, "I knew my job was liaison between the campaign organization Norman was developing and the premier's office, still staffed by folks who'd worked for Mr. Robarts." Armstrong became the first new person in the premier's office since Davis had taken over, creating a beachhead for blue machine political operations in Ontario at the highest level.

He worked attentively all summer with the campaign team, his role evolving by imperceptible degrees. The gradualness of the changes Armstrong brought to the operations of the premier's office and his well-bred manner helped ensure that none of the old guard became upset by the politicization of the province's top government operation. But that's what the special assistant to Ontario's premier was doing. Brian made certain the premier's staff responded to the campaign's requirements. He kept the premier's schedule focused on political activities. He ran interference with civil servants who wanted the premier's time, so the campaign team got everything it needed from Bill Davis in the run-up to the election.

Bill Davis had named Hugh Macaulay new director of organization for the party.

Hugh had grown up at Queen's Park, where his father, Leopold, had been a long-serving Toronto MPP, Cabinet minister, and twice a leadership contender. His brother Robert, also an MPP and leadership contender, had been "minister of everything" in John Robarts's government. Hugh was less flamboyant, more approachable, a gentle political fixer. Bill Davis first worked closely with Hugh when he chaired Robert Macaulay's campaign to succeed Les Frost.

Early in the summer of 1971, Atkins and Macaulay gathered every riding's campaign manager and nominated PC candidate at a Beaver Valley resort, southwest of Collingwood and away from all distractions. Norman's propensity to get people together in the countryside where they could relax, chat, drink, exchange ideas, and bond had again kicked in. He laid out the campaign strategy in broad strokes, enough for everyone to get a clear picture and buy into the plan before the election call, yet without any details that nosey journalists could report or Liberals and NDP benefit from if advance information leaked out.

The campaign chairman explained there would be a single PC brand that would identify *everything* in the campaign. By now Norman was seasoned in dealing with politicians and riding associations, and knew everyone in the party "needed to get accustomed to the idea," and that that would take time.

A common PC logo as the *sole* identifier was another blue machine innovation. "For the first time all candidates were being asked to use the centrally developed 'creative' for all signs and pamphlets," said Armstrong. Norman, the professional advertising man, wanted one single identity for the party across the entire province, not the variety previously displayed by local candidates. "The importance of this will become evident when the television advertising starts," he explained, tantalizing the candidates and their managers in hopes of getting their willingness to use the party brand on everything, without exception. The centre was assuming control.

———

In Toronto, the campaign's backroom group met at Theodore's Steak House every Monday morning, kicking off another week of preparations for the 1971 campaign. Meeting in a popular steakhouse would not normally help campaign secrecy, but Theodore's only served lunch and dinner so was closed in the morning and Norman had persuaded the owner to open exclusively for his breakfast group. Just around the corner from the Camp agency, Norman had entertained so many clients at the restaurant over the years that asking for a private Monday morning slot was like a request from a part-owner in the business.

As Ontario campaign chairman, Atkins sought to build wide consensus for what he was doing, so this group included diverse players of the party, not just individuals he'd worked with before. Participants were Norman himself, Hugh Macaulay, Brian Armstrong, Roy McMurtry, party president Alan Eagleson, Davis's executive assistance Clare Westcott, Cabinet minister Tom Wells, chief fundraiser Bill Kelly, and provincial PC director Arthur Harnett, an early parliamentary press gallery radio reporter who'd twice run for the PCs in his native Newfoundland. Macaulay was as keen as Atkins to include Armstrong because his direct continuous link to the premier and those working for him had to be tightly integrated with their planning of pre-campaign and campaign activities for Davis. Norman presented the plans he wanted put in place, asking for their constructive criticisms and ultimately their support. His approach was succeeding. The diverse campaign team for 1971 was harmonious.

Norman specifically wanted the Monday morning sessions to vet nominations for positions in the campaign organization, because no matter how well he knew talented individuals, someone present might have additional information, pro or con, for a more rounded assessment. In addition to personnel, they also reviewed a variety of pre-election activities, ruling some out, agreeing on others. One person could develop a seemingly inspired campaign idea, but explaining it to other seasoned players, and hearing their discussion of it, helped establish a surer footing for an effective campaign.

———

Another way to ensure the campaign would be close to flawless was by conducting trial runs.

MacMillan helped Atkins test the all-important Davis tour by conducting a few limited excursions with the prototype. Tom set up a series of events in eastern Ontario, then doubled back to oversee Davis performing in these local settings, his first opportunity to witness the premier's campaign style.

"He was very smart, a wonderful leader," MacMillan said, "but even he would admit that 'charisma' was not a word you'd associate with him in 1971." Bill Davis was "very low key, so the energy level in the room before his speech was also pretty low." In the hall "there was nothing going on. Some guy would introduce him, he spoke, and that was it."

Earlier, during Davis's leadership campaign, several of his organizers and supporters thought Davis a "terrible public speaker" and were elated when he'd finished and sat down. "He got through it." was their relieved reaction, not "He really wowed them!" or "What a stunning speech!" Simply, "He's done it."

Back in Toronto, MacMillan met with Atkins and DeGeer for a debriefing. "You know, for a campaign that is going to be as different as we want it to be," he said, "we need a way to fire up people in the room. We need a way to get the energy level up to make people receptive."

"What do you suggest?"

"I have friends who are musicians and think it would be great if we put them on the road so they can warm the crowds up before the leader gets to speak. Ike Kelneck is better than anybody I know at reading a crowd, getting them organized, and getting them 'up.' You should try him out and see what you think."

Atkins smiled. He'd always liked a campaign song, because he understood its importance in creating unifying power, message, and energy. It was no stretch envisaging the value that a talented band would add to a Bill Davis tour, though he could not yet imagine how making Kelneck's band, Jalopy, into the campaign's versatile house band, performing on the leader's tour and opening party events with upbeat music, would become one of the blue machine's most sensational campaign innovations.

The northern Ontario band Jalopy evoked high spirits and generated energy, which was just what the calm campaigns of Bill Davis and Bob Stanfield needed as leavening agents. The talented musicians were couples Bobby and Lynn Morandin, Roger and Reva Perreault, and Alice and Ike Kelneck. The airborne performers are Reva, Alice, and Ike.

———

Fully primed well before the 1971 election, the tour team was set to go.

Yet Atkins and DeGeer still wanted another "test drive," something more full-scale than MacMillan's events in eastern Ontario. There are always lessons to be learned. Better to do so before launching the premier's tour under full media gaze.

Sudbury was chosen for a complete dress rehearsal. The tour group laid on a program for Davis to speak to a service club, meet with union members, and address school children, before winding up at a banquet hall for a "fun raising" evening event. Atkins showed Davis the program to get his suggestions, but the premier agreed with the two-page itinerary as drawn up. He'd come to value Atkins's professionalism and was not one to micromanage.

Having a green light, the blue machinists shifted into operational phase. "We hired a DC-9 aircraft, alerted the Sudbury press, and selected a few reporters from the Queen's Park press gallery to travel with us," said DeGeer. A couple weeks before the event, Ross asked two members of the advance group "to go to Sudbury and put the plan together on the ground." Encountering a testy school principal, they quietly reconfigured Davis's event with pupils to bypass him.

Aboard the plane on tour day itself was Ward Cornell, affably smiling and chatting with everyone, creating good feelings all around. A legendary figure in Canadian broadcasting, Cornell was host of the "Hot Stove League" on CBC television's *Hockey Night in Canada*, a between-periods segment broadcast from Maple Leaf Gardens. "He was," said DeGeer, "very personable, highly knowledgeable, just a very nice man."

In the 1971 leadership race, Cornell had handled media relations for the Davis campaign, and Davis enjoyed his company. Atkins and DeGeer thought Ward's presence would help keep Davis, who tended to tense up inside, more relaxed. Even more, Atkins was certain that Cornell's media renown would benefit press relations in the full-scale leader's tour around Ontario once campaigning began in earnest.

When the troupe landed in Sudbury, they could glimpse through the plane's windows party faithful gamely waving welcoming placards, and beside them, the more subdued Sudbury press corps. The advance team had done its work well.

With the aircraft's steps in place, Bill Davis descended to the tarmac and began shaking a few hands. "Then Ward Cornell came off the plane and everybody made a beeline for him," recounted a chagrined DeGeer. "They were taking pictures of him, the reporters asked questions and jotted down quotes, and the TV people wanted to schedule a studio interview with him." Davis and his wife, Kathleen, were left on the sidelines, talking to the few remaining party stalwarts who had not huddled near the reporters to hear what legendary Ward Cornell was saying. "It was very embarrassing."

Advance man Hal Huff made a note: "No celebrities to accompany leader."

The agenda was full. The premier addressed a joint luncheon meeting of Sudbury's service clubs. Next came an afternoon union meeting at the Steelworkers Hall. But for Davis to speak to pupils, the savvy advance men had reconfigured the event from a single school into a spectacle at Bell Park, with principals from several all competing to get their students into this special event with Ontario's premier, the former education minister. Advance man Gord Petursson had hired off-duty uniformed police officers to direct local traffic. The official motorcade enjoyed easy passage to the park.

On arrival, Davis looked up to take in the unusual venue. He could see a rise, with stairs going to the top. "There were security guards and the rest of it," said DeGeer. "When we got to the top, we discovered an amphitheatre stretching out below us, filled with a thousand kids waving flags and singing 'Ontari-ari-ari-o' with Ike Kelneck's band, Jalopy, playing and everybody very, very happy. It was *unbelievable* what that advance team had created."

Bill Davis was "absolutely taken aback. He had not been forewarned," said DeGeer after that jubilant event. "You could see him puff up with new energy and confidence."

That same night, across town at the Caruso Club for the PC Fun Raising event, the six Jalopy musicians, Ike on accordion with all stops out, filled the place with the liveliest music likely ever heard in Sudbury. Kathleen Davis leaned across to her husband to shout, "You've *got* to use these guys in your campaign!"

Atkins booked Jalopy for the entire 1971 campaign, a unique gig to enliven whatever audiences the advance team assembled, wherever in Ontario the tour took them. The Sudbury test run, said DeGeer, cemented "a long, happy, and fruitful relationship between the abilities of the campaign team and Mr. Davis's confidence level going into an election."

———

The most "salutary message" from the Sudbury trial run was the one DeGeer also called "very embarrassing."

At the airport "everybody had been attracted to Ward Cornell." In spite of the publicity surrounding the PC leadership convention, thanks to the competitive race it had become, and notwithstanding that the premier had been the province's minister of education and minister of colleges and university affairs for a decade, "people simply did not know who Davis was," said DeGeer. "They just didn't know him."

Norman Atkins beamed. His pro-Lawrence delegates who'd chanted "Save Us from Dav-us" at the convention saw the education minister as too familiar, a well-worn representative of the tired Tory establishment. But to Ontario's voters, Bill Davis was a clean slate.

It meant the blue machine could reposition and repackage the young premier however polling research indicated would help him win. "This insight," said DeGeer, "was instructive in and of itself, most of all to Davis."

With the advertising and communications skills available to Atkins, presenting a fresh Bill Davis with contemporary ideas and a plan for the future was a delight compared to trying to sell voters on Bob Stanfield.

Norman assembled a secret consortium of the best available talent from different agencies, each a top specialist in a particular area of advertising. They included John McIntyre from the Camp agency, Art Collins from Foster Advertising, Peter Swain and Peter Simpson on the media-buying side, Ross Monk for print production, and so on, in effect a full-service agency made up of people on undisclosed secondment.

The entire outreach program, in all media, would be created by this consortium in-house as part of the campaign. By not having to pay arms-length agencies their 15 percent commission, this Tory entity could notionally pay itself the 15 percent, in effect recycling that amount of money to buy more advertising. Having its own advertising constellation also helped tighten secrecy about the campaign. And, consisting of leading performers from major agencies, this all-star team meant PC advertising could outclass that of competitor campaigns. After the election, they would disband. During the campaign, they'd be known appropriately by the nondescript name "Ad Hoc."

————

The provincial Tory campaign would itself be a "test drive" for the federal campaign expected the next year.

The new political technology and innovative methods the Progressive Conservative Party had been assembling at the national level under the direction of Malcolm Wickson and Atkins, after the 1968 loss to Trudeau, were being made operational in Ontario's 1971 electoral context for the first time.

Deep-market public opinion research, new types of political advertising, public relations, media work, the leader's tour, the use of a house band, and tightly disciplined event management had each been tested successfully, but now faced genuine trial in a full-scale election. Wickson as PC national director spent most of his time in Ontario close to Norman at the Camp agency's Eglinton offices in the run-up to the election, then during the campaign at headquarters on Adelaide Street. Malcolm wanted to learn all possible lessons first-hand, because in the looming Canada-wide effort for Stanfield, seat-rich and politically volatile Ontario would be key.

Roy McMurtry, who'd been designated the campaign's policy coordinator to ensure emphasis on progressive measures, had been finding the responsibility "vague and frustrating." Once the election was called, and the ministers went campaigning, he'd find their departmental policy branches even less helpful, bureaucrats regarding him "as just another backroom political operative who had to be humoured more than helped."

Darwin Kealey was in charge of a unit producing statements on issues and policies for use by candidates, another part of this same policy-focused activity at the centre. In the past, some Ontario PC campaigns had a centrally produced booklet, such as the blue-bound *A Record of Accomplishment* put out by Leslie Frost and Clare Westcott, itemizing the government's spending on highways, schools, rural electrification, hospitals, and other indicia of progress. Candidates could use from it what they wanted, as it suited their needs, according to their own judgment. For the 1971 election, Atkins established, with this new unit, the first of what would become a critical part of all blue machine campaigns going forward, a "research and information" component. The "PC Fact Book" became the approved source of consistent responses to frequently asked questions. A new mantra began to circulate: *Stay on message.*

Ward Cornell and Burke van Valkenburg, a creative radio man who'd built up a good business taping speeches at the Empire Club and conferences then selling the audio recordings, had each been part of Bill Davis's leadership team dealing with reporters. They continued into the 1971 election, but were shifted to backroom operations handling "media relations." Others on Davis's team, however, such as his loyal supporter lawyer Ed Kowal, were kept even further away by Atkins and those around him, making Ed understandably bitter. He was one of a number.

The machine's gears were moving, but largely out of sight. "People knew what individuals like Ross DeGeer, John Thompson, or Tom MacMillan were doing," said Jalopy's lead-man, Kelneck. "But Norman Atkins seemed a mystery and was remote." It was an observation echoed by others who never saw Norman. They knew he was "always around," he said, "like the organization's godfather."

Norman liked to run his show behind the scenes, working through his committee of those in charge of different divisions who reported directly to him, like a military commander.

———

"From rehearsals and explanations," said tour manager DeGeer, "we moved on to the real thing" the day the election was called.

Atkins and DeGeer decided to start the tour, symbolically, from Queen's Park. The boldly painted buses rolled up, dramatic visuals for television cameras showing a campaign beginning, a stunning display to intimidate the competition.

"We knew we had to be ready to roll the second the election was called, creating momentum and establishing the character of the campaign," Ross explained. That character, as Atkins envisaged, was "touring to meet the people face to face."

From the Adelaide Street campaign headquarters in downtown Toronto, Atkins coordinated the entire enterprise of putting the advertising together, reviewing creative content, guiding the media relations operation, and keeping tabs on the tour. The Dirty Dozen were linked in a close communications loop between the war room, the tour buses with the leader, the communications unit, the news media, and the PC logistics and policy teams. Brian Armstrong was on the leader's tour throughout the campaign, accompanying Bill Davis as primary liaison between all these components.

A bus tour like this had never been done before. Associate tour director John Thompson, otherwise working in a senior position for Greyhound Bus Lines, had arranged for the buses, got them outfitted as mobile homes and offices, and had them painted with the campaign colours and logo. Two were official, the Davis bus and the press bus, but Atkins insisted a third bus be fully prepared to trail the other two, out of sight, available as backup. The army had taught him to incorporate "redundancy" into any deployment of equipment.

Part of the entourage, as quartermaster Atkins also insisted, was a food truck providing hot and cold meals for the leader, his team, and the press corps. Nobody had to waste time looking for restaurants, or get left behind in one when service was too slow. The provisions vehicle also served a pancake breakfast in whichever town the tour started its day. Advance man Peter Groschel advertised locally that Ontario's premier would be in town and invited everyone to join Bill Davis for breakfast, which attracted good attention and drew crowds following their nostrils to morning bacon and grilling pancakes.

More pancake syrup than substantive policy was served with breakfast, although Bill Davis did address local issues, on which he'd been carefully briefed, when making his short remarks. People were also drawn by Jalopy's upbeat music, adding to their cheerful frame of mind. In terms of visibility and energy, these events gave steady boost to the campaign. People enjoying

Tory pancakes might not repay with their votes, but the experience of the local PC candidate and premier visiting face to face with the residents had lasting good effect both for citizens of the community and the riding's PC volunteers, wherever the tour went.

"It was a very slick campaign," smiled DeGeer.

———

Early in the election, the media advertising based on Bob Teeter's research and crafted by Ad Hoc was launched in record-breaking frequency, a political onslaught through television and radio still possible in an era without restrictions on the timing or volume of paid advertising.

Progressive Conservative publicity started in September, immediately upon the call of the October 21 election. Once the overwhelming waves of TV ads began, Bill Davis was no longer "a blank slate" to the public. After a few weeks of intense television bombardment, the premier beamed with satisfaction to DeGeer at one of the tour events, "They know who we are now, Ross!" The shy premier said "we" to mean himself.

The campaign made a happy discovery with radio. Burke van Valkenburg prepared short segments from tape recordings of Bill Davis's speeches (called an "actuality" in the news business), adding a concise newsman's introduction. For example: "Speaking in Peterborough today, Premier William Davis announced new funding from his Progressive Conservative government to revitalize canal transportation in the province" — then cut to something pithy the leader had said while delivering a grant cheque for repairs to the Peterborough lift lock on the Trent canal.

"We were pushing out actualities put together by van Valkenburg to the radio stations every day," said an astonished DeGeer. "Most of them would take the feed" — right from PC campaign headquarters. "We were recording our own stuff, a Davis speech, then the campaign team would determine the message of the day, Burke would edit and package it, and the Ontario stations were broadcasting it." The provincial radio stations became an unfiltered extension of the PC campaign, conveying the sense to the voters of an active and engaged young premier who was doing real things that made news.

———

Ike Kelneck of Jalopy even elevated the happiness index on the PC campaign plane during the 1971 Ontario election. Ike plays his accordion, Bill Davis his pipe, and Kathleen Davis beams delight that the band is part of their leader's tour.

Jalopy on tour had three musical set-ups. The smallest was portable, suitable for playing along a street and, like the Pied Piper, drawing people who'd end up at a Tory event. The instruments for this were a coronet, horns, a glockenspiel, and a set of walking snare drums. The second version was larger, used if travelling by bus or small airplane. It included, in addition, lights, an electric piano, some lightweight amplifiers, and a set of light drums. The big set-up, the third, required transport trucks to move the band's full-scale amplifier equipment and two-hundred-pound Hammond organ to an arena or stadium.

A campaign lesson Tom MacMillan learned, to the band's chagrin, came in Cobden: "Never have an event at five o'clock at night in eastern Ontario because people are out milking their cows." He'd invited people to meet Bill Davis at the Agricultural Hall, on the second floor. He told Jalopy there'd be "a huge crowd and I needed them early, so they arrived and schlepped all their equipment up the narrow staircase, including a big Hammond B-3." By a quarter to five, they were ready. But nobody came.

"The little pinwheel sandwiches were out, with the tea and coffee, but no more than eight little old ladies were sitting on the many chairs," said

MacMillan. Ike and the band were playing their hearts out to entertain these people, but the only response came when one lady beckoned the advance man over. He leaned down to hear her ask, "Could you ask the band to turn the music down? It's too loud."

But every campaign has lows, as well as highs. Another night, for a big Niagara Peninsula rally of five ridings, a huge auditorium was jammed and Ike and the band "just had the place rocking. Everybody was in the right frame of mind. Then Davis came on. It was a very powerful combination."

The daily itinerary for the Davis tour was created by Joyce McEwen on a typewriter during the night. As secretary to the tour unit, she often had to make insertions and updates, requiring retyping the entire schedule, using the mechanical equipment of the era. The basic itineraries and program, prepared days in advance, were often changed to respond to an unexpected opportunity or to stave off some potential disaster. Joyce McEwen got the itineraries to the tour bus and news media by working a combination of copying machines, telephones, and drivers to ensure everyone showed up at the right place on time.

Riding on the press bus was a "wagon-master," who ensured reporters had whatever they needed, from adequate time for filing their stories to cold beer. Working with the bus driver, the wagon-master also ensured the tour maintained its assigned schedule. Doug Caldwell, one of the Dirty Dozen, managed this operation, volunteering time away from his fledgling Caldwell Partners headhunting business.

———

Meanwhile, the local campaigns in each of Ontario's 117 ridings had received their allotment of materials from the Toronto headquarters.

Their acceptability was, DeGeer said, "something Norman was worrying about. He was creating a graphic look for the campaign that projected a unity to all Ontarians." Although echoing what Dalton did nationally in 1957, this was groundbreaking for Ontario provincial campaigns. And unlike the other details of the campaign, like the bus-based tour with pancake breakfasts and an uplifting band, or the dissemination of prepackaged radio news stories, the centrally produced campaign materials involved the sensibilities of thousands of party members and partisan workers across the province Norman could not afford to alienate.

In the empty Niagara Peninsula hall, Tom MacMillan stands in the centre of his blue machine campaign advance team describing what had to happen to transform the facility in the next eighteen hours. The transformation is seen in the photo below, when the Ontario Progressive Conservative leader's tour the following night included a Niagara Peninsula campaign rally that absolutely packed the same regional centre for a five-riding event addressed by Ontario premier Bill Davis.

At the Beaver Valley gathering of PC candidates and managers, he had already signalled his plan for a single graphic design, but now they and their local volunteers were seeing, for the first time, the common-look logo, uniform colours, and identical imagery and text. It was not that they'd object to something new if it were additional, but when it changed how local campaign signs had been made up for generations, or replaced the tradition of constituency pamphlets written on the candidate's kitchen table and produced in local print shops, that provoked resistance.

The fact a constituency could no longer produce its own materials rankled, since most Tories felt predisposed to local self-control. Many began to recall how Davis as education minister had, from the centre, consolidated hundreds of school districts, eliminated small local boards, and closed one-room schools to create larger schools, overseeing restructuring from the centre, changing the character of traditional local communities.

"Norman's ambition was that every sign have the same common look, which was new and not always accepted," said DeGeer. People were not accustomed to headquarters dictating what their signs should look like. The central campaign would have to convince them.

Negative feedback began pouring into Toronto headquarters. "A lot of this stuff came to my desk," said DeGeer, "so I had to call and persuade people that, as the campaign developed, this 'branding' was going to be an important part of winning. Politics and politicians being what they are, many candidates did not believe anything could be more important than their own picture, or their own policy statement."

In fact, Ad Hoc jumped through hoops producing brochures for each of the 117 ridings that included the common province-wide elements but also, in each case individually, the riding's name, candidate's name and photo, and contact information for the local PC campaign headquarters. Ad Hoc also produced the core PC pamphlet, featuring Bill Davis and the PC program, in some twenty-two different languages for Ontario's multicultural voters.

If pushback came from a number of ridings to the common-look campaign, a full-scale uproar was provoked by the Davis radio and television commercials. "They were outstanding, powerful commercials and their frequency was incredible. It quickly reached the point we were getting feedback from the ridings protesting, 'Stop, there is too much.'" Everyone available around headquarters had to field this barrage of calls. Norman Atkins, Hugh

Macaulay, Ross DeGeer, "anyone who picked up the telephone" was "sending them off, sympathetically, of course."

The inbound messages were mixed, said Ross. "People were calling to say, 'This is the right thing to do, stay with it, don't buckle.' Others were offended and hostile at how often they had to look at these commercials, some of which were not complimentary about the Opposition, an early stage of 'negative ads.' Some people even thought it was unfair."

Norman Atkins and Bill Davis stayed with the plan. "Mr. Davis was getting feedback when he was travelling around. He would just be sympathetic, and shrug it off."

———

Election day, October 21, ended with the PCs claiming a ninth consecutive term in office. The Davis-led Tories maintained a majority in the legislature with seventy-eight members, gaining eight more seats by taking seven from the Liberals and one from the NDP.

The victory was a triumph for Bill Davis who now had his own mandate, and for Norman Atkins and the much improved blue machine.

Their political union had been fully consummated.

CHAPTER 36

GOVERNING WITH BILL DAVIS

The politicization of government would now enter a new dimension in Ontario, offspring of the campaign marriage between Bill Davis and the blue machine.

During 1971, Dalton Camp wrote major speeches for the premier, Brian Armstrong metered the flow into the premier's office, Roy McMurtry occupied positions dealing with government policy and legal affairs of the provincial Progressive Conservatives, and Norman Atkins met regularly with senior cross-over players between party and government. In a parliamentary democracy, governance and partisanship are fused, so this early 1970s experience in Ontario was in no way unique.

Yet it did embrace new elements.

The new premier cherished politics more than his predecessors had. In the 1950s, conduct of Ontario public affairs under Leslie Frost had a clear line of demarcation between party and government. His political fixers, though close at hand, were not on the public payroll but paid by the party. Frost instructed those running party affairs he would attend only three PC events a year, not more, because he was premier of all Ontarians and wanted to be seen above partisan dimensions. Any time that Frost had for public appearances or platform speeches would go, almost exclusively, to large gatherings of provincial associations and public interest organizations.

In the 1960s when John Robarts replaced Frost, he too played down partisanship in public, though not so rigidly. He simply promulgated his theorem that "good government is good politics" and concentrated on the former so that he might in passing achieve the latter.

For the 1970s, Bill Davis, though acquiring much from both predecessors, did not share their partisan detachment. The Progressive Conservative Party was as central to his being and as basic to his vocation as was religion to a priest. Ontario was Bill's parish, Queen's Park his church, and Dalton, Norman, and their closely knit PC associates his sidesmen.

———

After the election, the Camp agency was awarded the Ontario government's tourism account.

Some Tories, aware this had become "the deal" for Camp and the blue machine in other provinces and even nationally, still expressed surprise Davis would go along with the quid pro quo arrangement, a number having negative attitudes about Dalton because of the Diefenbaker business, others dubious about the ethics of melding party interest and public business, believing the old style "spoils of office" politics had no place in modern Ontario.

This government advertising was not gratuitous patronage, however. "Whenever one of the government advertising accounts came up," said Dianne Axmith at the agency, "we had to make a competitive presentation alongside other agencies for the business." Bill Davis knew who his friends were, and the agency had an inside track because Davis also appreciated the creativity of Camp and those he'd drawn into his advertising galaxy.

The speeches Dalton wrote for him — "Cities are for people, not cars," when cancelling the Spadina Expressway — had policy punch and pithy phrases that outclassed standard provincial fare. The creative quality of Camp advertising, already previewed earlier with Dalton's successful hypopotamus campaign, would soon prove to be just as stellar.

Ontario's tourism officials felt anxiety about losing business to neighbouring New York State with its highly successful "I Love New York" campaign. The minister needed a response. The research department at the Camp agency discovered that when people were shown the province's travel literature, their eyes popped. The brochures about places and experiences

Ontario offered were stunning, yet virtually unknown to the travelling vaca-tioner. So Dalton, Norman, John McIntyre and others decided to create a theme to instill an exciting sense of pride, of discovery, and adventure.

They filmed Ontario's wide variety of unique scenes and linked that imagery to the attractive travel literature, creating a double whammy: engaging television and mass distribution of brochures. Some three million copies of roto inserts were distributed to households across the province. The theme, "very much in character with the province," said McIntyre, "had a soft-spoken quality." It was: ONTARIO: *Yours to Discover*.

The slogan was an invitation. The onus was on individuals and families to make the discovery, which they were free to do. Its simplicity appealed not only to Ontarians and Canadians but Americans, too, as results from Camp agency focus groups in the United States attested to as well. They considered ONTARIO: *Yours to Discover* "very polite, reflecting Canadian character." Also, "discovery" spoke to the sense of a different culture and foreign country which is why Americans would come to Canada. *Yours to Discover* held out that promise. The campaign was so positive that the Davis government added the slogan to the province's licence plates, where it still remains, decades later.

Meanwhile, on the political side, Atkins also became, in essence, full-time political organizer for the provincial Progressive Conservatives, operating the agency as a backroom hub for partisan organization.

The advertising offices on Eglinton Avenue transformed, said Paul Curley, "into the political office of the Ontario PC Party after the 1971 Bill Davis vic-tory." Tories John Andrews, John McIntyre, and Bob Byron all worked there under Norman's leadership.

Others coming to the agency for political strategy meetings, when not gathering downtown at the Albany Club, included Michael Gee who'd been appointed to run Caucus Services for Progressive Conservative MPPs at Queen's Park, Hugh Macaulay, and Terry Yates, longtime friend of Atkins's who, a successful Hamilton businessman and chartered accountant, had been named comptroller for the coming 1972 federal campaign. Hugh Macaulay made the place his second home. Spades Roy McMurtry, Paul Weed, Patrick

Vernon, and Eric Ford were regulars in the mix, the latter two now busy raising money for the 1972 federal campaign.

The agency was not only a place for planning, but operations. One of Bob Byron's specialties was arranging all point-of-purchase materials for the PCs, getting volume discounts on signs, billboards, T-shirts, sweaters, lapel pins, campaign hats, and logo-imprinted pens and coffee mugs. "Norman understood the value these things have," said McIntyre. From logos and pins to campaign innovation and high-level strategy, the blue machine was now truly a fusion, as Dalton had first envisaged in the late 1950s, of a political party and an advertising organization, capable of changing people's perceptions and influencing public affairs.

With so much activity, the Camp agency moved into larger premises at the northwest corner of Yonge and Davisville. Norman enjoyed his bigger office, spacious walk-out balconies, and separate capacious boardroom on the fourth floor. "He'd spring for muffins, croissants, and coffee," said his assistant Dianne Axmith about the change, "and more campaign meetings took place in the agency than at restaurants." It was a modern, newly constructed building with staggered levels. The Camp agency, as anchor tenant, more than quadrupled its Eglinton Avenue space.

Davis, after discussing the personnel change with Atkins, replaced Arthur Harnett by Ross DeGeer as provincial director of the PC Party. Roy McMurtry continued as general counsel to the party. Brian Armstrong remained in the premier's office as appointments secretary, the official gatekeeper organizing Davis's time and controlling access to power. Camp wrote speeches, gave advice, and took on special assignments for the premier. The Spades, whose identity was still unknown, were becoming more fully inserted into the conduct of Ontario's government.

———

The party meshed with government at the highest level of policy, too, in the way every premier or prime minister needs a "kitchen Cabinet" of trusted advisers.

In New Brunswick, Dalton and Norman had established such a link with Richard Hatfield, whom they so frequently entertained that at Robertson's Point he'd been given a permanent "guest room." Every significant initiative the premier took, from making New Brunswick officially bilingual to government support for manufacturing the Bricklin gull-wing sports car, had first been thrashed out at Robertson's Point.

As Bill Davis settled in to govern, a similar arrangement took form in Ontario. Weekly gatherings of a "Park Plaza Group" sought to harmonize government policy and party operations. Although kept quiet and certainly not an official body, the weekly session soon became a well established centre of power, convening throughout the year, except in summer, for an hour and a-half to two hours in a private suite at the Park Plaza Hotel, a couple of blocks north of the Ontario legislative buildings.

There Bill Davis regularly hashed out the politics of his government and party with Roy McMurtry, Hugh Macaulay, Ross DeGeer, Brian Armstrong, Dalton Camp, Norman Atkins, the Cabinet secretary, and, depending on the issues, invited senior officials. Among several reasons Davis welcomed this arrangement was his full access to Dalton's counsel in a venue nobody knew about, an artful way of handling his unsavoriness to many Tories. With the blue machine in the control room, the politicization of Ontario's government proceeded apace but, significantly, Bill Davis was the only elected representative in the room.

———

Ross DeGeer rightly considered himself "the lynchpin of the Spades's provincial connection" because he was now the Eglinton riding president, a member of the provincial PC executive, a campaign manager in provincial elections, and the party's executive director.

The Spades were all, at one time or another, also directors of the Albany Club. The incumbent president of the club would have the directors to his country place for a weekend of frivolity, barbecues, and talking politics. "We did a lot of eating, drinking, and arguing," said DeGeer. "In this setting was built teamwork, camaraderie, relationships, and trust. These were not a bunch of people who came in, worked hard, swept up, and then went away. We worked together politically for years, almost on a daily basis." As the years advanced, those running the Albany Club were the same people running the big blue machine — the same people who were increasingly involved in running Ontario and its governing party.

Following DeGeer's elevation as executive director, he launched an ambitious reorganization of the province-wide party apparatus. The innovations and overhaul of traditional approaches that had become a hallmark of the successful 1971 campaign were now broadened to change Ontario's Progressive Conservative Party itself. The blue machine advanced from being a campaign organization to part of the formal structure itself, in practice if not under the party's constitution.

"It was the ambition of Davis, Macaulay, and Atkins," said DeGeer about this change he was implementing, "to put in place an organization that would be more responsive to the kind of techniques we used during the campaign. To accomplish that objective, the centre became more directly involved with the riding associations."

This was especially important in constituencies the PCs did not hold but where vote margins were close enough for a win next time. "This meant," said the party's new executive director, "communicating with the riding executives more regularly than had ever been done before."

————

The overlay of central control and direction, introduced and imposed by Norman Atkins in 1971, was the start of a true "revolution" or reversal in the core relationship within the ranks and operational structure of Progressive Conservatives.

It began with the signs, the brochures, and the "common look" across the entire province. It was extended by the leader's tour, which transformed a general election across 117 ridings into a single centrally controlled presentation. It was reinforced by the centre's highly professional television messaging based on Canadian pioneering with American methods for "enhanced research." It was now being altered by headquarters's hands-on relationship with riding associations. It would soon embrace the all-important matter of raising and spending campaign money.

The creation of a cadre of regional party organizers, answering directly to the party's executive direction in Toronto, was also a break from the past. Leslie Frost, the province's premier from 1949 to 1961, never lost a by-election because he never called one until his quietly reliable personal organizer, Hugh Latimer, spent a lot of time in a riding where a vacancy had occurred. After enough time unobtrusively spying around and listening, Hugh then reported to Frost what the issues were, who the best PC candidate would be, and how well prepared the riding association was. Of seventeen separate by-elections in the Frost years, the PCs won them all.

Under Robarts, when party operations at first were directed by insurance broker Patrick Kinsella, some regional organizers were hired, younger men like Jerry Lampert who handled eastern Ontario. The direct link to the premier was severed. The PCs no longer won all by-elections.

Now DeGeer, in collaboration with Atkins and Macaulay, expanded this parallel party function with a complete network of regional organizers throughout the province, "which over time helped bring the party closer to the ridings." The closeness was that of a separate, centralized party operation. From the centre, all ridings can start to look the same.

Party headquarters in Toronto produced and sent monthly newsletters to riding association executive members in every constituency. "This in turn meant we could develop a more accurate membership list which had many uses as time went on," said DeGeer. "We also asked the newsletter recipients to pay $10, to defray the cost of the mailing, which was another innovation for the party." Money began flowing from the ridings to the centre. It had previously worked the other way.

The party had evolved from the ground up, in a province of vast distances and limited communications, with locals taking charge, organizing themselves, selecting their candidate, raising their own money and keeping it for their own needs, running their campaign, motivating voters according to local political culture and regional opportunity. For Conservatives, this autonomy and direct responsibility, begun as practical necessity, created a political orientation or philosophy. The provincial "party" was the Progressive Conservative *Association* of Ontario, a loose amalgamation of many separate organizations: riding associations, PC business associations, PC women's associations, PC Youth organizations, and campus PC clubs.

But now the centre was exerting new control. It was not only happening politically. The Davis government took bold measures to reconfigure governance itself, including by consolidation of a number of separate municipalities into regional governments which continued the premier's earlier steps as education minister to consolidate rural schools and expand the educational system.

———

With the premier's own interest in national politics, even the prime ministership itself, he and his blue machinist friends increasingly turned their eyes to the coming federal election. Bill Davis pledged to put all his resources behind Bob Stanfield's next campaign.

For this effort, the blue machine had a strong political axis of men who knew each other well as close friends. Finlay MacDonald was federal campaign chairman. Malcolm Wickson would run day-to-day operations of the national campaign. Both would harmonize with Norman Atkins's extensive reach and formidable resources, for another round of campaigning with Bill Davis across Ontario, this time for the Progressive Conservative national cause.

CHAPTER 37

BLUE MACHINE AXIS

The blue machine innovations made by Atkins, Wickson, and Lind, on full display in Ontario's 1971 election, showed what the Tories could bring to their 1972 re-match against Pierre Trudeau.

Ontario would be a major battleground for the election, so Atkins wanted to further strengthen the axis between blue machinists in Toronto and Ottawa through closer integration with the national party.

When Dalton was president, the blue machine's hold on the national party was direct. Since then, restless Frank Moores, Dalton's blue machine–friendly successor, had departed Ottawa to lead the Newfoundland PCs. It was time to prepare for the party's 1971 annual meeting, which would elect a new slate of officers. However, the contest was becoming quite bizarre, primarily because of those now counselling Stanfield.

The presidency was shaping up as a battle between two strong Tories, neither of them blue machinists. Donald Matthews of London, a wealthy contractor and member of John Robarts's circle, was in the race, as was Alberta's influential Roy Deyell. The people around Stanfield wanted to see the Albertan elected, to help secure that province's political base. In line with this thinking, they had Stanfield ask Atkins to run somebody from Ontario, because under the constitution the party's president and vice-president could not both come from the same province.

Stanfield interacts with Spades Don Guthrie and Roy McMurtry, and Newfoundland MP Frank Moores, who'd replaced Camp as PC party president. At this annual meeting in Ottawa, McMurtry was a candidate for national vice-president, as the party and the blue machine sought to juggle the talent lineup.

So the blue machine, following the leader's wishes, mounted a campaign for Roy McMurtry as party vice-president. The Atkins team, with no particular grievance against Don Matthews, set about to defeat him by supporting Roy Deyell. Atkins encouraged the newly elected PC Youth Federation's policy vice-president, Hugh Segal, to recruit youth voters for McMurtry. He did so keenly. "Having McMurtry, close friend of Davis, Camp, and Atkins, as second top person in the national party," enthused Hugh, "would blend the Ontario blue machine with the federal organization in a way that would achieve the required co-operation between Ontario and the feds if we were to win the coming 1972 election." Meanwhile, with mixed signals from the leader's office, Stanfield's own riding president nominated Don Matthews!

In the end, Matthews was elected PC national president and Deyell went on the executive as vice-president. McMurtry returned to his Toronto law practice and Ontario political focus.

———

A much simpler way to strengthen the Tory campaigners' axis between Ottawa and Toronto had, to Norman's relief, already been established when he and Wickson shared preparations for the 1971 Ontario election. After the Davis victory, partisan planning at the Camp agency continued uninterupted, with the two of them relying on the same talented team, the only difference being that for their next campaign, they'd all be working to elect Stanfield.

In November 1971, Norman invited the Dirty Dozen to dine at the Albany Club. He congratulated the advance men. "You did a great job for Mr. Davis," he said, "and now we would like you to meet Bob Stanfield and do for him what you did for the premier." Ontario's premier, also attending, urged the Dirty Dozen volunteers "to carry on and do what you have done provincially, federally."

Among the advance team recruits that night was Paul Curley. With a keen interest in politics dating back to his days at the University of Ottawa, Paul had been enlisted, along with Tom MacMillan, by his university buddy John Thompson to work in Darcy McKeough's campaign to become Ontario PC leader and premier.

Not long after the convention, Curley got a call from Hugh Macaulay, who asked him if he wanted to be an advance man for the Davis campaign in the coming election. Curley didn't know what he was being asked, but understood there was only one correct answer to the question.

Now a volunteer for the Davis campaign, Curley had only to cross the street: the PC headquarters on Adelaide Street faced the front door of Rio Algom, where he worked. From Norman Atkins he received a *Guide to Advance the Hon. Robert L. Stanfield, Federal Election, 1972,* a confidential sixteen-page manual, numbered and assigned to him by name. It was a condensed version of the handbook issued the year before to those advancing the leader's tour for Bill Davis, the Canadianized version of Jerry Bruno's manual for pulling off battlefield triumphs.

Several weeks later, Atkins and Curley were in British Columbia for the November 28 Grey Cup game at Empire Stadium. Davis, who'd been a varsity football player at the University of Toronto with McMurtry, was on hand too, cheering for the Toronto Argonauts, happy the team's colour was blue. Also in the stands was Peter Lougheed, who four months earlier, fully independent of the Camp-Atkins organization, had ousted Alberta's Social Credit dynasty in a stunning electoral upset to become the province's first Progressive Conservative premier. Lougheed, who'd played two seasons of pro football with the Edmonton Eskimos, displayed his enthusiasm for Toronto's rivals, the Calgary Stampeders.

In addition to a love of football, the two fresh Progressive Conservative premiers of powerhouse provinces came from very political families and were lawyers. Even the teams they supported were closely matched. The Argos and Stamps battled through a very tight game on the rain-slicked gridiron until Calgary finally claimed the celebrated Cup, 14–11.

After the game, Atkins spotted Curley and introduced him to Vancouverite Malcolm Wickson. The three went into a coffee shop to continue their discussion. Malcolm asked Paul more about his background, and learned he was bilingual, from Ottawa, had worked in Montreal, had a university degree and had also studied abroad, had worked in the private sector, and was now in Toronto. It was as if a halo appeared over Curley's head. For several weeks Norman canvassed other potential prospects for the job of Malcolm's executive assistant, and made endless soundings about Curley. In the end, the decision made, he telephoned Curley.

Curley quit his job at Rio, moved back to Ottawa, and reported for duty as executive assistant to the national director of a major Canadian political party, "not knowing what my job was or even why they wanted me to do it. But I was single, bilingual, and took the job."

———

Wickson in Ottawa was campaign chairman, Atkins in Toronto was communications coordinator for the national campaign, and Curley now was their resourceful and intelligent go-between.

Malcolm knew quite a few Tory operatives, having been national director since 1968, but to fill the campaign's organization chart, he and Norman increasingly tapped the blue machine's own roster of top organizers across Canada. "I kept in touch with everyone in the field and throughout the organization," said Curley, "to make sure each person knew what they were supposed to be doing." Keeping tabs on them all, he grew familiar with the blue machine's most trusted contacts, a national network of exceptional campaign organizers.

Malcolm Wickson, the "Good Shepherd" of the Progressive Conservatives, sits amidst his flock of "black sheep," including, at his right Robert Stanfield, Murray Coolican, and Gerry Nori, Ontario PC president; and at his left, Nate Nurgitz of Winnipeg. In the back, behind Stanfield, are Roy McMurtry and Brian Armstrong, then Tom MacMillan and Hugh Segal. The three standing at the very right are Paul Weed, Norman Atkins, and Hugh Macaulay. National tour director John Thompson sits in front of Nurgitz, and at the end of that row to right is Spade Eric Ford in dark-rimmed glasses. Seated in front of Stanfield are Michael Gee, director of Ontario PC Caucus Services, and Paul Curley. All present were key to the Tory organization.

"A lot of major federal PC campaign decisions were being made in the Camp offices," Curley observed, "long before a separate election headquarters in downtown Toronto was set up." At the Camp agency, election preparation teams were established with PC organizers for every province. Detailed arrangements were worked out with the secret specialist advertising consortium, code named PACE. Public opinion polling work was projected, with Bob Teeter and Fred Steeper coming to the agency from Detroit for meetings, figuring out better ways to project Stanfield's image that would align perceptions of him with public concerns about the economy. The 1972 tour planning team was assembled, including a specialized unit to organize everything with airplanes.

The Progressive Conservative's national campaign would be headquartered in Toronto. Curley, now an integral part of the Ottawa-Toronto axis, became "the guy who kept in touch with everybody in the campaign organization as Malcolm and Norman built the campaign itself."

One year after their Ontario election victory, the original 1971 Dirty Dozen advance team celebrated, inviting Norman Atkins and Malcolm Wickson to join them at Toronto's King Edward Hotel. Conditioned to create photo ops, advance men Peter Groschel and Tom MacMillan placed their lone table dead centre in the ballroom and had this memorable image shot from above.

Ontario was the primary battleground because the province's electorate was more volatile than voters in Canada's other regions and because a great many seats were in play.

In the four Atlantic provinces to the east and the four provinces to the west, Tories worked hard, held firm, and feared fickle Ontarians might deny them a national victory. What happened in Quebec, where Norman interacted principally with Richard LeLay, Stanfield's French-language press secretary, and Quebec PC organizer Jean Peloquin, would be a case unto itself.

Crucial to the Ontario theatre of battle was that Bill Davis wanted to play a major role in the national campaign. He led his entire provincial PC organization into action for Stanfield. Davis himself spent all available time working for the cause, appearing at meetings with the leader, speaking in individual ridings on behalf of PC candidates, peppering the province with timely phone calls. At

Norman Atkins and Malcolm Wickson, dining at the Albany Club, spent a great deal of time together building a strong Ottawa-Ontario blue machine axis for Progressive Conservative election campaigns.

Queen's Park, Brian Armstrong aligned his calendar to the campaign's needs. When not in Davis's office, he went downtown to work in the campaign office on Adelaide Street, to ensure maximum coordination.

The set-up was familiar, to Armstrong and most others, because the same building had been used as provincial campaign headquarters the year before. Some elements of the national campaign were being handled in Ottawa, but this was the main engine room for the Canada-wide effort.

Here Atkins and Wickson continued working closely throughout the election, taking special pride in collaborating with PACE to produce television commercials that campaign veterans considered "brilliant." Curley worked out of Ottawa at PC Party headquarters, travelled a lot, was on the campaign plane with the leader, and "followed up on a lot of stuff Malcolm did not have time to do. Like a 'gofer' I did whatever needed doing."

———

The word went out "all hands on deck" once the election was called for October 30.

Camp telephoned the Spades, and a few others, to tell them he would not contest the election. He explained to Bill Davis that he wanted to continue his new work, outside partisan politics, as a member of the Ontario Royal Commission on Book Publishing, to which John Robarts had appointed him in December 1970. The premier understood. He valued Camp's political assessments, proffered Tuesday mornings over private breakfast at the Park Plaza Hotel, but knew from his own grapevine that the former national president of

Roy McMurtry paces Dalton Camp as they count out laps in downtown Toronto, the two hatching political strategy in locker rooms as well as party backrooms. At this time, as Dalton was beginning to withdraw from certain political roles, Roy maintained contact as a friend who'd been concerned "leadership review" would cripple Camp's political future.

the PCs was still *persona non grata* with many Tories. Davis did not protest or urge reconsideration. Dalton ended their conversation saying he just wanted "to write and do other things."

––––––

The 1972 national leader's campaign, with tour maestro John Thompson and the Dirty Dozen advancing Stanfield, made the 1968 campaign's efforts appear amateurish.

As national tour director, Thompson had Bill McAleer alongside as a co-director; Murray Coolican was their assistant, Gordon Petursson manager, Bev Dinsmore comptroller, and Joyce McEwen secretary. They directed the national tour and ran five separate field teams of regional advance men, each with its own coordinator. The Dirty "Dozen" expanded with fresh recruits; some had no political track-record yet were still keen for action and highly enterprising. For this nation-wide effort, the field coordinators were allotted entire provinces and regions: Tom MacMillan, British Columbia and Alberta; Hal Huff, Saskatchewan and Manitoba; John Slade, Ontario; Richard LeLay, Quebec; and John Laschinger, the four Atlantic provinces. In concert with local PC organizations across Canada, more than sixty volunteer tour personnel would handle Stanfield's activities off Parliament Hill.

Slade, son of a lifelong Liberal, considered the national tour with Stanfield "quite a move for us, because it involved so much more planning and travel" than the Davis tour around Ontario. DeGeer drew more volunteers from the Junior Board of Trade. MacMillan brought in fellow Abitibi Paper employee Jim Howe.

It didn't take Tom and advance partner Peter Groschel long to discover that politics in the Pacific province "was pretty much a rat's nest of competing interests for the Conservatives." The duo managed to patch together working relationships with politically active PCs such as Tony Saunders and Don Hamilton. The latter ran a radio station and "understood a centralized campaign, something rare." Mostly, their experience involved encountering locals who insisted on doing the campaign their way.

MacMillan didn't have to be a psychic to foresee a planned Stanfield rally in Vancouver would be a forlorn assembly in a near-empty hall that television cameras could pan, deflating the national campaign. "They did not have as many bodies on the ground in British Columbia as local organizers thought," he said. Locals told Tom a thousand people would turn up at Hotel Vancouver. He doubted they'd see even six hundred.

First of all, the reception was for Stanfield, who was not very exciting. Second, the Conservative Party did not do well in British Columbia, whatever the event. In 1968, the PCs had not elected one MP anywhere in the province. But MacMillan knew pointing out the obvious would not boost numbers, so instead did what advance men are meant to: *create conditions for success.* "If you get more than six hundred people to the reception," he challenged, "I will jump into the bay with my clothes on."

The chance to punish a know-it-all from east of the Rockies was an appealing incentive. They "worked their asses off for the last ten days" and when Stanfield showed up, so did 602 supporters. "They were a long way from one thousand, but would have been a long way from six-hundred if I hadn't challenged them." On a cold autumn day, fully dressed, MacMillan took his dive off a pier into the cold waters of Vancouver's harbour, almost too chilled to hear the cheering. The stunt created a foundation of goodwill for future work among B.C. Tories, as his gutsy reputation spread.

The blue machine advance teams did not always have the option of a good venue, as this cramped stage in a small community attests. Ike Kelneck provides music, Stanfield speaks, television cameramen squeeze in, flags and posters detract from the focus, and local Tory chieftains sit wherever chairs fit.

At the other end of the country, John Laschinger checked a Nova Scotia community two days before the Stanfield tour was to arrive for a school auditorium rally. He discovered local PCs had erected a big sign for Bob Stanfield. Atkins had been adamant that all advertising and media, including signs, use only R.L. Stanfield. The intent was to achieve prime ministerial gravitas, as in R.B. Bennett. The need was common identity across the entire national campaign. Laschinger ordered the Nova Scotians to get "R.L." from the sign-maker to fit over "Bob." They labelled him "the jerk from Toronto."

In Alberta, MacMillan and Jim Howe found a complete contrast to British Columbia, a province where even the turf was Tory. Of seventeen federal ridings, now increased for the 1972 election to nineteen by redistribution, one was Rocky Mountain where PC candidate Joe Clark hoped to unseat a remaining Grit.

Gutsy advance man Tom MacMillan, by Vancouver's Bayshore Inn, plunged fully clothed into frigid Pacific waters after boosting numbers at a Stanfield event by vowing to do so if locals could get six hundred people to a reception for the campaigning leader, which they did. The Dirty Dozen's code was to "create conditions for success."

After meeting Clark at his campaign office in Drayton Valley, MacMillan, with Howe and Clark, began walking the streets, accompanied by the municipality's manager, discussing plans for a Stanfield breakfast as part of the national tour's Alberta swing. MacMillan noticed loudspeakers mounted on lamp posts everywhere.

The manager explained the system allowed someone to tell the whole town what was going on, just by flipping a switch at the recreation centre. MacMillan immediately saw Radar in the TV series *M*A*S*H*, broadcasting his announcements throughout the army base. The manager added, "We rent it out."

MacMillan reached into his pocket, counted out enough bills, and "cut the deal then and there" to acquire exclusive local broadcasting rights for the election. On the morning of the breakfast, "we were able to turn the loudspeakers on and invite the whole town to come on over and have breakfast with Bob Stanfield." And almost everybody did.

In Edmonton, however, when MacMillan tried to get an ugly wooden graphic representing Stanfield taken down from the arena before a big rally, Roy Watson, an Edmonton insurance broker who ran the northern half of the province for the PCs, realized he, too, was dealing with a jerk from Toronto. "You know, this is Alberta. This is how we do things. We won't be changing anything now."

———

It had been early February 1972 when Atkins asked John Thompson to organize a "national campaign tour" for Stanfield. The only guideline was to prepare for the federal election "with some of the philosophy that had been successful in the 1971 Ontario campaign for Davis."

John convened a tour committee and by March 29 presented its plan to the PC National Executive which approved its two key elements: the national tour would be based in Toronto, and it would have centralized authority over Stanfield's activities away from Parliament Hill. Not knowing when the election might come, the tour was prepared in segments that could be compressed or expanded.

For the pre-writ period, which turned out to last six and a half months, the initial tour objectives combined close analysis of Teeter's deep polling research and the need to compile an extensive library of film showing Stanfield in many different settings across the country for media use and campaign advertising. In this phase, Stanfield visited 136 communities, involving 402 separate gatherings. In sixty days of touring, his activities encompassed plant tours, radio talk shows, media interviews, "and all forms of practical campaigning," said Thompson. To reflect what polling showed as areas most probable for PC gains, the tour spent thirty-three days in Ontario, fifteen in the West, seven in Quebec, and five in the Maritimes. This segment cost $71,000.

Over the half year of pre-election touring, Stanfield's activities shifted from major rallies and nominating meetings to community functions, such as coffee parties, visits to old age homes, breakfast meetings, airport receptions, private meetings, and "issue events" to address aboriginal concerns and pollution

Robert Stanfield addresses one of the many large crowds the Dirty Dozen advance team created for him, while a blue machine cameraman films "library" footage for use in PC television commercials.

problems. By July and August, concentrating on Ontario, major emphasis again shifted, now to hotline shows and plant tours. There was no budget as such for this phase, just a guideline to not exceed $1,500 per touring day. By concentrating on Ontario, Thompson kept expenditures to an average of $1,173 a day.

Once the election began on September 12, leading to voting on October 30, he had three distinct tour phases with different objectives. Phase One would portray Stanfield as a credible alternative to Pierre Trudeau through a tour that was organized, efficient, dynamic, and determined. "We wanted to make the point that Robert Stanfield is determined to be prime minister and that this election is a two-way contest," said Thompson. The tour team sought to do this "in such as way as to draw out the undecided voters and to ease the fundraisers task." In the process, more film was added to the PC library showing "good geographical, people, Stanfield, and issue shots." Attention was drawn "to our first rate candidates across the country." And in contrast to the PCs' 1968 campaign, this tour was designed to make Stanfield "look like a winner and thus allow the press to come our way."

The blitz-like opening in September, touring coast to coast, covered a great deal of territory in short time, included a diverse mix of events. Stanfield was "well received everywhere" because "we went to strength," said Thompson.

Phase Two, from September 25 to October 17, was expected to be harder, because the tour concentrated on the campaign's three priority provinces, in Ontario for nine days, and British Columbia and Quebec for two each. Thompson anticipated this intense regional focus would make the tour seem duller, and the press duly complained that it was. All the same, Stanfield registered an impact in the regions visited, which made their ridings more receptive to the PC media campaign. "It was never our objective that the tour would catch fire in these regions," said Thompson, "only that we would allow for a great deal of participation by the riding organizations and flood the local media with evidence of Stanfield's interest in their riding."

During most of Phase Two, Stanfield — reading Camp's speeches — concentrated on attacking Pierre Trudeau and his management of the economy. This complemented the PC media campaign which started October 7 and continued for ten days, with commercials consisted of street interviews suggesting Canada had serious problems of unemployment, galloping prices, and excessive taxes, and that these were the responsibility of the Trudeau Liberal government.

By October 18, right on schedule with Atkins's strategy, the PC media campaign moved into its positive phase, as a response to the negatives about the economic problems highlighted in Phase Two. This was accomplished through four waves of commercials: "issue and answer," "Robert Stanfield the Alternative," "testimonials," and "crowd reactions" — all of them upbeat and constructive.

Phase Three ran from October 19 to 28. The tour's concluding goal was "to demonstrate the strength and substance of the P.C. and Stanfield alternative, as a solution to Trudeau and his government's mismanagement of the economy." This ten-day leader's tour was "going to strength, with due consideration for riding and area priorities."

Overall, the touring campaign ran for thirty-one days, with Stanfield visits to eighty-five communities and engagement in a staggering 218 events. Stanfield displayed athletic stamina. Tour director Thompson, devoted to spending control given his strong financial training, spent $228,300 of his $230,000 budget, averaging $7,475 per touring day, costed to $2,680 for each community visited and $1,092 per event. He also had a $45,000 budget for tour advertising, of which only $10,200 was used. For transport, the leader's tour chartered a dedicated DC-9 from Air Canada, and two sets of twin buses. The aircraft logged 69,318 miles (including 10,000 in empty return flights) and the buses clocked 50,000 miles with Stanfield aboard for 8,000 of them.

"No other national political figure in this country," Thompson calculated, "has travelled as far and met as many people in as many communities as did Robert Stanfield between February 16 and October 30, 1972."

———

Ike Kelneck's band, Jalopy, having so enlivened the Davis campaign tour, was indispensible for Stanfield's.

"They wanted the thing to work," said MacMillan of the band members. "They wanted people to be in the right mood for Davis because they loved Davis and it was the same for Stanfield. I think they liked all the leaders, in those early days. There wasn't anything they wouldn't do to advance the cause."

In Quebec at a Chicoutimi college, Jalopy warmed up the student audience before Stanfield's arrival. Kelneck spoke French. The band worked through its extensive repertoire. Organizers at the back of the auditorium gave Ike the signal to "s-t-r-e-t-c-h" the performance, so they kept playing. Stanfield had been delayed. The students enjoyed the upbeat music but were getting restless, after more than an hour. Again, "s-t-r-e-t-c-h" was being signalled. Stanfield's plane

Jalopy leader Ike Kelneck is at the keyboard, guitarist Roger Perreault is behind the lovely Alice, Reva, and Lynn, all of them performing on a sunny outdoor stage to attract crowds and pique enthusiasm before Robert Stanfield reaches the microphone with his 1972 campaign message.

had still not landed. Jalopy, having performed all suitable songs, began playing through their repertoire a second time. "S-t-r-e-t-c-h" signed the advance
man from the rear door. Band members urgently needed a toilet break and
wanted to rest their raspy voices and sore fingers. They'd been playing over
two hours. Students began leaving. Others angrily chanted "Give us Stanfield."
After Jalopy's two-hour-and-twenty-minute non-stop performance, a harried
R.L. Stanfield made his appearance while the musicians fled the stage. "That
was our toughest night," sighed Kelneck.

Integrating Jalopy into the PC campaigns changed the way entertainment
fused with politics, enlivened crowds, made everyone more receptive, and created a better environment for the leader. Decades later, Tom MacMillan would
look back over his many campaigns and innovations to state that his greatest
satisfaction came from "putting Ike Kelneck in touch with the Conservative
Party and all the good that came out of that over the years."

———

Wherever Stanfield spoke, his speeches were exceptionally good: consistent,
quotable, and content-solid. Each was the product of a clandestine operation
conducted deep in Toronto's Westbury Hotel.

The person writing the words Stanfield spoke, wherever he appeared across
Canada, was Dalton Camp. At this stage, Camp was in personal withdrawal
from the structured operations of election campaigns, and as a royal commissioner in Ontario also thought it best not to be visible in partisan efforts.
But even more, Dalton was now estranged from Stanfield, harbouring a hollow diffidence about being distanced to placate Diefenbaker loyalists. Yet he
felt responsible for Stanfield being leader, and still relished crafting political
speeches. When Bob asked for Dalton's help, in a secret face-to-face meeting
in a room at the Château Laurier, Dalton had agreed. He was familiar with
the scenario, played out from Prince Edward Island to Winnipeg, where a
party leader treated him like a married man might his mistress, desired for his
remarkable abilities and sophisticated understanding, but kept out of sight to
avoid disastrous reactions.

Hunkered down with Camp in his off-the-chart facility in Toronto were
Bill Grogan and Wendy Smallian. The place was only known to its three inhab-
itants and Atkins, Wickson, Stanfield, and Brian Armstrong, who jokingly

dubbed it "the bunker," a counterpart to Norman's "war room." Grogan was a seasoned Tory speech writer and senior assistant to Stanfield with whom Camp worked well. They bounced ideas off one another and settled on pithy phrases that packed maximum punch yet were consistent with the leader's own "voice." As researcher and assistant, Smallian, who'd earlier worked for PC caucus research in Ottawa, ferreted out damning statistics and dumb statements by Liberals, as requested by either man.

As part of their Château deal, all Stanfield's speeches would come exclusively from the bunker, to ensure consistency of voice and content. Camp and Groggan's texts ranged from the leader's grand vision of Canada's future to short modules that, like a hand of cards, could be rearranged, played, or kept back for a later round. The speeches incorporated party policy, reflected Teeter's opinion analysis, and contained Stanfield-like vocabulary.

Here again, as with tour, the PCs were now light years ahead of their 1968 campaign. Then Stanfield had to make up policy, in the vacuum created by the Diefenbaker chasm, on the fly. By 1972, drawing on devoted policy work by countless PCs over many months, the PC leader was able to call for discipline in government spending, more powers for the auditor general to fight waste and inefficiency, and banning strikes in essential services.

Stanfield also announced in his speeches how the PCs would require foreign-owned companies operating in Canada to have a majority of Canadians on their boards; provide a financial incentive for Canadians to invest in small businesses; co-operate with provincial governments in economic development; and emphasize re-training for unemployed workers. His speeches further advocated a range of tax, tariff, and financial measures to address voters' concerns about the economy, such as increased processing of natural resources within Canada, reducing personal income tax rates 7 percent, indexing tax brackets to inflation to keep taxes from creeping up as the cost of living rose, regularly adjusting old age security payments to offset inflation, and setting up residential land banks to reduce housing costs. Stanfield even said the PCs might introduce price-and-wage controls, if necessary, to control inflation.

Getting these speeches to the touring leader took advantage of a communications machine that was state-of-the-art for 1972. Once Camp and Grogan finished a text, Smallian typed the speech onto the special paper used for an early version of the facsimile machine. The paper was then put onto a roll, the equipment hooked up to a telephone and, as the roll began revolving, exposing the text line-by-line, the rhythm of its clackety-clackety-clackety beat in the bunker confirmed that another Stanfield speech was making its way to some distant corner of Canada.

Wherever Stanfield travelled, a member of the tour carried the counterpart machine which he hooked up to the telephone in his hotel room. Upon receiving the text, he'd hand it to the leader, so Stanfield could become familiar with his speech before going to the public event where he'd deliver other men's words and make them his own.

This way of creating campaign speeches was new. There was a common "voice" to them all, and consistent development of the campaign themes as honed from Teeter's research and party policy, which is where Brian Armstrong contributed to the work of Camp and Grogan. They followed the campaign from the bunker, especially watching the television newscasts to see what items got media play, and which did not. This synergistic loop enabled them to refine the speeches and torque Stanfield's message as the campaign progressed.

Until this point in Canadian elections, a speech writer travelled with the leader's campaign team, as Camp and Grogan had both done many times, because that was the only way to be in touch with what was going on and to hand material to the leader for his speeches. Absent a speech writer a leader might carry a well-used text and deliver the same message over and over. Sometimes a person might telephone long distance with suggested wording to be incorporated in the leader's soon-to-be-delivered speech, or otherwise get a note to him, but this patchwork approach, apart from lacking a reliable control system, was open to errors in transmission, especially as the number of people involved increased.

What Stanfield saw, and what he delivered from the podium, was exactly what Camp and Grogan had written and signed off on, consistent with deliberately established party policies.

———

The last of the 264 constituency nominations were taking place.

Ottawa-Centre was such a Liberal fiefdom that not even popular Ottawa mayor Charlotte Whitton had been able to win the riding for the PCs in Diefenbaker's 1958 landslide. Even so, campaign strategists sometimes entice a prominent person to stand for office in order to add luster to the party's lineup for national publicity purposes. Those in the backrooms understand the person's commitment lasts only until election day, after which he or she will resume normal life. The PCs got Edward Foster, a prominent Ottawa lawyer with Canadian Pacific Railways, to agree to be the party's standard bearer in hopeless Ottawa-Centre.

But Hugh Segal contested the nomination. Supported by young Conservatives from Carleton and Ottawa universities who swamped the nominating auditorium and outvoted others, Hugh became the party's official candidate.

Atkins was enchanted by this brazen display of organizational ability and, always seeking to "broaden the tent," as he put it, shone a spotlight on the presence of Segal as an articulate young Jewish person in the Progressive Conservative Party. Several times during the campaign, he called Segal to national headquarters in Toronto "to help on communications matters and do some free-time TV." The Liberals retained their hold on Ottawa-Centre, but just barely. Hugh came within five hundred votes of breaking through.

Hugh Segal was a leading PC student organizer at University of Ottawa when he successfully challenged a prominent CPR lawyer for a Tory nomination. Although he nearly won the seat, Hugh never did make it into the Commons, remaining instead in the blue machine backrooms helping elect others.

————

The 1972 election itself was odd, from start to finish.

The Liberals had surfed into office in 1968 on a crest of Trudeaumania, were still high in the polls, and seemed high on something else, too, with their sweetly mindless campaign slogan "The Land is Strong" and television commercials showing Canadian scenery. With the economy in a slump, Canadians were not looking for strength in the land so much as in political leaders.

The PC campaign, drawing on Teeter's polling, did not emphasize Stanfield, who'd been found "honest yet bumbling." Instead, the Tories simply presented a contrast to the Liberals' drift on economic issues, pledging "A Progressive Conservative government *will* do better." The PCs offered a long list of economic and financial measures to benefit hard-hit Canadians; the Liberals had few issues, fewer program details.

The most drama of the campaign came on election night, October 30, 1972, as Canadians became mesmerized by changing vote counts and seat tallies deep into the night. The PCs first held their advantage in Atlantic Canada, Stanfield's political base, with twenty-two seats, to fifteen for the Liberals. In central Canada, the Trudeau-led Liberals swept his base, Quebec, winning sixty of the provinces seventy-eight seats, while Social Credit picked up fifteen, leaving the PCs with two. Across Ontario, where the blue machine made its most intense push, the hoped-for dividend was paid. The PCs climbed from seventeen seats to forty, taking twenty-seven from the Liberals. Through the Prairies the PCs won most seats, including Alberta's Rocky Mountain where Joe Clark unseated the Liberal member with a comfortable five thousand vote advantage, including a surge of support in Drayton Valley.

All Canada waited up for the British Columbians, watching as the PCs picked up eight West Coast seats. It was enough. The PCs had broken through, winning more ridings than any other party. Stanfield went to bed as prime minister-elect with the narrowest of minority governments, 109 PC seats to 107 for the Liberals, 31 for the NDP, and 15 for Social Credit.

Overnight, recounts reversed the picture. In two ridings, a bare handful of votes would shape Canadian history. A British Columbia riding just narrowly came back into the Liberal column, putting the two parties at 108 seats each. In Ontario, the York-Scarborough outcome proceeded to a judicial recount and two weeks later, the judge confirmed that PC Frank McGee's apparent comeback had not materialized. He'd lost by four votes. Thanks to that slim difference, Pierre Trudeau continued as prime minister, his Liberal minority government supported by David Lewis and the NDP.

The outcome deeply chagrined the blue machinists, who'd put on a masterful campaign, but the result corresponded, reasonably well for once, with the popular vote. Canada-wide, the Liberals did have higher support at 38 percent, to 35 percent for the PCs. The NDP's 17 percent translated into thirty-one seats, and Social Credit's 8 percent, fifteen.

It was the closest election outcome in Canadian history.

CHAPTER 38

THE HIGH PRICE OF HARD POLICY

After the PCs' razor thin loss, most Tories believed it was only a matter of time.

In Nova Scotia, it had taken Stanfield a couple of elections to become premier. Nationally, after the crushing 1968 defeat, the party and Stanfield had almost edged the Grits out in 1972. Now blue machinists hoped his slow-and-steady approach would prevail in the next election. With a minority government, it could come anytime.

There were no major changes or shakeups. Paul Curley, off payroll, went to Europe, taking stock of his life for a number of months. At party headquarters, John Laschinger became national director. When Curley returned to Canada in the spring of 1973 and needed a job, he looked up Atkins, now promoted to director of operations for the next federal election. Malcolm Wickson would be national campaign chairman. Back in Ottawa, Paul reprised his role as Malcolm's assistant, working with candidates and the campaign organization to get ready.

Two features, however, one technological, the other human, did mark new dimensions for the blue machine at this time: an enhanced television production unit, and a bonding phenomenon known as "the Rough-In."

Television had increasingly transformed Canadian public affairs. By the early 1970s, it was the common vector through which all of the blue machine's most important elements were channelled and reconfigured: the leader's tour, party "brand" identity, the uniform scripted "message" from candidates, emphasis on TV training at campaign schools, hours of preparation and performance coaching for the televised leaders' debates, and carefully crafted commercials tied to deep polling analysis. To gain the advantages of television, more campaign money and staff resources were devoted to it than anything else.

Nancy McLean, an astute television counsellor and Tory backroom player, would identify the big blue machine in Ontario as "the beginning of the modern era of politics that spanned the seventies and eighties." Nancy and her husband, Barry, also a television producer, worked closely with Terry McCartney-Filgate, Toronto Film House–owner Don Haig, and others Dalton and Norman recruited to ensure the best television team in politics.

Nancy's colleague John Laschinger recalled her saying of the blue machine, "The hallmark was two things — it was professionalism and it was discipline." McLean and Lashchinger both observed that, while many members of the blue machine were highly committed Tories, their partisanship "never seemed to get in the way of the notion that good government equals good politics." This same professional standard also applied to everything done in the blue machine's television production.

———

As for "The Robertson's Point Interprovincial Tennis Classic & Rough-In," this get-away weekend for hard-core backroom organizers began in 1973.

The venue was the Atkins's family cottage by New Brunswick's Grand Lake, site of the inaugural encounter between Dalton and Norman in 1942. It had since expanded into a compound, with more buildings, and after Dalton married into the family, Robertson's Point had evolved into a Maritime mecca for political insiders who wanted to sip on current events and chew over elections. The place was no public drop-in centre, but a rarefied venue to which thoughtful and progressive players immersed in politics, journalism, and the uses of power were, if lucky, invited. No longer just an ordinary summer retreat, Robertson's Point had become a legendary place.

Summer verandah talk could be about pragmatic politics, which was Norman's forté, or soar into conceptual realms as Dalton endlessly dissected a seemingly intractable governance dilemma, or examine a proposed political solution by discussing the concept from many angles. They happily talked politics anywhere: a bar, a smoky hotel room, a dinner table, or one of Norman's campaign committee breakfast meetings in the back corner of a restaurant. But the best venue of all was together at Robertson's Point and, by the early 1970s, Norman saw potential here for something new.

After he and Dalton formed the Spades in 1966, getaway weekends in the Ontario countryside helped its hand-picked members bond. Their times away together in winter included snowshoeing and cross-country skiing, followed in late afternoon by talking politics in front of a roaring fireplace with drinks in hand, then dinners running well into the night as empty wine bottles accumulated. Fine wine and wide-ranging conversation helped the Spades normalize into a tight-knit and highly effective cadre. "I learned in those weekends," said Bill Saunderson, "that there was more to politics than politics."

Norman promoted such events because men who valued each other as friends would be inclined to not fight amongst themselves during a campaign's intense conflicting pressures. It made sense, he thought, and Dalton agreed, to try the same thing at Robertson's Point. The brothers-in-law thrived on hanging out with other men, good friends like Finlay MacDonald and Richard Hatfield, and a lengthening parade of others. Paul Weed had a nearby cottage. They'd mull over political possibilities, plot a campaign, and exchange political gossip about people and public affairs.

The first gathering brought together a dozen and a-half political friends, including Malcolm Wickson, campaign chairman for the coming federal election; Finlay MacDonald, now Stanfield's principal secretary; Brian Armstrong, premier Davis's principal secretary; Michael Gee, director of members' services for Ontario's PC caucus; Arthur Collins and Tom Scott from Foster Advertising in Toronto; John Andrews from the Camp agency; Jean Peloquin, a Quebec PC organizer; Richard LeLay, Stanfield's French-language press secretary; "Uncle" Nathan Nurgitz, campaign chairman for Manitoba; Michael Meighen, grandson of Tory prime minister Arthur Meighen and a candidate in Montreal's Westmount riding; Tom Hockin, principal of St. Andrew's College in Ontario; Paul Curley, Tom MacMillan, Hugh "the Backhand" Segal, and several Maritime organizers.

"I felt very proud to be invited by Norman and see the spiritual home of the big blue machine," said the Dirty Dozen's MacMillan, who attended the 1973 gathering and shared a bunk with Hockin. Still in his twenties, Tom found this "a pretty heady experience for a kid from Iroquois Falls," and was "enormously appreciative of being included." The tribal weekend appealed to all who came, making them keen for an encore. So Norman, who thrived as much on having a fresh squad of tennis players to beat as discussing back-shop politics, reconvened an expanded list of blue machinists in 1974. A Rough-In invitation was on its way to becoming a coveted honour, a right-of-passage into the blue machine's inner sanctum.

As each year passed, more of the chosen made the pilgrimage to Robertson's Point to relax, speak freely, laugh, trade campaign tales, play cards, swim in the buff, sing, eat, drink, snore in their sleep, belch, pass wind without apology, trade zingers, forget to shave, swear, eat steaks from the barbecue, smoke cigars, and play tennis on the compound's excellent clay court. It was, beamed MacMillan, "a classic guy's weekend."

The tennis was competitive. Norman, who'd been a New Brunswick provincial tennis champion, was still a top player, head and shoulders above everyone else. His legs were fast. His feet danced. His serve was bullet-like in speed and accuracy. His return was hard, whether forehand or back, and seldom outside the lines, though often on them. He was serious and unyielding to the end. Whether a person played twice a year, and one of the times was at Robertson's Point, or whether a devoted tennis enthusiast who was very good, everybody strove mightily to beat Norman, to no avail.

The "rough-in" part of the name, by which the event became known, came from an advertising term for how someone might start a thematic concept or publicity campaign by just "roughing in" a design to see what it looked like, a first jotting, a preliminary sketch of what might take shape. If the concept seemed to work, based on how others reacted and the person creating the campaign still viewed it after several days, he then might "rough it out" more fully, completing the sketch, providing details, polishing the look, even getting ready to book billboards and airtime. A rough-in is where a campaign starts, and if right, where it gels.

The common factor bringing these people together, said Curley, "was their admiration and loyalty to Norman." When a political campaign approached, "he had many who would willingly and quickly respond to his request to help." The Rough-Ins "became a breeding ground for campaigns."

MacMillan, who liked "dreaming up stuff," thought a logo was needed. He asked Lloyd Cook, an amateur artist friend, to try his hand at something, explaining the Rough-In was "basically tennis, drinking, and telling stories."

Cook created a graphic that stunned MacMillan, who'd not mentioned Dalton Camp. The design was the figure of a man, balancing a tennis racket and a martini glass, his face behind sunglasses and a big cigar, with a protruding tummy stretching a tennis shirt that was already too short, all held aloft on spindly legs. "The character closely resembled Dalton," said an astonished MacMillan. "It was almost karma that it happened that way." The Rough-In caricature appeared in many applications over the years, printed on invitations, signage, special-order tennis shirts for Rough-In participants, even the program for Dalton's sixtieth birthday celebration at the Albany Club.

The gatherings fostered a sense of communal belonging. Those attending had strong belief they shared a common purpose important to Canadian democracy. By mixing people for meals, conversation, tennis, entertainment, drinks and debates, the Rough-In melted divisions that would otherwise have existed. It was also a great way to transfer expertise. One of the greatest values of the Rough-In, said Segal, "was that it linked up generations of party supporters, strategists, advertisers, campaigners, organizers, policy wonks, young and old."

———

The 1974 election began when Prime Minister Trudeau, his government defeated in the Commons, set voting day for July 8.

The PC national campaign, following the model of the 1972 effort, was again primarily based in Toronto. Atkins's role, as it had been ever since he mastered the orchestration of operational logistics, was to bring the elements seamlessly together. "He recruited the players, to start with," noted Ross Monk, referring to the PACE II consortium members who worked in advertising for Norman. "Then we'd meet about three times a week as a group, typically Monday, Wednesday, and Friday, usually over breakfast, when everybody reported on their aspect of the campaign. We then knew what the others were doing so we could coordinate."

As an adman used to late nights, Monk "hated breakfast meetings because I had to get up early," but he recognized "everybody had another job, so we had to work it out with our other duties." In other words, most working on the campaign, even at these highest levels, were all volunteers.

"The level of trust was high," observed Art Collins, another advertising expert in PACE II. "It had to be. We were all working for the same goal."

"Because everyone had different assignments," said Monk, "each one's effort had to mesh with someone else's. You could not simply go off, do it by yourself, and just let things happen. It had to be a team effort. Everybody was focusing on a different aspect of the campaign, but all elements had to be brought together and work as one."

In the realm of image, the Tory leader was not contemporary enough, especially when juxtaposed to Pierre Trudeau. Monk despaired of getting a suitable photograph of the PC leader, saying "Mr. Stanfield was not very photogenic and it was really hard to get an image that could be used for posters and pamphlets." He went through ninety-seven pictures and in the end found "one that was good." It wasn't that Stanfield and cameras were enemies. His appearance just did not correspond to what the blue machine's advertising team and pollsters believed the public was looking for.

When it came to photos of Stanfield in the 1974 election, however, things got much worse. During the campaign, journalist Geoffrey Stevens, who the year before had written a biography of Stanfield, was tossing a football with the PC leader during a May 30 campaign stopover at North Bay. Press photographer Doug Ball captured many shots of Stanfield catching the ball in various poses, although one time he fumbled. That image, sent by Canadian Press across the wire-service, is what Canadian dailies ran on their front pages. The fumble was more devastating than any Liberal advertisement to diminish Stanfield could have hoped for in the age of image politics.

———

In 1974, the new "phone bank" system, another blue machine advance, was operational. It had been added to the arsenal after Ontario PC executive director DeGeer attended a Washington meeting of Republic Party candidates who were being instructed on this latest campaign innovation.

The phone bank, explained DeGeer to other blue machinists in Toronto, "is a system that allows a candidate to monitor the campaign by systematically contacting people on the voters' list in order to evaluate their voting preferences and also to identify issue hot spots. A well-run phone bank can have a letter in the hands of the person telephoned, responding to their particular issue and signed by the candidate, within twenty-four hours."

The operation consisted of rows or banks of telephones from which teams of volunteer callers dialed up the voters' on their lists. The party did not need to create such a costly facility, just arrange for after-hours use of offices and telephones with Tory-friendly companies, such as real estate firms or insurance businesses, where dozens of clear desks with unused phones otherwise sat idle after 5:00 p.m. and over weekends, prime time for PC workers to reach voters at their homes.

The method had been experimented with the Ontario PC campaign, with limited take-up, so a more extensive trial run in an Ottawa area federal by-election, facilitated by John Laschinger as national director, had helped the blue machinists adapt the operation to Canadian ways, including the follow-up policy letter, in full readiness for the 1974 campaign.

———

Another way of reaching voters had, by now, almost become traditional.

Brian Armstrong worked with Robert Teeter to design the opinion polling and, as the American pollster conducted his research, he joined him to interpret the results, adding an all-important Canadian perspective. Rounding out this process, Atkins again assigned Brian to also liaise between the campaign headquarters and the speech writing team of Camp, Grogan, and Smallian.

In this multi-part configuration was revealed the sophisticated stage that had now been achieved in the interaction between electorate and campaign, a level of heightened understanding that, depending on how it was used, could be richly persuasive, or deeply damaging, in presenting the party's "election platform" of policies.

The deep research conducted by Teeter was not to create policy stances, but to reveal which of the PC Party's many policies had most resonance with current concerns among voters. This guided the blue machine to emphasize *only those policies*, in order to make the leader and candidates relevant contenders for popular support. This quest to align a campaign platform with the public's beliefs, values, and interests was not new; it began the day electoral politics started. But its dynamic changed when the new age of democratic politics introduced the opinion survey into this equation.

At first, polling's impact was blunt, because the nature of sampling's use was primitively understood. In 1953, for instance, Allister Grosart wanted the Progressive Conservtive election platform centred exclusively on a whopping tax cut, and he generated an opinion poll substantiating his contention that the public really wanted it. In time, posters and savvy politicians had learned how such polls could be "cooked" by the wording of questions that triggered the desired answers. Teeter had now gone far deeper, earning more respect and achieving greater clout by his rigorous methodology and its accuracy in revealing voter impulses and concerns.

Heading into the 1974 election, the PC pollster had established, beyond any doubt, that the "paramount concern" to voters was inflation. Yet, for a campaign message, the crucial question was what to do with this key intelligence?

Camp believed an opposition party did not need to offer solutions, just identify the problems and lay them squarely upon the government. Get the people mad, then ride their wave of anger into office by just standing back to reap the whirlwind. "When a government is determined to bring itself down," he'd said in the 1952 New Brunswick provincial election, "the most important thing for its rival is to get out of the way and let it."

Yet Stanfield, thinking like a prime minister rather than as leader of the Opposition as he heard Teeter's finding, felt duty-bound to do something about inflation. His lifelong interest in economics made him agonize about the malaise of "stagflation" that had settled over Canada, a stagnant economy pummelled by inflation. Normally, there is either a slowdown, or price inflation, but not both together. He wanted to offer a remedy. In an abstract view of democracy, that was how responsible politicians ought to behave. In the world of electoral politics, this was not the way to win an election.

Stanfield pledged to implement price-and-wage controls. He was reactivating a proposal from the PCs' 1972 platform, but now strongly committed to make controls mandatory, no longer just an option if necessary. This time, it was not admen who foisted a message or policy onto the party as its campaign centrepiece, but the leader himself, acting in his conscientious way, which had pretty much always been Bob Stanfield's nature. This strong commitment to price-and-wage controls was the blunder of the campaign. The leader of the Progressive Conservatives had taken the high-risk step of basing an entire campaign strategy on a single, hard policy, responding to what the pollster said preoccupied voters. Suddenly the issue was no longer rampant inflation, but the PCs' controversial plan to deal with it.

Savvy Liberals knew they'd been dealt a wild card. With eyes blazing, Pierre Trudeau mounted a strident defence against the Tories to protect Canadians. "Do you want your wages frozen? *Zap* — you're frozen!" Opinion shifted. Editorial writers criticized imposing price-and-wage controls in peacetime.

Robert Stanfield at a press conference, with reporters following the distributed text he is reading about price-and-wage controls, prepared by Dalton Camp. More than a dozen record his remarks for radio, while television cameras (out of sight to the right) capture footage for the evening newscast.

Others said that kind of market manipulation and central economic control was what communists did, not conservatives.

Again, as in 1968, the campaign began slipping away from Bob Stanfield. Following the prime minister's lead, Liberal candidates at the doors and in all-candidate meetings, chiding the PCs and spreading alarm among voters, said with prices already soaring and putting needed goods and services beyond reach, the Tories would freeze wages and make things even harder to buy. "Vote Liberal! We would never freeze your wages."

Tom MacMillan, advancing the leader's tour, said of the price-and-wage controls campaign, "We were really battling uphill." For Paul Curley, "The campaign was not as much fun, and didn't work out as well, as in 1972. We were getting blown out."

A fracture line over the price-and-wage policy appeared throughout Progressive Conservative ranks. As the PC pledge caused further division in the party, many candidates wobbled. The controls policy even drove a wedge into the engine room of the blue machine.

Paul Weed was one of Norman Atkins's most faithful and loyal lieutenants, a grassroots organizer who knew every trick and could play the boldest of them with nerves of steel. If others chewed gum, Weed ate nails. Working in the national campaign headquarters alongside Atkins, he saw an election win evaporating. After so much hard work and innovative effort to craft a superior campaign machine, he grew bitter. His debates with Norman over the folly of campaigning on price-and-wage controls grew heated, but the campaign director remained committed to the plan because Robert Stanfield as leader had established it and Dalton was, even if unenthusiastically, supporting it. Paul Weed urged every way he could imagine to abandon the price-and-wage controls policy, while there was still time.

He could not understand Atkins's unyielding position. The two men, so close for so long, became estranged. Each cared deeply about politics, and winning campaigns. Norman, who preached "loyalty," was torn by conflicting ones. He sided with his leader, whom he'd personally helped launch into national politics.

After his close friend departed, Norman took out his list of Spades and, with a shaking hand, drew a line through the name of excommunicated Paul Weed.

———

Despite astute campaign planning and the latest innovations, the Stanfield-led PCs lost the 1974 election. In battleground Ontario the party dropped fifteen seats, the Liberals gained nineteen, and that made all the difference.

One Ontario seat the Liberals held was Ottawa-Centre. Hugh Segal, who'd come close two years earlier, ran again in 1974. Atkins made sure the PC riding association "had more support than usual." It would be a sweet victory, they hoped, but it was not to be. If Segal had spent more time canvassing the riding, that might have helped, but he was often working in campaign headquarters instead. Atkins, by mid-campaign, wanted Segal's talent for the national effort, figuring it better use of his time, given how the election was turning against the PCs.

Many workers inside the Progressive Conservative campaign, especially those cocooned within the bubble of enthusiastic belief at the Toronto headquarters, were shocked. Their plans had appeared so promising, and their efforts become so focused, that most remained convinced Stanfield was going to win. That's what Norman, who never wanted to change a campaign once it was underway, doggedly hoped would take place. That's what Paul Weed could see was not going to happen.

Although the Tories were stunned by losing the election, they were shocked even more when Pierre Trudeau's Liberal government, using its majority in the Commons, introduced price-and-wage controls.

CHAPTER 39

THE TRANSFORMATION OF BILL DAVIS

In the hollow calm that followed the party's loss nationally, two blue machine emissaries from Toronto arrived in Ottawa to recruit the national PCs' director of communications and planning, because Atkins recommended him as "a bright young guy who maybe could be helpful."

Arriving in Hugh Segal's office at party headquarters, Hugh Macaulay and Ross DeGeer got quickly to the point. "Would you be prepared to leave here and work for Premier Davis in Toronto in preparing the coming provincial election campaign?"

Segal declined, stating he was "not prepared to leave Mr. Stanfield until he decides whether he is running again."

Macaulay respected such loyalty to a leader, but was himself more loyal to another, Bill Davis. DeGeer, smooth and friendly but relentless when focused on an objective, was determined to see Davis re-elected. And Segal, flattered at being asked and knowing the next big election would be in Ontario, agreed to Ross's Plan B: he'd remain officially in his national position but become "a part-time campaign secretary, working directly with the Ontario campaign manager Norman Atkins who had charge of preparing and running the campaign."

In this role, Segal was soon attending campaign meetings, "making sure that when people agreed to do things, those things actually got done between

Progressive Conservative campaign chairman Norman Atkins and party leader Bill Davis relax at the Ontario premier's Georgian Bay summer home, sharing morning news from the political arena. Atkins, at the controls of the blue machine that engineered his provincial campaign victories, worshipped Davis as a political hero.

meetings." His relationship and friendship with Atkins strengthened as they began working together almost continuously.

Norman, for his part, had gone to New Brunswick after the federal PC loss. From Robertson's Point, he turned his attention, as communications and organization adviser, to the provincial PC campaign, hoping for at least one victory before year's end. On November 18, 1974, the Hatfield-led PCs won re-election, giving anxious Norman a needed boost. He'd seen Teeter's bleak polling numbers for Ontario, where an ominous provincial election loomed.

———

Back in 1971, after the provincial election, Bill Davis and Norman agreed he'd work full-time in charge of the blue machine apparatus. They wanted close links between the PC Party and the Davis government, laying down solid tracks to carry the premier through a successful re-election campaign.

Now Atkins looked at the dire prospects and shook his head. The premier would have to call an election in 1975 but his image had sagged, and so had the PCs' standing in opinion polls.

Since the 1971 high point, when Davis as a dynamic premier led his government to introduce 150 new legislative measures and program initiatives in as many days, and won a big majority in the provincial election, Tory fortunes had spiralled downward.

Political scandals touching the premier, his ministers Darcy McKeough, Dalton Bales, and Bert Lawrenece, and the inept handling of them, had tarnished the government. Les Frost had peremptorily fired Cabinet ministers Bill Greisinger, Clare Mapledoram, and Phil Kelly for buying pipeline company shares, taking advantage of insider information, and won public support and sympathy for his decisive action to uphold ethical conduct. By contrast, Bill Davis dithered, delayed, and stonewalled when it appeared that conflicts of interest touched his ministry, and lost support for being slow to respond.

The Davis government had been very active on other fronts, yet, ironically, was paying a price for this, too. Protest greeted new restrictions imposed by the government's environmental plan to protect the Niagara Escarpment. Elsewhere, land-use policies to prevent sprawl of single storey factories and housing subdivisions onto prime agricultural land met opposition from farmers who wanted to become multi-millionaires by selling to developers. The government had intervened massively in Ontario's regional and local politics, forcing historic municipalities into "regional governments" with new names and little cohesive identity. This generated a third wave of antagonism, this time from displaced local office holders, heritage-minded citizens, and taxpayers underwriting bigger bureaucracies and the higher costs of overlapping jurisdictions, because major sections of the province now had *four* levels of government: federal, provincial, regional, and local. From Queen's Park, all these initiatives seemed necessary, but they upset the status quo and, from those directly affected, generated ill-will toward the Davis PCs.

Compounding these problems was the most ironic twist of all: a government resolved to be highly political had become dramatically less so. Davis had revamped the top policy and administrative structure of Ontario in line with recommendations from a Committee on Government Productivity. This committee consisted of senior public servants and business executives, none of them *politically* mindful. Appointed by Robarts, they reported to Davis.

The committee's big idea was to cluster departments into what were called "policy fields," each coordinated by a super-minister. Davis's top Cabinet members, anxious to be "super-ministers," got the positions and ever since had been spending their time in meetings at Queen's Park coordinating policy. Swallowed whole by the new bureaucratic labyrnth, lost in a twilight zone away from operating departments, the most politically astute, ambitious, and articulate senior PC ministers had been sidelined by their own government.

Having disappeared inside Queen's Park meeting rooms, the top ministers no longer circulated the province to discover what was going on, the task of every politician. Nor were they giving speeches explaining the government's programs, the leadership task of every politically accountable minister. Indeed, when a few intermittently did reappear in the sunlight to tell Ontarians what they were up to, their speeches were boring expositions about restructuring public administration and government "productivity." Their focus on policy became how it was processed, not what it accomplished for the people.

This left Ontario's public affairs field wide open for issue-oriented and eloquent New Democrat leader Stephen Lewis. With a free run hammering at real issues, from mercury poisoning at the Grassy Narrows First Nation Reserve in northwestern Ontario to the paving over of prime farmland in southern Ontario, Lewis and the NDP got media play and won public support. Even the Liberals gained strength, because they too connected to realities upsetting Ontarians in the *political vacuum* created as the best PC politicians morphed into administrators, playing roles designed by corporate executives and bureaucrats who disdained politics as much as they discounted democratic governance.

Furthering this anti-political process, Premier Davis replaced Keith Reynolds, who'd been Robarts's deputy minister and Cabinet secretary, with James Fleck, an associate dean of administrative studies at York University who'd been secretary to the Committee on Government Productivity and become wedded to its non-political approach to government. Fleck lacked the instinct for flexibility, compromise, and the free exchange of ideas and information necessary for politics. He understood administration, not governance and accountability. He had no network of friends in the civil service to keep him informed. Under Fleck's stewardship, Bill Davis spent time in unnecessary meetings with the wrong people while becoming increasingly distanced from his ministers and caucus.

The seed of destruction in the Committee on Government Productivity's work, now sprouted and nurtured daily, deliberately, and directly by Jim Fleck as the Ontario premier's deputy, was the hoax that to achieve "modern" government, some abstract private sector idea about "productivity" had to trump politics.

———

The disquiet among Bill Davis's publicly elected members of caucus, and rumblings by Progressive Conservative Party members who knew Queen's Park should be the seat of *government*, not merely the headquarters for its administration or top office of an operation "run like a business," had to be addressed. The premier also knew that opposition parties, not only his own backbenchers, were increasingly restive about the legislature's marginalization. He responded by appointing a three-member commission to improve operations of the provincial legislature.

Dalton Camp was chairman. Davis valued Camp's work as a royal commissioner dealing with Ontario's beleaguered book publishing companies, and he'd also listened to Dalton's intermittent suggestions about the need to update the provincial legislature. Having Dalton chair this commission would keep him close at hand operationally, yet at a discrete distance politically. This creative mission would provide Dalton income, and, even more, support his quest to emerge from the political backrooms into a public role for which he was eminently qualified. Davis appointed two other commissioners, for partisan balance and their experience as elected legislators: Douglas Fisher, former New Democrat MP, and Farquhar Oliver, previously an MPP and Ontario Liberal leader.

The Camp Commission's reports led to fundamental changes. For the very first time, strong rules would govern election finances: limiting donations, restricting campaign spending, requiring audits, and disclosing everything to the public. The Davis government's 1975 Election Finances Reform Act, based on the Camp Commission's November 1974 recommendations, was pioneering legislation in North America that completely transformed Ontario politics. The act became a model for election finance laws in other Canadian jurisdictions, beginning with Alberta, which copied the Ontario statute directly, just dropping its more onerous provisions.

Dalton Camp, Roy McMurtry, and Bill Davis confer at the margins of a social event, the Ontario premier's standard drink of orange juice and rum virtually untouched, also standard. They agreed fundamental reform of election finances was needed.

For Dalton, this transformative change brought the delight of true accomplishment, an enduring legacy. Davis's decision to act on the commission's recommendations had lasting effects for him, as well. Although the premier's dire standing in the polls heightened his appetite for launching a revolution in ethical conduct of campaign finances, it nevertheless took real political courage to reform the role of money in elections. Electoral politics would never be the same.

————

Despite this positive change, the atmosphere at Queen's Park for the Tories remained negative. Between 1971 and 1975, the news media had become hostile and taken Davis and his government to task over a litany of shortcomings. "The press," as polite Brian Armstrong expressed it, "had not been kind to Mr. Davis and he had fallen out of favour." Atkins fretted. DeGeer considered the *Globe and Mail* "the official opposition."

In an ill-advised response, Bill Davis even escalated the ill-will. Addressing the Canadian Club in Toronto, Ontario's premier criticized the *Globe and Mail* for slanted coverage and critical editorials. "The battle is joined," responded combat-ready Richard Doyle, the newspaper's editor.

In 1974, one of the *Globe's* reporters at Queen's Park, Jonathan Manthorpe, who with Ross H. Munro and John Zaritsky formed Doyle's troika of avenging Press Gallery warriors, published *The Power and the Tories,* covering Ontario politics since 1943 when the PCs came to power. The book had a Duncan Macpherson front cover showing Davis, successor to the Tory Crown handed down by Drew and then Frost, pulling a blindfold over the eyes of a voter. A substantial part of Manthorpe's book dealt with the operations of the Davis years.

On balance, it seemed another nail in the Tory coffin. Many PCs felt, as Eddie Goodman put it, "after thirty-two years of Tory power, time appeared to be running out for the Davis government." The party had lost five straight by-elections under the supposedly astute blue machine. Opinion polls portrayed declining public trust in the Davis-led PCs.

In November 1974, Hugh Macaulay went to see Goodman, the Tory's highest velocity political operative, at his downtown Toronto law office. Eddie had been on the sidelines the past three years. Hugh slumped in a chair, spoke like a defeated man, and asked Goodman to take over his position as Bill Davis's director of party organization and adviser.

"I have done everything I can for Davis and it isn't working," he sighed, adding he thought Goodman had "the experience and energy to turn things around."

Eddie knew the timing was all wrong. "It's impossible for anyone to come in cold from the outside and take charge in the manner required to get us out of this mess." But he was prepared, he added, "to join the group and work as an assistant to you."

That "group" was the weekly Tuesday morning breakfast club at the Park Plaza which, Macaulay had informed Goodman, was "the only formal meeting we have." This advisory committee, he explained, consisted of the premier, himself, Dalton Camp, party fundraiser Bill Kelly, campaign chair Norman Atkins, party president Alan Eagleson, party legal adviser and Davis confidant Roy McMurtry (not yet an MPP), and party executive director Ross DeGeer. Davis having awoken to the urgency of replacing his deputy minister, Jim Fleck, had brought in Ed Stewart, his reliable and politically intelligent deputy minister from the education ministry. Stewart, explained Macaulay, was also now a regular on Tuesday mornings.

Eddie was surprised, when showing up at his first Park Plaza breakfast meeting, that no members of Cabinet were present. He found this high-level group's composition "clearly an unsatisfactory state of affairs that would lead inevitably to friction" with the elected PC politicians. Goodman knew other major players like Darcy McKeough had to be in the mix. McKeough had returned to Cabinet in 1973 as provincial treasurer, following time in political purgatory after he'd resigned over an alleged conflict of interest.

Whatever value the Tuesday meeting provided in crafting Ontario's public agenda was offset by the drag it placed on the PCs politically. As word of its operation filtered out, ministers grew resentful about being excluded from the premier's "kitchen Cabinet."

The big blue machine, facing an election, occupied political terrain utterly unlike that of 1971. Bill Davis was no longer a political "clean slate" on which the campaign could create an optimal image, but someone with a well-known reputation, and not a good one. The scandals had attracted a bad odour, identified in Teeter's polling as "an issue of trust." Ontario was experiencing an economic slowdown. The mood was grim.

Another problem for campaigning, polling revealed, was that no single issue dominated, which would make it harder to galvanize the electorate. Going into the 1975 campaign, Teeter's research indicated the Davis government was likely going to lose.

"The consternation had reached the point we had to change colours, in a sense," said DeGeer. Such thinking led to an unprecedented chameleon-like manoeuvre. Ontario's Tories switched established party colours and changed their logo. It was an advertiser's brazen ploy: switch identity to remain in office. Elect *us*, not those other PC guys.

"We ended up with a bilious yellow," he sighed. "Some people argued we should use what we had in the past — red, white, and blue — but we needed to present a different face." In part to fool the public, in part to distance themselves from themselves, the blue machine redesigned the Ontario PC logo and switched to blue and *yellow* for all signs, advertisements, and campaign materials. It was, acknowledged DeGeer, "an effort to be different."

A sign of just how much control had now passed to the campaign's central organizers was demonstrated by how, in 1975, the blue machine strove to create the impression of a new party and was able to pull it off unhindered. The practice of polling produced analysis that anticipated defeat; this led to a backroom decision to repackage a tradition-fused party by changing its identity, which, in turn, was followed by imposition of abrupt and unpalatable change upon everyone in the party, province-wide.

————

The election was called for September 18.

Dianne Axmith, by now as much involved in Atkins's campaign operations as in client work at the agency, located premises for a central Davis re-election campaign headquarters on Toronto's Adelaide Street, filled it with equipment, and lined up volunteers to run the place. During the election, Atkins and Hugh Segal saved commuting time by sleeping in the permanent Tory suite at the Park Plaza Hotel, where Axmith picked them up every morning, drove them to headquarters, and updated them en route about new developments.

Norman again asked Brian Armstrong to negotiate terms of the televised leaders' debates on behalf of the Progressive Conservatives, as he'd done for the 1971 provincial election. The PC debate strategy for 1975 was to prevent the two opposition leaders ganging up on the premier. The Tories also wanted to avoid the shouting matches three-way debates often degenerate into, when each candidate, knowing so much rides on the brief encounter, tries to score a point while another is speaking: a noisy contest of voices that turns off most voters. "We wanted to have one-on-one leaders' debates because we wanted Mr. Davis to be able to take Liberal leader Robert Nixon head on," said Armstrong of the key point he successfully negotiated.

Teeter's firm was in the field polling and Armstrong was, in his now customary role, liaising between the pollster and the campaign organization, delivering the results and helping interpret and apply them. Ten days before voting, Davis and the PCs were ten points behind the Liberals. Defeat was imminent.

Atkins called a summit meeting. It took place in Bill Davis's Brampton home. Joining Davis were Atkins, Armstrong, and Teeter, as bearers of the opinion sampling's bleak tidings; along with party president, Alan Eagleson;

director of party organization, Hugh Macaulay; Davis's political assistant, Clare Westcott; and chief party fundraiser, Bill Kelly. Everyone was tense.

Downstairs in the recreation room, the premier heard that he would soon go into history as the man who presided over the collapse of Ontario's Progressive Conservative dynasty.

Eagleson came on exceptionally strong in challenging Davis. He said the premier had to go after Liberal leader Nixon "as hard as he was capable of doing" in their televised leaders' debate. It was slated for broadcast in just a few days. Davis was reluctant.

Alan was a bare-knuckle fighter, but Bill was not. Eagleson won. The plan was set. Others present reiterated that the losing PC leader had to become more aggressive, but only "the Eagle" advocated extreme fighting. In the coming couple of days, in preparing for the debate, Alan, more than anyone else, got Bill Davis "up" for heavy combat in the two-way debate, the final chance for confrontation before the fateful day of voting.

When the Davis entourage arrived at the CTV studios, the leader was pumped but nervous, and extremely uncomfortable with what he now believed he had to do. He'd been persuaded, in the interests of the party, the government, and the province, that he must do the deed to serve the cause. "He went into that studio and did everything that we asked him to," said one of those present, "but, boy, was he uncomfortable doing it." So flustered was Davis that at one point he called the debate's moderator, Fraser Kelly, a man he'd known well for years as a Queen's Park senior political reporter, by the wrong name.

Davis effectively proceeded to call Robert Nixon a liar. He said to his face he was running a dishonourable campaign of misinformation and untruth. Nixon, never having experienced Bill Davis like this, appeared stunned. In CTV's studio viewing room, the PC leader's wife, Kathleen Davis, watching what was happening, began to weep.

The big blue machine did not rely on this debate alone to turn the tide. Art Collins of Foster Advertising, working in the special PC consortium of advertising specialists, created a number of negative commercials. One of them, which got extensive television play after the debate, right up to the blackout period for paid partisan election advertising, was the "weathervane" commercial. The television ad showed a rooster weathervane turning this way and that, suggesting Bob Nixon just blew in whatever direction the winds pushed him — in short, intimating that he was a man without principles.

Others in the Progressive Conservative Party, traditionally more inclined to follow best practices from Britain, would not have glommed onto these American campaign innovations with the same sly pleasure Dalton Camp and Norman Atkins did. Pollster Alan Gregg, now helping with the campaign, was a strong advocate for the positive effect of negative ads. "They work," he'd concluded, after tracking polling patterns and election outcomes in the United States.

The first time the blue machine had used negative "attack" ads in Canada was in the early 1970s. The PCs edged into this territory with the 1972 federal election, with advertisements stating "Trudeau Has Failed!" Those TV spots incorporated, said Brian Armstrong, "what we called 'streeters' at that time. We had people interviewed on the street about why they thought the Trudeau government was bad for the country." By the 1974 election, the campaign team pushed this technique by introducing what came to be called "dirty streeters." The film crew on the street interviewed critical Tories posing as random passersby.

The accelerating trend continued in 1975. For the desperate final week of the Ontario campaign, the hard-edged "weathervane" attack ads ratcheted the ploy a full notch higher. By September 18, it was still uncertain, however, if the combination of a hard-knuckle debate and single-minded negative ads about an untrustworthy Liberal leader would be enough.

On election night, Atkins and Segal were at the Brampton headquarters, with Davis, watching results come in. The premier, it was gradually revealed, would be leading a minority government. Both men circulated the campaign headquarters cheering up dismayed people like Kathleen Davis. "Look, you are still in government. You held on." A minority looked pretty good to them, based on what they had seen elsewhere, and based on what had been expected in Ontario that day.

The Tories lost twenty-seven MPPs. The party's ability to retain even a minority hold on power was only due to vote splitting in Ontario's electoral triangle. The Davis-led party received just 36 percent of the popular vote, province-wide. Some 63 percent of the electorate had voted non-PC, divided 34 percent to the Liberals and 29 percent for the NDP. In a legislature expanded to 125 seats, the PCs managed to win fifty-one, the NDP thirty-eight, and the Liberals, thirty-six. The chagrined Grits, who'd been set to take power, had been relegated to third spot.

At his Georgian Bay retreat on Townsend Island, Bill Davis keeps up pressure on Roy Mc-Murtry to seek election to Ontario's legislature. Roy ran and lost in a 1973 by-election, but won a seat in 1975 and promptly entered Davis's Cabinet. McMurtry inscribed this picture for Norman Kempton Atkins, joking he "really was too young and innocent to be a politician!!"

The PC campaign had a decidedly altered look, with different colours, new logo, and harder edge attacks. Its passive and dismissive slogan, "Your Future. Your Choice" was the best the blue machine brain trust could come up with, believing there was no single issue. The more inspired New

Democrats had countered with "Tomorrow Starts Today" and were now the Official Opposition.

————

Bill Davis found himself in the same position as George Drew, back in 1943 when he'd begun Ontario's Tory "dynasty," a premier who could be defeated at any time but who nevertheless held power and was grateful to be facing *two* opposition parties.

Just as Davis had been sufficiently shocked, after almost losing the PC leadership, to take dramatic action by placing his fate with the Camp-Atkins blue machine, he was again sufficiently traumatized, by almost losing the government, to adopt a new way of conducting politics.

His sombre gaze into the abyss of defeat galvanized a political transformation in William Grenville Davis. "He began to reinvent himself," noticed Armstrong, as sensitive a close-range observer as anyone. "Over the course of the next three or four years, he went from being an embattled leader of a scandal-ridden party to a folksy, bland 'Mr. Ontario' personality whom Ontarians grew to love. In the minority situation he became much more at ease with himself."

That the raw edge of political uncertainty in his daily life and in that of his government should produce a man at ease with himself may seem a paradox. What it really shows is just how deeply imbued with politics Bill Davis truly was. The more he came into his own, the greater his confidence, no matter how awkward or challenging the situation. This enabled him to take a firmer grip on the big blue machine. Bill Davis, with Norman Atkins, would now achieve an infinitely more effective integration of government operations and campaign politics.

For openers, Davis and Cabinet secretary Ed Stewart accepted Atkins's recommendation that Segal become the premier's legislative assistant, to help the PCs weather the coming storm as a minority government and enhance direct communication between the blue machine and daily operations at Ontario's legislature. Segal had been Stanfield's legislative assistant in Ottawa during the Trudeau minority government, but nobody at Queen's Park had such experience because Ontario's last minority government was back in 1943. The Davis government set about to navigate in the legislature and survive, despite having fewer votes than the combined Opposition.

On New Brunswick's Saint John River heading to Robertson's Point for a session of blue machinists are, from the left: Bruce Fountain, Ross DeGeer, Norman Atkins, Bill Kelly, Bill Davis, and Brian Armstrong.

Another big change came in the composition of the premier's Tuesday-morning breakfast group. From the start, Bill Kelly, the Ontario PCs' fund-raiser, was a Park Plaza regular, as was Hugh Macaulay, Davis's reliable political fixer, and Ross DeGeer, executive director of the Ontario PCs. Dalton Camp had participated until 1975 when the sessions were opened up at Eddie Goodman's behest to key Cabinet ministers Darcy McKeough, Tom Wells, Bob Elgie, and Dennis Timbrell. Roy McMurtry, elected in Eglinton in 1975, continued to participate, now as a minister. Norman was miffed that Dalton was no longer at the Tuesday breakfasts, and whined about it.

Goodman, one of the best connected Tories, who transitioned easily between the PC Party, the legal community, business and philanthropic worlds, and the Jewish community, and a forceful and effective deal-maker in any backroom, was present and fully accounted for on Tuesday mornings after 1975. From 1978 to 1984, Tom Kierans would also become a Tuesday-morning regular, at Davis's direct invitation, to provide policy analysis, particularly on economic issues. The premier's principal secretary of the day was included, successively Brian Armstrong, Hugh Segal, then John Tory. Davis's deputy minister, Ed Stewart, was never out of sight.

Flowing into this summit gathering were the views of the civil service and the wider political public. Ed Stuart, as Ontario's senior civil servant in the Cabinet office, distilled the views of the province's army of public servants to report on the possibilities and pitfalls for any proposed course of action. At the same time, Roy McMurtry and Norman Atkins both had open phone lines and took time to listen to more people in one week than most individuals would connect with over a month, and apart from being extensive, their networks were diverse. Bill Davis's natural political instincts for balance were rewarded, getting the aggregated and integrated views from all three about handling a matter.

These senior players discussed and shaped significant government policies on a routine and continuing basis, which enabled those running elections, and between campaigns running the party's media relations, to have accurate understanding of what the PC government was really doing so it could handle the "messaging" and ensure the leader succeeded in maintaining public support for his initiatives. It also helped those in high office, receiving and inwardly digesting weekly field reports from the party's executive director, to guide the government away from potential electoral difficulties and toward popular stances.

Although this had been the intent of the Tuesday sessions from their inception, by 1975 it seemed no such care had ever been taken, given how many problems the Davis government faced and its declining support. Those days were over. This remix was the make-over of the blue machine's politicization of Ontario government.

Armstrong witnessed from the centre how "during the testing years after 1975, striving to maintain his minority government, Premier Davis's Tuesday Morning Group became central to running the province of Ontario." When Segal came into it, he characterized the group's purpose as being "to meet on a weekly basis, look at issues coming and going, and make sure that they didn't get away from the government, and that the government had ample time to reflect upon them. We would give our best advice, and the premier would take that to caucus and Cabinet where the real decisions would be made."

Yet there was no escaping the inherent problem of how decisions were taken and power exercised. In the eyes of ever more Tory ministers and MPPs, the "real decisions" were reached at the Park Plaza, not at Queen's Park. With the blue machine so closely connected to Ontario governance at its top levels, initially to ensure that campaign messages properly reflected the intent of goals set by Bill Davis, his Cabinet and the PC Party, it was only a matter of time before the flow reversed. Even insiders like Clare Westcott began to push back, saying it was not appropriate for backroom organizers like Atkins and Segal "to meddle into policy and goals of Ontario's government and the choices between provincial programs." Westcott, not part of the Park Plaza Group, was hardly alone in taking exception to the hushed-up existence of the blue machine's Tuesday breakfast sessions.

"People resented the tight control this group had on power," said John MacNaughton. "The MPPs and ministers knew that every Tuesday morning a group was meeting at the Park Plaza to set policy, discuss issues, and plot the course of the government and party. They asked 'What am I doing here, all the work to get elected, so others can make the decisions and I'm a rubber stamp?'" John Tory, when he came on the scene, dutifully played down the breakfast meetings, the agreed-upon message to keep elected representatives onside.

———

Time passed. The government was not defeated. Yet by 1977, two years of minority government "was taking its toll on a lot of people, including the insider volunteers," said the party's executive director, DeGeer. "Some people were anxious for an election, but there was no overarching issue that could be turned to our advantage. Nonetheless, we had a general election in 1977."

Bill Davis engineered the vote because Robert Teeter's 1977 polling showed the Progressive Conservatives could regain a majority. DeGeer became campaign manager, under chairman Atkins. Segal was on the campaign bus with Davis, enjoying a role he numbingly characterized as "the legislative policy linkage person."

In this campaign, the still novel "phone bank" got its best workout to date. Ontario's 1975 provincial election had not yet given enough time to win acceptance of this new practice in most ridings. By the 1977 Ontario election, the blue machine "used the phone bank technique to great advantage," said DeGeer. "We were light years ahead of anything the Opposition was doing." It was to be another example, however, where using a new and better method did not translate into more votes.

On June 9, election night, the PCs increased representation by seven seats, still in minority territory, with 40 percent popular vote. The other 60 percent of the popular vote split 32 percent for the Liberals, 28 for the NDP. Polling statistics and the Ontario electoral system, on which the blue machine's political strategists had depended to their detriment, had confounded them.

Alberta premier Peter Lougheed, Quebec premier René Lévesque, Quebec youth minister Claude Charron, Ontario premier Bill Davis and wife Kathleen, at Grey Cup game. New Brunswick's Richard Hatfield is behind Lévesque. For many blue machinists, interest in sports was on a par with devotion to winning political campaigns.

The 1977 Ontario election changed little in the legislature — Bill Davis began and ended the campaign with a minority government — but it sure triggered change within the big blue machine. Disenchanted volunteers went back to their businesses, less enamoured now by politics than they'd been in the heady days of 1971. Changes were made in the caucus office and at PC Party headquarters. Segal departed to John Labatt Limited in London as director of corporate relations. DeGeer moved into the premier's office as liaison between Davis, the party, and the caucus.

Moving around personnel was not difficult. What was harder to deal with was the polling. "This was the first time in our work with Market Opinion Research," said Armstrong, intermediary between the pollsters and campaign organization, "that they had been wrong about the outcome."

Bill Kelly was livid. He'd pulled in all his favours to raise millions of dollars for the campaign, not a pleasant chore when donors were less than enthusiastic about Davis and the provincial PCs, and had, anyway, contributed millions to a campaign only twenty months before. Because of Kelly's vehemence, the blue machine was now in the market for a new pollster.

"Bill Kelly was absolutely adamant that we had to change pollsters," said Armstrong. "We had spent all this money on an election campaign thinking we could win, based on intelligence that told us we would, and the intelligence was wrong."

After the 1977 fiasco, with no resolution about who would be the new pollster, the Ontario PCs did no surveys for a long time. Atkins and others in the federal organization had worked well with Teeter for years, and felt comfortable in the relationship. Kelly remained adamant, however, there'd be no money for an Ontario campaign in which the American pollster was involved.

———

Norman, with Dalton's counsel, remained involved with PC politics in the Maritimes, including two provincial elections in 1978.

In Nova Scotia, the resurgent PCs claimed a thirty-one-seat victory on September 19, defeating the Liberals, who dropped to seventeen seats, as the NDP advanced to a total of four, in a House of Assembly increased to fifty-two members. Next month, in New Brunswick, where Norman had been communications and organization adviser for an October 23 election, the campaign was what Dalton called "a closely run thing." The PCs won with thirty seats to twenty-eight for the Liberals.

As for Ontario, with another election possible anytime, Norman insisted Davis ask Hugh Segal to come back from his public relations job at Labatt's to help prepare the campaign and assist in "negotiating various energy and related matters with the federal government." Blue machinists held that if a leader wanted someone to work at a senior level, he had to ask himself, so the link was real, the loyalty direct, and the commitment personal, in both directions. Atkins, like Camp, knew from experience that when a party leader asks, people will not refuse.

Segal resurfaced in Queen's Park as secretary to the Policy and Priorities Board of Cabinet, with the status and hefty salary of a deputy minister. The Policy and Priorities Board, universally known in upper echelons as simply P&P, was the executive body directing Ontario's government, a more formal administrative body than "the breakfast group" that gathered with the premier Tuesday mornings. Segal's directing role as secretary of P&P, with clout as a deputy minister officially part of Ontario's government and public administration, was cover for the fact he'd come back to Queen's Park explicitly to "prepare for the coming election." He did so from the very centre of government, remunerated from the public treasury, fusing the blue machine with the operation of government.

While all this provided riveting interest for those in Tory backrooms, the larger national political scene remained an even more compelling source of political intrigues, as well as stunning changes, for Progressive Conservatives.

CHAPTER 40

JOE CLARK FROM THE BACKROOMS

After the 1974 federal election, Bob Stanfield knew it was time to go. He'd racked up his third loss as leader, despite a superb campaign organization. He would dutifully suffer the party members' anger about the price-and-wage campaign and absorb the recriminations over defeat. Waiting that out was the least he could do. It was also the most.

By autumn 1975, believing those resentments largely dissipated, Stanfield made public his decision and asked the party to organize a leadership convention for the winter of 1976. That would give his successor time to establish authority in the party and make a fresh connection with the electorate. As contenders tested their prospects to succeed Stanfield, two men who'd long fantasized about becoming prime minister now faced the unreality of their dreams.

Bill Davis had been reduced to a minority government in Ontario. The premier's lustre from his sweeping 1971 victory, the first for the Camp-Atkins operation in Ontario, was tarnished by scandals and public administration that, despite the big blue machine's best efforts, resulted in two successive minority governments. Around Queen's Park and in the Albany Club, the prospect of a Davis bid for the federal leadership was discussed, only to rule it out. "We were trying to hang onto government," said Armstrong, "and Bill Davis was essential to that."

Dalton Camp also pondered his chances. Back in 1967 he'd been forced by John Diefenbaker's explosive animosity and the waiting daggers of The Chief's loyalists to subordinate his ambition, placing his superb campaign apparatus in service of Stanfield instead, biding his time for a later leadership run. A decade later, Camp now evaluated his prospects with different eyes. He did not have a seat in Parliament. His two efforts to gain one had failed, his record of non-electability diminishing his appeal. Eight years had gone by since he'd been party president, and though other blue machinists held senior party offices, he'd not maintained familiar and frequent contact with PC players across Canada the way he had in the 1950s and 1960s. The PCs, having gone through three elections with a bald Maritimer, would not want another. And experience had recast his attitude about public affairs and politics from one of enthusiastic engagement to that of detached disdain. He now preferred to write about how politics should be, rather than shape it himself. Finally, his marriage to Linda had ended. He was entering a second life with a new wife, Wendy Smallian, from the bunker. They were building a costly new home in rural New Brunswick, all of which represented a further retreat from political life, as well as dissipation of all his money. Dalton would not be a candidate, either.

But many others were entering the race, including Claude Wagner, a PC member of Parliament and before that Quebec's hard-hitting attorney general in Liberal Jean Lesage's government. Claude had been recruited, with help from Brian Mulroney, to run federally as de facto leader of the PCs in Quebec.

Mulroney himself entered the race, a double surprise. The same man whose adroitness in political backrooms had helped entice Wagner to switch parties and become a Tory MP was now going to challenge him for the leadership. It was also surprising because Mulroney had no seat in Parliament himself, nor had he ever bothered to try getting one.

MP Joe Clark declared his candidacy for the leadership and mounted a clean campaign, with a raft of policy statements on major issues, to which few gave heed because he was not a contender who would win. A couple of weeks before the convention, this commonly held view was made manifest when Clark held a press conference in Toronto to which not a single reporter showed up.

By 1976 the blue machine had evolved into two primary operations. One was a powerful campaign organization, with control of theAlbany Club and the Camp advertising agency, run by Norman Atkins. The second, a political team deeply enmeshed in the governance of Ontario, run by Bill Davis.

Norman, Davis, and Hugh Macaulay went to the convention at the Ottawa Civic Centre, all insider spectators, none backing any of the candidates. "Our people were all over the place," said Armstrong, "but the big blue machine as such was not assembled to work for anybody." He himself ran British Columbia MP John Fraser's campaign. Hugh Segal worked for MP Claude Wagner. Bill Saunderson helped Brian Mulroney. "Spades sort of spread out in the 1976 leadership race," said Saunderson, but none supported Joe Clark.

Joe had worked as a summer student at the Camp agency. The blue machinists saw him as a junior, "the kind of guy who, if you were in a meeting," said Camp cuttingly, "would be the one you'd send out for coffee."

Hugh Macaulay and Norman Atkins, as uncommitted voting delegates, relax and enjoy the 1976 leadership race. Hugh inscribed this picture for Norman, teasing: "Wasn't this when we decided to move to Horner?" Dief loyalist Jack Horner, who hated Dalton Camp for disloyalty, lost his bid for the PC leadership then joined the Liberals for a Cabinet seat.

On the first ballot, Joe was in third place, well back of Claude Wagner and not very close to Mulroney, who was in second spot.

With nine other candidates, the voting continued through four ballots. With each round, Clark, as a pristine compromise choice, picked up surprising support. On the second and third ballots, he pulled ahead of Mulroney. By the fourth, he bested Wagner, nudging in front of him by just sixty-five votes out of 2,309 cast. The next morning, the *Toronto Star*'s headline feigned shock about the PCs new leader, "Joe WHO?"

————

The relatively obscure thirty-six-year-old Albertan was certainly known to PC backrooms.

Joe had been elected to Young Progressive Conservative Party offices, both on campus and in the national party. He'd worked with Camp and Atkins, not only at the agency in Toronto but also in Fredericton, helping run the 1964 thinkers' conference. As Stanfield's speech-writer on Parliament Hill, he'd interacted with the blue machine when Dalton, out of sight, was also writing speeches for "RLS," as these backroom players referred to the leader.

Clark had also become familiar in Alberta's political backrooms working for Peter Lougheed to establish a PC Party in their home province. After failing in his bid to become an elected Alberta MLA, Joe continued working behind the scenes as Lougheed's chief assistant.

Clark differed from Stanfield in three obvious ways: he was a couple of generations younger, he could speak French, and he owed nothing at all to the blue machine. He'd won the leadership, indeed proven he could accomplish the impossible, without Camp's strategy or Atkins's organization.

Another difference was that, without any taint of Dalton Camp helping him win, and being an Albertan rather than someone from the suspect East, Tories who'd loved Dief could like Joe. This was yet another of the least expected results from Clark's ascension to the leadership. In so many ways, the party had not been able to recover from the Dief-Camp-Stanfield imbroglio until Joe, an unencumbered player, supplanted them all.

A fifth change was that Clark brought spunky aggressiveness to the role of leader. Gone was Stanfield's circumspect diffidence. Joe had emerged from Tory backrooms a true Grit fighter, as hard as Camp, though without Dalton's mellower humour. Challenging Liberals mattered to the new leader. Even as a student he'd subverted his university education to an overriding impulse to engage in PC politics.

After becoming leader, Clark made overtures to the blue machine. He held meetings in 1976 and 1977 with Atkins and others in Toronto, trying to persuade the Ontario-based team to co-operate with him federally. Yet he did not ask for the machine's support in any official capacity, just to back his efforts in the federal party.

Atkins and other blue machinists were devoted Tories who, in principle, would be supportive because Clark was the Progressive Conservative Party's leader and winning against Pierre Trudeau's Liberals would vindicate their defeats at his hands in 1968, 1972, and 1974. Yet they held back. "I don't think either Dalton or Norman could see Joe as a potential prime minister," said Armstrong. "They never seemed to click, although both respected Joe for what he stood for, which politically were the same things they believed in."

———

The leader's lacklustre invitation, and their sense Clark was not really worth making the effort for, left Atkins and his colleagues reluctant to dilute their efforts at the national level. The blue machine already faced huge problems in Ontario keeping the Davis minority government afloat.

Clark was more than content with this situation. He'd not solicited the blue machine's active participation, which effectively required turning campaign operations over to Atkins, because Joe was building his own organization. Knowing how Lougheed and he had brought fresh faces and formed new relationships to create a successful campaign team, he felt confident he could do the same nationally, bolstered by winning the leadership his own way, and based on what he'd learned in Alberta.

Although the Camp-Atkins enterprise had taken roles in Alberta for federal elections, principally advancing the leader's tour for Stanfield and providing Canada-wide PC brand campaign signs and advertising, blue machinists had no traction on the ground provincially. While not unmindful of new campaign techniques and the potency of the Camp-Atkins organization, Lougheed, and Clark working closely with him, had refused to set up a franchise branch. Instead they'd forged a made-in-Alberta political team run by Albertans, a separate blue machine.

A principle the blue machine had unequivocally established was to not go into an election without knowing what you'd encounter. Deep polling and its sound interpretation was as important as a well-crafted and fully funded budget.

Market Opinion Research would continue to conduct field research for the national PCs under Clark, but with a new twist. A young Canadian pollster, Allan Gregg, who'd worked in Clark's leadership campaign, would carry out all analysis and interpretation of Teeter's data as principal Progressive Conservative strategist. Gregg's presence was something of a riddle.

At Ottawa's Carleton University, Allan had acquired the skill sets of a political behaviourist, focused not on the human art of exercising power but rather the "science" of opinion sampling and analysis of data. By taking politics into the realm of formulae and random sample interviews, behaviourists purport to discern the whole through their "representative samples." Citizens become "demographics," values are quantified, beliefs can be manipulated. Eager to develop this frontier area of political research, Allan ventured into the political laboratory of the United States, to learn from one of America's most innovative survey researchers, Richard Wirthlin. This Republican pollster was developing a sophisticated "hierarchical values map" of the electorate by which he could model the dynamics of an election, based on the insight that it is a person's values that drive his or her voting preferences, more than any causal linkage to lower level triggers of policies, programs, traits, issues, and partisanship.

Known to Clark as a fellow Albertan, Allan started working on Parliament Hill in PC caucus research, then at PC headquarters in the run-up to the 1979 general election. "It was a time when the big blue machine had been banished from the federal scene," Gregg said. "Joe Clark thought the election campaign should be run by volunteers, not the usual cast of backroom boys. He wanted to open the process up to new people." Gregg was certifiably a new person. And he was on the inside track with the new national leader.

The role Brian Armstrong had played federally as polling liaison with Teeter vanished once Clark sidelined the blue machine, but Brian himself was seasoned and well respected. Because the secret blue machine cadre, the Spades, remained unknown, even at the highest levels of the party, and because polite and deferential Armstrong appeared neutral to all factions, Clark named him official agent for the federal party. As Allan Gregg could see, Armstrong "was about the only guy in the campaign close to Norman Atkins and his crowd."

The official agent was legally responsible for full compliance with the stringent new election finance laws that now governed acquiring and spending money in campaigns. It was a key post.

"When I first got involved in politics," Armstrong said, "the most important person was the campaign manager." But by the 1980s, "significant changes in election finance laws meant the most critical people were the accountant or official agent, then your lawyer, and then maybe your campaign manager. The consequences of being offside the election finance law had become very serious."

From the beginning, Canadian election campaigns had been funded by a well-established system of corruption. The party in power asked for and got cash from contractors and companies whose fortunes depended on government orders, which the governing party controlled. The party in opposition sought funds from the same sources, which they also paid, like an insurance premium, in case voters changed the party in power.

Until well past the mid-twentieth century, this covert nexus between money and political power was the norm. Systemic corruption was pragmatic. It was the only way the political organizers knew to get the money needed for elections. "In the case of Ontario, up until the rules for campaign financing changed as a result of public pressure and recommendations from the Dalton Camp Commission," said DeGeer, "all fundraising was done between the chief party fundraiser and corporations." Once changes in election financing were introduced in Ontario, with corresponding reforms federally, the new era of election financing spread to other provinces.

The PCs knew that under this new regime, they had to change fundraising methods. "In the mid-1970s we took the biggest leap of all," said DeGeer. Among the possible new methods, he was convinced that a systematic direct mail fundraising program offered the surest way of yielding a great deal of money. Strong opposition to this concept arose from the party fundraisers and most Toronto ridings. "The meetings held around this subject were laden with acrimony."

Soliciting campaign funds by individual letters to many people for small amounts had been proposed by Phil Lind to Wickson and Atkins for the federal PCs after he'd learned about this new grassroots Republican practice in the United States. Hugh Segal had in turn gone to Washington to meet with Bobby O'Dell, a Nixon fund raiser, who'd found "when the big donors went away, the little people kept sending $10 or $20."

At the national level, as well as in Ontario, the PCs began experimenting with direct mail. The Ontario PC organization started modestly into direct mail solicitation. "We used our own lists, supplemented by a purchased list," reported DeGeer. "We broke even with the first one." After the Election Finances Reform Act took effect federally in the mid-1970s, the national party created a new entity, the PC Canada Fund, with highly successful yet unassuming Hamilton businessman Terry Yates its first chair.

In 1976, Atkins and Wickson got Yates named comptroller, the same year they also orchestrated Paul Curley's election as national treasurer of the PCs. Yates, Wickson, Atkins, and Curley knew the federal party's finances were appalling, with debts totalling a couple million dollars. When new party leader Joe Clark asked Yates for a plan, he said direct mail would solve the party's money problems and unlock new opportunities. The consensus was to support an ever-expanding initiative.

"We got a donor base," said national director John Laschinger, "and were raising $6 or $7 million a year through direct mail." In Ontario, by the time Ross DeGeer departed in 1978 to become Ontario's agent general in Britain, "the direct mail program had been taken over by the chief fundraiser," he said, "and we were raising much more money from this source than any other."

Thanks to this blue machine innovation, PC campaigns became well-funded, and in time Liberals and New Democrats would implement the direct mail approach, as the nature of money-raising in Canada changed course and Canadian politics was radically transformed.

———

In the more public realm of politics, meanwhile, the Liberals were adrift under Pierre Trudeau.

High unemployment, high inflation, and record-breaking spending deficits were discouraging Canadians and crippling Canada with staggering national debt. The Grits had let vacant seats in the Commons accumulate, thinking a general election, or a rise in the polls, or a change of leader, or PC disintegration under Clark, would address, somehow, the fact citizens in seventeen constituencies were now unrepresented. When none of those solutions occurred, Trudeau called all by-elections for the same day in October 1978, a micro-election, having decided he'd wait until the full five years allowed by the Constitution before calling a general election.

Because the Spades had backed David Crombie's successful election as Toronto mayor, they now supported his run for Parliament in Toronto-Rosedale against John Evans, president of the University of Toronto and widely touted as potential successor to Trudeau. Atkins was busy with Ontario politics for Bill Davis, so the Spades designated Bill Saunderson, who'd continued to raise money for Crombie, to be his campaign manager as well. When the by-election was held, Crombie was elected MP, as were most of the seventeen

When Joe Clark became national Progressive Conservative leader in 1976, Ontario premier Bill Davis supported him for his federal election campaign in the seat-rich province, although Clark did not really want "the big blue machine" as part of his revamped organization. Bill now came armed with two pipes and tobacco pouch fully drawn.

other PC candidates that day, confirming beyond doubt that voters had soured on the Trudeau Liberals.

Saunderson was now regarded in Ottawa by the Tory backrooms as a great organizer and was understandably pleased to get a call from Joe Clark asking him to be campaign chair for Ontario in the coming general election. Saunderson realized that Clark and Atkins didn't get along very well, which is why he supposed the leader had bypassed Norman and asked him. But the leader had asked. Saunderson agreed. That was the rule.

In the 1979 national election, Bill Davis threw his full support behind the federal party, working hard to get Clark elected, making many public appearances across the province with the PC leader.

In Ottawa, Paul Curley was national campaign manager, working under campaign chair Lowell Murray, but of necessity on the phone to Atkins all the time. Norman was not visible on the campaign's organization chart, but the veteran campaigner's directions were indispensable in guiding Curley.

When Curley needed a fill-in because the person running the leader's tour left the campaign, Atkins suggested Armstrong. It would be in addition to his role as official agent. Although Armstrong was just starting a planned vacation in California, upon hearing from Curley that Atkins had recommended him for the role, he cut his holiday short, returned to Canada, and helped run Joe Clark's road tour as professionally as he had Bill Davis's in 1971. Clark, all the while, believed he was forging ahead without the blue machine.

The Clark-led PCs won 136 seats, with the highest popular vote of any party in seven provinces, and huge Ontario gains, particularly in the area outside Toronto. However, the party only won two constituencies in all Quebec, where in the backrooms Mulroney and his supporters speculated about Clark flaming out and Mulroney taking over. Among the Liberal losses were several high-profile Cabinet ministers. Pierre Trudeau announced his decision to step down as leader.

When sworn in as prime minister, one day shy of turning forty, Joe Clark occupied a tenuous position. Despite the electoral system's output, in the country at large the PCs' popular support had only been 36 percent, contrasted to 40 percent for the seat-losing Liberals. And though Clark's 136 MPs outnumbered the 114 Liberals, they fell short of the 142 needed for a Commons majority. The NDP would not prop him up, but Quebec's six Social Credit MPs could readily do so.

Prime Minister Clark remained attentive to building his national campaign team, imperative because of his government's precarious roost. The next election could be imminent, and he wanted to win it big.

For his revamped version of the PC Party's national operation, one of the people he wanted was Paul Curley. After the PCs' electoral rout in 1974, he had returned to Imperial Oil and been transferred to Calgary. Three years later, Atkins tracked him down in Alberta and explained that he and Wickson, looking ahead, wanted Curley to run for the national treasurer's job. "Given that I was living in Calgary," he said, "had all these friends in Ontario, and knew a lot of guys from Quebec, I ran for national treasurer of the party and won." That put Curley on the party's national executive in one of its most powerful positions. As a result, he was able to keep involved in the federal party, interacting with the new leader, Joe Clark, while continuing in the employ of Imperial Oil. Clark valued Paul's talent and his Alberta connections and knew he was ideal for the new version of the party he sought to create.

Another person Clark wanted, on becoming leader, was long-time backroom presence Lowell Murray. The two had worked together in Stanfield's office. Clark asked him to chair the federal election campaign, and they both agreed on Curley as their choice for director of operations in the federal campaign.

He agreed, took a leave of absence from Imperial Oil, and went back to Ottawa, which is how the May 22, 1979 election came to be chaired by Lowell, with Curley directing all operations. Within a week of Clark winning and becoming prime minister, and with his job done, Curley returned to Calgary and Imperial Oil.

Over the summer, Murray and Clark both called him, this time requesting he become national director of the Progressive Conservative Party and, from that position, "get involved and run the organization to get prepared for the next campaign." Both the PM and Murray knew they needed major help on the campaign front, but refused to call in the blue machine. They wanted to avoid reviving the party's searing internal recriminations of the prior decade and a-half, with which Atkins and Camp were directly associated.

Curley wrestled with his dilemma. He enjoyed being part of Imperial Oil's operations and did not want to leave. He liked working in well-crafted election campaigns with Norman and Malcolm, but they were being sidelined by the Clark entourage, and, if he accepted their offer, he'd be moving beyond Norman and the main campaign organization from which he'd sprung and with which he had closest affinity. But, as Norman had taught him, when the leader asks, you say "Yes."

In September 1979, Paul arrived in Ottawa and took up his new position. Because Wickson and Atkins were still his main resources for skillful election-eering, he remained in close contact with his two mentors, in effect conducting an end-run around Clark's idea about "new and younger people," not blue machinists, running the campaign.

While busy with his backroom organization to win votes in the country, the PM was less attentive to the front parlour where he needed to marshal votes of MPs to stay in power.

In the Commons, the Social Credit MPs from Quebec, whose views and values aligned with those of his own party, had votes he needed. What they did not have were quite enough members to qualify for official party status, a designation that provides a parliamentary budget for research staff and imparts to individuals in the diminished party a sense of relevance and worth. Having worked hard in Alberta to defeat the province's long-entrenched Social Credit regime, Joe had difficulty seeing in their "Créditiste" cousins from rural Quebec as a different political formation, a group of men ready, and more than willing, to help keep his minority government in office.

Previously, when established political parties failed to win enough seats for official party status, they'd benefitted from other parties agreeing to lower the qualifying number, a compassionate understanding springing from the sober-ing insight, "There, but for the grace of the Electorate, go I." Prime Minister Clark's calculus had no metric for generosity to other parties. So no change to the rule was made. The Créditiste MPs could only bide their time, in humili-ation, until a confidence vote presented itself.

One did on December 13. The Créditistes abstained from supporting the Conservatives and the Clark government was defeated in the Commons. Hubris had overpowered the PM's ability to count votes, something parlia-mentary politics and prime ministership require. He even disregarded the urgent alarm from assistant Jodi White to delay the vote while three PC members returned to Ottawa. Somehow, normal rules about numbers did not apply to Clark.

When Curley met up with Clark after the vote, the prime minister was jubilant about his government's defeat. Clark, it turned out, was not apprehensive, but keen to be defeated. Hadn't an earlier PC leader and prime minister from western Canada, John Diefenbaker, gone from a minority government in 1957 to the biggest victory ever a year later? Clark made the comparison a number of times, tantalized, thinking history would repeat itself.

Making things even better, the Liberals were leaderless.

The Grits had not looked at history, however, but current opinions polls, which showed them twenty points ahead of the PCs. Such numbers had emboldened them, despite being leaderless, to defeat the government.

That night, Clark asked Curley, as they rode from Parliament Hill together in the back seat of the prime minister's limosine, to be national campaign chairman for the election whose date he would set for February. He agreed, but said he had many questions he needed answered. After the newly named campaign chairman got the best answers he could get from Clark, he climbed out of the limousine and walked through snow drifts to his apartment, while Clark continued on to 24 Sussex. As soon as he got inside, Curley phoned John Thompson in Toronto, telling him he needed him right away. Thompson packed his suitcase and was with Curley in Ottawa next morning.

"We scrambled," said Curley. "Nothing was ready and we were twenty points down. There was no damn way we were ever going to win the election. But we put together a reasonable campaign." In crucial Ontario, the relatively inexperienced Bill Saunderson again chaired the province's section of the 1980 federal PC campaign for Clark, applying the best he'd learned from Norman, but without being Norman. "We came back some eleven points," noted Curley.

The vote in the Commons bringing down the government was on a proposed tax increase of eighteen cents per gallon on gasoline. It was contentious because Clark had campaigned on not increasing taxes. "The consumers of Ontario were against it," according to Allan Gregg's polling, and that is where the swing in seats from PC to Liberal made all the difference in bringing Pierre Trudeau back to power, after he rescinded his resignation and led the Liberals into the election.

Gregg also reported, not from polling data but his contacts in Ontario's big blue machine, how strongly "the Davis people were against the gas tax hike." The public could also tell, because the Liberals ran ads quoting Bill Davis's criticism. The premier did not, this time, campaign for Clark.

The Liberals gained 4 percent and thirty-three seats, the PCs lost 4 percent and thirty-three seats, the NDP edged up 2 percent in popular vote, gaining five more seats for a total of thirty-two. The Créditistes won five seats. Some modest changes occurred in a few provinces, but it was again Ontario's pendulum voters who caused the change of government: the fifty-seven PC seats in 1979 were reduced to thirty-eight in 1980, while the thirty-two Ontario Liberal seats climbed to fifty-two. Pierre Trudeau, resurging from brief retirement, now led a majority government, bringing down the curtain on a brief turn in power for Joe Clark's Progressive Conservative government.

The ardor of Davis and the Ontario blue machine to work for Clark had been cooled by the gas tax, but their displeasure about that specific issue only reinforced their general sense that Clark was not the right leader for the party. There was widespread and profound annoyance that a national PC government had been foolishly forfeited.

———

Under the Progressive Conservative constitution, as Dalton Camp's legacy to the Tory Party, a leadership review had to take place at the party's annual meetings following an election loss.

A review requires a secret ballot in which all delegates approve, or not, the leader continuing in office. For the meeting at Winnipeg in January 1983, Clark's surprising problem with numbers again proved an impediment to his political career. The party-ratified constitution required approval by only a simple majority for Clark to remain leader. But Joe made up his own rule about numbers, to replace the constitution's provision. He announced, with bravado, that he wanted well over *two-thirds'* support if he was to continue to lead the party.

The votes were cast and counted. Clark received a significant endorsement to continue. Instead of the minimum 50 percent plus one, delegates in Winnipeg had given him a strong 67 percent vote of approval, effectively meeting his own high standard. But when news of the vote count reached Clark in a backroom huddle with his advisers, Lowell Murray heard that respectable number, only to inexplicably declare, "It's not enough!" Clark, oddly, agreed. Joe had always seemed challenged by the arithmetic of politics, but now he was guided by Lowell Murray, whose own sense of these matters was evidently just as deficient.

Joe Clark, PC leader and briefly prime minister, resigned, despite party delegates recon-firming his role in the party's leadership review, to run again for leader. At this resulting Ottawa convention in 1983, Brian Mulroney won in their second match-up.

Clark returned to the convention hall, approached the podium, and began to deliver what all delegates and news media expected would be an acceptance speech. Instead, he stunned everyone with an arrogant declaration that he needed a higher level of support than the party's own constitution stipulated, and the generous one these very delegates had just given him.

Clark announced he was resigning. He called on the Progressive Conservative Party of Canada to incur the expense and effort of holding another convention. He declared he would be a candidate for the same office two-thirds of the PC delegates had just voted he should continue to hold.

Lowell Murray nodded approvingly.

Brian Mulroney, who actually seemed to want the job of leading the Progressive Conservatives and understood that winning in a democracy only required getting more votes than anybody else, could not believe his ears. He was stunned, overcome by ecstasy.

When the convention took place in Ottawa on June 11, Mulroney defeated Joe Clark on the fourth ballot and became leader of the Progressive Conservative Party of Canada. Neither Atkins nor Curley, who was now work-ing closely with him at the agency in Toronto, played a role in any of the leadership campaigns or at the convention.

CHAPTER 41

THE PERFECT CAMPAIGN

After the 1980 federal election that ended Joe Clark's government, when Liberal strategists and Pierre Trudeau proved how a down-and-out leader could recover and return to his former glory, blue machinists hoped to accomplish something similar for Bill Davis in Ontario.

Norman Atkins, still campaign chair, began to prepare for the next provincial election but was stymied in even his three preliminary steps of completing the organization chart, developing a budget, and conducting a poll. What hobbled him was the icy standoff over pollster Bob Teeter with the Ontario PC's chief fundraiser, Bill Kelly.

Kelly remained incensed that in 1977 millions of dollars he'd raised were wasted and that the province itself put through a costly election triggered only by Teeter's urgent claim that the PCs had re-entered majority territory with provincial voters. He became even more adamant that Teeter had to go after being stung by the American's big final invoice for that campaign. Norman, however, remembered Teeter's finer days and also knew the decision to call that provincial election had not been taken by Teeter but by Davis with Kelly's concurrence. He balked at making the American the scapegoat.

Allan Gregg's remarkable ascendancy at this juncture not only marked a major transition in the technical sophistication of the blue machine's backroom, but helped solve Atkins's conundrum.

Immediately after the PCs won the 1979 federal election, Gregg incorporated his public opinion and market research firm, Decima Research. In 1980, he had complete charge of polling research and analysis for the federal PC campaign. When Clark lost the election, things did not look great for him. "We were all disgraced and the big blue machine was laughing," he said. It seemed impossible that a young pollster who'd been a key part of Clark's team and its wreckage would have any prospects with the blue machine, least of all in Ontario where Atkins's operation was a solidly entrenched component of Bill Davis's party and government.

Allan Gregg, groundbreaking PC pollster, in 1983.

Gregg, however, was in the right place at the right time, thanks to conditions created by Teeter. "His mistake was in not fully understanding the Canadian system and the impact of incumbency on local voting," opined Gregg. "Because he got the numbers wrong, that created an opening for me in 1981."

Gregg insinuated himself into the Ontario PC operation, his friends on the inside helping. Advertising talent Tom Scott at the agency, a blue machinist with whom Allan had worked earlier, recommeded Gregg and helped him gain trusted access. Atkins made his painful move to replace Teeter. Bill Kelly, who not unlike Dalton Camp and Clare Westcott also had general disdain for polling, was only partly mollified. "If you are right," he told Gregg bluntly, "I will pay you and if you are wrong I will not."

Replacing Teeter by Gregg let the Tories be more open about who was surveying opinion for them. It was no longer an American being kept under wraps, but a Canadian, and a young and rebellious one at that, good for the party image. On an operational level, too, this was more practical, because analysis of field research had increasingly been handled by Canadians anyway, Gregg nationally in the 1979 and 1980 campaigns, and Brian Armstrong in the Ontario elections and nationally for the Stanfield campaigns.

This change in the campaign's polling component meant Armstrong's role for the 1981 Ontario provincial election shifted, too, as had been the case federally. "With Allan taking public opinion research to a new level, it was no longer necessary for me to be involved," said Armstrong. For a change-up, Norman asked Brian to run the campaign's legal services branch, newly important in light of the election finance rules. He'd already gained valuable experience as the official agent for the party in the recent federal elections.

With these matters settled, Norman proceeded to roll things out, getting people in their slots and convening regular meetings of his election committee. Hugh Segal left the Cabinet office and public payroll to join the premier's political staff and was on the tour bus with the leader, as he had been through the 1977 general election. Norman hung a large sign in the campaign headquarters: MAJORITY IS THE PRIORITY!

The campaign seemed only about getting power for power's sake. "Majority to do what, exactly?" asked a miffed John Thompson.

———

Partisan elements aligned better for the PCs in 1981. Intensely eloquent NDP campaigner Stephen Lewis was off the scene. Liberal veteran Bob Nixon had faded away.

A seasoned Bill Davis faced two inexperienced opposition leaders, New Democrat Michael Cassidy and Liberal Stuart Smith. Although this seemed a clear advantage, Norman envisaged how a televised leaders' debate would give the unknown opposition leaders more prominence, and greater opportunity to wound the Tory premier. Hashing this out with his planning group over breakfast, the blue machinists decided they simply did not want a televised leaders' debate. Atkins sent Segal to negotiate with the other parties and broadcasters. To the approval of everyone at PC headquarters, smiled Segal, "a TV debate never transpired because we couldn't reach an agreement."

With television having assumed such importance in elections, it seemed perverse that debate arrangements remained subject to pressurized negotiations at the start of each campaign, rather than being provided for with dispassionately established rules in the Election Act to inform electors about the parties and their policies in advance of voting. Yet with parties unwilling to update the electoral system, this democratic shortcoming for an orderly and well-rounded mandatory schedule of televised debates was another example of campaign arrangements beneficial to incumbent parties rather than voting citizens.

With that risk of a televised debate avoided, the focus turned to integrating the leader's tour, supporting key riding organizations, and recruiting strong new northern candidates like Mike Harris, Ernie Eves, and Alan Pope.

For the campaign itself, a focus was needed. Segal enthused about a government incentive program he'd been crafting in the Cabinet office for a couple of years, with the stultifying name "Board of Industrial Leadership and Development for Ontario." This he proposed as the centrepiece for the 1981 PC campaign, "the platform for which we sought a mandate." Segal tried to popularize his project with an equally ineffectual acronym, BILD. He tried to describe it with enthusiasm: "a mixed economic, social, and environmental program well ahead of its time to bring new investment, new jobs, new growth, and new innovative technologies to various parts of the Ontario economy, like biotechnology and new metallurgy, and a host of related activities." His friend Atkins embraced it, but others around Davis, such as Clare Westcott, were not charitable. "Norman and those guys came up with some lemons, like the BILD program, for the government, which was not necessarily part of their job," he said, critiquing this extension into government policy by campaign organizers.

BILD may have been a campaign platform, but Atkins knew a bigger theme was needed. He worked with Tom Scott at the agency to craft an inspiring yet generic "Help Keep the Promise" campaign. This slogan, aligned with polling research, was to convey an upbeat message, invite participation, hold out a future prospect, and suggest people could vote for Davis and still bring about massive economic change for Ontario's betterment. Even BILD fit within that.

———

With so much at stake, careful polling, which had already been used to test this slogan, was crucial. For the 1981 Ontario election, there would be something new in market research. Gregg would run "a very focused polling program in twenty-six bellwether ridings."

This integrated program was a major innovation. With the big blue machine's reputation on the line, after two Ontario elections in which the PCs barely clung to power, Gregg "took the polling to an entirely different level," said the one witness who really knew, Brian Armstrong. "He developed a model of the province that was quite remarkable in terms of its ability to predict results on a riding by riding basis."

This information enabled the campaign to know in advance which ridings PCs would easily hold and those that Tories had little or no chance of winning. With that information in hand, all the financial, advertising, and leader's tour resources could be deployed on the swing ridings having potential to be captured. In a number of ridings, the margin of victory turned simply on the number and strength of candidates splitting off the opposition vote. If the mix was right, this would enable a PC candidate to win, even with a low plurality of total votes cast. Election campaign strategy did not need to be based on miracles if it could rely on the first-past-the-post electoral system.

———

Up to this time, the way political campaigns linked polling information and election advertising was general, not specific; obtuse, not precise.

If the party was ahead in the polls, the ads sought to reinforce with voters a sense of confidence and security, in the hope that reassurance would prevent wavering and slippage of support. If the party was behind, campaign advertising might either denigrate the more popular opponent or highlight a specific issue that party strategists prayed could catch favour with electors and turn the tide. With the help of Bob Teeter's work over the past decade, a new high had been achieved in aligning the values voters held with the qualities personified by Bob Stanfield, although this never helped him form a government.

Meanwhile, the blue machine had also made strides improving campaign messaging, first by deploying the talent and innovations of the Camp agency, next by forming ad hoc consortiums of advertising experts during elections, and third by creating a highly professional television production team. Furthermore, the blue machine had, across the board, brought advertising, party logo and colours, and all aspects of campaign messaging under strong central control from headquarters, presenting voters with a uniform image and politically consistent communications.

Now another major advance was about to be implemented.

For 1981, Gregg and Atkins invented a new approach by using "K-Tel" type advertising combined with daily opinion tracking, calibrating the impact of their election advertising as revealed by a rise in polling numbers, and direct follow-up with voters. The magic came through the fusion of all three.

The K-Tel method had been invented by Saskatchewan farm boy Philip Kives, who'd acquired an instinctive knack for innovative ways to market and sell products such as cookware, sewing machines, and vacuum cleaners. Kives realized that instead of appealing to just a few people at one time, he could extend his reach through television to demonstrate a product for masses of people all at once. He made a five-minute TV commercial to sell a Teflon non-stick fry pan, using what he'd learned as a successful demonstration salesman about appealing to people. He began to reach large audiences with telling effect. Orders poured in. He spread his television ad throughout Canada. The success of Kives's long and informative commercial marked the birth of the world's first "infomercial."

This powerful new approach to advertising that joined the salemanship of *Kives* and the medium of *television* he dubbed "K-Tel." With K-Tel International, Kives went on to enjoy runaway success peddling slicing machines, knives, and compilation music albums of top hits, selling millions of units in thirty-four countries. He was inducted into the Canadian Professional Sales Association Hall of Fame for creating the first infomercial and changing the face of advertising in the world. As Kives's success became legendary in the late 1970s, people in the marketing world took note. Even though sophisticated folk dismissed his cheap products and low-budget, long-winded, repetitive commercials, others paid close attention to something that worked, especially members of the advertising team at the Camp agency.

Unlike "spot" commercials for major brand products slotted into the costly prime-time advertising periods of the shows with the highest audience ratings, ads that lasted only sixty seconds, or thirty, or even just fifteen, K-Tel's infomercials were five minutes long. That was plenty of time to make a point over and over, the power of good communication being repetition. They also cost far less because they aired during off-peak periods. Broadcasters also used them as fillers for unexpected or unfilled blanks in their schedule of commercials.

The Ontario PCs' 1981 infomercials were focused on the twenty-six ridings chosen by Gregg as winnable. Merged with this barrage of Tory K-Tel type advertising were the two other elements. "We would track the numbers daily," explained Gregg, who was analyzing polling feedback, and this was "tied directly into a huge direct mail campaign, targeted at swing voters in our bellwether ridings."

Not a single electoral district outside the twenty-six targeted areas was gained by the Progressive Conservatives. Of those twenty-six ridings, twelve elected PC candidates. On March 19, the Liberals held their thirty-four seats, neither gaining nor losing any, but the NDP forfeited a dozen, all to the Davis-led PCs. A relieved premier and a vindicated blue machine, with seventy of the legislature's 125 seats, were again running Ontario with a majority government.

"The 1981 Ontario election was," said Gregg, "without question, the most sophisticated and technically advanced campaign I was ever involved with."

"I would say the victory of 1981 was the ultimate proof," purred Segal, "that there is such a thing as a perfect campaign." It had "a perfect message, perfect leader, and perfect platform." It all came down to turning enough votes in twelve of twenty-six swing ridings, while not making gaffes to lose any others. It meant avoiding a province-wide televised debate in which Ontarians might have judged for themselves between three leaders and their plans. Far from being a democratic free-for-all, the "perfect" campaign was a shrewd plan for working the electoral process, applying new techniques to create the desired result. As Segal said, it came together "based on the discipline that Atkins brought to the process."

It was a result that pros in all campaign backrooms would envy enough to emulate.

———

In Norman's thinking, there would never be a "perfect" campaign, but there could be exceptionally good ones to be proud of.

Whether a campaign was for a commercial product at the agency or an election to political office, he wanted it to start from the right premise and be professionally executed. That is why, on the political side, as Allan Gregg observed, "The big blue machine was responsible for the professionalization of Canadian politics."

Under Atkins, the blue machine did more than integrate diverse specialists with complementary talents. It fused the universe of advertising campaigns and the arena of electoral politics. What differentiated it from other campaign organizations and made it more professional was the degree to which it broadened talent at the top, from brokers and bill collectors to pollsters and lawyers, salesmen and marketing types to accountants and entrepreneurs.

Diversity of talent and range of skills was the blue machine's profile, and in the way Norman relentlessly sought to bond these exceptional people resided his genius as a campaign organizer.

Between election campaigns and leadership races, he kept the machinery tuned, sometimes organizing anniversary celebrations, other times deploying it for non-partisan causes, for example ramping up a new organization for diabetics in the early 1980s.

Atkins was interested in this medical condition, and so was Arden Haynes, president and CEO of Imperial Oil, long-running sponsor of NHL hockey and closely connected with league president John Zeigler, who made sure the Juvenile Diabetes Foundation was a beneficiary of the annual money-raising All-Star game. Atkins and Haynes met, thanks to Paul Curley, and their conversations led to agreement that a better national organization could be created by merging Juvenile Diabetes and other scattered entities to form Diabetes Canada, a single, focused, strengthened operation. Atkins took charge of organizing the effort. Haynes agreed to raise $5 million. With Curley in the mix as friend of both, their drive to reconstitute Diabetes Canada soon resembled an election campaign.

Atkins tapped Robert Stanfield to be honorary chairman. Curley, as if running a leader's tour, put together a schedule. Imperial Oil's corporate jet flew Haynes and Stanfield across the country for meetings with governments and corporations and speeches to service clubs. Blue machinists George Potton and George Stratton advanced the tour, utilizing many of Atkins's political connections in each western province to organize press conferences and meetings for Stanfield and Haynes. Dalton Camp was aboard the flights, helping craft Stanfield's speeches for the events in Winnipeg, Regina, Calgary, and Vancouver.

When the new entity, Diabetes Canada, came into being, Atkins, Haynes, and Curley served on its board. Once Haynes raised the millions of dollars earmarked for the Juvenile Diabetes Research Foundation, and with the organization up and running, the three smoothly transitioned off the board and left operations to others.

———

The more time Dalton and Norman spent on their carefully crafted campaigns to advance the wellbeing and careers of other people's offspring, the less time they had for their own.

"Norman was never home," said his wife, Anna Ruth. That could not surprise anyone about a man running an unending succession of campaigns. Even for elections in Ontario, and Toronto itself, he'd be away from home, largely because of the commuting time to and from Markham. For the Allan Lawrence leadership campaign, he and Ross DeGeer stayed in a penthouse near Maple Leaf Gardens and close to their Westbury Hotel campaign headquarters. For the 1981 provincial election, Norman and Hugh Segal lived out of the PC suite at the Park Plaza Hotel.

"I did double duty," Anna Ruth said about raising their three sons, Peter, Mark, and Geoffrey, "and put their father on a pedestal. I kept the home front intact. A son wants the attention of his father, to be noticed and to earn his respect. But because Norman was never home, I raised them to know that he cared."

"She lived in the background," said Geoffrey about his mother. When he was home, Norman's two main activities were hosting meals with political friends and phoning dozens of people to keep tabs on everything. "Norman always loved people around. I entertained *all* the time," laughed Anna Ruth.

"Norman loved the one-on-one conversations," she added, which contributed to his addiction to telephone use. "He was on the phone all the time," she said, "which made it hard for me as wife and mother to get his attention for the boys." Norman did not bring home big briefcases of work, but always had his well-worn book of names and phone numbers handy in his suit-coat pocket.

Norman's family, like Dalton's, were supportive and proud of the major role being played, but bore the cost of an absentee campaigner.

"It was just one campaign after another, not just away from home, but often out of province," Anna Ruth sighed.

And once, even out of the country.

CHAPTER 42

CLANDESTINE CAMPAIGNS

As Dalton and Norman learned early, secrecy is a campaigner's handmaid.

Ever since the secret ballot was introduced, electoral politics came flavoured with uncertainty. The advent of opinion polling sought to peel back that veil over voter intent, but an element of mysterious unpredictability still accompanied the outcome. And secrecy shrouds more than the intent of voters. Familiar reference to "smoke-filled backrooms" is folksy shorthand for the clandestine campaign operations of those hidden away while waging our country's electoral wars.

Out-of-sight operation has long been desired to shield activities that may cross an ethical boundary or breach an election law, hide questionable uses of campaign money, or obscure politically sensitive plans from rival parties and snooping reporters.

On a human level, keeping the presence of backroom organizers from public attention is also understandable because a leader wants to be seen as master of his or her own destiny rather than some puppet of campaign engineers. This secretive instinct is multiplied when the campaign guru is imported talent and the leader keen to avoid allegations of "outside interference." A campaign organizer is desired for magic, but not to be identified as the magician.

For Camp, these normal features of Canadian campaigns were quickly learned and willingly applied: staying in hotel rooms under assumed names, working in Maritime elections away from the campaign headquarters, writing campaign speeches for others to deliver, and newspaper "editorial advertisements" signed by a fictitious character. It added appealing intrigue to the game.

By the mid-1960s, tainted by his role in "dumping Dief," Dalton's familiarity with secrecy was magnified. He directed Stanfield's 1967 leadership campaign by remote control and surreptitious rendezvous. To advise Duff Roblin, he accompanied Manitoba's premier on fishing trips to isolated northern lakes or meeting him secretly in a suburban home. Dalton wrote Stanfield's election speeches from a top-secret "bunker" well off Norman's organization chart. Dalton advised Bill Davis in the privacy of a hotel suite over breakfast. He met with New Brunswick Premier Dick Hatfield privately at Robertson's Point.

It was one thing to be secretive for the sake of the campaign, another to be secreted like a pariah. Yet Camp and Atkins understood this phenomenon, too. They played the game themselves, hiding as best they could the American identity of pollster Bob Teeter. They'd even raised the stakes by forming their clandestine Spades, which had a secret bank account that operated unacknowledged to influence campaigns for the interests of the blue machine. The Albany Club, a private organization run like an upscale Tory backroom, its major events "off the record," further enhanced this secluded nature of their campaign politics.

When Dalton and Norman sought to help Prince Edward Island Tories with their election campaigns, they discovered each time how secrecy is especially hard to maintain in the closed-loop society of a small island. The PEI experiences had conditioned them for a Newfoundland campaign, and Dalton's venture with Flora MacDonald to St. John's in 1962 to help the island Progressive Conservatives gave a foretaste of what might be in store again.

But nothing could have prepared Norman and his team for what they experienced in 1979.

———

The blue machine was called in by Newfoundland's new Progressive Conservative premier, Brian Peckford, who wanted help to win his first provincial election that year. Norman agreed to take control as communications coordinator of the campaign, and be his adviser on campaign organization. Peckford was adamant their support remain "behind the scenes."

The new premier owed his position to Frank Moores's inability to stay with anything long. After becoming an MP in 1968, Frank was elected president of the PC Party of Canada a year later, thanks to the campaign by Norman Atkins and the Spades. Frank then left national politics to become PC leader in Newfoundland and Labrador. The next year, in 1972, Frank was premier. Seven years later, Frank wanted to leave public office and trade on his connections in politics and government as a lobbyist. When he came to see Dalton for advice about extricating himself from the premiership without harming the PC Party or forfeiting power in the province, they plotted a course of action. Moores then effected the transition, announcing his departure in January 1979, with his successor, Brian Peckford, a rural school teacher and MLA, elected party leader March 17, 1979.

Preparing now to obtain his own mandate from the provincial electorate, the new premier asked Atkins to run the campaign, as the final step in the plan Camp had devised for Moores. Dalton had convinced Moores to prevail upon his successor to retain the services of the blue machine, a gambit that would also help ensure continuing business for the Camp agency with the Newfoundland government. Peckford went along, reluctant because of his cherished sense of independence and especially because he knew the political risks if news leaked out.

Atkins immediately prepared his organizational chart, but then waited for the 1979 federal election to end before placing his calls. When Brian Armstrong picked up the phone, he listened eagerly as his political mentor made yet another offer he could not refuse. Having just become a partner of his Toronto law firm, orchestrating a temporary absence for yet another election campaign was now easier.

The Camp-Atkins organization was Ontario-based, despite its Maritime origins and continuing strong connections in Nova Scotia and New Brunswick, so Newfoundland Liberals, if they discovered the truth, would gain ground appealing to nativistic distrust of anyone "from away," mock provincial Tories for importing Toronto "experts," and accuse Peckford of thinking nobody local could run a campaign.

The strong team Atkins assembled, and brought quietly to St. John's in the spring of 1979, included himself and Armstrong, political operatives John Laschinger, Nancy McLean, Chris Urquhart, and Derrick Ellis, with John McIntyre from the Camp agency to prepare layouts of advertisements, pamphlets, and other campaign material. "We essentially ran that entire campaign for Peckford," said Armstrong.

This trimmed-down blue machine got some help in avoiding detection by the fact the news media, and political attention generally, was focused on the nation's capital where Joe Clark was putting together his Cabinet amidst intense speculation about who from Newfoundland would be included, and whether John Crosbie might become finance minister.

To increase their cover, these Ontarians secreted themselves in a sleazy hotel. They stayed in the nondescript place, said Armstrong, "because it was out of the way and Peckford and Atkins thought nobody would find out we were there. We in fact ran the whole campaign without anybody ever finding out."

As far as the provincial Progressive Conservative organization, "Only one or two guys at the senior levels, including the premier, knew we were doing all this." Using a couple of rental cars to move between their hotel and the back parking lot at the quiet legislative buildings, where they operated during the day to run the campaign, ensured that no cab drivers would make a connection. With the legislature dissolved, members were away campaigning and political reporters were elsewhere covering the election events, not a vacated building.

Atkins was overall campaign manager. Laschinger handled organization on the ground, working with constituency associations, passing himself off as a local but always from a distant part of the province. McLean handled everything to do with television. Urquhart did the media buying. Armstrong wrote all the copy, and interpreted any survey data, although for this election the campaign conducted relatively little opinion research. Ellis and McIntyre laid out the advertising.

In the election's opening days, before Premier Peckford hit the campaign circuit, Atkins and Armstrong joined him in his office, getting all candidates nominated. "Peckford just started calling these guys around the province and saying, 'You are going to be the candidate.' He would have to work on them a bit," said Armstrong, "and cajole several until they agreed. But there was no nominating meeting, no hint of democracy in any of this."

With PC candidates "nominated" in the province's fifty-two ridings, Peckford filed his list with the chief electoral officer then left St. John's to meet his standard-bearers in their towns, villages, or outports, and encourage local voters to mark their ballots for these outstanding community leaders. Atkins and Armstrong looked at each other, shaking their heads at the conduct of a democratic political party in late twentieth century Canada. "These guys were essentially appointed as the party's candidates," said Armstrong. The blue machinists, though having experienced many backroom styles, "had never seen anything like this before." They clearly did not know Canada's smaller political parties.

Norman's war room was the premier's office. With Peckford away campaigning, he and Norman stayed in touch, talking on the phone every day, Atkins at Peckford's normal end of the line. Whether placing calls, reading staff memos, signing off on ads, or contemplating a next move, Norman had never run an election like this, nor operated from a more sumptuous campaign office. For campaign operations, the blue machinists "took over the entire upper floor of Newfoundland's legislative building." Their staff conferences took place in the Cabinet room.

A feature of the campaign making it possible for the blue machine to get the PC message across effectively was that "the press in Newfoundland and Labrador at that time wasn't terribly competitive," said Armstrong. "Whatever we put out as a press release, they would run." Atkins, as a result, pulled back on the paid advertising component of the campaign. They did not need to spend much on advertising because the radio stations, television broadcasters, and newspaper editors would run "whatever we wrote without much scrutiny."

Armstrong also wrote forceful speeches for Peckford about Newfoundlanders standing up for themselves, being proud of their heritage, asserting provincial rights, and no longer beseeching central Canada or Ottawa for help. At one point, Laschinger turned to Atkins to ask, "Do you really think a Toronto-based agency is going to get this government's advertising?" They all realized, the more these pro-Newfoundland speeches resonated with voters, the perilous risk of the whole campaign exploding if their top-secret mission was discovered.

The Liberal leader, Donald Jamieson, was a former Trudeau Cabinet minister, legendary in the province as a rich-voiced broadcaster. Being "a household name," however, also meant Don had been around quite some time "and his star had begun to fade," while Brian Peckford was fresh and forceful.

Peckford succeeded brilliantly in the June 18 election, with the effective force of the hidden blue machine that nobody noticed. With just over 50 percent of the popular vote, the PCs claimed thirty-three seats, while the Liberals with 40 percent got nineteen. The New Democrats' 8 percent support produced no representation.

The voting results satisfied Norman, since they had notched up another victory, but the election's aftermath disappointed him, signalling, as Armstrong said, "the beginning of a change in the way politics was being done." The Canadian tradition was that someone in advertising who ran a winning party's campaign "would be favoured with a significant amount of government advertising business afterwards. Dalton had built the Camp agency, in part at least, on that principle."

The Camp agency had lucrative tourism accounts in New Brunswick, Nova Scotia, Prince Edward Island, Manitoba, Newfoundland, and Ontario. "It was all as a consequence of Dalton's work and commitment to the party in those provinces. Mr. Davis had honoured that tradition and given the Camp agency the Ontario tourism account when we won in 1971," said Armstrong.

With Peckford things were different. The blue machine's involvement, while seemingly welcomed, had never been his idea, but a deal between Moores and Camp. When he won handily, he felt that the victory was due to his own amazing talents and strong personal appeal, not the result of unknown organizers working behind the scene. Who, after all, had handpicked all the winning candidates? Who had appeared in public to raise support by his personal appeals to get most of them elected? And hadn't the new premier crusaded to keep more of the province's benefits for the people of Newfoundland and Labrador? That applied across the board, from offshore oil and gas to "the spoils of office."

Peckford took the tourism business away from the Camp agency, which it enjoyed under Moores, and handed it to a local agency, keeping all revenue within the province. The premier picked a St. John's firm, using the same direct personal approach by which he'd selected his candidates. "Norman found that disheartening and disappointing. Loyalty meant a lot to him," said Armstrong. "He saw Peckford's behaviour as an act of disloyalty after what Norman had done for him. We had all been down there working for nothing to get Mr. Peckford elected. Norman expected the premier would want him to continue in some role in the province." Even the invoices for out-of-pocket disbursements went unpaid a long time. Dalton himself had to make several calls to Peckford to get payment.

Yet in 1982, with another election in Newfoundland, Atkins, unable to refuse a direct ask by a party leader, answered Peckford's appeal and returned to St. John's as campaign communications adviser for the provincial PCs in the April 6 election. The Progressive Conservatives won with 61 percent of the popular vote to the Liberal's 35 percent support, a result that translated to forty-four seats for the PCs and eight for the Liberals.

———

Norman's reputation, enhanced in 1981when the PCs regained a majority government in Ontario, was spreading.

Senior representatives of United Bermuda Party, the governing party that anticipated a strong electoral challenge from the rising left-wing and union-supported Progressive Labour Party, discreetly contacted him in Toronto. With both climate and politics enticing him, Norman signed on as senior consultant to the UBP and began laying plans for a 1983 general election. Norman asked Brian Armstrong, given their experience running clandestine campaigns on islands, to join him.

"Although we had never taken a cent for working in a campaign in Canada," Brian said, they decided they'd need to be paid. "If they wanted our help, we would provide it as political consultants, not as Canadian volunteers trying to affect the internal politics of another country, which would be inappropriate."

The United Bermuda Party accordingly hired the Camp agency, through which billings for campaign organizing went to Norman and Dalton Camp. Armstrong's services were also billed by the agency so his earnings similarly flowed through to him. The duo began making regular trips to Bermuda through spring, summer, and fall of 1982. They met with the new leader of the United Bermuda Party, dynamic, entrepreneurial, and outspoken John Swan.

Swan was a charismatic and progressive leader atop a conservative and centrist party. The UPB advocated moderate social and fiscal policies, held a majority of seats in the legislature, and worried about the growing strength of the island's Progressive Labour Party. Bermuda's government mostly ran domestic affairs. Britain still directed the country's foreign and defence policy and security activity. Bermuda was simultaneously in the American orbit, a result of the strong U.S. economic and military presence, and its intelligence operations, on the island.

The CIA closely followed Bermudian politics and island activities, snooping everywhere to ensure no American interests or assets were in jeopardy. The agency quickly became aware that Canada's blue machine was operating locally, with Canadians masterminding the United Bermuda Party's upcoming election campaign. "The CIA, we later learned, knew everything that we were doing down there," said Armstrong.

Others did not, however. Secrecy was as important to the plan for Premier Swan as it had been for Premier Peckford in Newfoundland. Instead of being holed up in a decrepit hotel the way they had been in St. John's, however, for this campaign the Canadian team luxuriated in the magnificent Southampton Princess Hotel, crowning a height of land from which they could overlook the entire island.

Once the election writ was issued, Atkins and Armstrong immediately flew to Bermuda. Armstrong set himself up in a Southampton Princess suite for the entire four weeks of the campaign, with Atkins coming and going as he continued to deal with business in Canada as well. Brian slept in one of the suite's two connecting rooms and converted the other into "a sort of bunker where the writing was done."

His primary role in the election was to write speeches for Premier Swan, advertising copy for the campaign, and policy papers for the party. Armstrong kept all the material for this top-level work in the second room. Atkins locked the outside corridor door of the bunker and hung a DO NOT DISTURB sign on the door handle where it remained for the next four weeks.

This precaution was necessary because Bermuda's political life was polarized between union and non-union forces. Southampton Princess employees were unionized. "We were concerned that if these folks came in to clean the room, they would quickly find out what was going on and word would get out. More than that, campaign intelligence would get out." The unionized workers strongly supported the UBP's rival, the Progressive Labour Party.

Besides locking the corridor entrance to the bunker, they also locked the interior adjoining door between the two rooms, and always double-checked that both rooms were secure whenever they left, even just briefly. The staff, Norman quipped, must have thought "this was one of the most outrageous honeymoons to ever take place at the Southampton Princess, because the DO NOT DISTURB sign remained in place for a month." All the while, the CIA's tap inside their rooms caused no disturbance. John Swan's plans for enhanced Bermudian relations with the United States and the CIA's evaluation that the UBP was a safer choice for U.S. interests than the leftist PLP meant that American intelligence officers were content to simply monitor the blue machinists' progress.

In addition to Atkins and Armstrong, the Canadian team included John McIntyre from the Camp agency, and Canadian camera crews brought in to film Premier Swan.

Taking a page from their Ontario election playbook, featuring non-traditional colours for the PC Party and a new image for Premier Davis, the blue machine completely revamped the public presentation of the United Bermuda Party. "We redesigned their party logo," said Armstrong, "and we gave them new colours. We wrote a campaign song for them. We did 'the whole nine yards,' just as we had elsewhere."

The revamped UBP campaign worked its magic, in harmony with the party's dynamic new leader, who'd had the smarts to recruit Atkins and use his services to maximum effect. Like Brian Peckford in 1979 Newfoundland and Bill Davis in 1971 Ontario, John Swan had automatically become premier upon his election as leader at a party convention, but had yet to win a general election in his own right. Just as those two Canadian premiers won substantial majorities in their inaugural outing with the blue machine, the premier of Bermuda was victorious on February 4, 1983. The Opposition Progressive Labour Party had, again, been thwarted.

For the flight back to Toronto, Atkins and Armstrong celebrated their first overseas election win by upgrading their tickets to first class and toasting themselves with champagne all the way home. Norman overcame his shyness and traded campaign stories with fellow passenger across the aisle, John Aird, Ontario's lieutenant governor and veteran Liberal seasoned in backroom politics.

Atkins hoped by participating in the Bermuda election in a pivotal way that the Camp agency would have an entree to the government's tourism business. It was a huge account, tourism being a pillar of the island's economy. But Premier Swan, bent on decolonizing Bermuda, refused to even give Atkins the chance to bid on any government advertising. It remained with an island agency, at least a few more years before being transferred to a New York firm.

As with Newfoundland, this Bermuda experience, despite the election win, left a bitter taste in Norman Atkins's mouth. "It also did for me, too," said Armstrong, "because it would have been gratifying for me to have seen Norman given that opportunity. It would have been a great account for the Camp agency, and great fun to represent the government of Bermuda, travelling there on a frequent basis to do that business." Both Norman and Brian overlooked that they had been duly paid for services rendered.

Several years later, when the Swan government's mandate was running out, the premier's senior campaign representatives contacted the Camp agency for another round of professional service in the upcoming election. Armstrong went to Bermuda with Elizabeth Roscoe of the agency to investigate. Back in Toronto with Norman, they discussed prospects and decided to decline this request to work for the United Bermuda Party.

The blue machine's first international campaign had also been its last.

CHAPTER 43

SHIFTING GEARS WITH BRIAN MULRONEY

After winning the leadership on June 11, 1983, Brian Mulroney focused on getting himself into the Commons, which he did within two months through an August by-election of convenience in Nova Scotia. The first-time MP quickly began putting together a campaign team for the coming general election.

Bill Davis urged that Mulroney invite Norman Atkins to head his national campaign. Atkins was the party's most knowledgeable and successful campaign organizer, with a solid record of wins or well-runs campaigns nationally and in many provinces, Davis reminded Mulroney, who knew it very well. Mulroney also knew the Camp-Atkins blue machine had been in the driver's seat during Stanfield's leadership, but not Clark's, and the only federal election the PCs won, in the succession of five under those two leaders, had been Joe's win in 1979. But Davis's strong recommendation carried clout.

Behind Davis's 1981 win had been the blue machine's new four-part approach to bellwether ridings, with Allan Gregg's polling and constituency modelling, the focused K-Tel type television commercials the Camp agency developed, the barrage of direct mail contacts from PC campaign headquarters, and the concentration of the leader's tour in the swing seats that gave the majority. These prized backroom secrets, of course, would not have been known to someone familiar only with the public results of the 1981 Ontario victory. The federal PC leader weighed his options and made the call to Atkins late in the summer of 1983.

PC leader Brian Mulroney, centre, with 1984 election campaign team at PC headquarters in Ottawa. Mulroney inscribed this photo for Atkins, "Norman, look what we got each other into! Good luck and 'bon courage!' Brian"

Immediately after Mulroney asked him to chair the PCs' national campaign, Norman invited Brian Armstrong to join him at Robertson's Point. The two Spades sat on the verandah of Atkins's yellow cottage, talked over roles, discussed the ideal individuals for each, and then filled in the campaign organization chart.

"For a national campaign committee, you are looking at 125 people," said Paul Curley, who'd chaired the previous national campaign in 1980 and was fully back in the loop with Norman. For 1984, every province established its campaign committee based on the same criteria Norman had, resulting in "a single national campaign organization with ten provincial campaigns replicating the same model." Norman could pick all those people, said Curley, because he had "an unbelievable network of contacts from which to put together probably the best campaign organization this country ever saw up to that point, and probably ever since."

To chair the Nova Scotia committee, for instance, he turned to Fred Dickson, his friend from Acadia University who'd worked with him in provincial elections. In Nova Scotia, a single Tory organization existed, so the same people worked in provincial and federal elections, two sides of the same house.

"I followed Norman's guidance and philosophy and put together a 'mini-blue machine' in Nova Scotia," said Dickson proudly. Mini-blue won provincial elections in 1978 and 1981 and was now gearing up for both federal and provincial contests in 1984. With his friend and mentor chairing the 1984 national campaign, Dickson wanted to be sure his Nova Scotia efforts met the high standards Atkins was known for. "Needless to say, Norman demanded perfection. There were to be no screw-ups; that was for sure."

More blue machinists were part of the 1984 national PC election effort, and proud campaign chairman Atkins stands with his upbeat and talented tribe of Tory warriors.

For the national organization Norman was assembling for 1984, this professionalism and devotion of Dickson's machine in Nova Scotia was typical of Atkins's extended organization in most provinces.

———

By this date, Atkins's election performances had risen to grand master's level.

Norman "was like a military general leading the organization," said Curley, "putting the players in the right spots, providing the overview and broad strategy. Our job was to implement."

Norman knew what needed to be done, thanks to years of accumulated experience in the army's logistical operations, campaigns with Dalton, running the agency, and witnessing from his director's chair the dynamics of government, communications, and events. "He managed to make it so you always felt really good," said Allan Gregg, "and that you were lucky to be in the room." He allowed people to nurture great respect for each other. "You were welcome, as long as you performed well."

He would even whine people into action. Nancy McLean teased Atkins about this way of motivating others, calling Norman's style "management by whining." Gregg said, "I would rather say 'yes' and not like what I had to do than deal with saying 'no' to Norman."

The organization chart for 1984 was complete, daunting for its high calibre of talent, diversity of people, and depth of experience. But just as there's a difference between fantasy baseball teams and those playing on real baseball diamonds, campaign organizers can also assemble a dream team on a chart but not get buy-in from the leader. Perhaps some prior run-in, or a suspected character flaw of an individual in the proposed organization, would cause Mulroney to nix a particular choice.

So it was with Allan Gregg.

————

Atkins as campaign chairman and Armstrong as the blue machine's pollster liaison both wanted Gregg to run polling and strategic development for the coming campaign.

"Yet Mr. Mulroney and his folks were absolutely death on Gregg," said Armstrong. There seemed to be "an institutional paranoia that infected that group of guys around Mr. Mulroney," he ventured. Atkins was blunter, calling them "the cronies." Neither of them had seen such a reaction as from the Mulroney group in politics anywhere before. "The level of paranoia was unbelievable."

The cronies all thought Gregg "was too close to Joe Clark." As Armstrong noted, Gregg was a friend and admirer of Clark's, "and Mr. Clark had brought him into politics and given him his start. So they thought he was a Clark guy." A related fear about the pollster was Gregg's collaboration with CBC Radio journalist Patrick Martin and Queen's political studies professor George Perlin on a book about the recent Progressive Conservative leadership convention and process leading up to it. The book, entitled *Contenders: The Tory Quest for Power,* had not yet been published when these discussions took place. Since Gregg was close to Clark, and Mulroney had taken the leadership prize from him, the cronies feared some kind of publishing reprisal was in the works.

The main source for this apprehension was Mulroney himself, since he knew better than anybody all that had taken place behind the scenes for him to gain power. "They were absolutely paranoid about what this book was going to say about the new leader of the party," said Armstrong, who'd begun puzzling with Atkins how to ensure they got Gregg as campaign pollster.

Armstrong met with Charlie MacMillan, a professor at York University who'd become Mulroney's policy guru. "Norman has designated me, on the organization chart," said Armstrong, "as the person in charge of research." They both understood that did not mean policy study but opinion research. Armstrong's name had been inserted as a proxy for Gregg's. His real job was to find a way to get Gregg to do the polling research.

"You can do what you want," said MacMillan in his chippy, direct way, "but you had better not bring Gregg back in here because he is writing a book about the leader and Mulroney just won't have it."

The next formal step was for the blue machine to issue a request for proposals to contract polling work for the Progressive Conservatives federally. Armstrong oversaw the competition. At the end of the exercise, Decima, Gregg's firm, was chosen. Then Atkins and Armstrong had Gregg conduct a poll, the first opinion sampling Decima and the blue machine did for Brian Mulroney.

When ready to present the results, Atkins and Armstrong got together with Mulroney in a secret weekend meeting at the Camp agency in Toronto. As they presented the findings, and especially how Gregg had interpreted the numbers, the aspiring prime minister was impressed. He did not like Gregg, or at least was highly suspicious of him, but could see he needed his kind of talent to win.

Charlie MacMillan, PEI native and York University professor, was a close policy adviser to Brian Mulroney, and both were determined to have nothing to do with pollster Allan Gregg.

Atkins was able to persuade the leader that he could not put together a winning campaign without Gregg's strategic input, and Mulroney was now able to understand why. As someone who avidly consumed opinion research, Mulroney understood that deep polling would help him determine his tack when trying to persuade others to support his approach to an issue.

Still, it was not going to be easy. Mulroney did not want Gregg's face seen anywhere in Ottawa, in the campaign organization, even the remotest corner of the party's most secret backrooms. He did not want to have to acknowledge that Gregg, who'd worked for ill-fated Joe Clark, was now on his campaign. The thrust of backroom appeals made on Mulroney's behalf by his supporters, when building support for him to win the leadership, was that Brian would be a *total* change from Joe.

Teeter had to be hidden because he was American, Gregg because he was "Clark," and in both cases Armstrong was the buffer and go-between. "It was a strange role I had to play," he said, "first with Market Opinion Research in the early 1970s, now between Allan and the campaign group in the early 1980s." Gregg did all the work. Armstrong became the face of polling, presenting the results and analysis.

Shortly before Prime Minister John Turner called the 1984 general election, Armstrong appeared at a Wednesday morning PC national caucus of MPs and senators to outline the results of a poll Decima had just completed. Unlike the published polls in the media, which had motivated John Turner's decision to request the Queen to cancel her state visit so he could call an election, the numbers Gregg's polling team extracted from people they'd surveyed looked quite good for the Mulroney-led PCs.

Mulroney came across well in the poll for quality of his leadership, ranking higher in a number of categories than Turner. As Armstrong got about halfway through his presentation, Mulroney, knowing precisely what was most important for his caucus to understand, leaned across the head table and "whispered" instructions in a voice intentionally audible throughout the large room, provoking laughter while heightening interest, "Tell them more about the leadership stuff."

The blue machinists were relieved that the most advanced polling techniques and political analysis would be at their service, despite this cloak-and-dagger hassle. Gregg and Armstrong negotiated the agreement for Decima to do the polling work and all data analysis for the campaign. Gregg would do the same modelling for the country as a whole that he'd pioneered in the 1981 Ontario election, to find the winnable ridings that could give the Tories victory.

––––––

Another part of Atkins's dream team was having Paul Curley work closely with him as campaign secretary. Mulroney associated Curley with Clark, too. "I was out of favour with the Mulroney guys," said Curley. But the PC leader appreciated that the person closest to his campaign chairman would be bilingual, and harboured no fears about Curley.

Brian wanted the election campaign run out of Ottawa, a change from the recent pattern of essentially Toronto-based operations, so Norman spent most of late 1983 and the first nine months of 1984 in the capital, living at Finlay MacDonald's townhouse, where Dalton Camp also stayed when he was in and out of town and where Curley now also resided. Camp and MacDonald were part of the campaign's "brain trust" helping devise strategy.

Living in Ottawa full-time for almost a year, Atkins left the Camp agency in Segal's hands, where he remained to take care of business. Norman had brought in Hugh from the premier's office, after the return to majority government, to be a vice-president of the Camp agency and president of Advance Planning, the public relations and public affairs firm Dalton had started years before, as part of his structured outreach beyond advertising. Advance Planning had languished, with Dalton's changing interests, and Segal's mission was to revive it.

During the campaign, Segal's handling of business at the agency would be interrupted only a couple of times by political assignments from Norman, first to support Brian Armstrong in negotiating the televised leaders' debates, second to help Mulroney with preparation for the the English-language debate.

As soon as the election was called for September 4, the blue machine campaign team assembled for action. Armstrong left his Toronto law practice and arrived in Ottawa to work full-time in a unit housed at party headquarters, separate from the primary campaign headquarters, with Atkins, Gregg, and Tom Scott. Scott, on loan to the campaign from Foster Advertising as part of Atkins's backroom advertising consortium, had already worked effectively with Gregg and Armstrong in the 1981 Ontario campaign. Now reassembled, the trio began merging research and interpreting polling results for the national PC media campaign.

Bill Davis again campaigned actively for the federal PCs, as he had for each of Robert Stanfield's elections and Joe Clark's first. In addition, he motivated his caucus and the Ontario PC organization to to campaign with enthusiasm for Mulroney. This support was always important in a province electing so many MPs.

Bill Saunderson, after taking a break from campaigns, told Atkins he wanted to get back into the game. Norman named his fellow Spade comptroller for the 1984 campaign. "I was privy again to the Norman Atkins style of meetings," Saunderson beamed. "They had actually gotten better. Norman had refined his style. The 1984 campaign was classic."

Saunderson's work as comptroller carried more gravitas thanks to the election finance law reforms. Now if campaign spending exceeded statutory limits, people could go to jail and election results might be nullified. Saunderson would encounter "some real problems" because members of the campaign team reassured him they were within spending limits, only to turn up in distress after the campaign with a sheaf of invoices for expenses they'd forgotten about "because people didn't always send bills until the election was over."

Another part of the 1984 campaign, Brian Mulroney's inspiration, was the creation of an advisory group of influential Progressive Conservatives across Canada, including Peter Lougheed in Alberta and Bill Davis in Ontario, whom he called intermittently to consult about the campaign. Working the phones had long been a built-in characteristic of the PCs' new leader. He'd developed a majestic telephone manner, abetted by his rich baritone, calling people, getting information, making them feel included and valued. Each "adviser," of course, was also a highly influential political player who could, in turn, mobilize campaign resources. Mulroney kept them inspired to take emphatic action.

Mulroney, like Atkins and McMurtry, was a master at reaching out to people this way. "He was thoughtful," said Curley. "He'd phone someone whose spouse was in hospital, or whose father had died. I'd hear the next day, 'I can't believe the leader, with all he has on his mind, telephoned me last night.'"

With Mulroney, the Progressive Conservatives had a leader more adept in the backrooms than anyone before him. Even Joe Clark, who'd grown up in student politics, graduated to roles as a party organizer for the PCs in Alberta under Lougheed, and worked for Camp in party operations at Ottawa and at the agency in Toronto, could not command clout among backroom players to match the engaging demeanour of Mulroney. He was also the first leader of a national Canadian party who really wanted to study polling results, even sometimes the raw data, because he could comprehend the implications for himself. He'd assembled a robust team of loyal fundraisers, delegate dealers, and news media allies to succeed in replacing Joe Clark. Becoming leader of the national party before ever having once run for election to Parliament, Mulroney had well-earned credentials for adeptness in backroom politics.

Other innovations now hallmarks of a blue machine campaign were deployed for 1984. An intensive program of campaign schools for candidate training, and others to instruct campaign managers and official agents, had taken place in advance of the election call.

Mulroney   Tour   Calendar   –   Campaign   '84

And The Winner Is?

The leader's tour for Brian Mulroney during July and August in the 1984 federal election was tightly organized, blending polling information with strategic timing for greatest impact, covering all key areas and communities in a sequence for building momentum.

"Every element of the national campaigns in 1984 was probably the best the country had seen up to that time," reiterated Curley, with "real coordination of all the components of advertising, communications, and polling. Everybody knew what their role was, everybody understood the objectives, and everybody understood who was making the final call — it was the national campaign chairman, Norman, with the support of Mulroney."

———

The special promise of Brian Mulroney was to break the Liberal grip on Quebec.

He'd campaigned for the PC leadership by asking why Tories should start each election conceding the Grits sixty-five or seventy seats. In the most recent election, indeed, Liberals had taken all but one of the province's seventy-five seats. Brian's message was that, as a fully bilingual Quebecer with strong organizational skills, he would change that.

For much of the twentieth century, the default position of the province's voters had been to take refuge in the Liberal Party, an imperfect bargain because Liberal governments in Ottawa got used to winning these seats and took the province and its elected representatives for granted. But when Quebecers decided to send an electoral message telling Ottawa to stop ignoring them, they seldom turned to the Conservatives. They swung instead to fresher political formations, such as the Bloc Nationale, and the Ralliement créditiste du Québec. On top of that, Conservatives were punished by the voting system. Tories received far more votes across the province than got translated into proportionate representation in the Commons. Judged by its number of MPs from Quebec, the PCs appeared effectively extinct as a party, although often more than a million supporters voted for *les bleus.* In 1980, their 372,587 votes in Quebec resulted in only one seat in the Commons.

Such long-term voting trends and the electoral roulette of the entrenched voting system made Mulroney's boast seem improbable of fulfillment. "*Le tonneur bleu*" or "blue thunder" — the Quebec version of the blue machine — had mounted valiant efforts in Quebec for Robert Stanfield and then Joe Clark in 1968, 1972, 1974, 1979, and 1980, with little to show for the effort.

While the Atkins's operated blue machine did its best to work with PC organizers in Quebec over these years, Mulroney steadily solidified his own connections and support within the same ranks. All the while, some fine organizers had been drawn into Quebec federal PC activity by Robert Stanfield, and others had developed loyalties to Joe Clark. In the backrooms, if not at the ballot boxes, Quebec PCs were quite alive.

Richard LeLay, Stanfield's French-language press secretary, was also key with the Mulroney team in the 1984 campaign, and thirty years later, reflecting on those days and consulting his numerous documents of the period, could effectively trace "how the Mulroney victory in 1984 was the fruit born of the particular extension of the fierce determination of the group of individuals associated as 'big blue' — Atkins, Lind, Wickson, Curley, MacDonald, Camp, Meighen, to name just those alone." The essence of the support for the PCs, believed LeLay, was "creation of a strong and motivated partisan membership, an organization directed by effective and performing managers, as well as ideas and a program that was clear, coherent, and articulated."

Yet on the ground, *le tonneur bleu* was an operation unto itself, working with Quebec rules, not under Atkins's control. Brian Mulroney in 1984 was able to draw the personnel of *le tonneur bleu* into an integrated campaign with two further fighting battalions inside the province.

One was his own team of hardened Conservative organizers who'd loyally carried Brian through two leadership campaigns. Bernard Roy, his close friend since law school, was chair of the 1984 Quebec campaign. Roger Nantel ran all PC campaign advertising in Quebec, quite distinct from that in the rest of the country. Bernard and one or two other members of the Quebec campaign came to Ottawa for national campaign meetings, to ensure the lines of communication were open, but national campaign chairman Atkins was involved with action in Quebec only in connection with the leader's tour.

Mulroney's other battalion was the provincial Liberal organization of Premier Robert Bourassa who, for cause, felt abused by Ottawa's Liberals under Pierre Trudeau and was prepared to send an ally, instead, to the prime minister's office. This, said Curely, "was a whole different campaign. We didn't know much about it, except that Bourassa and Mulroney would meet in the premier's 'bunker' in Quebec City" to lay plans, discuss the campaign's progress, and envisage what might come from a new PC government in Ottawa, which time would reveal to be the Meech Lake Accord, an inspired act by federalist Quebecers to reintegrate their province constitutionally, as PM Mulroney would say, "back into the Canadian family."

Not only was the crucial Quebec operation quarterbacked by Mulroney, the leader also made sure his loyalists were in key positions throughout the overall campaign structure of provincial committees, too. "But whoever was on these provincial committees," said Curley, "they all bought into Norman's plan."

Ike Kelneck and his band, Jalopy, an integral part of the blue machine since 1971, now raise spirits with Mila Mulroney in 1984. Jalopy had also contributed musical energy to the federal campaigns of Stanfield and Clark, but for the first time had natural stage performers in Brian and Mila.

By the time Mila and Brian were making the leader's bus tour through the many ridings of populous southwest, central, and eastern Ontario on days thirty to thirty-four of the campaign (August 8–12), a surge to the PCs had begun and they were both in their element joyously meeting and greeting voters.

The campaign plans were agreed to, a clear focus was on winning, yet beneath the surface, perhaps better seen in retrospect than at the time, twinning two campaign organizations, one loyal to Atkins, another to Mulroney, created a deep rivalry within the PC Party.

———

The campaign was only days old when a gaffe threatened to sour everything.

On the leader's tour, Brian Mulroney strolled to the back of the PC campaign's chartered aircraft to speak with reporters. They talked about the raft of Liberal patronage appointments outgoing Prime Minister Trudeau required his successor John Turner to make. One of the many was Montreal MP Bryce Mackasey, labour minister in Trudeau's Cabinet, appointed Canada's ambassador to Portugal. Mulroney, who fancied himself a friend of many in the press corps, misjudged the relationship by seeking to treat them that way. He also erred by thinking that speaking with reporters at work covering an election campaign was somehow "off the record."

He rambled on about the many appointments and, when asked specifically about Mackasey, became jocular. He was sort of fond of the fellow Montrealer with shared Irish heritage. He quipped that he did not really blame "old Bryce" because as everybody knows, "there's no whore like an old whore." He further undermined his own *public* criticism of Turner's appointments by adding, as a throwaway line, "You know, if I had been in Bryce's shoes, I would have been right there with my nose in the trough like the rest of them." Everyone laughed. Mulroney made his way back to the front of the plane, delighted with the easy, companionable relationship he enjoyed with reporters.

Not all journalists believed that what a leader said in private, when it differed from his public stance, was to be protected by some unwritten rule. Nor were all reporters covering the campaign interested in seeing Mulroney and the Progressive Conservatives win. The "old whore" statement was duly reported and became an immediate sensation. Mulroney's boomerang delivered a double blow, one hit for the course language used by a would-be prime minister, another for the acknowledgement that he would have behaved no differently from the Grits if able to be a patronage recipient.

The news on television sets in the PC campaign headquarters, set to all channels to monitor coverage in a comprehensive manner, shocked Atkins.

The election reports were barely over before he was, Armstrong said, "fielding phone calls from campaign organizers outraged at this development and demanding some kind of action, in response, from the campaign." Atkins tried desperately to reach Mulroney and the tour group.

When Mulroney called in, Atkins took the phone and lit into the leader with rare vehemence. He described the news story as "a potential disaster for the campaign." He insisted that Brian apologize for his comments. Only that might help put the issue to rest.

Mulroney resisted. Who was Atkins to tell *him* what to say? He had been cocooned and did not realize the rapid and far-reaching negative fallout from his very public off-the-record comments. The leader was being told by his press secretary and several "cronies" in his entourage that he needn't worry because the news story would be "a one-day wonder" that nobody would remember by voting day in September.

Atkins, however, was passionate about the misstep. He would not back down. He insisted on a meeting to discuss it. Camp and MacDonald accompanied him, as part of the brains trust on campaign strategy, reinforcing Norman's effort to persuade the PC leader, and other advisers with him, that an apology not only had to been made, but offered sincerely.

Brian Mulroney "made very elegant and eloquent apology at a Winnipeg campaign stop at the beginning of the next week," said Armstrong, "and the issue died an instant death after that." If things had turned out differently, it would have affected the election outcome in quite a significant way. "If he had not apologized," it became clear in hindsight, "then he would never have been able to take the high ground so effectively against Mr. Turner in the debates."

————

Atkins asked Armstrong, because of his experience negotiating terms for the televised leaders' debates in three Ontario elections, to do the same for the 1984 national campaign, and requested Segal, who'd negotiated out of existence the TV debate for the PCs in the1981 Ontario election, join him.

Alongside Armstrong and Segal were Michael Meighen and CTV broadcaster Tom Gould. The four joined the other parties' representatives in a downtown Toronto hotel, where CBC hosted the negotiations. What intrigued them most was the impression that John Turner did not want to debate at all. He and his Liberals, after all, appeared to be riding a crest of popularity. In contrast, the blue machine desperately wanted to pit underdog challenger Mulroney against Turner, encouraged by those many "leadership" attributes Decima's private research kept generating that showed the Tory leader out-distancing the Grit chief.

Shortly before the debate, Armstrong and Gould went to the studio to advance the arrangements, so they could brief Mulroney about the studio set-up, where he would stand, how many cameras there would be, and the location of each. Gould was thoroughly professional about everything, said Armstrong, and "Mulroney was really comfortable working with him."

When the dates drew near for the debates, Atkins scheduled Brian Mulroney to be in Ottawa at Stornoway, the Opposition leader's official residence, where Segal, Lowell Murray, Bill Neville, and Lucien Bouchard began covering with him the full range of policies, issues, and tactics.

Meanwhile, the only person to appear at the TV studio on John Turner's behalf was Israel Asper, dispatched by the Liberal campaign to advance the debate. The talented Winnipeger, who'd led the province's Liberal Party and since launched into broadcasting with the Global Network, appeared on his own and spent little time looking over the studio or its intended set-up.

Brian Mulroney turned in a masterful performance during the French-language debate, relaxed, eloquent, focused on key issues, and reassuring. He shone even more brilliantly in the English-language debate, delivering his knockout blow to John Turner when the PC leader excoriated the prime min-ister for making the Grits' extensive patronage appointments.

"I had no option," shrugged Turner, suggesting his hands were tied.

"You had an option, sir," rejoined the Opposition leader, his index finger pointing with stinging accusation as if in a courtroom. "You could have said 'No!'"

Conventional wisdom emerged that the defining moment in the 1984 election campaign was this nationally televised debate. But for blue machine insiders, as Armstrong said, "if Brian had not apologized and the issue had stayed alive during the election campaign, he would never have been able to admonish Turner on the patronage issue, never have been able to take the high ground the way he did so well." To Armstrong, "the turning point in that campaign was not the debates, but when Norman Atkins went toe to toe with Mr. Mulroney, told him he had to apologize, then put the people together who could persuade him it had to be done."

Devoted to the Progressive Conservative cause, Ontario premier Bill Davis fully supports the campaign of national leader Brian Mulroney throughout the province, feeding him the names of folks between puffs on his pipe. Brian is delighted by requests for his autograph.

Following the two televised debates, the PC campaign's insiders knew Mulroney was on the ascendant, a feeling supported by Decima's nightly "rolling polls." Wanting to ensure nothing came unstuck in the crucial closing stages, Atkins assigned Armstrong to accompany the leader's tour on the airplane, performing anew the role he'd mastered when touring with Joe Clark and Bill Davis in prior campaigns.

At every stop, as directed by Atkins, Armstrong found the nearest payphone and called headquarters to report to Norman directly on how the event went, what the leader had said, and "the temperature of the water." Brian Mulroney at this stage had his stump speech well honed. There were no more incidents of loose chatting with reporters in the back of the plane or on the press bus, no more need for confrontations over the need for an apology.

As the results began to be broadcast, PC leader Brian Mulroney and his key organizers watch the televised results and realize he is on his way to becoming Canada's new prime minister, despite the large lead of the Turner-led Liberals at the start of the campaign.

On September 4, the 211-seat win for the Progressive Conservatives was a campaign triumph for Brian Mulroney and a landmark accomplishment for Norman Atkins and the big blue machine.

The New Democrats, led by Ed Broadbent, remained almost unchanged from the 1980 election, holding about the same level of popular support, around 19 percent, and losing just one of its seats to end with thirty. The real electoral battle had been fought between the Liberals and Conservatives. The Grits plummeted from 44 percent popular support in 1980 to 28 percent, and lost 135 MPs to end up with only forty members in the Commons. The Mulroney-led PCs climbed above 50 percent in popular support and won 211 ridings, a gain of 110 members in the 282-seat house.

With his historic PC majority, Brian Mulroney, a fully bilingual Quebecer leading the Conservative Party, rightly took satisfaction that four out of every five ridings across his native province had elected a PC member to Ottawa.

Norman Atkins, flashing the "V" of victory, was national campaign chairman for the Progressive Conservatives in 1984 when the big blue machine was at its zenith. His skill, seasoning, and campaign mastery helped Brian Mulroney win the largest number of Commons seats for any party in Canadian history.

The national tour included campaigning by bus, a well-honed operation since the 1971 Davis campaign in Ontario. Seated and listening to Brian Mulroney are Pat MacAdam and Brian Armstrong, while standing, Charlie MacMillan and press secretary Bill Fox follow the planning.

To the cheering Progressive Conservatives, campaign manager Norman Atkins, Prime Minister Brian Mulroney, and party president Bill Jarvis link hands and bask in electoral glory.

CHAPTER 44

THE SEE-SAW CAMPAIGN

After the PC victory, Norman, Dalton, Finlay, and their inner circle felt it crucial to forge a strong connection with the government, including the prime minister's office and party headquarters.

The pattern Bill Davis developed following his big win in 1971, with the Park Plaza Group and Brian Armstrong as his principal secretary at Queen's Park, offered a model for Prime Minister Mulroney, they believed, to fuse the political direction of his government with ongoing operations of a fully integrated campaign organization. In short, Atkins, Camp, and MacDonald wanted to ensure the blue machine's operational presence at the heart of Canadian government.

Finlay MacDonald urged the case for putting top campaign organizers and fund raisers in the Senate, a principal role of the appointed house, so they could be in Ottawa, close to the PM and members of caucus, to advance partisan electoral interests while on the public payroll. MacDonald saw himself as a perfect candidate for this role, as did Camp. They got Stanfield to ask the PM to do it. On December 21, 1984, Mulroney named his first senator, a Christmas present for MacDonald. His presence in the Senate secured a beachhead for the blue machinists.

To achieve more direct, hands-on coordination at the top, they had earlier urged Brian Armstrong to consider working in Prime Minister Mulroney's office as a deputy chief of staff, to function as a trusted liaison between the party's campaign organization and the PMO. Mulroney had appointed Bernard Roy chief of staff. They envisaged Armstrong as his deputy. Roy and Armstrong agreed to discuss how this might work in practice, and met at Ottawa's Westin Hotel.

Armstrong began by asking what Roy had in mind. The chief of staff replied he'd not thought about it very much. To fill the void in their conversation, Armstrong suggested he needed to organize the office "on the basis of someone to run the staff and someone external working with caucus and Cabinet on issues of substance to advance the prime minister's agenda — one staff role, one policy role." Bernard, however, "saw himself doing both roles and did not know how I would fit in." When Armstrong asked to see an organization chart, Roy was unable to produce one, even as a sketch. Armstrong never did see one, at any stage.

Learning from his years in the Ontario premier's office how crucial the structure at the centre is for the complex task of running a government, Armstrong worried that another big Progressive Conservative majority

At a Château Laurier meeting, Canada's new prime minister wears a "Day 1" button as Norman Atkins delivers prepared remarks, alongside PC Party organizers Jean Bazin, Paul Curley, and John Laschinger. At the time, a popular ad campaign for legendary American stock brokerage firm E.F. Hutton was "When E.F. Hutton talks, people listen." Mulroney, in the euphoric glow of early days, inscribed this goodwill picture, "When Norm Atkins speaks, E.F. Hutton (and their Canadian clients) listen!"

government could implode, from misdirection and confusion at the centre, as it had with John Diefenbaker's. He spoke with several seasoned players, including Bill Neville, who'd been Joe Clark's "North Star" as chief of staff and was on the Mulroney transition team, only to learn that Neville himself had been trying to advise about the PM's office set-up, as well, without apparent interest since Mulroney and his confidants believed they'd get no constructive lessons from how Clark's office had been run.

Armstrong met with Atkins and Segal, reporting that he feared the PMO "did not know what they were doing" and, most important, Mulroney had not asked him to join his staff. Working for Bill Davis had begun when the premier asked directly. Armstrong "thought it telling that Mr. Mulroney did not make the offer personally."

"If you feel uncomfortable," said Segal, "go back to law."

Armstrong returned to Toronto and revived his sagging law practice. In Ottawa, the PMO soon became overwhelmed. Basic management at the centre was lacking. The PM faced a succession of issues, which was normal, but there

Brian and Mila Mulroney host Ontario's "big blue machine" to a formal dinner at 24 Sussex Drive. Included are Bill Davis, Clare Westcott, Norman Atkins, Eddie Goodman, Ed Stuart, Bill Kelly, Hugh Segal, their spouses, and the Davis family. The elegant celebrations proceeded, while behind the scenes Mulroney ensured he kept the blue machinists from taking too much control.

was a persistent escalation of many of these into crisis or scandal, a situation that, eventually, diminished the PM's support.

Meanwhile, the blue machine had also been trying to install one of its own at PC headquarters. After the 1984 election, Norman advocated strongly for the PM to appoint Jerry Lampert national director.

Lampert had abundant administrative and organizational qualifications, but Mulroney and his own organizers wanted a Quebecer as national director. Lampert did not speak French, a shortcoming at any time, a fatal flaw for a party finally having solid phalanx of fifty-eight Quebec MPs and strong ground organization in the province. The saw-off was to appoint Lampert and Gisele Morgan, a highly knowledgeable Quebecer connected with the francophone team, as co-national director responsible for Quebec.

The compromise did not hold long. When Elections Canada completed its review of the 1984 financial reports several months later, Marcel Masse was cited for having overspent in his election. Elections Canada notified Lampert it would be making an investigation, and the national director briefed the PM's chief of staff, Bernard Roy, because Marcel was a Cabinet minister. When the CBC interviewed Lampert, sensing a scandal, he was asked if he'd informed anyone in the PMO and replied that he had. When the CBC asked Bernard Roy, he denied he'd been told. "This put everything into a tailspin," said Lampert, "and it got very strange."

This occurred just days before the summer of 1985's Rough-In, and phone lines buzzed with urgent instructions to Norman and others to "get this thing sorted out." Quebec organizers who'd been attending the Rough-In in prior years were instructed not to go. Only Jean-Carol Pelletier, who'd grown up on Champlain Street in Baie Comeau with Brian Mulroney, felt secure enough to venture against his friend's orders. Pelletier, director of PC caucus research, travelled easily between all the party's factions, even the competitive clusters around Mulroney and Clark.

At the Rough-In, Jerry treasured those "who gave me a lot of support and good counsel and showed the magic of 'big blue' in trying to work out political problems together." The inbound phone messages conveyed from the top that Jerry had to be gone immediately, but Norman pushed back and bought time. He arranged a smooth transition. When Lampert left for British Columbia, Brian Mulroney's choice for national director, his fearless yet diplomatic friend from Baie Comeau, Jean-Carol Pelletier, moved in. He would remain national director for the next five years.

Long-time PC organizer Jerry Lampert, after a major role in the 1984 campaign, was pro-moted by Atkins to be new national director of the federal party. Controversy with Mulroney made the appointment short-lived. Here Norman ponders Jerry's update on the confronta-tion, and the difficulties of fusing the blue machine with the PM's own organizers.

"Mulroney came to power as prime minister with a strong core of former university friends and supporters, from St. Francis Xavier, plus a core of Quebecers who were with him for years," said Lampert. "They were very protective of Mulroney and when they came up against another group, the blue machine that was led by Norman, there were conflicts." Atkins's nominee had not lasted. It took a few weeks for Lampert's phasing out, but "in the end, the Mulroneyites got what they wanted."

In the more immediate afterglow of the September 4 victory in 1984, well before those organizational flaws and power struggles came to light, Atkins and Segal hit Ottawa with a different display of their event-planning prowess.

Four weeks after the Progressive Conservatives swept to power, a two-day conference in Ottawa registered over two hundred senior executives to learn about "The New Government: Players & Priorities."

The event was Norman's brainchild. The entity organizing and hosting the conference, Strategic Planning Forum, was half-owned by Advance Planning and Communications, whose chairman was Atkins and president, Segal. In conspicuous circulation was Dalton Camp, now more recognized as a political columnist and broadcaster than former PC Party national president.

The upbeat conference included major speeches on foreign policy by External Affairs Minister Joe Clark, Canada's economic prospects by Finance Minister Michael Wilson, and the promise of Canadian energy markets by Pat Carney, minister of energy, mines and resources. The roster of speakers also boasted a dozen other movers and shakers from the realms of polling, business, economic organizations, and public service. Although Atkins's name was absent from the glossy program, he was the one who made the calls, assembled the talent, devised the plans, and personally circulated the rooms ensuring everything from food trays to podium services were just right.

"While the Tory government benefitted from having a friendly platform from which to convey its message to the private sector," noted political writer Ron Graham, "Strategic Planning Forum took the profits and the publicity."

———

Also that same fall, Atkins and a hand-picked team of blue machinists worked with Fred Dickson and his "mini-blue" machine in a Nova Scotia provincial election, jointly applying all their best methods. When the votes were counted on November 6, 1984, the PCs climbed to their biggest win yet, with 51 percent of the popular vote across Nova Scotia and forty-two of the fifty-two seats in the House of Assembly.

But by 1987, fortunes would turn in neighbouring New Brunswick for Premier Richard Hatfield. After a dozen years as a popular and progressive premier, he'd pushed the limits of personal behaviour and the five-year constitutional term of office beyond anything blue machinists could offset with a valiant campaign. In the October 13 election, the Liberals, led by Frank McKenna, won in every constituency, getting 60 percent of the popular vote and 100 percent of the seats. The PCs had 29 percent of the popular vote and the NDP, 11 percent, meaning some 40 percent of New Brunswick's electorate were left without any voice in their provincial assembly, and the government itself was denied the benefits of scrutiny and critique of its measures by opposition lawmakers.

Another exceptional electoral outcome in this period occurred in Ontario, in two stages. In 1985, the province's Tory dynasty crumbled under Bill Davis's successor, Frank Miller. "The dumb thing Frank did when he became leader," Clare Westcott said, "was declare his first act would be to get rid of the big blue machine." Without the blue machinists, Miller barely managed to win a hastily called general election, emerging with only a minority government. Defeated in the legislature, the PCs were replaced by a Liberal-NDP coalition, which Lieutenant Governor John Aird had accepted so Liberal leader David Peterson could form a government and become premier. The second stage came in the next election, in 1987, when the Liberals won ninety-five of the 130 seats at Queen's Park, while their coalition partner New Democrats slipped to nineteen seats. The PCs plummeted to third-place standing, losing thirty-six members from the total elected two years earlier, leaving them with only sixteen seats.

As if to prove that Tory support was falling almost everywhere, Nova Scotia PCs headed into a provincial election on September 6, 1988, and dropped fourteen seats to the Liberals. However, they did manage to retain, with twenty-eight seats, their modest majority in the fifty-two-seat assembly, and hence control of government.

None of these provincial outcomes augured well for the Mulroney PCs, as many saw declining support for the federal Tories contributing to the diminishing appeal of Conservatives everywhere, something unhelpful to anxious Norman Atkins, fretting about the national re-election campaign he would chair sometime late in 1988.

———

As early as June 1986, amidst signs of declining PC fortunes, the PM, hoping Norman could reprise his triumphant role from 1984, appointed him to the Senate and asked him to again chair the national campaign.

The campaign's operational headquarters were back in Toronto this time, but all major committee meetings still took place in Ottawa, drawing on facilities and services readily available in the country's political capital, and better in every way for campaign meetings with the all-important Quebecers. Each week, Atkins went to Ottawa for these meetings. Segal travelled with him as liaison between the campaign committee as a whole and the Toronto-based advertising, communications, and polling group.

Also working in Toronto with Segal, in addition to Tom Scott who ran advertising and communications, was Allan Gregg in charge of polling, Nancy Jamieson with the group "translating polling into communications," and Bill Liaskas who created radio and television free-time broadcasts. Together this group also produced all the commercial advertisements.

For the 1988 campaign, Atkins again named Bill Saunderson comptroller. "We did accrual accounting," he said, to avoid the problems of overspending this time. "As soon as an order was placed, that became an expense," said Saunderson. "It was on the books as a commitment, deducted from the allowable amount we had to spend."

Running campaigns at the federal level, Saunderson dealt with a lot of difficult and sensitive problems. "I have to be careful what I say," he tiptoed, "but all those Quebec guys operated a lot differently than we did, as I found when controlling the money." Quebec was one of the places the national PC organization had trouble at the end of the 1984 campaign, but with the lesson learned, Saunderson said, "it was much better in 1988 because Norman had installed people to ensure that we did it properly. He knew that things had to be done right."

———

The 1988 election, which the PM announced for November 21, became a heated battle over "free trade" with the United States.

Voters often find it hard to distinguish between Progressive Conservatives and Liberals, but never more than in 1988 when the two parties switched policies. In the 1911 election, the free-trade Liberals championed a Reciprocity Treaty between Canada and the United States in a red-hot electoral battle against protectionist-minded and tariff barrier–loving Conservatives. In 1988, the Conservatives fought for the new Canada-U.S. Free Trade Agreement with the United States while the Liberals opposed it with all vigour possible.

Not only had the parties reversed their historic positions, but Brian Mulroney had repealed his own recent articulate opposition to "continentalism." When campaigning for and winning the PC leadership, he advocated protecting Canada from American encroachment. Since then, he'd adopted the free-trade recommendations of Liberal Donald MacDonald's royal commission report, discovering value in accelerating economic flow between the two countries. The PM pulled off this historic about-face without even a debate in caucus.

The 1988 federal election was going to be difficult. Progressive Conservative strategists actually wanted to *avoid* the free trade issue. "The problem was that while people did not understand its long-term and intangible benefits," said Allan Gregg, taking the soundings, "the immediate threats of free trade were tangible and real. We did not want the electorate to focus on those liabilities."

The nationally televised leaders' debate between Brian Mulroney and John Turner, however, caused them to do precisely that. "The emotion Turner displayed in the debate," said Gregg, "played a central role in this turn of events. The debate caused people to say that Turner actually believed free trade would threaten Canada's social programs, and if he feared that, maybe they should, too."

Gregg's nightly tracking showed the number of people supporting the PCs had begun to decline, partly "because Mulroney was carrying a lot of baggage," and partly due to Turner's impassioned performance in the debate, which the Liberal campaign was repeating in its televised commercials.

Atkins phoned Gregg and stated, with calm simplicity, "We need to figure out how to change this." They met on a Sunday, after Decima had completed further research and Gregg had done his analysis, including work with focus groups revealing "that the bridge that joined fear of free trade with an increased tendency to vote Liberal was Turner's credibility, rooted in emotion."

The counteracting response from the PCs, they decided, had to "play to the innate cynicism voters had toward politicians — 'Turner said what he said not because he believes it, but because he wants your vote!'" The strategy was to "bomb the bridge" and destroy the Liberal leader's credibility.

Launching this bridge-bombing campaign, Canada's finance minister, Michael Wilson, said brazenly in public that John Turner was "a liar." Willard Estey, "the grandfather of Medicare in Saskatchewan" and a distinguished lawyer who'd just retired from the Supreme Court of Canada, said unequivocally that free trade would not put healthcare in jeopardy. These and other statements formed the basis of the blue machine's campaign to destroy Turner's credibility.

"We used 'streeter' advertising that employed real voters voicing their disbelief of Turner's motives, together with very tight shots of Turner's face. We hammered away," said Gregg. "The numbers stopped going down, and then reversed."

What was stunning were the number of PC advertisements, more flights of television ads after the televised leaders' debates than ever seen before, "aimed at people who stayed home and watched shows like *Oprah Winfrey* and such, because they were the people our polling told us were undecided," said Segal. Many people on the bus with the leader's tour, including the journalists, never saw the ads because they were travelling, "but the voters we needed to get to were carefully reached in the campaign and craftily put together on that basis."

The drama was explained by Gregg, who said when he'd "first started on the knee of Norman Atkins, he talked about 'the rule of eight.' You could never manage more than eight points of popular-vote shift over the course of a campaign." The 1988 election had two *fifteen-point* swings. Mulroney and his candidates lost support going into the campaign, and again after the debate. "We lost it twice and won it back twice during that campaign," said the Tory pollster.

In this see-saw campaign, the PC response, which focused on John Turner's "Ten Big Lies," came from polling research "that kept telling us that people misunderstood free trade," said Segal. "What John Turner and others had been saying made people believe free trade was about American guns flooding into Canada, about giving up our water to the United States, about doing away with Medicare."

The tabloid newspaper, *Ten Big Lies*, was prepared by the PC campaign, under Norman Atkins's direction, with content prepared by Harry Near, and Segal contributing based on Gregg's research. With lightning speed, bundles of the tabloid were distributed in all major urban ridings across Canada, at bus stops, subway stations, and any public place people congregated or travelled in large numbers.

The newspaper's blunt message was supported by a series of campaign television and radio ads in which Simon Reisman, who'd been John Turner's deputy minister, talked about how Turner was "wrong on free trade, probably lying." Mr. Justice Emmett Hall, whose major public contributions included extensive support of Medicare over many years and chairing a royal commission on medical services, was heard by Canadians saying he had read the Free Trade Agreement "and there was nothing in it that would hurt Medicare in any way, shape, or form."

RIGHT: The morning after the Mulroney PCs win a second majority government on November 21, 1988, national campaign chairman Atkins, standing beside a blow-up of Brian and Mila and the leader's campaign itinerary, holds up the *Ottawa Citizen* with the headline "TORY MAJORITY!" The front page includes a story, "Ontario Defies Predictions, Helps Push Tories to Win."

SEPT. 29
PRIME MINISTER - U.N. ADDRESS
SEPT. 30
OCT. 1
WRIT DROPPED
OCT. 2
OTTAWA
-Media Tour Briefing
-HQ Event
OCT. 3
GEORGETOWN
LAMBETH
OCT. 4
CALGARY
RED DEER
OCT. 5
B.C. INTERIOR
OCT. 6
SASKATCHEWAN
OCT. 7
WINNIPEG
OCT. 8
QUEBEC
OCT. 9
MONTREAL
-Return Ottawa
OCT. 10
THANKSGIVING
OTTAWA
- DOWN
OCT. 11
OTTAWA
-DOWN
-GOVERNMENT BUSINESS
OCT. 12
TORONTO
- Summit Plaque
- Economic Speech
- Party Event
OCT. 13
NEW BRUNSWICK
NEWFOUNDLAND
OCT. 14
NEWFOUNDLAND
NOVA SCOTIA
OCT. 15
P.E.I.
OCT. 16
OTTAWA
- DOWN
OCT. 17
OTTAWA
- DOWN
- GOVERNMENT BUSINESS
OCT. 18
ONTARIO
OCT. 19
ONTARIO
OCT. 20
MONTREAL
OCT. 22
-DEBATE PREPARATION
HAMILTON
Mrs. Mulroney
SUN
MON
TUE
WED
THU
SAT
OCT. 23
-DEBATE PREPARATION
OCT. 24
DEBATE
(French)
OCT. 25
DEBATE
(English)
OCT. 26
QUEBEC
OCT. 27
TORONTO
OCT. 29
OCT 30
OTTAWA
- DOWN
OCT. 31
HALLOWEEN
OTTAWA
- DOWN
- GOVERNMENT BUSINESS
NOV. 1
BRITISH COLUMBIA
NOV. 2
BRITISH COLUMBIA
NOV. 6
OTTAWA
-DOWN
NOV. 7
QUEBEC
NOV. 8
U.S. ELECTION
MONTREAL
NOV. 9
ONTARIO
NOV. 13
QUEBEC
NOV. 14
ONTARIO MUNICIPAL ELECTIONS
OTTAWA
VANCOUVER
NOV. 15
CALGARY
WINNIPEG
NOV. 16
MONTREAL
NOV. 20
QUEBEC
NOV. 21
ELECTION DAY
THE OTTAWA Citizen
TORY MAJORITY!

According to Segal, the *Ten Big Lies* was part "of one of the most remarkable comebacks after the infamous debate in 1988. We went from six points ahead to fourteen points behind across the country, and could have very easily lost that election, had the *Ten Big Lies* comeback campaign not been put in place."

When the Mulroney PCs won a second majority government, with 169 seats, Allan Gregg attributed it "to Norman Atkins's hand on the tiller. He put the keel deep enough in the water to stay the course." Normally, when you get into campaign trouble, he added, the first thing that happens is your detractors cut and run. "They say the advertising is bad, and so forth. There was not one word of panic at all during that campaign."

Of some fifty election campaigns Gregg worked on, he classed two as "the most exceptional" — the Ontario 1981 election as "the most technically advanced and sophisticated," and the 1988 national election as "the most brilliant."

CHAPTER 45

DISMANTLING THE MACHINERY

Ontario's motto, "*As it began, so it remains,*" applied to the Progressive Conservatives themselves. Just as the province heralded a rise in PC fortunes in 1943, so it remained a place foretelling the party's fate toward the end of the century. Where the big blue machine came into greatest prominence was where it would also be destroyed.

After Ontario's Davis-led PCs won re-election in 1981, the secure comfort of a majority in the legislature induced an easy-going complacency. The Tories became less alert than they had been with a minority government. And even though the PCs had more seats, it was the same old story: they'd only earned them with 44 percent of the popular vote. Vote splitting had kept the Tories in power since 1943, and in 1981 had saved their day once more by dividing the 55 percent of non-PC support, 34 percent to Liberals and 21 percent to New Democrats.

The electoral system made Ontario's PC Party, the Tory governments, and the big blue machine appear more powerful than they really were. In addition, the Davis government itself was running down. Cabinet needed an overhaul. But instead of tapping the new energy and fresh thinking of ambitious younger MPPs, the premier kept worn and self-important veterans in place. Loyalty trumped renewal. Many practices needed to be updated, but even decisions so routine as adding a driver's photograph to provincially issued licences bogged down for lengthening rounds of further reconsideration because there was little rush and less decisiveness.

Such lethargy became oddly mixed with strange initiatives and stranger distractions. The premier stunned everyone, even most members of his Tuesday-morning circle of insiders, by announcing the Ontario government had purchased 25 percent of Calgary-based oil and gas company Suncor. "Suncor was one of those decisions everybody realized, as soon as it was announced, as dumb and wrong," said John MacNaughton. "Who could think you'd get a 'window on the oil industry' by buying shares of just one company, and a minority interest at that, and of an American-owned company?"

The Davis government, oscillating between sluggish performance and shocking decisions, also got distracted by national politics. In early 1983, Joe Clark, despite getting two-thirds approval in the mandatory "leadership review," perversely resigned, called for a leadership convention, and declared himself a candidate for the job he'd just been confirmed in but tossed away. That alone was enough to get people's attention. It certainly drew consuming interest from those meant to be focused on governing Ontario.

At Queen's Park, Bill Davis, having again assumed the lustre of a successful political leader with a majority government, gave renewed consideration to running for the national leadership. The idea of being PM had danced in Davis's imagination since youth, and accounted for many of his adult actions. If ever he was to make his move, it had to be now.

Over at the Camp agency, Hugh Segal, Bill Kelly, Norman Atkins, and key blue machinists had, since 1981, been actively building a Davis campaign organization across the country, in anticipation of making William G. Davis Canada's next prime minister. They would prove support for Davis in a tangible way by putting together enough committed support from party leaders in many provinces, then go to Ontario's premier and say, "Look, you have a chance at this thing!" They convened a dinner for Davis at the Albany Club, a show of support to pressure him, announcing the names of prominent PC players who were behind him. They draped the room with a large banner from the 1981 election, its same provincial slogan BILL DAVIS NOW FOR ALL THE RIGHT REASONS notionally reapplied to the federal scene.

These efforts faced stiff opposition from PC premier Peter Lougheed in Alberta. He had never been beholden to the blue machine because he'd built his own campaign organization. Beyond Peter's partisan independence and Albertan sentiments about central Canada, his hostility to Bill Davis becoming national leader of his party also incorporated the political fallout from Davis's support for the contentious constitutional amendment package negotiated by Prime Minister Pierre Trudeau, and Ontario's support for the Trudeau government's National Energy Program, which Albertans saw as favouring Ontario at their expense.

Ontario's premier, already facing such iron-clad opposition from Alberta, learned that in his very own backyard a Toronto-based group, spearheaded by Hal Jackman, was mounting a strong "Draft Lougheed for Leader" movement and gaining support from many influential Ontario Tories.

History made clear that the route to 24 Sussex could never run through a provincial premier's office, but ironically it took another premier to save Bill Davis the embarrassment of showing he'd failed to learn this lesson.

The blue machinists who'd taken Nova Scotia's premier through three unsuccessful national elections hadn't got the point, either. "I wanted him to run," said Atkins. The night Davis announced he would not, Norman was interviewed on CBC national television by Barbara Frum for *The Journal*, and all but burst into tears.

Without their candidate of choice heading to the August 1983 PC leadership convention, members of the big blue machine either remained neutral or scattered to different campaigns. Bill McAleer ran Joe Clark's re-re-election campaign. Roy McMurtry supported fellow Toronto progressive Tory David Crombie. Davis attended the convention, as did Atkins, Armstrong, Curley, and most other blue machinists, observing it all and remaining neutral, more easily done because of their hollow feeling inside.

———

As the months passed, Davis reconciled himself to having reached the end of his political road. He dealt with matters that had troubled him, clearing his conscience as well as his desk. A second stunning and controversial move, after Suncor, was to repudiate his own 1971 decision on funding Roman Catholic separate school education for grades 11, 12, and 13. Saying no to such funding had contributed electoral support to his majority PC win that year. But in June 1984, with full support from his Cabinet, he reversed that very decision and said yes, driving away electoral support not only from many Protestant Tory voters, but also from others seriously concerned about implications of religious schools and public funding.

By October 1984, Davis was ready to bow out completely. He invited Atkins and McMurtry for lunch and served up the news. Both were shocked and tried to change the premier's mind. Roy believed Davis the only person who could satisfactorily explain to voters extending separate school–funding, and that without him doing so the PCs would likely lose. Norman, deeply attached to Davis personally and apprehensive about the fate of the blue machine without him, became deeply morose. Later, he would call it "one of my saddest days in politics."

Bill Davis made another decision with adverse long-term consequences for his party. He stipulated that only party members in good standing *for a year* could vote to elect delegates to the Ontario PC leadership convention to choose his successor. Hotly contested conventions are a primary growth engine for parties. Candidates and their supporters recruit new voting members, who swell party ranks, add momentum, and bring refreshing perspectives.

Davis had been appalled by the sensational news when "instant Tories" in a few ridings had given a voting edge to Brian Mulroney's convention forces but a black eye to the national PC Party. He vowed the quality of party membership in Ontario would not be sullied by rounding up indigent voters and handing them a paid membership card and a few dollars on their way into a meeting hall to vote as instructed. The premier's high-minded decision contributed further to the demise of his beloved party by freeze-framing it at an earlier date in time. No recruitment, no renewal.

Roy McMurtry might have been a strong contender to succeed his friend, except he'd spent his Cabinet years in the same portfolio, failing to gain a breadth of government experience. He'd long been diffident about his political ambitions anyway, and had not prepared for a leadership run. He began to call members of the big blue machine. Norman volunteered to chair his campaign and recommended Brian Armstrong for campaign manager. McMurtry reached Armstrong vacationing in England. "When you get back, I'd like to talk with you about my campaign." Soon the two were together in Toronto, discussing the nature of the leadership race.

As Armstrong put it, the provincial PC Party had gone through "a strange transformation during the period of the minority government and then in the period after 1981 with a majority in the legislature." He itemized a sequence of controversial measures taken by Premier Davis that had "antagonized the right wing of the party," such as imposing rent controls and acquiring a shareholder interest for Ontario's government in Suncor. Armstrong felt the government "had fallen out of touch with the grassroots of the party." The youth wing "had become much more conservative than progressive. Resentments had built up."

While feelings about "not listening to or paying attention to regular party members" focused on the leader, it was hard for Tories to openly criticize likeable Bill Davis. So they redirected antipathy instead toward the big blue machine and the cadre of advisers around the premier, men like McMurtry and Atkins and their increasingly infamous backroom colleagues.

"All these elements have coalesced around Frank Miller," summed up Armstrong, "and give life to his campaign for the leadership." Miller was health minister, then provincial treasurer, in the Davis Cabinet. He and two other ambitious ministers, Dennis Timbrell and Larry Grossman, had been openly campaigning, even though Davis had not yet resigned. McMurtry had not even made quiet plans.

"We are seriously behind the eight ball," concluded Armstrong. Still, with Atkins chairing the "McMurtry for Premier" campaign, a credible effort, if not a winning one, could be mounted. McMurtry declared his candidacy, several weeks after all the others had done so. "We put together a great team," said Armstrong. "A lot of people who'd worked for Norman in Ottawa in the 1984 campaign joined us, including Bill Saunderson, Paul Curley, Bill McAleer, and George Stratton. Freddie Watson drove the tour bus. We fought hard against tremendous odds."

Delegates from across Ontario arrived for the Toronto convention in early February 1985. Because the McMurtry campaign had few committed delegates, the blue machinists looked for ways to demonstrate support. They'd developed a bloody-minded attitude that, if they could not win, they would have a lot of fun losing.

Someone in the group, gazing at the McMurtry campaign bus parked by the convention facility at the CNE grounds, got the idea to run a free shuttle bus service between the downtown hotels, where delegates were staying, and the CNE site, using many such buses as mobile billboards. Soon, twelve big buses were circulating around Toronto with the McMurtry colours, sometimes empty, but visually dominating the routes.

Another gambit was to have singer Burton Cummings perform at a McMurtry event. It morphed from political gathering into a Cummings concert, with over six thousand in attendance. "Cummings loved it," said Armstrong, and then became "part of the cheering section for Roy on voting day." The convention's third night brought more of the same when Rompin' Ronnie Hawkins, a longtime friend of McMurtry's, gave a fabulous concert that again attracted thousands of people, few of them delegates voting for the new premier of Ontario.

Segal, working on Larry Grossman's campaign, quipped of the McMurtry effort, "They have surrounded us with buses and singers."

This showy but desperate exercise revealed that not only had the Davis government run out of steam, but so had the big blue machine, deploying its resources in a diversionary and costly way, coming late into play with more show than substance.

Opinion polls indicated Roy McMurtry was the only candidate among the PC leadership contestants who could beat David Peterson and the Liberals. But those surveyed included few delegates to the convention. On the first ballot, McMurtry got three hundred votes and, forced to drop out, supported the next most progressive candidate, fellow-Torontonian Larry Grossman. This enabled Grossman to pass Timbrell on the second ballot. When Timbrell, also from Toronto, dropped out, he too supported Grossman for the dramatic final ballot.

Then another deep sentiment across the province that united Ontarians came into play: antipathy toward Toronto. On February 8, Frank Miller, from small-town Bracebridge, won the leadership of the Ontario PC Party, surpassing all three Toronto candidates to become Ontario's nineteenth premier.

As Brian Armstrong had clearly understood, all the feelings within the ranks of Ontario's PCs against their own government's direction and the legendary blue machine had "coalesced around Frank Miller."

––––––

From Ottawa, Prime Minister Mulroney offered McMurtry a dignified way out, passage to London as Canada's high commissioner to the United Kingdom. As well as distancing him from Ontario provincial politics for a spell, Mulroney hoped the move would also provide McMurtry with increased stature so that, on his return to Canada, he would be in a position in a few years to run for Parliament and enter his Cabinet.

Whatever that future might hold, members of the blue machine in Ontario were dejected when Roy resigned to take up his foreign posting. "A lot of us were disappointed because we'd hoped he would be a force for moderation in the Miller government," lamented Armstrong. "When Roy went, there was nothing left for us there."

"At that point," he said ruefully, "the big blue machine started to come apart."

———

A man of intelligence who chose to disguise it, Frank Miller lacked instinctive aptitude for politics. Fate had placed the new premier beyond his natural realm, where he was pulled one way by his hardline advisers who wanted a break from the past, and pushed the other way by moderates who understood that reality required bringing the party's competing groups together.

Although he'd vowed that his first act would be to "get rid of the big blue machine," the leader began a unity drive. Frank started to reach out, but possessed neither the skill nor, really, the determination to reconcile the smarting factions. His attempt was decidedly perfunctory with the blue machinists, most of whom he called, none of whom he asked to help. When Armstrong heard from Miller, he inquired what role Norman Atkins would have in the upcoming provincial campaign. Though the conversation went on awhile, it ended without Miller making any commitment about anything. "It was odd, because if the leader asks you to do something, you usually do it," said Armstrong. "But this was different."

Ontario's novice premier, making an absolute break in continuity, turned to Patrick Kinsella to run his election campaign. Kinsella, an insurance broker who'd been executive director of the Ontario PCs in the late 1970s but had long since departed for British Columbia to become a deputy minister in the Social Credit government, then backroom strategist and chief of staff to Socred premier Bill Bennett, was out of touch with Ontario players and issues.

When the leader told Norman he'd named Kinsella, Atkins said simply, "That is fine, Premier. You have made your choice. Good luck."

Attorney General Alan Pope, the PC member from Timmins representing Cochrane South, met several times with Miller to discuss the coming campaign, especially its timing. The premier did not heed the northern Ontarian's urging to wait before calling an election. Alan knew that with Atkins and the blue machine's key players removed, rebuilding the apparatus behind the scenes would take time, and was essential before the PCs would be ready for a province-wide campaign.

Yet the PCs were up in the polls, some 20 percent ahead of the Liberals, the usual bump of support following a televised leadership convention, approval that can melt in a hot campaign when partisan opponents and aggressive media pounce on any glitch. Miller was innocently confident. Just six weeks after becoming premier, having thought he'd done his full duty by naming a new campaign chair, he called an election. The Tories he led were unprepared to fight.

For the first time since 1970, the extensive group of individuals who had coalesced in Ontario around Bill Davis as the blue machine would not be mobilized in a provincial campaign. A number tried to support the effort, for the party's sake, but were fairly aggressively pushed aside. This was now "Miller's Ontario," they were told.

When it came to a televised leaders' debate, the new premier, relatively unknown to most Ontarians, refused to participate. With weak organization, inability to handle the Catholic school funding imbroglio, and facing an effective Liberal campaign, the PCs were reduced to minority government on May 2. Edged out in popular vote by the Liberals, who got 38 percent to 37 percent for the Tories, the PCs lost eighteen seats yet still managed to emerge with fifty-two members. But the Liberals were close, with forty-eight, and the NDP held the balance of power with twenty-five MPPs.

As the results began emerging, Segal phoned Robertson's Point to inform the banished blue machine organizer. Norman was sick to his stomach. He couldn't sleep at all that night.

At Queen's Park, Miller's PC members were outvoted on June 18, on a motion stating the Opposition had no confidence in the government, ending more than four unbroken decades of Progressive Conservatives governing Ontario.

Later that same day, a number of blue machinists gathered for drinks at the Park Plaza Hotel's roof garden bar. Looking west as the sun set for the last time on what Frank's narcissistic inner circle had promoted as "Miller's Ontario," they raised their glasses and bid nostalgic farewell to Ontario's Tory dynasty.

———

Miller lost power, but no new election occurred when Lieutenant Governor John Aird consented to David Peterson's Liberals forming a government because they had a two-year pledge of support from Bob Rae's New Democrats.

Eddie Goodman challenged the pact as unconstitutional, but what Tory really wanted another election? The prospect of winning back power as long as Frank Miller headed the party was not realistic. Compounding the dilemma for the PCs was the incredibly shrewd manoeuvre by the two opposition parties. The Liberals now had twenty-four months to implement a program the NDP had agreed to support. This not only broke the Tory grip on power, but broke through a psychological barrier for the majority of Ontarians who had only known Progressive Conservatives governing their province. The people would have two full years to get used to something different.

When the Liberal-NDP alliance expired, Liberals won ninety-five seats in the ensuing provincial election, the NDP nineteen, and the PCs sixteen. When Miller resigned after losing the premiership, Atkins chaired yet another provincial leadership race, this time for Larry Grossman. The peppery Torontian won the convention, but failed to lead the party back in the 1987 general election, unable to budge the diminished Tories from their reassigned bottom position in Ontario's electoral triangle. The PCs trailed the NDP, and Larry even lost his own Toronto riding, triggering yet further leadership changes.

PC member of the legislature Mike Harris believed he could not get elected leader of the Ontario Progressive Conservative Party at a traditional convention where most voters were constituency delegates. "The big blue machine still has its tentacles into most ridings, through the control of appointments, the running of election campaigns, and other ways," he said. "That means it also has a lot of control over who becomes a riding's delegates to a convention, and which candidate they'll support."

Raising this spectre of a blue machine bogeyman now vanished, Harris accelerated the democratization of party leadership selection. "Moving from the pressure-cooker atmosphere of a delegated convention to 'one-member, one-vote' is what will help me win," he emphasized. With the revamped leadership selection system that resulted, he became leader of Ontario's Progressive Conservatives, chosen by rank-and-file members in the direct balloting process that was part of a larger democratizing overhaul of the party.

In the spring of 1990, with Harris just elected PC provincial leader, Liberal premier Peterson hoped to catch the Tories off guard, divided, and unprepared. He called a premature Ontario general election for May. Peterson was also seduced by polling results in which he glimpsed an even larger Grit majority than the overwhelming one he already had. Senator Keith Davey, the Liberal's astute campaign mastermind, tried to persuade Peterson of his folly, pointing out that it was the premier's personal approval rating that considerably exceeded other Ontario party leaders, not the strength of the Liberal Party when measured against the PCs and NDP. If anything happened to turn voters against the premier himself, cautioned Keith, the bottom could fall out. But even a "Rainmaker" cannot dispel hubris. David glowed with his vision.

Ontario voters found the opportunistic premier lacking common sense. His ratings plummeted as more people decided they'd prefer the province's first socialist government to his. He was rewarded for his inexplicable gamble and the province's unnecessary election by an NDP upset victory. The New Democrats, led by Bob Rae, formed a majority government with seventy-four seats to thirty-six for the humiliated Grits.

The Conservatives came in third, again, with twenty members. The PC campaign organizers, after several bumpy rides and bad defeats, had lost their cockiness as critics of the now legendary big blue machine.

————

This plight of the Progressive Conservatives in Ontario was a harbinger of more widespread Tory fate.

Another province where the blue machine had held great sway, New Brunswick, birthplace of the Camp-Atkins campaign organization, was no longer controlled by Progressive Conservatives. A stunning result in the October 13, 1987 general election saw the Liberals win every seat in the fifty-eight-member legislative assembly. By September 23, 1991, when the next election took place, New Brunswick's voters elected forty-six Liberal members, but only three Tories. Regardless of popular support and electoral system distortions, the political reality and public image of the PCs was again that of a party in the wilderness.

Next door in Nova Scotia, two years later, voters ousted the Progressive Conservatives. The Tories won just nine seats as the Liberals took forty. Newfoundland and Labrador's Progressive Conservative government, elected in 1985, had been replaced by a Liberal government in 1989 and the Grits would go on to win three more elections in 1993, 1996, and 1999. Prince Edward Island's Progressive Conservatives, in office from 1979 and re-elected in 1982, lost to the Liberals in 1986, in 1989, and again in 1993.

Quebec was not only without Tories, but even the party's remnant forces in the Union Nationale had dissipated, its federalist *bleus* making their home with Quebec's Liberals, the nationalist *bleus* entering the ranks of the Parti Québécois or Action démocratique de Québec. Manitoba was undergoing another of its periodic political realignments, with Progressive Conservatives back in power after election wins in 1988, 1990, and 1995, only to be replaced by the New Democrats in 1999 and for a number of elections thereafter.

Saskatchewanians elected Progressive Conservative governments in 1982 and 1986, but by 1991 the NDP had taken over, winning three more consecutive majority governments after that. When the New Democrats were supplanted, it was by a coalition of non-socialists calling themselves the Saskatchewan Party.

Alberta remained solid Progressive Conservative through the 1990s, continuing with the majority governments that started with Peter Lougheed's stunning win in 1971, and the creation of an indigenous Albertan blue machine. But after more than four decades in office, through a dozen consecutive election wins under a succession of rejuvenating leaders, this PC dynasty appeared as tired and disconnected as the Social Credit regime it had earlier replaced. In its final stages, it cycled through a rapid succession of leaders until, in 2015 it was displaced in another stunning upset as the New Democratic Party led by Rachel Notley formed a majority government.

British Columbia, like Quebec and Saskatchewan, was a province where the Conservatives had morphed into other identities, first through a coalition with Liberals, then through a merger with Social Credit, and, with the demise of Social Credit, by means of a reinvention as Liberals yet again. This time, however, it was the Liberal name that identified their unified front in British Columbia, unlike in victorious election campaigns in 1945 and 1959 when the amalgamated centre-right forces had been called Conservative. Certainly there was no provincial PC Party now.

This shift from Progressive Conservatives in the provinces removed the party's pillars, and the foundation of the Camp-Atkins blue machine. It represented a complete reversal of the building-block strategy Bill Rowe and Dalton Camp had pursued, as federal organizers in the mid-1950s, to win nationally on the underlying structure of Tory strength provincially.

By the early 1990s the consolidated operation known as the big blue machine no longer existed.

———

Against this backdrop of sagging PC support in the provinces, and following the retirement of Brian Mulroney as leader, the federal party went into a general election in 1993 under Kim Campbell. The B.C. MP and Mulroney Cabinet minister had won the PC leadership with organizational support from Norman Atkins and Dalton's son David Camp of Vancouver. Dalton even wrote her convention speech.

When Prime Minister Campbell called the election, the PCs stood 12 percent above the Liberals in the polls, thanks to the temporary uptick following a televised leadership convention, augmented by pride and fascination Canadians felt in having a female prime minister. The Campbell-led PCs, with a distracted leader and a disconcerting campaign, then set a world record.

No other party in any democratic country before had gone from a strong majority in the legislature to only two seats. The Tories lost 154 MPs in a single election. The two elected, Jean Charest and Elsie Wayne, no longer had official party status in the Commons. The calamity for the party extended to the grassroots, where 2,186,000 PC supporters found themselves shortchanged in Commons representation. Jean Charest took over and, as is common for party leaders in the political wilderness, advocated electoral reform.

Within eight years of Brian Mulroney leading the Progressive Conservative Party to the largest win in Canadian history, the national PCs had been carved apart, the party's nationalist supporters in Quebec reassembled within Lucien Bouchard's sovereignist Bloc Québécois, and its supporters west of the Ottawa River who embraced economic liberalism having decamped for the Reform Party tent.

The failure to combine the Mulroney team of organizers successfully with the Camp-Atkins blue machine contributed to the PM's inability to establish the "Tory dynasty" he'd boasted about at party functions. Having two factions of campaigners in the same party made this potential difficult to realize, an updated replay of the gulf between Dief loyalists and Camp supporters, though its bitterness never that open or widespread.

The estrangement between Brian and Norman not only personified this internal party dilemma, but exacerbated it. When the former prime minister wrote his memoirs, he continued in print what had been his pattern in practice: to denigrate, diminish, and dismiss the contributions of his backroom rival. It was sad, and unnecessary, because Brian Mulroney's significant accomplishments in Canada's highest public office had become his true legacy. Only political insiders cared about who got credit for him getting there, or the way his election campaigns had been run. When Mulroney arrived for his book launch at Toronto's Royal Ontario Museum, the former prime minister said to Paul Curley, anticipating Atkins's response to his *Memoirs*, "Your friend is not going to be happy."

Beyond doubt, the big blue machine was busted. Its structure had been dismantled. Its un-patentable innovations copied by other parties, equalizing the advantages, leaving Canadian politics changed forever.

CHAPTER 46

THE BLUE MACHINE FACTION

The big blue machine was a faction among Canadian Progressive Conservatives.

It was unlike other factions that rise and fall over time, those grouped around a fresh policy orientation (like the progressive Port Hopefuls in 1942), or a plot to gain power (like the Four O'Clock Club of Diefenbaker's ministers who tried overthrow and replace Canada's prime minister in 1963.) It was, uniquely, a faction devoted to winning political campaigns.

The blue machinists were skillful, hardened, diverse individuals held together by a code of performance and a bond of human affiliation. They were more akin to a sports team or squad of commandos than a typical political organization, although winning power, not claiming a trophy or seizing an installation, was their mission. Blue machinists included Tories of long standing, converts from Liberal ranks, and apolitical inductees who embraced the brand and its projects more for adventure than because of attraction, at least initially, to the philosophy of Canadian political conservatism.

One hallmark that ensured they would remain a faction was their embrace of slick campaigning. Being "slick" in politics is tricky. A pejorative meaning suggests "a slick character" might be a cheat, a term you'd never want applied to your party's candidate or office holder. A different sense of "slick," however, is exactly what a campaign should be: "dextrous, not marred by bungling, carried smoothly through." Ross DeGeer smiled with pride describing the blue machine's convention campaigns for Bob Stanfield and Allan Lawrence at Maple Leaf Gardens as "very slick!" Yet that slickness dismayed voters, distanced journalists, and even caused many Tories who benefitted from it to recoil.

"The very thing that personified success," said DeGeer about this irony, "became the issue against us. While the U.S. influence and slick campaigning that went on in 1971 was the reason for our success, it was used against us with great effect. We were being chastised and criticized during the campaign for being 'too slick.' Even though we knew that *slick works.*"

That quest for slick performance was like a bonding agent for those who hung together as operators of the machinery. On October 21, 1981, on the tenth anniversary of their Davis 1971 campaign victory, the Dirty Dozen threw a dinner for themselves at the Albany Club to honour their own accomplishments and celebrate "A Decade of Slick." Their guest of honour was American Jerry Bruno, legendary advance man for the Kennedys, whose book of tips for running campaign tours had become their bible.

"We celebrated. We thought we were good. We knew we were," said John Laschinger. Down to minute details, the celebrants had planned their event with the same attentive skill they'd deploy on a major campaign event. The evidence of being professional, or "slick," was everywhere — from the prestigious room chosen at the historic Tory club, to the professionally designed glossy printed program, savvy choice of menu items, and finely tuned speaking arrangements. Specific limits of time had been allocated for each individual. A Decade of Slick was their spotlight event to illuminate what the campaign business was really all about.

"The purpose of an election campaign is deadly serious," said Laschinger, one of the seasoned backroom warriors present. "But we also make campaigns fun, professional, and exciting."

These blue machinists celebrated themselves because they believed they were the best. The night grew long as after-dinner drinks flowed. "We had fun celebrating our success, not caring what anybody else thought." Everyone spoke well past their allotted time, "and told b.s. stories." It was an odd mix of smugness and sincerity. In that room were dedicated specialists who'd come to love the electoral game, most of them never having done more than vote in an election before being recruited by Norman Atkins, Ross DeGeer, or a friend who valued their talent and character for somebody's campaign.

On October 21, 1981, the blue machine's Dirty Dozen threw a dinner for themselves at the Albany Club to mark ten years since the Davis election win in Ontario. Front, left to right, are Ross DeGeer, Gord Petursson, legendary American advance man Jerry Bruno, who was their inspirational role model, John Shepard, and Paul Curley. Rear, l-r: John Laschinger, John Slade, Norman Atkins, Tony Stampfer, Bill McAleer, Bill Neish, Malcolm Wickson, Brian Armstrong, John Thompson, Tom MacMillan, and Peter Groschel.

They believed their electoral work indispensible for a democratic society. "It was our chance to make a difference," said another of the advance men. "Our fathers were not in politics."

———

The original members of the blue machine had been drawn like disciples to Dalton Camp, a luminous presence in a Tory wasteland. As time passed, they and additional recruits were kept together by Norman Atkins's ability to spot talent, turn individuals into a team, and foster, through them, the ambitions of his brother-in-law.

Conducting this work full-time and to the exclusion of normal family life, Atkins became as devoted to it as might a grand master to the workings of a secret fraternal lodge. Norman kept lists of the faction's members, identifying the separate units of the Camp-Atkins political machine: the Eglinton Mafia, the Spades, the

Allan Lawrence Leadership Campaign Team, National Club Group meeting with Bill Davis, the Restaurant Group, the Park Plaza Group, the '71 Ontario Provincial Election Team, the Dirty Dozen, the '72 Federal Election Team, the Robertson's Point Interprovincial Tennis Classic & Rough-In, the '74 Federal Election Team, the '75 Ontario Provincial Election Team, the '77 Ontario Provincial Election Team, the Albany Club executive, the '81 Ontario Provincial Election Team, the '84 Federal Election Team, Blue Thunder, the '88 Federal Election Team.

Each campaign formation was a hand-picked group, a fraction from the whole. Such exclusivity brought important benefits to the blue machine, but separate status also guaranteed never rising above being a component within the Progressive Conservative Party. Being in the blue machine was never about being a Tory, but about being part of a group that made Tories successful.

Norman, a maestro of clubiness, knew he could best promote his code of "loyalty, friendship, and communication" by a shrewd and companionable

Those whose careers were intimately entwined with Norman Atkins's gathered at the Albany Club to pay tribute to the engineer of the blue machine. Dalton Camp speaks with humour. Waiting his turn (lower right) is a pensive Robert Stanfield who, by this date, regretted having distanced himself from Camp and Atkins to curry favour with the Diefenbaker loyalists.

mixing of diverse individuals. Special shared identity as part of the Eglinton Mafia, or the Spades, or the Dirty-Dozen would impart a deeper hold, beyond mere party affiliation.

He expressed this through the Rough-In, to which women began to be invited, just as he took a driving role to have women admitted to membership in the Albany Club, on the basis that loyalty to the PC cause was not gender restricted. Among those he invited to join the formerly all-male Rough-In were Jodi White, Diane Axmith, Elizabeth Roscoe, Kellie Leitch, Marjory LeBreton, Effie Triantofolopolus, Gina Brannan, Joan Peters, Nancy Jamieson, Rita Mezzanotte, and Jocelyne Côté-O'Hara. The first year women came, an earring was added to the Camp-like character in the logo, and the image printed on white sweatshirts for all participants. Blue machinists always appreciated a nice touch, and some humour.

As the event's reknown spread throughout Norman's larger tribe, the number of invitations climbed and the Rough-In outgrew the Robertson's Point facilities. The gathering then rotated through different, larger venues in Quebec, Ontario, and Manitoba. By the early 1980s, Norman needed to accommodate some seventy-five of his top political operatives, so made a deal with one of his Ontario organizers, Art Ward, who owned Wigamog Resort in Haliburton. With three tennis courts, a tennis practice wall, two pools, and a lot of card tables, Wigamog remained the Rough-In's venue for the rest of the group's days.

Whatever the location, Norman brought in new players each year to strengthen the network, including its Blue Thunder section in Quebec. Rodrigue Pageau started coming in 1980, sharing some of his techniques that would make him a highly effective double-agent organizer for Brian Mulroney's leadership campaign while appearing to be organizing for Joe Clark. Marcel Masse, already prominent in Quebec provincial politics as a leading Union Nationale minister and later a key Mulroney Cabinet minister, joined in. Richard LeLay was another regular, as was Jean-Carol Pelletier.

The growing roster of attendees was important for cohesiveness of the blue machine. Norman fostered team camaraderie among individuals who'd never met before. The common denominator of all, said Paul Curley, "was their admiration and loyalty to Norman." When a political campaign approached, "he had many who would willingly and quickly respond to his request to help." The Rough-Ins "became a breeding ground for campaigns."

In the early 1970s Norman Atkins gathered his core team at Robertson's Point for a guy's weekend that included tennis, grilled steaks, drinks-in-hand, and politics.

Each year more blue machinists, keen for a coveted invitation, turned up for Norman Atkins's tennis classic and PC campaigners Rough-In. Each year a different logo-imprinted sweatshirt was issued, but every year Atkins — a former New Brunswick tennis champion — claimed the trophy with his intensely competitive play.

The "classic guy's weekend" became co-ed when women were invited, about the same time the Albany Club admitted women members. The sweatshirts issued that year were white and the Dalton Camp–like figure of the logo got an earring.

The tennis was hard-hitting, the ribbing by the attentive spectators even harder. John Tory and other blue machinists watch play, relax, chat, and hurl comments at Norman Atkins who, despite hosting the Rough-In, was resolved to beat all comers, and did.

Those participating acquired a sense of communal belonging and strong belief they shared a cause important to Canadian democracy. Mixing people for meals, conversation, tennis, entertainment, drinks and debates, melted divisions between them and created an ideal method to transfer expertise. For a person who had managed ten campaigns, or done the advertising for them, or run the media buy for them, or conducted the leader's tour for them, to hang out with a younger person wanting to get more involved in electioneering and explain how all that works after a couple rounds of tennis and over a beer, was, said Segal, "a rare and wonder-filled opportunity."

———

Some names run consistently through most of Norman's groupings of blue machinists, his own in them all. His lengthy list of Quebecers in Blue Thunder was "subject to change," as if Norman was unsure of just how the Quebec-based projection or affiliate of the blue machine operated, or was even constituted, because many would be seen by Joe Clark and by Brian Mulroney as being part of *their* team of organizers, not Dalton's and Norman's.

A second revelation is that the names of various individuals who'd been instrumental (his tested friend Paul Weed, for example) were crossed out after Norman cut them adrift, like retouching a photograph to remove a person from history. Also, others who'd participated in key events were omitted from his lists, perhaps through a failure of memory, or clerical error, but, likely, just because those individuals considered themselves more a component of the blue machine than Norman ever did.

Most surprising of all was the fact Atkins's records, as he kept them after reaching the Senate in 1986, only focused on Ontario and Ottawa in the 1970s and 1980s. Although Norman was himself at the centre of the blue machine, and had matured as a young man amidst its origins and evolutions in the Maritimes, he'd started to envisage this special Tory faction narrowly in time and geography. Spinning his rewrite of history, the senator prepared a memorandum asserting "the big blue machine really got its start with the Spades." That happened in 1966. He'd forgotten about coming back to Canada in 1959 from military service, showing up at the Camp agency for a job that blended advertising and campaign organization, and Dalton's work as an organizer and campaigner in the 1950s that was the foundation for all that followed.

Norman had changed his citizenship and the name he went by. Why not change the creation story? If spies are licensed to kill, admen are licensed to spin.

The truer narrative is that everything Norman Atkins was able to do politically was built on the innovative campaign work Dalton had engaged in since the 1950s. This included election wins in New Brunswick and Nova Scotia, significant connections in Manitoba during the Duff Roblin years, the various campaigns involving John Diefenbaker, and making Bob Stanfield national PC leader against very long odds in 1967. Norman increasingly became part of all that, not just by following and expanding Dalton's methods but also by absorbing and applying Dalton's insights and values.

It was in New Brunswick where the first PC win came, that the first government advertising contract had been proffered, where the pattern of close personal interaction in casual settings with party leaders began, and the Rough-In was launched. Robertson's Point, from the beginning, was to the blue machine what the Montreal Forum was to the Canadiens hockey club in the glory years of repeated Stanley Cup championships.

———

So the blue machine was more. But it was also less.

As a faction, and a generally secretive one at that, the blue machine was not as broadly representative as the party itself, nor could it embrace all the diversity found throughout the far ranging Tory domain. The independent PC dynasty in Alberta was proof of that, and so was the edgy coalition with Mulroney's ground forces in Quebec. The blue machine was never designed to be a welcoming big tent. It was always just a faction because that larger umbrella function remained the exclusive role of the Progressive Conservative Party, to which the machine was connected as a tightly disciplined backroom operation.

Secrecy was essential to the blue machine's nature: plotting how to beat Grits and win power was something Liberal informants sought to find out about, as did persistent journalists, so guarding against spies and leaks was imperative. That very secrecy, though essential to its operation, caused resentment and suspicion within the PC Party itself, feelings that over time would be the blue machine's undoing, as Ontario showed. The large majority of Tories who were not at the machine's controls began to see themselves as pawns rather than players: Cabinet ministers excluded from the Park Plaza Group, MPPs and candidates whose speeches, signs, and schedules were centrally determined by the blue machine's war room with no input from them.

———

Another feature of this political machine is that the renown was larger than the reality. Both Camp and Atkins were in the advertising business, and exceptionally good at it, so understood how it advanced their purposes to be seen, not as fallible humans, but as men operating a superhuman "machine," which is how their strong and innovative operation impressed reporters and rivals alike at Maple Leaf Gardens in 1967 and again in 1971.

Clare Westcott certainly exaggerated when he dismissed the machine as "a fiction." Jerry Lampert, the political organizer who briefly became PC national director, came closer to the mark in talking about "the mythology" of the big blue machine. Early on, after the 1952 PC breakthrough campaign in New Brunswick, Dalton the giant-killer was savvy enough to chuckle about "the myth of my own reputation."

Nobody knew better than Atkins, the advertiser adept at making something larger than life, the importance of perception. At the start of the 1984 election, the national PC campaign chairman gathered his political operatives at the Albany Club to talk about the campaign plan and about attributes of political loyalty. He concluded by exhorting them, about the big blue machine: "Remember, we have a mythology to live up to."

Lampert in that campaign was co-director of operations with Harry Near and witnessed the machine at peak performance. While Near handled the practicalities of the leader's tour, Lampert liaised with all ten provincial committees, travelling the country, ensuring they had whatever was needed to run successful campaigns, acquiring in the process a rare overview of the machinery's parts. "There was a lot of mythology around the 'big blue machine' and what it was and how it operated," Jerry concluded.

"At the end of the day, it was a very small group of people who just rolled up their sleeves and got the job done. People had the impression the machine was thousands and thousands of people rushing out to do the job of electing

Davis, or whomever. It had a lot of volunteers, but a small group really made it work. The mythology grew out of that, because it was successful."

———

The blue machine was neither a fiction nor an invincible enterprise.

The reality is that it enjoyed "success" often enough for people to remember the wins; they linger in history but also endure as memorable because the blue machinists commemorated and celebrated their victories with trophies, pins, and Albany Club banquets. They made themselves legendary in their own time.

The causes of its success were twofold: blue machinists pioneered new dimensions to political campaigns that gave them a competitive advantage over others, and they made their impact for decades because they were semi-institutionalized through the Albany Club and the Camp agency and PC Party offices, which gave the advantages of experience, corporate memory, and longevity as an organization.

For instance, this political faction took effective control of the Tory Party's longest-running base of operation, the Albany Club, during the quarter-century

This dinner at the Albany Club, although a black-tie affair, seems casual by normal standards, with no head table and an interactive setup. The Club, founded in 1882 by John A. Macdonald and other Tories, functioned as unofficial head office of the Conservative Party ever since. The blue machine effectively took over the Club for a quarter century, helping to institutionalize its campaign operations.

of its most effective performance, using the prestigious facility for meetings, events, recruitment, bonding, and control. The Tory institution, founded in 1882 by the same man who formed the party itself, stipulated as a condition of membership, "No person shall become a Member of the Club unless a *Conservative*," with the party's well-being further embedded in rules both written and unwritten.

The Albany Club held sway over Tory politics in John A. Macdonald's home province, the most reliable place over the years for producing provincial Tory governments, sending the bulwark of Conservative MPs to Ottawa, and funding party operations across the country. Supporting the national party's budget was possible because Toronto was home to head offices of companies operating nationwide, and Tory collectors, invariably members of the Albany Club, raised cash locally for the federal party.

Yet even at the Albany Club in Toronto, the blue machinists were never more than a very strong faction; others who were not its initiated insiders continued to have roles at 91 King Street, too, intermittently serving as president, routinely booking the club's rooms and facilities, all of them, blue machinists or not, Conservatives.

As for the blue machine's other two bases of operation, in the Progressive Conservative Party it could never be more than a very small fraction, while at the Camp-Atkins advertising agency with its extensive political operations, it had exclusive control.

———

The cumulative record of numerous campaign innovations that history rightly credits to the blue machine transformed elections, and by extension, the conduct of public affairs, because this faction wielded power where it mattered, when it mattered, and not for just a single election but continuously over many years.

Although the blue machine's impressive operational bases gave it more influence and endurance than other factions that intermittently appear in political parties, its operations were fundamentally different from the machine politics of New York Democrats at Tammany Hall, or the Union Nationale power brokers in Quebec operating from the UN's own private Rennaisance clubs in Quebec City and Montreal and influencing voters through its own French-language tabloid daily newspaper, *Montréal-Matin*.

As a human enterprise, the "machine" made mistakes. Its assiduously fostered reputation for success helped camouflage screw-ups, false starts, and errors in judgment, but could not prevent them. Mistakes are inevitable, and the Dirty Dozen even created their own version of Jerry Bruno's "Grand Clong" award, presented to advancemen who committed a monumental campaign blunder.

Gaffes and hillarious stories live on in legend, exchanged and embellished even today at gatherings of blue machine veterans, reassuring proof that, despite the psychological benefit of the blue machine's reputation, its renown was often just a shield from scrutiny, and that behind it were individuals trying their level best, yet not immune from human error, in the tumultous course of intense election campaigns when hundreds of jostling characters and events interact in chaotic harmony.

CHAPTER 47

FINAL PASSAGES

Dalton Camp came of age in an era where boys modelled themselves on heroes found in books and on movie screens, characters who, through creative editing, were more luminous than anyone could ever be in real life.

Forced by his father's death to return from the United States, one of the teen's disappointments was to find Canada a land without heroes. "In the United States," he recalled with longing, "we had new ones all the time, men like Charles Lindberg." Winston Churchill became a lifelong hero to Dalton, but in Canada nobody came close to his exceptional attributes. Over time, disappointment blunted Camp's impulse to look for greatness in others. He began to delight in exposing with wry humour, in the fine tradition of Stephen Leacock, the foibles of all-too-human political leaders with whom he'd become intimately familiar. As time passed, however, the critiques grew harsher, his humour more acidic.

When pollster Allan Gregg first met Camp in the 1970s, he thought him "a bitter old man" who "complained about everything." Gregg also discerned how Camp "thought he should have been prime minister. I think he believed that the Progressive Conservative Party missed a great opportunity and that he'd taken a bullet for the party."

Camp wrote brilliantly, but his speeches were delivered by others. He plotted masterful campaigns, but his strategies got other men elected to high office.

He toiled in backrooms while shallower men took centre stage. Dalton aspired to be prime minister but watched as first Joe Clark and then Brian Mulroney, both of whom earlier worked for him organizing campaigns and political events, bypassed him and took up residency at 24 Sussex. All the while, many others he'd drawn into politics got elected to Parliament, something he'd twice attempted but never pulled off. A discouraged Dalton Camp looked on, not with pride, but chagrin. He had not become the hero he'd envisaged himself to be.

It is a punishment living in other men's shadows when ambitious to make something memorably worthwhile of one's own life. As PC Party president, Camp endured bitter and blighting recriminations for seeking, in all the ways he knew, to preserve Progressive Conservative unity when it was being splintered by John Diefenbaker's erstwhile supporters and ardent adversaries.

On the morning of November 15, 1966, pacing together outside Ottawa's Château Laurier Hotel at the start of a day on which Canadian political history was about to be made, Roy McMurtry voiced concern that Dalton Camp's campaign for leadership accountability in the Progressive Conservative Party, in face of former prime minister John Diefenbaker's adamant refusal to step aside, would likely end Dalton's own ambitions to eventually become prime minister.

"When we're talking about the founding party of our country," replied Camp evenly, gazing out over the strong wide flow of the Ottawa River, "the fate of one man's political future is just not that important."

What McMurtry feared would be the fate of a man he admired, Camp seemed prepared to fatalistically accept, perhaps even with a nod to Nemesis for his own role in creating the personality cult around Diefenbaker, a flawed hero, in the first place.

Yet "taking one for the party" over Dief demanded personal self-effacement to a degree he could not have imagined in 1966. Dalton had been forced to exist as a *hidden persona,* working for leaders like Duff Roblin and Bob Stanfield who'd only meet him in clandestine ways. He was, as his brother-in-law Norman complained, "kept under wraps" by Bill Davis. He was stung by the venom of Diefenbaker loyalists, something that did not dissipate but instead grew more poisonous as time passed and legends grew. In the 1980s, when Brian Mulroney asked Camp to work for him in Ottawa as a special adviser, he tucked him obscurely into the Privy Council Office, on hand if needed but out of the way, claiming that hiring Camp was his means "to purge him of the stain of 'disloyalty' unfairly placed on him by the Diefenbaker diehards."

Dalton was a prized political mistress to men publicly wedded to their lofty positions, self-protective of good appearances, noble upholders the PC Party's sanctity. They "kept" him with government business accounts for his advertising agency and fees paid for speeches he wrote but they never credited to him, even in the permissive era of openly acknowledged speech-writers.

Part of what made Dalton toxic was how his critics nursed and spread smouldering hatreds over his role in the Diefenbaker battles. Another part stemmed from resentment among Tories over how wealth was flowing to Dalton and Norman through the Camp agency's advertising contracts from PC governments. Even friendly PC backroom insiders like Nova Scotia's Fred Dickson mentioned that. Mulroney, himself a direct beneficiary of blue machine support, also gave gratuitous vent to this disdain. After the 1984 landslide win, "the largest advertising contract the federal government issued was awarded to Norman through Camp and Associates," he said, without adding that he himself approved it.

That was Brian, playing the game while taking shots at it. He described with condescension how Camp went to provinces where elections were underway, ensconced himself in the largest suite of the best hotel, wrote superb speech modules for the PC campaigners, then after the successful election outcome, collected the grateful government's advertising account and moved his caravan on to the next campaign, until ultimately "selling his business for a handsome multiple."

———

By 1979, when Camp published his brilliant yet bleak book *Points of Departure*, he'd synthesized the dual personality which circumstances had forced upon him.

That year he put into print what he'd already improvised in practice as a personal survival mechanism for quite some time. He'd coped by transferring identity to an alter ego he named "the Varlet." In English, the term *varlet* can apply to a medieval page preparing to be a squire, or "a menial, low fellow, a rascal." His identity was this second one: the rapscallion.

In Camp's mind, his transposition into the Varlet as a separate objectified identity suited him. As this other person, he was able to write in the third person, a participant who was simultaneously a detached observer. Yet even Dalton's self-saving re-emergence through the Varlet was, he lamented, only "passing solace to an ego consigned to the shadows of anonymity."

Over his years in party politics, explained Camp, his "transference of so much private thought, blood, and nervous sweat to prime ministers, premiers, and aspiring opposition leaders" had yielded "only tangential gratifications, such as the applause of unseen audiences, distant editorial approbation, or an oblique electoral triumph."

His forlorn quest to ascend to neutral political ground, combined with his enduring drive to engage others through his exceptional talent as a writer, propelled Dalton to obtain journalist credentials and join the media tours accompanying party leaders Pierre Trudeau and Joe Clark during the 1979 federal election, ostensibly an informed insider who was yet detached and dispassionate. It was a brave step, and bold, attempting to recast himself as independent analyst covering a general election campaign. His resulting book's apt title suggested its author was himself heading in unknown directions. The brilliance of his political analysis, combined with insights, candour, and artistry, make *Points of Departure* as searing and exceptional as his 1970 memoir, *Gentlemen, Players & Politicians*, which covered Dalton's initial involvement in New Brunswick politics from 1948 up to successful completion of the first Diefenbaker campaign in 1957.

But by 1979, as told in *Points of Departure,* a different aspect accompanied everything Dalton observed. Camp's personal estrangement from politics soured his view of election campaigning, even though many practices he witnessed followed patterns he himself had first devised. His end-of-the-Seventies account was a three-part mixture: observant campaign coverage, flashbacks to people and events forming background to the election, and personal angst.

The paradox was that he could not leave politics alone, even though his growing cynicism about it was destroying him personally and casting an obscurant shadow over his lifelong accomplishments. Tortured by his uncertain identity, Dalton by this date was weary of playing backroom organizer and éminence grise, "a career given over to conceptualizing political strategies and reducing them to more or less precise expression" for the benefit of other players in the spotlight of Canadian politics.

The more his personal quest for a role in national leadership eluded him, the greater his turmoil. The more intense this distemper became, the harsher grew his scrutiny of others. Believed to be the Tory Party's saviour by some, a traitor by others, Camp now aspired only to ascend high enough to "give all alike the benediction of his cool."

He'd travelled far: organizing for George Drew, helping smash entrenched Maritime Liberal machines, being John Diefenbaker's loyal campaign manager, making creative efforts as national PC president to support The Chief during his tenure in office, forcing a leadership review when it became his destiny to do so, and becoming the single most divisive man in the party's entire history. At that point, Camp said, "he began to enter back doors, ride service elevators, and occupy hotel rooms pre-registered under assumed names" and endure "the dark nights of a prolonged penance."

It was a Faustian bargain Dalton had contracted: trading excursions into public life for incursions into his most inner self.

———

Beneath Dalton's tortured contradictions, though, was an enduring, staggering talent, which occasionally broke out like a ray of sun through a storm cloud.

On September 18, 1980, when the same Allan Gregg who'd found Dalton a "bitter old man" attended Camp's sixtieth-birthday celebration

On September 18, 1980, Dalton Camp's friends hosted a black-tie dinner at the Albany Club to celebrate his 60th birthday. The six seated at the table, l-r, are Robert Stanfield, Dalton Camp, Roy McMurtry, Nate Nurgitz, Norman Atkins, Hugh Segal. The sixty others present included Tory players, elected politicians, party office holders, the Spades, pollsters, journalists, and future party leaders.

Dalton Camp

Gentleman, Player and Politician

60th Birthday Dinner
The Albany Club
Sept. 18, 1980

The title of Camp's 1970 political memoir, *Gentlemen, Players and Politicians*, seemed apt for Dalton, his singular self. Norman Atkins, with his creative team at the Agency and blue machinists, fashioned Dalton's Albany Club birthday banquet in 1980.

About the author:

Dalton Kingsley Camp was born in New Brunswick, lives in
New Brunswick, thinks like a New Brunswicker. But, having made
unique and broad ranging contributions to national politics, he
knows this country from coast to coast as few other observers of the
Canadian scene do. As journalist and author, he continues to
maintain a bristling interest in public affairs that unfailingly provides
his readers with penetrating insights and pungent prose.

The fact that 60 years of a life with more than its share of
turbulence have not diminished his elfin humour, capricious
good looks, droll and diligent sense of the politically absurd, or his
enduring concern for the pushed around, put down, and passed
over is - well - touching.

Dalton Camp has not always been an easy man to comprehend, deal with, or work for.

But, by God, he has never forgotten his friends.

Nor they, him.

Is there a higher accolade?

A synopsis of Dalton's qualities appeared, along with the Rough-In logo, on the back of
the printed birthday keepsake. The happy celebrant inscribed the author's program.

at the Albany Club, he was "blown away," saying, as he listened to the guest of honour, "I could not believe anybody could be so smart." He was glimpsing a version of Dalton once again himself, enjoying a happy moment in a familiar setting with true friends. Gregg, thinking *I am in the presence of greatness*, henceforth placed Camp and Pierre Trudeau in the same rank as "towering intellectuals."

Here, for a shining moment, was the old Dalton, the articulate Canadian who'd inspired others to not quit the PCs but stay; to not vote Liberal again but join with him in a higher quest; dozens of talented individuals from across Canada to form a campaign-ready battalion and follow him.

Even so, the surfacing of the Varlet betrayed Camp's deeper reality. He'd intermittently experienced bouts of depression, calling them visits from his "black dog," using Winston Churchill's own term for his dark days of despondency. Struggling to reconcile how his life's bargain, like Faust's, had transformed him, Dalton seemed to come unmoored and drift.

He not only reinvented himself as an anti-hero for his book, but, in his new guise the Varlet left his long-cherished wife Linda and married Wendy Smallian, a comrade from an election campaign bunker and seen by some close friends of the Camps as resembling an earlier version of Linda herself. Dalton built a new home on an elaborate scale, isolated in rural New Brunswick. He spent his considerable proceeds from sale of his half-interest in the agency until the money was gone.

He did not get appointed to the Senate, his brother-in-law did, which provoked him to write a column he had to edit before sending it for publication. In 1986, he accepted as consolation prize a position in the Privy Council Office at Ottawa, a move so improbable and inappropriate that few could comprehend Prime Minister Mulroney offering it or Camp accepting it. Before long, Dalton bitterly regretted the mistake, one more in a lengthening parade of them.

Dalton sat in his New Brunswick writing shed, itself at a remove even from his isolated house, pounding out columns for Canada's largest English-language daily, the *Toronto Star*, a Liberal newspaper that persisted, over his repeated objections, in ending his pieces with a tag line that reminded readers the columnist had once been president of the Progressive Conservative Party of Canada. Whether the publisher hoped to indicate the *Star* was tolerant, or Camp had recanted, was never clear.

ALTON CAMP COLUMN
STAR
7/86

①   ATTN: IAN URQUHART

ROBERTSON'S POINT, N.B. -- Norman K. Atkins, godfather to the Big Blue Machine, was summoned to the Senate yesterday ~~[struck out]~~ from his summer retreat here by Prime Minister Brian Mulroney. Neighboring cottagers, some of whom have never made the acquaintance of a Senator, *have begun* laying in supplies and putting out more flags. In these parts, *news of* the appointment of Atkins *was* greeted with instant approval. Besides, any ~~[]~~/*excuse* for a party.

Having a Senator on the premises gives Robertson's Point extra <u>cachet</u>, but there is larger significance outside this vacation compound. Atkins has been going to the Senate for two years, nominated by his friends immediately after the hugely successful 1984 Tory election campaign in which he served as chairman of the party's organization. Not much later, he was drafted *in* the media as *the* obvious candidate to fill the Ontario vacancy, *although* ever feckless, the media last week nominated Eric Nielson instead. *however,* The Prime Minister, whose *only* authority in this matter is absolute, was ~~[struck out]~~ *marching to his own drummer.*

In fact, Mulroney and Atkins had never discussed the possibility of a senatorship until the weekend of the cabinet shuffle. After vetting Atkins on the new cabinet, the Prime Minister -- almost by the way -- made the offer. Having had considerable time to think about it, Atkins needed *little more time to accept,* ~~[struck out]~~

⟶ 2

In 1986, when, influenced by Bill Davis's intervention, Prime Minister Brian Mulroney appointed Norman Atkins to the Senate, his brother-in-law sent his column to the *Toronto Star* expressing mixed views. Written on his trusty portable typewriter at Robertson's Point and corrected by hand, Dalton did his best to bring humour to the milestone in Norman's life, as he again saw someone junior to him advance further.

Things became still more confusing when Camp, trying to recast his political identity, began identifying himself as a "Red Tory." The concept had become so detached from the meaning University of Toronto political scientist Gad Horowitz originally intended, when coining that term in 1965 to explain how it was that Tories and socialists shared communitarian values, that it lost all salience at ground level in Canadian politics. Dalton contributed to this confusion by arguing in public that one's stance on capital punishment determined whether or not one was a Red Tory.

From a studio in Fredericton, Camp charmed national radio audiences on Peter Gzowski's CBC network program, *Morningside*, dissecting the week's political events with New Democrat Stephen Lewis and Liberal Eric Kierans. They engaged with intelligent partisanship, civility, and humour. It was Camp at his mature best, talking about politics the way he always had, with others whom he respected for their informed opinions and clear thinking.

These national CBC commentaries, Toronto *Star* newspaper columns, and the books he assembled to place previously published opinion pieces in the hands of a wider readership, all benefitted from the Varlet's detachment from public affairs. Yet, simultaneously, they perversely chronicled a growing detachment from the very Tory partisanship that Dalton Camp had thrived on, and, indeed, done so much to incubate, for decades.

A collection of his late 1970s and early 1980s offerings, published under the weird title *An Eclectic Eel*, gave a further glimpse of how Dalton now saw himself. The Varlet had become an eel. Using an "anonymous" quote, he said his role was to be, "Like eels at the bottom of the fish barrel, who keep them all awake up there."

A compilation of columns for a 1995 book entitled *Whose Country Is This Anyway?* testified to Camp's emergence as a scourge of the New Right, big corporations, and predatory Americans. His "clear-minded, witty, and hard-hitting" views on Canada's so-called neo-conservatives were applauded from the political left by June Callwood, Rick Salutin, and Linda McQuaig. At this point, concluded John Pepall, a Toronto lawyer and Conservative writer, "Camp was simply beyond caring."

———

There was, however, much that others could care about in Dalton Camp's life. Wherever he'd landed, Dalton could always convey, better than commentators or reporters who'd never experienced politics from the inside, candid realism about public life, including its bleaker and ironic backstage dimensions.

492 THE BIG BLUE MACHINE

For enduring public good, that same realism infused five volumes of recommendations from the Camp Commission on Ontario's Legislature. Implemented by the Davis government, the landmark changes in Ontario election finances and legislature operations remain a constructive and enduring part of Dalton's legacy, and, by extension, Bill Davis's as well. It was pioneering legislation in North America, transforming elections and the parties who contest them, a fitting marker for a man who'd created and sponsored many other innovations that had also altered forever the conduct of Canadian politics.

Within the Progressive Conservative Party, to which he'd devoted the best of his best years, another of Camp's legacies was the breakthrough amendment to the constitution requiring "leadership review" to ensure a democratic party itself enshrines the principle of democratic accountability.

There was much to lament, too.

The Varlet had tried to restructure his difficult personal narrative by spinning it from a different perspective, reaching back into medieval times for his identity as a low rascal. Yet had he reached even further into antiquity, a more telling image could have been found. For there was, by its end, the unmistakable quality to Dalton Camp's life of a Greek tragedy.

———

Norman Atkins looked for heroes even more.

From their first meeting at Robertson's Point in 1942, observers could see "he worshipped Dalton like a hero." When Norman's father died, the man who'd become his friend in boyhood years, then his brother-in-law, next his "older brother and friend," even became something of a surrogate father. "Hero" was far too weak a word to describe Norman's view of Dalton.

As Dalton withdrew into himself and other pursuits, away from the advertising agency and the PC Party, Norman found a new friend who became a political hero to him, Bill Davis. He celebrated Ontario's premier as "the epitome of a great leader" and relished his close relationship with "Billy."

"Norman wanted a similar relationship with Brian Mulroney to the one he enjoyed with Bill Davis," explained his friend Paul Curley, "but it wasn't on. Mulroney was just not that kind of guy." As a result, an estrangement between Atkins and Mulroney began, because Norman did not accept that the closeness he had with Ontario's premier wasn't going to be possible with

Canada's prime minister. His injured feelings worked themselves out in very human ways. Norman had "not taken credit for the wins in Ontario," noted Tom Kierans, "the way he tried to claim it Ottawa."

Atkins had seemed astute, at that first caucus meeting on Parliament Hill in September 1984, to direct attention *away* from his political backroom organization and on to Brian Mulroney, not just because the new PM was a public figure and the party's champion of the hour, but because political parties ripple with spreading circles of resentment. Staying in the background was safer. Atkins's long-time friend and PC backroom colleague in Nova Scotia, Fred Dickson, said that Norman was "extremely modest, in fact, too modest." That self-effacing quality had enabled him, in his best years, to master the party's backrooms by fusing effective teams of disparate individuals, many of whom had very large egos.

Yet, not getting sincere credit from Mulroney, even in private, created a downward spiral in their feelings about one another. The less Brian acknowledged his value, the more Norman claimed it. John Laschinger, as a blue machinist, always warned his colleagues, "Be careful not to take too much credit if you're an organizer." He quoted Atkins's aphorism, "Organizations don't win elections, they lose them," only to then add, "Norman forgot that sometimes you win because of the candidate, not the organization." Laschinger put it in a nutshell: "Norman thought he'd won the campaign for Mulroney and made him prime minister. Brian resented that."

Thinking he might shore up faltering relations with the big blue machine by naming Dalton Camp to the Senate, the PM received an intervention from Bill Davis to the effect that Norman Atkins had done far more for him than Dalton, and that, with Norman's much closer control over the campaign apparatus, he'd serve Mulroney better in the upper house, the way party organizers always do, being able to work full time on the party's next campaign at public expense. Meanwhile, Mila Mulroney and Norman had a lengthy lunch at the National Arts Centre, with the main entrée a senatorship. The PM named Atkins to the Senate in 1986, saying about the appointment in a cutting way that getting into the Senate "had been Atkins's best campaign of all."

Brian Mulroney was happy to benefit from what the blue machine could deliver, yet remained jealous of any credit it got. He said, "I asked Norman Atkins to be the national campaign chairman for the simple reason that I wanted Davis personally onside in the election."

While the prime minister greets guests, Norman Atkins whispers to Mila Mulroney in the entranceway of their official residence. Most political events have many versions, depending on who is describing them, and Norman's acquisition of a seat in the Senate was no exception.

He recounted how, when telling Ontario's premier how pleased he was that members of the big blue machine were playing a major role in his federal campaign, Davis clarified the relationship in the somewhat self-serving way one political leader might when speaking to another in confidence. "Brian, the big blue machine is the best at getting the buses to meet your plane, taking you to a room overflowing with supporters.... But the leadership, strategy, and message for the campaign, that's what I do. The real big blue machine? You're looking at it right now." — meaning himself.

In other contexts, not filtered through Brian Mulroney's effort to denigrate Atkins for thinking he had a role winning a campaign that he'd chaired, Bill Davis was never that dismissive of the Camp-Atkins political formation's role in helping him win elections, nor so forgetful of its role in the Park Plaza Group he himself had instituted to do far more than address bus scheduling and airplane logistics.

———

Following his death in March 2002, Dalton's remains were laid to rest deep in New Brunswick's heartland at the Lower Jemseg cemetery of St. James Anglican Church, a final resting place of locals since the 1850s, just 150 kilometres from where he'd been born eighty-one years before.

———

Upon becoming a senator, Atkins moved his trophy-laden office to Ottawa. Departing the agency, Norman sold Camp & Associates to a group of senior employees who wanted and got 100 percent of the business, not just his half-interest, so that their efforts could be fully rewarded.

Further changes followed at the agency. Hugh Segal had joined as an equal shareholder to develop the public relations and government lobbying side of the business, but when he, too, left for Ottawa, in 1992, to become chief of staff to Prime Minister Mulroney, the principals bought Hugh's interest. "We then," said Dianne Axmith, made Paul Curley "an offer he couldn't refuse," enabling him to expand his public relations business as an affiliated operation, which he did by getting successful Tom MacMillan and others to join him. Axmith herself had risen from Atkins's initially reluctant assistant to president of the agency. With Atkins and Segal departed for parliamentary precincts, the principals renamed the firm "Axmith, McIntyre, Wicht." After Axmith and Wicht retired, John McIntyre, who, as husband of his daughter Gail, had the strongest enduring link to Dalton, renamed the firm Agency 59 to commemorate the year 1959 when his father-in-law first launched his advertising business.

Atkins's departure from the agency coincided with another major change in his life: the end of his marriage. He had spent so many years travelling and working long hours on campaigns that he and Anna Ruth had grown apart. In Ottawa, after a time spent living with another senator, his friend Finlay MacDonald, he found a new partner in Mary LeBlanc.

Norman encountered a difficult time, too, with his political relationships. The Progressive Conservative Party in which he been a major player all his life had agreed to merge with a successor entity of the Reform Party, the Canadian Alliance, a culmination of Preston Manning's failed experiment. The goal was to present a unified conservative front and prevent further easy Liberal romps to majority government facilitated by vote splitting. Over 90 percent of constituency-elected PC delegates to a national convention voted to ratify the merger.

Norman was uneasy, knowing how Dalton in his final years had railed against the "right wing" in Canadian politics. Yet Bill Davis, to whom Norman had become closer as Dalton grew more distant, helped engineer the merger, at the request of his party's leader, Peter MacKay, and had negotiated its terms. It made more sense, Davis understood, to be together than apart. If one favoured moderate or progressive policies, the best way to achieve them was to stay involved, advance them as a player on the field, and get back into office to implement them. It also was an example of Davis being "loyal to the leader," chided the former premier gently, a principle Norman professed.

In the seductive comfort of the Senate, however, Lowell Murray, with whom Norman had been closely acquainted for years, pointed out that it made no difference to their generous salaries if they "held out on principle" and continued to sit as self-styled "Progressive Conservative" senators. In Canada's unaccountable legislature, a senator's affiliation can be whatever he or

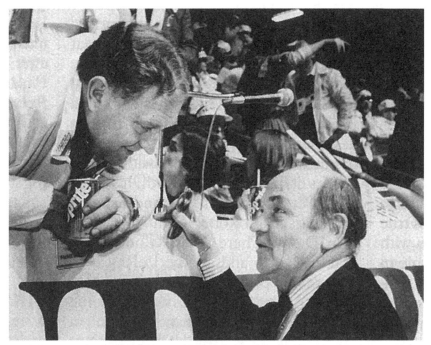

Across the decades Norman Atkins and Dalton Camp shared political goals in Tory campaign backrooms and leadership conventions. Here they exchange views between front-row seat and convention floor. Their resilient partnership enabled the brothers-in-law to direct and transform Canadian campaigns between the 1950s and 1980s.

she designates, even the name of a legally defunct political party. Norman and Lowell huddled in isolation with other holdouts like Joe Clark and Sinclair Stevens, also in denial that another necessary turn had been taken in the Tory Party's long and winding road for survival, failing to embrace engagement as a better strategy than separation.

As a result of his partisan identity crisis, Norman worked out a series of questions for his Senate assistant Christine Corrigan to pose in interviews with some fifty blue machinists, ostensibly for a book about his career as a campaign organizer. Included were questions concerning their views about Norman's appointment to the Senate and his remaining a "Progressive Conservative" after the merger — Norman's own variant on deep polling research. How much easier if, as for so many years, he'd just been able to follow Dalton's reassuring lead on this sort of thing.

———

When Norman died, at age seventy-two in September 2010, his fellow Tory senator and former business partner at the Camp agency Hugh Segal authoritatively pronounced, "He was, and will forever be, father emeritus of the big blue machine." By that standard, Dalton Camp would be in perpetuity the operation's "*grand*-father emeritus."

"Dalton Camp's determination to live a life of ideas and a life full of action," Norman himself had acknowledged in his final Senate speech the year before, "was an inspiration to me." Indeed, it had been, from the very first day his brother-in-law and mentor brought Norman into the fray with him. Atkins's career began with Camp's efforts, not to build a political machine, but bust one, their first cause to unseat an entrenched Liberal regime — "the corrupt McNair machine" as Camp called New Brunswick's power juggernaut in his 1949 radio broadcast — and replace it with a Progressive Conservative government. Norman was a junior helper, absorbing Camp-style politics throughout his formative years.

Atkins, in turn and by extension, became instrumental in redesigning election campaigns for more than half a century. His pioneering use of extensive organization charts and campaign timetables on headquarters' walls matched the campaign blueprint in his mind, because he wanted to be certain everyone on his diverse teams understood the structure and implemented his plan. His insistence on budget control as a management tool introduced a new campaign orderliness to a field not previously known for businesslike practices. His early adaptation in Canada of the latest American polling techniques reoriented how election strategies and campaign advertising were shaped.

Norman's legacy in revamping election advertising also took fresh directions with the formation of an in-house consortium agency of top specialists from different firms, K-Tel messaging for political penetration through television, and more aggressive attack ads. His early support for direct-mail fundraising techniques adapted from the Republicans in the United States helped PC Canada Fund build a lucrative mailing list of sixty-five thousand donors which, when coupled with a super computer, put the Tories in the green and made Grits green with envy. He transformed campaigns by introducing autocratic central control, imposing an identical party brand across all ridings and uniform messaging in all election materials, an exclusive emphasis on the leader through the focus of commercials, and making the leader's tour a media-friendly campaign centrepiece. A born and bred American, Norman saw Canadian elections rather like U.S. presidential campaigns.

The same camaraderie he'd enjoyed at Appleby, Acadia, and in the army he fostered as a bonding agent in his campaign teams through the Rough-Ins, the Spades, the Albany Club, and every Tory campaign backroom he occupied. Probably no one convened more breakfast campaign meetings than Norman Atkins. In time, he took a lead to include women in his male dominated enclaves, including the Rough-In and Albany Club, and promoted their careers, though he remained most at ease in the company of other men. He knitted it all together, uniquely, using his competitive advantage of supply-chain management skills honed in the exacting environment of the United States Army quartermaster corps, an exceptional training ground for a Canadian campaign organizer.

Norman did not accomplish any of these things alone. He always worked in close harmony with others. But whatever he did, Norman saw the way forward by following Dalton's light.

Looking back today at the dramas and conflicts that defined the big blue machine's campaigns, or how this partisan entity redirected the nature of Canadian politics, or even at Norman's non-partisan campaigns for Juvenile Diabetes and Acadia University, it is clear why Atkins told his fellow senators, in his final speech, "Life is all about showing up and truly involving oneself in one's community."

He showed up, involved himself, and accomplished results that impacted Canadian political history. His accomplishments came by recruiting and coordinating the willing, and allowing each to perform to their maximum, so long as each played according to his musical score and under his director's baton.

Norman followed Dalton but he was not Dalton. He did not use big words. He was self-effacing. As a speechmaker, he was a nervous journeyman, but in the craft of political campaigning, he was an undisputed master who let his deeds speak for themselves. Sometimes, they had to.

"When Norman died," noted Tom Kierans, "Mulroney's quote was 'he made the trains run on time.' That was it. Atkins was a master technician, but Brian would never acknowledge than anybody but he had anything to do with his victories. He understood politics, more than anyone else, in his view. In Ontario, Davis would give much greater credit to those who fashioned victories."

When he died, it could not have surprised anyone who'd known him that Norman Atkins's remains would be buried in Lower Jemseg alongside the grave of his political mentor, business partner, brother-in-law, and best friend.

"Dalton and Norman were one with each other again," said Atkins's resilient wife, Anna Ruth. "They did everything together, complemented one another's skills and, in the end, lie buried side by side in New Brunswick."

Their companion tombstones nestle serene beside Lower Jemseg's stone church, atop a small hill near the flowing Saint John River, in a province both men cherished as home.

Norman would follow Dalton anywhere.

ACKNOWLEDGEMENTS

Paul Curley, Tom Kierans, Michael Meighen, Paul Little, Phil Lind, and L. "Red" Storey, understanding the value of appraising Canada's legendary but misunderstood big blue machine, suggested that I chronicle this contentious saga of political history. I am grateful for their faith that I could pull it off.

They supported the telling by giving time and sharing information, as did so many others who were either insiders of the blue machine or who had it under close personal observation. Individuals who helpfully provided insights and accounts through formal interviews, telephone interviews, and correspondence through letter and email, between 2006 and today, included: Michael Allen, Brian Armstrong, Dr. Stephen Ash, Anna Ruth Atkins, Geoffrey Atkins, Dianne Axmith, Chad Bark, Derek Burney, Bob Byron, John Carter, Art Collins, Christine Corrigan, Paul Curley, Michael Daniher, Dorothy Davey, William G. Davis, Fred Dawkins, Ross DeGeer, Fred Dickson, Arthur Dollery, Bob Donaldson, Nancy Donaldson, Patricia Dumas, Rob Flack, Pierre Fortier, Ian Fraser, Jane Frost, Michael Gee, Mort Glanville, Allan Gregg, Don Guthrie, Win Hackett, Peter Harder, Bruce Hatfield, Hal Jackman, Bill Jarvis, Bill Kelly, Ike Kelneck, Tom Kierans, Jerry Lampert, John Laschinger, Allan Lawrence, Richard LeLay, Phil Lind, Joe Martin, Jack MacKay, Hugh Macaulay, Jim Macaulay, Tom MacMillan, Karen MacMillan-Aver, John MacNaughton, Bill McAleer, John McIntyre, Ross McKean, R. Roy McMurtry, David Meynell,

Percy Mockler, Janet Mulvagh, Harry Near, Nate Nurgitz, Dr. Kelvin Ogilvie, Bill Parker, Marilyn Pfaff, Jean Peloquin, Jean-Carol Pelletier, Joan Peters, Jim Ramsey, Jim Ross, John Rowsome, Bill Saunderson, Tom Scott, Hugh Segal, John Slade, George Stratton, John Thompson, John Tory, Tom Trbovich, Fred Watson, Clare Westcott, Jodi White, and Russ Wunker.

While their interviews underpin this story, it is a saga I know also from direct personal experience as both participant and observer. In the writing I have also drawn on my extensive archives of Conservative Party history, which include a number of original documents dating from the 1930s, hundreds of party publications, personal files for party events, and correspondence with individuals over six decades within the Progressive Conservative Party. Over those years I have as well diarized notes of events and conversations with most individuals mentioned in *The Big Blue Machine*, including Dalton Camp, Norman Atkins, Earl Rowe, Les Frost, John Robarts, Charles MacNaughton, Bill Davis, Frank Miller, John Diefenbaker, George Hees, Duff Roblin, Bob Stanfield, Joe Clark, Roy McMurtry, and Brian Mulroney, but extending also to hundreds more with whom I've shared political highlights and heartaches, both within PC ranks and across party lines.

Many other writers have researched and chronicled aspects of this story, and in acknowledging their work I thank them for it. The former trickle of books about Canadian politics became a flood during the period covered by this book, roughly the 1940s to 1990s, and our country is enriched by this preservation of a written record. Geoffrey Stevens has been a notable contributor to the big blue machine's heritage with books about the lives and times of such individuals as Dalton Camp, Norman Atkins, Robert Stanfield, Flora MacDonald, and individuals connected with them. Claire Hoy has written richly detailed accounts of the Ontario and Ottawa versions of political campaigns in which Camp and Atkins were central. Historian Bob Plamondon has added cohesiveness to accounts of the Conservative Party's history and personalities. Many more provided accounts of political history through memoirs — among them Dalton Camp, John Diefenbaker, Eddie Goodman, Hal Jackman, Bob Coates, Brian Mulroney, Roy McMurtry, Duff Roblin, John Laschinger, Heward Grafftey, and Hugh Segal — valuable for information not previously available and perspectives not otherwise possible. Joe Martin, whom I first met working together in Duff Roblin's leadership campaign in 1967, historian of the Albany Club of Toronto, was most helpful in providing a great deal of information about "the unofficial head office of the Tory Party."

Even if a clear and dispassionate view is hard to achieve, this book's effort to present a balanced portrait is my tribute to the exceptional men and women of the big blue machine, most of whom I know or knew during their lifetimes, many as good friends, a number of whom helped make my own lifetime in politics and decade in the House of Commons possible. For all of that, I give full acknowledgement and respectful thanks.

Bringing this book to print has been the handiwork, which I am also keen to acknowledge, of my friends at Dundurn, today Canada's largest independent publishing house. For more than forty years Dundurn's founder, Kirk Howard, has carried out his mission to "define Canada for Canadians" through publication of thousands of books, some eight of them mine. Carrie Gleason, Dundurn's editorial director, combines professionalism and a pleasant nature to make her a pillar of stability in the hectic universe of book publishing. Kathryn Lane, Dundurn's managing editor, has supervised the production of this book and lent her valuable advice on ways to strengthen it. Dominic Farrell, who has edited this book, is a key member of the Dundurn team with whom I've worked often before, each time valuing anew his ability to help me tell the story in the best way possible and using fewer words to do so. Courtney Horner, senior designer at Dundurn, has overseen layout and design. Gary Long of Fox Meadow Creations in Sault Ste. Marie designed the front cover. Edmonton lawyer Johnson Billingsley proofread the manuscript and, as with prior books, helped improve what you find here. To all I am most grateful.

PHOTO CREDITS

43: Camp Family; 128: PC Party Archives; 131: PC Party Archives; 150: PC Party Archives; 157: Atkins Family; 158: PC Party Archives; 160: PC Party Archives; 163: PC Party Archives; 166: Camp Family; 178: Courtesy Joe Martin; 209: *Toronto Telegram*; 221: Author; 224: PC Party Archives; 228: *Toronto Telegram*; 230: PC Party Archives; 255: *Toronto Telegram*; 258: *Toronto Telegram*; 259: *Toronto Telegram*; 261: *Toronto Telegram*; 266: *Toronto Telegram*; 267: *Toronto Telegram*; 293: Paul Curley Collection; 312: Atkins Family; 325: Kelneck Collection; 332: Kelneck Collection; 334: PC Party / Tom MacMillan Collection; 346: McMurtry Archive; 349: Albany Club / Tom MacMillan Collection; 350: Tom MacMillan Collection; 351: Paul Curley Collection; 352: McMurtry Archive; 354: Kelneck Collection; 355: Photography West, Vancouver; 357: Kelneck Collection; 359: Kelneck Collection; 363: Segal Family; 373: Tom MacMillan Collection; 376: Atkins Family; 380: McMurtry Archive; 386: Atkins Family; 388: Atkins Family; 391: Office of the Premier, Ontario; 395: Atkins Family; 401: PC Party Archives; 407: Kelneck Collection; 409: William C. Stratas; 427: PC Party / Paul Curley Collection; 428: PC Party Archives / Paul Curley Collection; 430: Scott Grant; 434: Paul Curley Collection; 437 (top): Kelneck Collection; 437 (bottom): PC Party Archives; 441: PC Party Archives; 442: Scott Grant; 443: PC Party / Atkins Family; 444 (top): Patrick MacAdam; 444 (bottom): PC Party / Atkins Family; 446: PC Party / Atkins Family; 447: PC Party / Macaulay Family: 449: PC Party / Atkins Family; 455: PC Party / Paul Curley Collection; 471: Albany Club / Paul Curley Collection; 472: Albany Club / Paul Curley Collection; 474–475: Paul Curley / Gina Brannan/ Atkins Family; 479: Albany Club / Tom MacMillan Collection; 486: Albany Club / Author's Archive; 487–488: Author's Archive; 490: Dianne Axmith; 494: Atkins Family; 496: PC Party / Paul Curley Collection

BIBLIOGRAPHY

Aiken, Gordon. *The Backbencher*. Toronto: McClelland and Stewart, 1974.

Amys, Jack. *The Albany: A Celebration*. Toronto: Yorkminster, 1981.

Armstrong, Alvin. *Flora MacDonald*. Toronto: J.M. Dent, 1976.

Armstrong, Joe C.W. *Farewell the Peaceful Kingdom: The Seduction and Rape of Canada, 1963–1994*. Toronto: Stoddart, 1995.

Blizzard, Christina. *Right Turn: How the Tories Took Ontario*. Toronto: Dundurn, 1995.

Bothwell, Robert. *The Penguin History of Canada*. Toronto: Penguin Canada, 2006.

Bothwell, Robert, and J.L. Granatstein. *Our Century: The Canadian Journey*. Vancouver: McArthur & Company, 2000.

Boyer, J. Patrick. "George Drew and the Revival of the Conservative Party in Ontario, 1938–1943." M.A. thesis, University of Toronto, 1975.

Bruno, Jerry, and Jeff Greenfield. *The Advance Man: An Offbeat Look at What Really Happens in Political Campaigns*. New York: William Morrow, 1971.

Butler, Peter M. *Polling and Public Opinion: A Canadian Perspective*. Toronto: University of Toronto Press, 2007.

Camp, Dalton. *An Eclectic Eel*. Ottawa: Deneau, 1980.

———. *Gentlemen, Players & Politicians*. Toronto: McClelland and Stewart, 1970.

———. *Points of Departure.* Ottawa: Deneau & Greenberg, 1979.

———. *Whose Country Is This Anyway?* Vancouver: Douglas & McIntrye, 1995.

Caplan, Gerald, Michael Kirby, and Hugh Segal. *Election: The Issues, The Strategies, The Aftermath.* Scarborough, [ON]: Prentice-Hall, 1989.

Coates, Robert C. *The Night of the Knives.* Fredericton: Brunswick Press, 1969.

Courtney, John. *The Selection of National Party Leaders in Canada.* Toronto: Macmillan, 1973.

Creighton, Donald. *Canada's First Century, 1867–1967.* Toronto: Macmillan, 1970.

———. *The Story of Canada.* Toronto: Macmillan, 1971.

Crosbie, John. *No Holds Barred.* Toronto: McClelland & Stewart, 1997.

Davey, Keith. *The Rainmaker: A Passion for Politics.* Toronto: Stoddart, 1986.

Dempson, Peter. *Assignment Ottawa.* Toronto: General Publishing, 1968.

Diefenbaker, John George. *Memoirs — The Tumultuous Years: 1962–1967.* Toronto: Longmans, 1977.

Doern, Bruce, and Peter Aucoin, eds. *The Structures of Policy-Making in Canada.* Toronto: Macmillan, 1971.

Editors of the Toronto Telegram. *Balloons and Ballots: The Inside Story of Robert Stanfield's Victory.* Toronto: *Toronto Telegram*, 1967.

English, John. *The Worldly Years: The Life of Lester Pearson, 1949–1972.* Toronto: Alfred A. Knopf, 1992.

Goodman, Eddie. *Life of the Party: The Memoirs of Eddie Goodman.* Toronto: Key Porter, 1988.

Granatstein, J.L. *The Politics of Survival: The Conservative Party of Canada 1939–1945.* Toronto: University of Toronto Press, 1967.

Graham, Roger. *Old Man Ontario: Leslie M. Frost.* Toronto: University of Toronto Press, 1990.

Haliburton, E.D. *My Years with Stanfield.* Windsor, N.S.: Lancelot Press, 1972.

Hoy, Claire. *Bill Davis: A Biography.* Toronto: Methuen, 1985.

———. *Friends in High Places: Politics and Patronage in the Mulroney Government.* Toronto: Key Porter, 1987.

———. *Margin of Error: Pollsters and the Manipulation of Canadian Politics.* Toronto: Key Porter, 1989.

Humphries, David. *Joe Clark: A Portrait.* Ottawa: Deneau & Greenberg, 1978.

Jackman, Henry N.R., ed. *The Letters and Diaries of Henry Rutherford Jackman: Volume 5, 1961–1965.* Toronto: Harmony Printing, 2005.

————. *The Letters and Diaries of Henry Rutherford Jackman: Volume 6, 1966–1969*. Toronto: Harmony Printing, 2006.

Johnston, James. *The Party's Over*. Don Mills, Ontario: Longman Canada, 1971.

Kingwell, Mark, and Christopher Moore. *Canada: Our Century*. Toronto: Doubleday Canada, 1999.

Kornberg, Allan. *Canadian Legislative Behaviour*. Toronto: Holt, Rinehart & Winston, 1967.

Kruhlak, Orest, Richard Schultz, and Sidney Pobihushchy, eds. *The Canadian Political Process*. Toronto: Holt, Rinehart & Winston, 1970.

Laschinger, John, and Geoffrey Stevens. *Leaders and Lesser Mortals: Backroom Politics in Canada*. Toronto: Key Porter, 1992.

Levine, Allan. *Scrum Wars: The Prime Ministers and the Media*. Toronto: Dundurn, 1993.

MacDonald, L. Ian. *Mulroney: The Making of the Prime Minister*. Toronto: McClelland & Stewart, 1985.

Malvern, Paul. *Persuaders: Influence Peddling, Lobbying and Political Corruption in Canada*. Toronto: Methuen, 1985.

Manthorpe, Jonathan. *The Power and the Tories: Ontario Politics, 1943 to the Present*. Toronto: Macmillan, 1974.

Martin, Joe. *The Role and Place of Ontario in the Canadian Confederation*. Toronto: Ontario Economic Council, 1974.

Martin, Patrick, Allan Gregg, and George Perlin. *Contenders: The Tory Quest for Power*. Scarborough, ON: Prentice Hall, 1983.

McDougall, Alex K. *John P. Robarts: His Life and Government*. Toronto: University of Toronto Press, 1986.

McDougall, Bruce. *Ted Rogers*. Toronto: Burgher Books, 1995.

McLaughlin, David. *Poisoned Chalice: The Last Campaign of the Progressive Conservative Party?* Toronto: Dundurn, 1994.

McMurtry, Roy. *Memoirs and Reflections*. Toronto: The Osgoode Society, 2013.

Meisel, John. *Working Papers on Canadian Politics*. Montreal: McGill-Queen's University Press, 1972.

Moore, David W. *The Superpollsters: How They Measure and Manipulate Public Opinion in America*. New York: Four Walls Eight Windows, 1995.

Mulroney, Brian M. *Memoirs: 1939–1993*. Toronto: McClelland & Stewart, 2007.

Newman, Peter C. *The Distemper of Our Times.* Toronto: McClelland & Stewart, 1968.

————. *Renegade in Power.* Toronto: McClelland & Stewart, 1963.

————. *The Secret Mulroney Tapes: Unguarded Confessions of a Prime Minister.* Toronto: Random House, 2005.

Nimmo, Dan. *The Political Persuaders: The Techniques of Modern Election Campaigns.* Englewood Cliffs, [NJ]: Prentice-Hall, 1970.

O'Leary, Grattan. *Recollections of People, Press, and Politics.* Toronto: Macmillan, 1977.

Oliver, Peter N. *Unlikely Tory: The Life and Politics of Allan Grossman.* Toronto: Lester & Orpen Denys, 1985.

O'Sullivan, Sean. *Both My Households: From Politics to Priesthood.* Toronto: Seal Books, 1986.

Page, Christopher. *The Roles of Public Opinion Research in Canadian Government.* Toronto: University of Toronto Press, 2006.

Paikin, Steve. *Public Triumph, Private Tragedy: The Double Life of John P. Robarts.* Toronto: Viking, 2005.

Peacock, Donald. *Journey to Power: The Story of a Canadian Election.* Toronto: Ryerson, 1968.

Perlin, George C. *The Tory Syndrome: Leadership Politics in the Progressive Conservative Party.* Kingston: McGill-Queen's University Press, 1980.

Plamondon, Bob. *Blue Thunder: The Truth about Conservatives from Macdonald to Harper.* Toronto: Key Porter, 2009.

Regenstreif, Peter. *The Diefenbaker Interlude.* Toronto: Longmans, 1965.

Roblin, Duff. *Speaking for Myself: Politics and Other Pursuits.* Winnipeg: Great Plains Publications, 1999.

Sawatsky, John. *Mulroney: The Politics of Ambition.* Toronto: Macfarlane Walter & Ross, 1991.

Simpson, Jeffrey. *Discipline of Power: The Conservative Interlude and the Liberal Restoration.* Toronto: University of Toronto, 1980.

Slade, Arthur. *John Diefenbaker: An Appointment with Destiny.* Toronto: XYZ Publishing, 2001.

Smith, Denis. *Rogue Tory: The Life and Legend of John G. Diefenbaker.* Toronto: Macfarlane Walter & Ross, 1995.

Soderlund, Walter C., Walter I. Romanow, E. Donald Briggs, and Ronald H. Wagenberg. *Media and Elections in Canada.* Toronto: Holt, Rinehart & Winston, 1984.

Speirs, Rosemary. *Out of the Blue: The Fall of the Tory Dynasty in Ontario.* Toronto: Macmillan, 1986.

Stevens, Geoffrey. *Flora Power: No Boundaries, No Limits.* Toronto: McClelland & Stewart, Publication pending.

———. *The Player: The Life & Times of Dalton Camp.* Toronto: Key Porter, 2003.

———. *Stanfield.* Toronto: McClelland and Stewart, 1973.

Stewart, Walter. *Divide and Con: Canadian Politics at Work.* Toronto: New Press, 1973.

———. *Shrug: Trudeau in Power.* Toronto: New Press, 1971.

Stursberg, Peter. *Diefenbaker: Leadership Gained 1956–1962.* Toronto: University of Toronto, 1975.

———. *Diefenbaker: Leadership Lost: 1962–1967.* Toronto: University of Toronto, 1976.

Taylor, Charles. *The Pattern of Politics.* Toronto: McClelland & Stewart, 1970.

———. *Radical Tories: The Conservative Tradition in Canada.* Toronto: House of Anansi Press, 1982.

Thorburn, Hugh G. *Politics in New Brunswick.* Toronto: University of Toronto Press, 1961.

Thorburn, Hugh G., ed. *Party Politics in Canada.* Scarborough, ON: Prentice-Hall, 1972.

Van Dussen, Thomas. *The Chief.* New York: McGraw Hill, 1968.

Walker, David. *Fun Along the Way.* Toronto: Robertson Press, 1989.

Weston, Greg. *Reign of Error: The Inside Story of John Turner's Troubled Leadership.* Toronto: McGraw-Hill Ryerson, 1988.

Williams, John L. *The Conservative Party in Canada: 1920-1949.* Durham, NC: Duke University Press, 1956.

INDEX

urged to run for Parliament
in Peel riding by, 213
John Diefenbaker
advanceman for, 225
creates cult of personality
around, 136, 140–44
defends against coup at-
tempt, 196, 209
harmonious relationship
with, 22, 134
cooling of relationship
with, 152
initial encounters with, 128,
129, 132
launches leadership review
to oust, 216, 233
becomes politically toxic as
result, 301, 313, 483
requests Camp's help in
backroom operations,
129, 132, 143
runs campaign advertising
for, 135–36
similarities and differences,
132–34
speech-writer for, 129, 138,
148, 149, 152, 160
See also Diefenbaker, John;
leadership review; Stan-
field, Robert
George Drew, 78, 93
huge tax cut as 1953 cam-
paign plank, opposes, 101
Liberal days, 13, 16, 46, 51–52,
77
disillusioned by corporate
nature of Liberal Party,
50–52
Gregg, Milton, campaigns
for, 46–47
King, Mackenzie, relationship with, 48–49
Liberal Review, columnist
for, 45–46, 50
McNairn, John
assigns Camp to interact
with Liberal ad agen-
cy, 47, 48, 76
campaign tour in New
Brunswick election,
with, 47
force of premier's political machine, acknowl-
edged by, 12, 47

invites Camp to meet
top Liberals in Otta-
wa, 44
Maritime Liberal strate-
gy for national con-
vention, participates
in, 49
New Brunswick Young
Liberals, employment
by, 50–51
quits Liberal Party to retain
liberal values, 52, 77, 298
retaliation of Liberals for
joining PCs, 68–69
works against Liberals
in 1952 provincial
election, 80–81,
85–89
Roy McMurtry
converted to PCs by, 13, 214
leadership review campaign,
supported by, 223–9
personal friendship between,
229, 352, 483
See also Park Plaza Group;
Spades; Camp, Dalton
Brian Mulroney
appointed to Privy Council
Office by, 483, 489
uneasy common interest in
the blue machine, 23–24,
493
Progressive Conservative advertising and communications
guru, role as
advocates informed use of
television, 131
communications initiatives
within party, 117, 119,
120, 130
director of national election
advertising, 159,
rivalry with McKim
vice-president Allister
Grosart, 163
Progressive Conservative organizer, career as,
ascent in party backrooms,
103–05, 107
building-block strategy and
other party organizing
work with PC national
director Bill Rowe, 108–
10, 113–14, 115–18

benefits of build-
ing-block approach,
146, 154
reversal of, 467
campaign manager, in individual constituencies, for
Richard Donahoe, Hali-
fax (NS), 114–15
Doug Everett, Charlotte
County (NB), 46
Hugh John Flemming,
Royal (NB), 176
centralizing campaign
control by, 137–38,
143–44,
director of national cam-
paigns, 159,
Atlantic Canada, 150,
184
general distain for opinion
polls, 409
1962 federal election, 183–84
inspiration for big blue
machine, 137, 138
political initiatives as, 104,
106–08, 115–16, 117,
119, 130–32, 137, 139–
40, 145, 146, 199
presidency of PC Party, 14,
196, 208, 209
challenge by Maloney,
Arthur, 223, 228, 229
reputation as campaign
strategist, 89–90, 91, 103
Second Century Dinners,
organizes, 117
Duff Roblin
campaign support for,
177–79
effort to recruit as national
PC leader, 237
Royal Commission on Book
Publishing, member of,
352, 379
Bob Stanfield
campaigns in Nova Scotia,
96–101, 114–16
federal leadership and,
235–46, 251–68
make-over of, 248–51
first encounters, 96–97, 98
gets funds for advertising
in 1957 federal election
from, 146